MUSIC
THE ARTS
AND IDEAS

Patterns and Predictions
in Twentieth-Century Culture

BY

LEONARD B. MEYER

THE UNIVERSITY OF CHICAGO PRESS

CHICAGO AND LONDON

For my favorite Quintet:
Lee and Marion
Muffie
Carlin
&
Erica

THE UNIVERSITY OF CHICAGO PRESS, CHICAGO 60637
The University of Chicago Press, Ltd., London

81 80   9 8 7 6

ISBN: 0–226–52140–0 (clothbound); 0–226–52141–9 (paperbound)

Library of Congress Catalog Card Number: 67–25515

MUSIC
THE ARTS
AND IDEAS

PREFACE

This book is an attempt to understand the present—to discover some
pattern and rationale in the perplexing, fragmented world of
twentieth-century culture. The search began with music, and music has
remained both the main focus of attention and a valuable source of
ideas and concepts. But questions about music continually led to questions about the other arts and, more broadly, about the ideas and beliefs
that characterize our culture.

At first I supposed that an underlying order would reveal itself if
some basis could be found for deciding which of the several currents of
contemporary music would become "the style of the future." I formulated the question many times, and in many different forms: how will
twentieth-century music develop? which existing tendencies will be the
dominant, consequential ones? why, after fifty years, have we not
arrived at a stylistic consensus? and so on. But none of the "answers"
seemed satisfactory. Mostly they turned out to be plausible platitudes.

Then it occurred to me that, because it presupposed a particular kind
of answer, perhaps the question itself was the wrong one. Perhaps our
time would be characterized, not by the cumulative development of a
single style, but by the coexistence of a number of alternative styles in a
kind of "dynamic steady-state." It is the exploration of this hypothesis
which forms the central core of my book.

As I remember it, this possibility suggested itself in a general and amorphous way just after I finished reading Herman Hesse's *Magister Ludi*. Then I began to engage in my own intellectual "Bead Game" —playing with ideas, seeing what their logical consequences and psychological implications might be, questioning the necessity and validity of opposing viewpoints and accepted formulations, and asking whether empirical evidence from other disciplines and other areas of culture supported the hypothesis. In so doing, I have not hesitated to consider and speculate about fundamental problems—for instance, about the nature of history and our relationship to it, the organization and prerequisites of complex hierarchic structures, the relationship of the arts to culture, and so forth.

From this point of view, my book is somewhat self-indulgent. I have tackled and conjectured about problems, not only because they were relevant, but because they fascinated and challenged me. Nor have I tried to be cautious and circumspect in dealing with them. Consequently, there will undoubtedly be a number of dissenting—even outraged—reactions to what I have written. Fine. I am by no means confident that everything in the book is incontrovertible and correct, that the answers proposed are final truths. But I am sure that the issues broached and problems posed are important, exciting, and fun.

A book about contemporary culture is speculative for other reasons too. First, because the meaning of the present will be definitively established only when its implications—its consequences—have become the facts, problems, and perplexities of some future present. And second, because, however much one may try to be detached and impartial— observing relationships and movements rather than judging them—it is impossible to stand outside of culture. For the models and categories we use in conceptualizing and ordering the world are necessarily limited to, if not determined by, those which are provided by our particular culture. If I have adopted a position close to what is called "analytic formalism" in chapter 8, it is not because formalism is per se a better or more valid position than any other but because it is the one best suited to the task at hand—the task of comprehending the multiplicity of twentieth-century thought and culture.

What I am presenting, then, is a theoretical construct rather than a chronological account. Because its main thrust is explanation rather than documentation or description, no attempt has been made to cover all aspects of contemporary music—let alone the other arts and culture generally. Much has been left out: major composers not mentioned, significant movements slighted, interesting concepts neglected. I have admittedly been very selective, and, given the wealth of diverse and divergent material presented by a culture as rich and variegated as ours,

Preface

I can only hope that my selection has not been too much influenced by the hypothesis being considered.

The book is divided into three parts. The first, "As It Has Been," consists of five essays already published. Although it seems, in retrospect, that I was moving toward a new conception of the present, these essays were written before the formulation of the central thesis of this book. Since it deals for the most part with the understanding of traditional music and established aesthetic values, Part I acts as the base and as a point of reference for what follows. Part II, "As It Is, and Perhaps Will Be," states the main thesis of the book, tries to show that a considerable amount of evidence supports it, and considers what its consequences might be. Part III, "Formalism in Music," returns to an explicit consideration of music and examines problems having to do with the theory and practice of highly complex experimental music.

The debts owed to the ideas and work of other writers and scholars are so numerous and obvious from the references in the text that it would be pointless to list them here. If some chapters seem overburdened with footnotes and other "trappings and suits" of scholarship, it is not because I wish to impress or to pretend to an erudition which I do not possess but because the views and opinions of others—artists, historians, scientists—are my data. It is with *their* view of the world, whether right or wrong, that I am concerned. In other cases I have leaned heavily upon the work of others because I lack their knowledge and competence in a particular field. This is the case, for instance, with the many quotations from Professor Nagel's book.

The debts owed to my students and colleagues should also be acknowledged. These are the result of many, many discussions—sometimes heated, often lengthy—in which ideas have been tried out, objections argued, and evidence examined. When I think about this sort of exchange, four people especially come to mind: Leo Treitler, John R. Platt, Robert McMahan, and Grosvenor Cooper. Though I doubt that any of them will agree with all, or even most, of this book, I am certain that each of them will find it interesting, suggestive, and thought-provoking. And that is what I hope other readers will find as well.

Grateful acknowledgment is made to the journals in which a number of the chapters of this book first appeared: *The Journal of Aesthetics and Art Criticism,* Vol. XV, No. 4, June, 1957 (chapter 1), and Vol. XVII, No. 4, June, 1959 (chapter 2) ; *Journal of the American Musicological Society,* Vol. XIV, No. 2, Summer, 1961 (chapter 3) ; *The Yale Review,* Vol. LII, No. 2, Winter, 1963 (chapter 4) ; and *The Hudson Review,* Vol. VI, No. 2, Summer, 1963 (chapter 5).

CONTENTS

PART I

Prelude: As It Has Been

INTRODUCTION

T HE ESSAYS reprinted as Part I of this book are largely concerned
with the ways in which culturally experienced listeners—including composers and performers—perceive, understand, and evaluate the traditional tonal music of the West. In this sense, they treat of music "as it
has been."

The first two chapters deal with the nature of musical experience and
the problem of musical value. In both, concepts borrowed from information theory are used to explore and illuminate the ideas presented and
the questions raised. Though I would now tend to be more circumspect
in the use of information theory (see chap. 10) and somewhat more
cautious in making broad generalizations about value—implying, for
instance, that these are generally cross-cultural—there is nevertheless
much in these essays which still seems relevant, at least to an understanding of tonal music, and which I still find interesting and provocative. Indeed, several of the ideas merely broached or prefigured in these
essays become concepts of considerable importance in Parts II and III
of this book.

"On Rehearing Music" has been included both because it touches
upon the question of the nature of style change, which is discussed at
some length in chapter 7, and because it leads from the syntactic
concerns of the first chapters to the cultural-ideological ones considered
in the two following chapters.

The last two essays emphasize that critical judgments and aesthetic attitudes are based upon and derived from ultimate, and perhaps a priori, metaphysical-cultural beliefs. "Forgery and the Anthropology of Art" underestimates, I now believe, the extent to which the ideology of Western culture has already changed. Though I would not alter its denouement—would not, that is, maintain that forgeries can now be exhibited with impunity—the essay does call attention to the conditions under which a past stylistic syntax might become a viable mode of composition in the present; and it is conjectured in chapter 9 that such conditions may be about to, or perhaps already, prevail. "The End of the Renaissance?" takes us into the present, but to the present still conceived of as a transient deviation from the main stream of Western ideology and art. Since writing the essay, I have found it more and more apparent that the viewpoint of "radical empiricism" is but one expression of the deeper and more widespread shift in cultural beliefs described in chapters 8 and 9.

No substantive changes have been made in the texts of these essays. Here and there new footnotes have been added or existing ones extended. All additions or extensions are preceded by an asterisk (*). Occasionally a footnote has been deleted because the gathering together of these essays made it redundant.

CHAPTER

I

Meaning in Music and Information Theory

I have dealt elsewhere at some length with the central importance of the arousal and subsequent inhibition of expectant tendencies in the shaping of musical experience.[1] In that analysis of musical experience many concepts were developed and suggestions made for which I subsequently found striking parallels—indeed equivalents—in information theory. Among these were the importance of uncertainty in musical communication, the probabilistic nature of musical style, and the operation in musical experience of what I have since learned to be the Markoff process. In particular, it would seem that the psycho-stylistic conditions which give rise to musical meaning, whether affective or intellectual,[2] are the same as those which communicate information. It is this hypothesis which I propose to explore here.

The hypothesis is of particular interest because, if it can be substantiated, then the seemingly disparate and discrete worlds of physical phenomena, bio-social behavior, and humanistic creation can, at least from this point of view, be brought together and subsumed under a

---

[1] Leonard B. Meyer, *Emotion and Meaning in Music*; in particular, see chaps. 1 and 2. (Short titles are given in the footnotes; full references will be found in the Bibliography.)

[2] *Ibid.*, pp. 35–40. The differentia between the affective response and the intellectual response to music lies in the dispositions and beliefs which listeners bring to musical experience rather than in the musical processes that evoke the responses.

single fundamental principle—the law of entropy. And thus Eddington's famous suggestion that "there are the strongest grounds for placing entropy alongside beauty and melody" will have received concrete exemplification.

Let us begin with a general definition of meaning. As Morris R. Cohen puts it:

> . . . anything acquires meaning if it is connected with, or indicates, or refers to, something beyond itself, so that its full nature points to and is revealed in that connection.[3]

Meaning in this sense resides in what both Cohen and George Herbert Mead have called the "triadic relationship" between a stimulus, the thing to which it refers, and the individual for whom the stimulus has meaning.[4] While meaning is thus a mental fact, it is not arbitrarily subjective. The relationship between the stimulus and the thing to which it refers is a real relationship existing in the objective world, whether physical or social. For ". . . *what* anything means is in no wise created by our apprehension, but is presupposed by the latter." [5]

Under this general definition two types of meaning must be distinguished. (1) A stimulus may be meaningful because it indicates or refers to something which is different from itself in kind—as when a word refers to or denotes an object or concept which is not itself a word. This type of meaning we shall call "designative meaning." (2) A stimulus or process may acquire meaning because it indicates or refers to something which is like itself in kind—as when the rumble of distant thunder on a sultry day and the piling up of storm clouds (antecedent natural events) indicate the coming of a rain storm (a consequent natural event). This type of meaning we shall call "embodied meaning."

Music gives rise to both types of meaning. Music may be meaningful because it refers to things outside itself, evoking associations and connotations relative to the world of ideas, sentiments, and physical objects. Such designative meanings are often less precise and specific than those arising in linguistic communication. This does not, however, make them less forceful or significant.[6] Or music may be meaningful in the sense that within the context of a particular musical style one tone or group of

---

[3] *A Preface to Logic*, p. 47.

[4] *Ibid.*, p. 29, and Mead, *Mind, Self, and Society*, pp. 75–76.

[5] Cohen, *A Preface to Logic*, p. 28.

[6] Meyer, *Emotion and Meaning in Music*, chap. 8.

tones indicates—leads the practiced listener to expect—that another tone or group of tones will be forthcoming at some more or less specified point in the musical continuum.

Although these two types of meaning are logically separable, there is in practice an intimate interaction between them. The "character" (designative meaning) of a piece of music will, when well-defined, influence our expectations about subsequent musical events (embodied meaning), just as our estimate of the character of an individual will influence our expectations about his behavior in a given set of circumstances. Conversely, the way in which expectations are satisfied, delayed, or blocked plays an important part in the characterization of the designative meaning of a passage, in the same way that we make inferences about an individual's character on the basis of his behavior in a particular cultural situation.

Since in past analyses of musical meaning considerable confusion has resulted from a failure to specify which aspect of meaning is being considered, let us state at the outset that this study is concerned with those meanings which arise within the context of the work itself—that is, with embodied meaning. And except where the term "designative meaning" is explicitly used, the word "meaning" is to be understood as referring to embodied meaning.

Style constitutes the universe of discourse within which musical meanings arise. There are many musical styles. They vary from culture to culture, from epoch to epoch within the same culture, and even within the same epoch and culture. This plurality of musical styles results because styles exist not as unchanging physical processes in the world of nature, but as psychological processes ingrained as habits in the perceptions, dispositions, and responses of those who have learned through practice and experience to understand a particular style. What remains constant from style to style are not scales, modes, harmonies, or manners of performance, but the psychology of human mental processes—the ways in which the mind, operating within the context of culturally established norms, selects and organizes the stimuli that are presented to it. For instance, the human mind, striving for stability and completeness, "expects" structural gaps [7] to be filled in. But what constitutes a structural gap will vary from style to style. Thus a melodic skip of a third which is a structural gap in the diatonic-chromatic tonal

---

[7] A structural gap is a form of incompleteness in which one or more of the tones comprising the normal complement of pitches in a tonal system is left out. In this connection, see *ibid.*, pp. 130–35.

system of the West would not be a gap in a pentatonic tonal system in which such a skip is given as normative.

Once a musical style has become part of the habit responses of composers, performers, and practiced listeners it may be regarded as a complex system of probabilities. That musical styles are internalized probability systems is demonstrated by the rules of musical grammar and syntax found in textbooks on harmony, counterpoint, and theory in general. The rules given in such books are almost invariably stated in terms of probability. For example, we are told that in the tonal harmonic system of Western music the tonic chord is most often followed by the dominant, frequently by the subdominant, sometimes by the submediant, and so forth. Or we are informed in texts on counterpoint that, after a large melodic skip, the melody usually moves in the opposite direction, filling in the tones passed over. Ethnologists dealing with primitive or folk music have often implicitly acknowledged the probabilistic nature of tonal systems in their notation of scales as well as in their discussions of tonal progression. Indeed, some have compiled elaborate statistics of the frequency with which a given tone, interval, or progression occurs in the music of the culture under consideration. The problems involved in such statistical analyses of music are discussed toward the close of this chapter.

Out of such internalized probability systems arise the expectations [8]—the tendencies—upon which musical meaning is built. But probability is not the same as expectation. Or, to put the matter in another way, we must distinguish between active and latent expectation—between the fact of probability and the awareness that an individual has of alternative probabilities.

In a sense our whole mental existence is built around our expectations

---

*[8] I should now prefer to put these matters in somewhat more objective terms, referring to the *implications* which, given experienced and knowledgeable listeners, musical events have (or are felt to have) for one another, rather than to the *expectations* which listeners entertain about the future course of musical patterning. The difficulty with the term "expectation" is that it is often understood in a simplistic way. Though the experience that "expectation" is intended to describe may be *felt* as a single, composite goal-directed motion, in reality it is always the product of a complex set of interrelated variables in which musical events imply one another in different ways, to different degrees, and on different hierarchic levels. Moreover, as pointed out in chapter 12 (p. 310), the several shaping forces of music may not act in concert—may not support one another—in the articulation of structure and process. At any particular moment, disparate, or even contradictory, goals may be implied by a complex musical event.

about the normal (probable) continuity of events. We "expect" to get up Monday morning, to eat breakfast, to see that the children get to school, to go to the office, and so forth. But we are as a rule unconscious of such expectations. They are *latent* expectations, the norms of behavior which are taken for granted once they have become fixed habit patterns. Such expectations become *active*, either as affective experience or conscious cognition, only when our normal patterns of behavior are disturbed in some way. If, for instance, we oversleep or breakfast is delayed, then we become aware of our expectant habits. We are aware of the necessity of getting to the office, of making choices and decisions.

In short, the probability relationships embodied in a particular musical style together with the various modes of mental behavior involved in the perception and understanding of the materials of the style constitute the *norms* of the style. Latent expectation is a product of these probability relationships. And expectation becomes active only when these norms are disturbed. In other words, such latent expectations are necessary conditions for the communication of musical information, while the disturbances of these norms are the sufficient condition for musical communication.

Let us now return to an explicit consideration of meaning. Meaning arises when an individual becomes aware, either affectively or intellectually, of the implications of a stimulus in a particular context. As long as behavior is habitual and "unthinking" the stimuli presented to the mind are neither meaningful nor meaningless. They cannot be said to be meaningless, because this implies an active negation of meaning. Rather our experience of such stimuli stands in the same relationship to the meaningful-meaningless axis as the concept of "amoral" stands in relation to the moral-immoral axis. That is, such stimuli are neutral with respect to meaning. For example, as we drive along a highway countless stimuli (on-coming cars, pedestrians, buildings, billboards, etc.) are "seen," but as long as our habit responses "take care" of these stimuli we do not really observe them. They are not meaningful. They do not indicate or require any action on our part. Only when our habits are disturbed do these stimuli become meaningful—e.g., if an on-coming car swerves into the middle of the road and a judgment of speed and distance must be made, or if a detour sign requires a decision as to the future route, or if a particularly striking landscape calls attention to itself.

Similarly in music, a tonal process which moves in the expected and probable way without deviation may be said to be neutral with regard to meaning.[9] Musical meaning, then, arises when our expectant habit responses are delayed or blocked—when the normal course of stylistic-mental events is disturbed by some form of deviation.

Three varieties of deviation may be distinguished. (1) The normal, or probable, consequent event may be delayed. Such a delay may be purely temporal or it may also involve reaching the consequent through a less direct tonal route, provided that the deviation is understandable as a means to the end in view. (2) The antecedent situation may be ambiguous. That is, several equally probable consequents may be envisaged. When this takes place, our automatic habit responses are inadequate, for they are attuned only to a clear decision about probabilities. And (3) there may be neither delay nor ambiguity, but the consequent event may be unexpected—improbable in the particular context.

The first two modes of deviation are very similar in their basic psychological effect. For whenever there is a delay in the antecedent-consequent relationship (as in 1), the mind becomes aware of the possibility of alternative modes of continuation. It weighs, though perhaps unconsciously, the probabilities of the situation in the light of past events, the present context, and the possible influence of the delay on the future course of events. For even though one mode of continuation may seem much more probable than any of the others, it is still only probable, not certain.[10] Thus both varieties of deviation (1 and 2) arouse active expectation because of the necessity of envisaging alternative consequents—of estimating the probabilities of an uncertain situation.

Sometimes such uncertainty is slight and evanescent, as when a chromatic tone is introduced within a standard cadential progression or when the portamento of a violinist delays the arrival of a substantive (expected) tone ever so little. At other times uncertainty may reach heroic proportions, as it does just before the E minor theme in the development section of the first movement of Beethoven's Third Symphony (mm. 248–80). Here the destruction of the rhythmic organization, the weakening of melodic motion, and the arrival at a harmonic impass create a musical situation bordering on chaos. And the tremen-

---

[9] Such stimuli may of course have designative meaning; that is, they may be meaningful because they refer to or designate extra-musical concepts, moods, actions, and so forth. And they may also appear to be meaningful because they constitute elements of a larger hierarchic structure which is meaningful.

[10] An antecedent-consequent relationship with complete certainty (a probability of unity) will not occur because it would be a meaningless tautology.

dous impact of the new theme, when it arrives, is clearly a product of the uncertainty of the antecedent situation.

Our definition of meaning can thus be revised to read as follows: Musical meaning arises when an antecedent situation, requiring an estimate of the probable modes of pattern continuation, produces uncertainty about the temporal-tonal nature of the expected consequent.

Here we see our first clear relationship between embodied meaning and information. Information is measured by the randomness of the choices possible in a given situation. If a situation is highly organized and the possible consequents in the pattern process have a high degree of probability, then information (or entropy) is low. If, however, the situation is characterized by a high degree of shuffledness so that the consequents are more or less equi-probable, then information is said to be high.

Both meaning and information are thus related through probability to uncertainty. For the lower the probability of a particular consequent in any message, the greater the uncertainty (and information) involved in the antecedent-consequent relationship. "Information is . . . a measure of one's freedom of choice in selecting a message. The greater this freedom of choice, and hence the greater the information, the greater is the uncertainty that the message actually is some particular one. Thus greater freedom of choice, greater uncertainty, greater information go hand in hand." [11]

The third variety of deviation discussed above, however, does not involve the active expectation of alternative consequents.[12] No uncer-

---

[11] Warren Weaver, "Recent Contributions to the Mathematical Theory of Communication," p. 273.

*[12] The greater the number of alternatives envisaged in a given situation, the greater the amount of time required for selecting any particular one (see Paul M. Fitts, "The Influence of Response Coding . . . ," p. 47). Or, looked at in another way, the greater the number of decisions required of the central nervous system in a given amount of time, the slower must be the rate of information if communication is to be accurate (see pp. 272–73). Consequently highly chromatic movements, which present the listener with a relatively large number of alternative sets of implications, tend to be slower than movements which are largely diatonic. Conversely, the greater the time allowed for "envisaging," the greater will be the number of alternatives actually considered. It is perhaps for this reason that in fast movements the improbable and the irregular are understood as surprise or as wit, while the same or similar progressions in slow movements are experienced as affect. In the former case, the listener has time to consider only a few of the possible modes of continuation. He is set and ready only for the highly probable. The less probable comes as a surprise and, seen as unexpected but somehow

tainty is aroused by the antecedent stimulus situation. Deviation occurs because the consequent was not the one expected, the probable one. (However, it conveys a maximum of information.) An understanding of the relationship of this mode of deviation to meaning and information necessitates a further analysis of the experience of meaning.

The meaning of an antecedent event depends upon its relationship to the consequent to which it refers. Since this relationship changes as the music unfolds, so does the meaning attributed to the antecedent event. Meaning, then, is not a static, invariant attribute of a stimulus, but an evolving discovery of attributes.

The development of embodied meaning may be differentiated into three stages.

1. *Hypothetical meanings* are those attributed to the antecedent tone or pattern of tones when the consequents are being expected. Unless deviation is present, hypothetical meanings will not arouse uncertainty or give rise to information. For, although any consequent is never more than a probability, as the probability of any particular consequent increases, the less probable alternatives are excluded from expectation. Thus, the more structured the situation, and hence the more dominant one mode of continuation over others, the less likely is the listener to envisage alternative consequents unless some deviation is present. This tendency of the dominant probability to exclude the less probable from consciousness is important because it explains why in a probabilistic world we are capable of surprise—that is, it accounts for the fact that the less probable becomes the unexpected.

Though the consequent which is actually forthcoming must be possible within the style, it may or may not be one of those which was most probable. Or it may arrive only after a delay or deceptive diversion through alternative consequents. But whether our expectations are confirmed or not, a new stage of meaning is reached when the consequent becomes a concrete musical event.

2. *Evident meanings* are those which are attributed to the antecedent stimulus in retrospect, after the consequent has become a tonal-psychic event and when the actual relationship between the antecedent and consequent is apprehended.

Evident and hypothetical meanings do not, however, arise and func-

---

"right," is interpreted as wit. (Repartee is rapid in a witty exchange.) In a slow tempo, alternative implications have time to be considered and the ambiguity perceived in the situation, evoking a feeling of doubt and uncertainty, is usually experienced as affect.

tion in isolation from one another. Evident meaning is modified by the hypothetical meanings previously attributed to the antecedent. That is, the consequent is not only that which actually follows, but it is that which follows as expected, arrives only after a deviation, resolves an ambiguity, or is unexpected.

Furthermore, the comprehension of the antecedent-consequent relationship in the light of evident meaning involves a revaluation of the hypothetical meaning of the initial stimulus and of the function of the completed progression within the larger context of the phrase, period, or section. Such revaluation then becomes the basis for future probability estimates and future expectations.

This process of revaluation is the mental counterpart to the "feedback" process in automatic control and information theory. For both feedback and revaluation are processes whereby future behavior, whether of automatic systems, motor reflexes, or expectations, is conditioned and controlled by the results of past events. Such mental feedback occurs both where the consequent was the one expected and where the consequent was unexpected.

If an antecedent event arouses no uncertainty and the consequent arrives precisely as expected, then meaning will be neutral, information nil, and feedback is superfluous—performs no function.[13] If the antecedent event has aroused uncertainty, feedback operates upon the arrival of the consequent (whether the one expected or not) causing the listener to modify his opinion of the hypothetical meaning initially attributed to the stimulus. That is, hypothetical meaning (expectation) is understood as having been confirmed, altered by temporary delays or deviations, clarified through the resolution of ambiguities, or mistaken because the improbable occurred. No matter which of the possibilities takes place, the information fed back to the initial situation, adding, so to speak, a new dimension to both hypothetical and evident meaning, acts to influence and direct the subsequent expectations of the listener—his estimates of future probabilities.

The presence of the feedback mechanism also throws light upon the genesis of meaning and information in those cases where the antecedent arouses no uncertainty, but in which the consequent is not the one latently expected. Such situations arise as a result of a discrepancy between the choices understood or felt to be available and those which were actually available. That is, the situation was less structured (more shuffled and higher in entropy) than the listener believed. One might

---

[13] See Arnold Tustin, "Feedback," p. 13.

put the matter somewhat differently by observing that while no uncertainty *was* felt, subsequent developments tell us that it *should have been* felt. And it would have been felt, had the "true" nature of the situation been understood.[14] It is important also to realize that such unexpected, improbable occurrences remain in the memory and influence the listener's later estimates of probability for the balance of the piece.

Not only does hypothetical meaning undergo a drastic reinterpretation in such cases, but so does our opinion of the information contained in the experience. For while the seemingly certain series of latently expected events makes it appear that the consequent will add little or no information to that already implicit in the antecedent, the situation was actually much higher in entropy and in information than it was thought to be.

3. *Determinate meanings* are those which arise out of the totality of relationships existing on several hierarchic levels between hypothetical meaning, evident meaning, and the later stages of the musical situation. As the music unfolds in time, later events are continually being related to earlier ones and vice versa. A recurrent theme or melody, for instance, is not only modified by the fact that it has been heard before, but its recurrence also modifies our opinion of its original meaning. In short, determinate meanings arise only after the experience of the work is a timeless memory—when all the implications of the stimulus on all hierarchic levels are realized and their interrelationships comprehended as fully as possible.

The fact that a given stimulus in some sense implies and is involved in later musical events points to still another relationship between musical meaning and information: the probabilities arising out of a musical progression (viewed on a particular hierarchic level) increase as the progression unfolds. For example, the implications of a group of two or three tones are more uncertain—lower in probability—than those of a phrase which is almost complete. Similarly on a higher level, the implications of a single section are lower in probability than those of a series of sections. In short, the more complete the section, the higher the probability relationship between those terms already established and any future sections.

"A system which produces a sequence of symbols (which may, of course, be letters or musical notes, say, rather than words) according to certain probabilities is called a *stochastic process,* and the special case

---

[14] A musical example of this is analyzed in Meyer, *Emotion and Meaning in Music,* pp. 48–49.

of a stochastic process in which the probabilities depend upon the previous events, is called a *Markoff process* or a Markoff chain." [15] The fact that music, like information, is an instance of a Markoff process has important practical and theoretical ramifications.

If music is a Markoff process, it would appear that as a musical event (be it a phrase, a theme, or a whole work) unfolds and the probability of a particular conclusion increases, uncertainty, information, and meaning will necessarily decrease. And in a closed physical system where the Markoff process operates this is just what does occur— probability tends to increase.

Uncertainty is, so to speak, "built into" the initial stages of a Markoff process. Such uncertainty is systemic in nature and it tends to decrease as the series progresses. *Systemic uncertainty* necessarily exists at the beginning of a piece (or part of a piece) of music where the relationships between tones, the intra-opus norms, are being established. And if music operated only with systemic uncertainty, meaning and information would necessarily decrease through the functioning of the Markoff process.

But music is not a natural system. It is man-made and man-controlled. And it is able to combat the tendency toward the tedium of maximum certainty through the *designed uncertainty* introduced by the composer.

On the basis of this analysis we should expect that designed uncertainty would be gradually introduced to compensate for the tendency of systemically caused information and meaning to decrease. That is, we should expect designed deviations, delays, and ambiguities to be introduced as systemic probability increases—as the pattern approaches completion. This expectation is borne out by the practice of musicians. C. P. E. Bach, for example, writes that "embellishments are best applied to those places where the melody is taking shape, as it were, or where its partial, if not complete, meaning or sense has been revealed." [16] Curt Sachs tells us that in primitive music a new note—one which is necessarily a deviant from the established tonal system—"generally ventures to appear only toward the end of the phrase, when the nucleus has been well established." [17]

Finally, it should be observed that as probability increases so does the

[15] Weaver, "Recent Contributions to the Mathematical Theory of Communication," p. 267.

[16] *Essay on the True Art of Playing Keyboard Instruments*, p. 84. For a discussion of the relationship between embellishment and deviation, see Meyer, *Emotion and Meaning . . .* , chap. 6.

[17] *The Rise of Music in the Ancient World*, p. 37.

apparent significance and information of "minor" deviations. The more certain we are that a particular consequent will be forthcoming, the greater the effect of deviation.

Music, like language, contains considerable redundancy. Redundancy is that portion of a message which "is determined not by the free choice of the sender, but rather by the accepted statistical rules governing the use of the symbols in question." [18] Just as letters can be left out of a written statement or words omitted from a message without affecting our ability to understand and reconstruct the word or message, so tones can be omitted from a musical passage without affecting our ability to grasp its meaning. A striking instance of this in music is found in solo sonatas for a string or woodwind instrument where chords are only partially stated and melodic "lines" are mentally constructed on a minimum of material. Or, if some of the tones of a melodic line are drowned out by the accompaniment, they can in most contexts be reconstructed in the mind of a listener practiced in the particular style. In short, because of the redundancy present in musical styles we are able to understand incomplete musical events, if what has been omitted is statistically probable.

Redundancy is of particular significance because it is one of the factors which allows for those important places in the experiencing of music where the listener's habit responses are able to "take over"—where the listener can pause, albeit briefly, to evaluate what has taken place in the past and to organize this experience with reference to the future.

Redundancy also serves to combat noise. It seems possible to distinguish between two kinds of noise: acoustical noise and cultural noise. Acoustical noise results from poor building acoustics (echoes, dead spots, etc.), poor transmission systems (which we leave to the hi-fi-natics), or just plain extra-musical sounds (talking, airplanes, and mosquitoes, if one is a devotee of summer concerts). Cultural noise, as I shall use the term, refers to disparities which may exist between the habit responses required by the musical style and those which a given individual actually possesses.

There appears to be positive correlation between cultural distance, whether historical or anthropological, and cultural noise. That is, the more distant a culture is from our present set of habit responses, the greater the amount of cultural noise involved in communication. The obvious exception to this rule is found in contemporary music. Here

---

[18] Weaver, "Recent Contributions . . . ," p. 269.

"noise" is the result of a time-lag between the habit responses which the audience actually possesses and those which the more adventurous composer envisages for it. It is also interesting to speculate whether some of the difficulties which audiences have with modern music do not result from the fact that the redundancy rate of this music is at times so low as to be unable to counteract the cultural noise which is always present in a communication situation. One might put this matter somewhat differently by saying that in their zeal to "pack" music full of meaning some contemporary composers have perhaps so overloaded the channel capacity of the audience that one meaning obscures another in the ensuing overflow.[19]

Since noise, whether cultural or acoustical, generally creates uncertainty, it would seem that noise is beneficial—for, as we have seen, uncertainty is important in the arousal of meaning and information. One must, however, distinguish between desirable and undesirable uncertainty.[20] Desirable uncertainty is that which arises within and as a result of the structured probabilities of a style system in which a finite number of antecedents and consequents become mutually relevant through the habits, beliefs, and attitudes of a group of listeners. Undesirable uncertainty arises when the probabilities are not known, either because the listeners' habit responses are not relevant to the style (cultural noise), or because external interference (acoustical noise) obscures the structure of the situation being considered.[21]

---

*[19] See chapter 11.

[20] See Weaver, "Recent Contributions . . . ," pp. 273–74.

*[21] The nature of the relationship between a musical style and the culture from which it arises is a complex and perplexing one. More often than not, scholars have assumed what they set out to prove, namely, that some sort of congruence exists. They have sought to show that particular attributes of a style can be equated with (or even derived from) culture or some specific facet of it. Or, they have attempted to relate the "spirit" of an age to the styles of art produced in it. Whatever the validity and value of this sort of enterprise—and it is at times open to serious question (see chap. 7)—another way of looking at the matter merits consideration. I should like to suggest the following:

A culture, like a musical style, is a learned probability system. Indeed, it is not uncommon to speak of the "style" of a culture. Conversely, it does no violence to the facts to refer to the "behavior" of a musical work. Since both music and culture are learned probability systems, might it not be fruitful to analyze and compare them in terms of their formal structures and syntactic processes rather than in terms of the particular "content"—events, beliefs, progressions and referential meanings—of the culture and its art? One might ask questions such as: how, in specific terms, are the norms of both styles articulated? what sorts and degrees of deviation are permitted? what constitutes tolerable levels of ambiguity and un-

These differences can be clearly and concisely illustrated by examples of linguistic communication. In the case of desirable uncertainty, one is uncertain simply about how a sentence in a familiar language will be completed. In the case of undesirable uncertainty resulting from cultural noise, one is in doubt about how a sentence in an unknown language will be completed. Here no consequent can be envisaged and none has any meaning or communicates any information when it arrives, since all seem equally probable (or improbable). Finally, where undesirable uncertainty is a result of acoustical noise, one is uncertain about how a sentence will be completed because external interference obscures or obliterates the antecedent upon which prediction depends.

The fact that musical styles are probability systems inevitably raises the complex problem of the possibility of a statistical analysis of style and the construction of devices for composing music on the basis of the probabilities inherent in the style of Western music. While I do not share the deep-seated antipathy felt by most humanists toward anything that smacks of statistics, I feel that the many difficult problems involved in any statistical approach must be recognized if such studies are to have anything more than a curiosity value.

The mere collection and counting of phenomena do not lead to significant concepts. Behind any statistical investigation must be hypotheses that determine which facts shall be collected and counted.

> An estimate of a probability which is made simply on the basis of unanalyzed samples or trials is not likely to be a safe basis for prediction. If nothing is known concerning the mechanism of a situation under investigation, the relative frequencies obtained from samples may be poor guides to the character of the indefinitely large population from which they are drawn.[22]

Since the nature and structure of the sample being studied is a result of a knowledge of the mechanism of the situation, a statistical investigation, if it is to have any relevance to music, must be based upon a sophisticated and sensitive understanding of the processes involved in the experiencing of musical style. Some of these problems are discussed in what follows.

---

certainty? and so on. I am not at all sure that this is possible. For instance, I do not know in what ways syntactic probability systems might be defined and differentiated, classified and compared. Nevertheless, even an attempt at such a study would, I think, prove rewarding and illuminating.

[22] Ernest Nagel, *Principles of the Theory of Probability*, p. 59; and also see Norbert Wiener, *Cybernetics*, p. 35.

Meaning in Music and Information Theory

1. The samples collected must take account of the tendency of systemic uncertainty to diminish and of designed uncertainty to be introduced as the music unfolds. And there may well be a difference between the probabilities of systemic origin and those introduced by design.

2. Tonal probabilities exist not only within phrases and smaller parts of a musical structure but also between them. These probabilities are not necessarily the same. For instance, it seems more likely that a phrase or melody will begin with a skip than that a progression of phrases will initially involve a large skip. Thus the statistical analysis of stylistic probabilities must be architectonic—different sets of probability must be discovered for different hierarchic levels.

3. It is a mistake to suppose that probability remains relatively constant throughout musical works. Quite the contrary. Some parts of a work tend to adhere much more closely to the normative and probable than do other parts. For instance, the development section of a sonata-form movement involves much more deviation—much more use of the less probable—than do the exposition and recapitulation. And this difference of probability between parts holds even in the case of short melodies. Thus serious statistical and methodological errors arise if probabilities are computed on the basis of a total "average" frequency over the entire piece. Subsystems must be analyzed within the larger probability system. And since the differences between subsystems will vary from style to style, so must the estimates of probability.

4. In defining the limits of a sample and discussing the probabilities involved, it is important to be cognizant of the historical development of musical styles. The fact that a given progression occurs in a large majority of cases is not a sure sign that it is psychologically probable. And conversely, the mere fact that the frequency of a particular progression is low is no certification of its improbable character. For instance, though the perfect cadence occurs infrequently in the later music of Richard Wagner, it is nevertheless presupposed as a norm; and when Wagner avoids the cadence, as he does time and time again, his resolutions are felt to be less probable deviants. Later in the nineteenth century the situation with regard to the perfect cadence becomes even more complex. For now the frequency of irregular cadential progression has influenced probability to such an extent that the probabilities are in doubt and the cadence becomes ambiguous.

5. Not all the probabilities embodied in a musical composition are determined by frequency. Some are based upon the nature of human mental processes—ways of thinking. For example, even though the frequency with which a large structural gap is immediately filled in is

low in a given sample, the felt probabilities are high that it will be filled immediately. For this reason one of the preliminaries to a statistical analysis of musical styles must be a description and analysis of the constants involved in the psychology of thought.

These observations raise a further question: Is it possible to develop an accurate mathematical picture of musical style which could serve as a basis for the quantification and measurement of musical information? Norbert Wiener's statement that "the human sciences are very poor testing grounds for a new mathematical technique" [23] seems persuasive both in theory and in the light of the statistical investigations of music carried on thus far.

But the case is not, I think, completely hopeless. Two things are required. First we must arrive at a more precise and empirically validated account of mental behavior which will make it possible to introduce the more or less invariant probabilities of human mental processes into the calculation of the probabilities involved in the style. This account need not necessarily be statistical itself.

> . . . probability statements do not always occur singly and are often part of a more or less inclusive *system* of statements or a *theory*. In such cases the estimation of the numerical values of the probabilities and the subsequent testing of such values may be made on the basis of *indirect* evidence which in some cases may even be nonstatistical.[24]

Second, and this is ultimately dependent upon the first, it is necessary to develop a more precise and sensitive understanding of the nature of musical experience.

The impossibility of measuring musical information precisely at present does not weaken or invalidate the theoretical position adopted in this essay. Rather it should act as a cue for further study and experimentation. Much might be learned, for instance, by making a more discriminating study of stylistic probabilities, introducing hypothetical mental constants with arbitrarily assigned numerical weightings, taking into account the various difficulties discussed above—then studying the resulting melodies. What sort of melodies, for instance, would arise if we assumed a numerical value for the mental tendency of a melodic process to continue itself, or took account of the differences in probabilities between different hierarchic levels or introduced random deviations in some parts but not others? Or, having arrived at a tentative probability scheme, what effect would changes in one variable—say the presence

---

[23] *Cybernetics*, p. 34.

[24] Nagel, *Principles of the Theory of Probability*, pp. 23–24.

of chromaticism—have on the resulting melodies? Such experiments, carried on by students who understand the mechanism of musical communication, might reveal much not only about music but also about some of the constants in human perception.

The preceding discussion has shown that embodied meaning and information arise out of the same processes. This does not, however, assert that they are identical. The differentia between them lies not in the nature of the processes involved, but in the psychological attitude taken toward the processes. For though both information and meaning are manifestations of the probabilities present in antecedent-consequent relationships, each has a different focus of attention. In the case of meaning, attention is for the most part directed toward the antecedent, though of course the consequent is, as we have seen, of vital importance. In the case of information the greater part of attention is concentrated upon the consequent. To put the matter briefly, in meaning, the musical process is considered and evaluated from the viewpoint of antecedents; in information the same processes are examined and assessed from the viewpoint of consequents.

This study has intentionally avoided the perplexing problems of value and value theory. Without entering into the many heated discussions raging in these areas, it seems permissible in closing to suggest that the viewpoint adopted here might prove fruitful in the analysis of value. For, aside from the obvious fact that something without meaning or information is, almost by definition, valueless (indeed what we mean by "trite" or "banal" is the most probable means of achieving the most probable end), it seems that valuations, evaluations, and perhaps values as well arise only as the result of the uncertainties involved in making means-ends choices—that is, in predicting alternative antecedent-consequent probabilities.

Furthermore, it seems plausible to regard "value" as an experience which, like meaning, evolves and changes, rather than as a fixed rigid attribute of particular stimuli. From this point of view, *valuation*, the estimate of probable consequents within a means-ends continuum, would be a correlate of hypothetical meaning; *evaluation*, the apprehension of what has actually taken place, would be a correlate of evident meaning; and *value*, the ultimate comprehension of an experience when it is timeless in memory, would be a correlate of determinate meaning.

Thus value, information, and meaning might profitably be considered as being different, though related, experiential realizations of a basic stochastic process governed by the law of entropy.

CHAPTER 2

Some Remarks on Value and Greatness In Music

As every musician must be, I have been concerned with the nature of value in music and have in moments of impetuous rashness even asked myself the $64,000 question: What makes music great? In grappling with these perplexing problems I have changed my mind many times, testing first this view then that; finding this objection then another to what I thought at first to be tenable positions. Nor have I as yet arrived at any fixed opinions or final conclusions.[1]

Indeed, instead of providing positive answers neatly confined to the area of aesthetics (as I should have preferred), my attempts to understand the nature of value in music have led to still further questions about the nature of value in general and ultimately to the rarefied realm of metaphysics. Since my ideas on these matters are still in flux, I shall present neither an explicit theory of value nor a definitive account of greatness. Rather, in pointing out relationships and correlations between value in music and value in other areas, I shall hope to suggest

---

*[1] I now feel that, though the account of value given in this chapter is relevant to our understanding of the values of Western art music at least since the Renaissance, it may not be applicable to the musics of other cultures—particularly those in which musical-aesthetic experience is not established in the culture as a specific conceptual-behavioral category—or to the art of transcendentalism (see chaps. 8 and 9, *passim*).

viewpoints and avenues of approach which will perhaps provide fruitful insights and may later lead to plausible conclusions.

Whatever the difficulties, uncertainties, and hazards may be, the question "What makes music great?" is one that anyone deeply concerned with his art must attempt at least to answer. And if some scholars make a point of avoiding such questions altogether as the positivists do, or throw them into the vast nets of cultural context as the social scientists have often done, or surreptitiously substitute the plausibility of technical jargon for basic questionings as humanists sometimes do—so much the worse for them. We cannot—nor can they for all their rationalizations—really escape from the problem of value.

This is true in two senses. The first is perhaps obvious, yet nonetheless important. We are in fact continually making value judgments for both ourselves and others. As an individual I can listen to and study only a limited number of musical works during my lifetime. I must choose between works, exercising value judgments. As a teacher I decide to use this work for teaching rather than that. And though I may select the work for didactic reasons rather than because I think it is a masterpiece, even as I chose it for this reason I am aware of the distinction between a work which is great in its own terms and one which will serve to illustrate a given point clearly.

The second reason why the problem of value is inescapable for someone concerned with music—or any art for that matter—is that a system or ordering of values is implicit in his account of how and what art communicates. Indeed, as soon as we say it communicates, we introduce values into the discussion. At one time I subscribed to I. A. Richards' statement that "the two pillars upon which a theory of criticism must rest are an account of value and an account of communication." [2] It has seemed increasingly clear, however, that these two are as inextricably linked to one another as are means and ends. When you discuss one, you are of necessity implying the other. For instance, if your account of musical communication is primarily in terms of the referential and associative states which music can arouse, then your judgments as to value are going to be different from those which would arise out of an account of communication which emphasized the more exclusively intra-musical meanings which I shall call embodied or syntactical.

At first it seems that the problem is not really very difficult. After all

---

[2] *Principles of Literary Criticism*, p. 25.

there are certain technical criteria for excellence in a piece of music. A good piece of music must have consistency of style: that is, it must employ a unified system of expectations and probabilities; it should possess clarity of basic intent; it should have variety, unity, and all the other categories which are so easy to find after the fact. But these are, I think, only necessary causes. And while they may enable us to distinguish a good or satisfactory piece from a downright bad one, they will not help us very much when we try to discriminate between a pretty good work and a very good one, let alone distinguish the characteristics of greatness.

Indeed the tune, "Twinkle, twinkle little star" possesses style, unity, variety, and so forth. And if we then ask is Bach's B Minor Mass better than "Twinkle, twinkle"—using *only* these technical categories—we shall, I am afraid, be obliged to answer that they are equally good, adding perhaps, "each in its own way." I shall return to the "each in its own way" argument presently. But for now, it seems to me that, granting listeners who have learned to respond to and understand both works, the statement that these works are equally good is preposterous and false.

Nor are length, size, or complexity *as such* criteria of value, though, as we shall see, complexity does have something to do with excellence. Thus some of Brahms's smaller piano pieces are often considered better works than, for instance, his Fourth Symphony. And I am sure that each of us can cite instances of this for himself. Perhaps it would be well at this point to turn to particular musical examples to see what we can learn from them.

Because a relatively thorough examination of even two brief pieces would involve a complex and lengthy analysis, I have chosen to discuss, briefly, two fugue subjects: the first is from Geminiani's Concerto Grosso Op. 3 No. 3; the second is from Bach's Prelude and Fugue in G Minor for organ. Since only the themes will be discussed, it should be pointed out that good themes do not necessarily give rise to good total works. And though it is difficult to write a good fugue on a really poor subject, an unprepossessing theme—such as that of Bach's Fugue in C-sharp Minor from the *Well-Tempered Clavier*, Volume I—may act as the basis for a very fine work.

Even though it goes against critical canon I intend to treat the themes as entities in their own right, but as themes, not as complete works. For considered in themselves they will serve to raise some of the basic considerations which are involved in value and ultimately in greatness. And these considerations apply with equal force to complete works, even those of the greatest magnitude. In short, reversing the procedure of

Value and Greatness in Music

Plato, who inquired as to the principles of justice in the individual by considering the nature of justice in the state, we shall try to learn something about the value of whole works by considering the nature of value in a small segment.

Here then are the two themes:

Example 1. A: Geminiani, Op. 3 No. 3. B: Bach, Prelude and Fugue for Organ.

They are certainly not equally good. And at first glance we observe that the Bach theme has more rhythmic and motivic variety, that it covers a larger range, and so forth than Geminiani's theme. However, there are good themes which lack obvious variety. In any case, it seems safe to say that variety is a means to an end, not an end in itself.

Looking at these two themes more closely, we see that they are quite similar in their basic melodic structure. Both begin on the fifth degree of the scale, move to the tonic (in the Bach, through the third of the scale), and then skip an octave. This skip creates a structural gap, a sense of incompleteness. We expect that the empty space thus outlined will be filled in, made complete. This melodic incompleteness is complemented by the rhythmic instability of this first musical shape. That is, the first separable musical events in both themes are upbeats which are oriented toward the stability of downbeats.

In a sense the structural gap and the rhythmic upbeats have established musical goals to be reached. We expect the melodic line to descend and ultimately to come to rest on the tonic note, reaching a clear organizing accent in the course of this motion. And so in fact they both do. *But* with crucial differences. The Bach theme moves down slowly with delays and temporary diversions through related harmonic areas. It establishes various levels of melodic activity with various potentials to be realized. Furthermore, these delays are rhythmic as well as melodic (see analysis under Example 1). The Geminiani theme, on the other hand, moves directly—or almost directly—to its goal. The second measure is chromatic and contains a potential for different modes of continuation. Of these the return to the B is certainly the most probable, but only slightly so. However, once the B is reached, the descent to E seems almost inevitable. And when the theme falls to this obvious consequent with neither delay nor diversion, it seems like a blatant platitude, a musical cliché. Nor are there any rhythmic resistances. The initial upbeat perpetuates itself without marked disturbance down to the final note which arrives on the obvious downbeat.

Thus it seems that, here at least, value has something to do with the activation of a musical impulse having tendencies toward a more or less definite goal and with the temporary resistance or inhibition of these tendencies. The importance of the element of resistance can be made even more apparent if we rewrite the Bach theme in such a way that this element is eliminated.

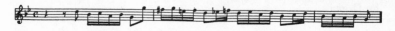

Example 2

The theme is now as banal as Geminiani's.

From these considerations it follows (1) that a melody or a work which establishes no tendencies, if such can be imagined, will from this point of view (and others are possible) be of no value. Of course, such tendencies need not be powerful at the outset, but may be developed during the course of musical progress. (2) If the most probable goal is reached in the most immediate and direct way, given the stylistic context, the musical event taken in itself will be of little value. And (3) if the goal is never reached or if the tendencies activated become dissipated in the press of over-elaborate or irrelevant diversions, then value will tend to be minimal.

The notion that the inhibition of goal-oriented tendencies is related to value is not a new one. Robert Penn Warren writes that "a poem, to be good, must earn itself. It is a motion toward a point of rest, but if it is not a resisted motion, it is a motion of no consequence. For example, a poem which depends upon stock materials and stock responses is simply a toboggan slide, or a fall through space." [3] John Dewey's position is quite similar. "Impulsion forever boosted on its forward way would run its course thoughtless, and dead to emotion. . . . The only way it can become aware of its nature and its goal is by obstacles surmounted and means employed." [4]

---

[3] "Pure and Impure Poetry," p. 251.
[4] *Art as Experience*, p. 59.

Value and Greatness in Music

More recently information theory has developed concepts in which the relationship between resistance and value seems to be implicit. In order to understand how information theory relates to these considerations, it is necessary to examine the nature of goal-tendency processes in more detail.

Musical events take place in a world of stylistic probability. If we hear only a single tone, a great number of different tones could follow it with equal probability. If a sequence of two tones is heard, the number of probable consequent tones is somewhat reduced—how much depends upon the tones chosen and the stylistic context—and hence the probability of the remaining alternatives is somewhat increased. As more tones are added and consequently more relationships between tones established, the probabilities of a particular goal become increased. Thus in Bach's theme the probability of any particular tone following the first D is very small, for the number of possible consequents is very large. As the line moves downward through the B-flat and the A, the probabilities of the G become very high and it is partly the satisfaction of this motion which closes out the first pattern as a musical event. This pattern, after the octave skip, now becomes the unit of motion and the basis for probability estimates on a higher architectonic level. Note that the variety of events in this theme, as well as the delays already noted, makes the particular sequence of events seem much less probable than the sequence of events in the Geminiani theme.

Here information theory becomes relevant. It tells us that if a situation is highly organized so that the possible consequents have a high degree of probability, then if the probable occurs, the information communicated by the message (what we have been calling a musical event) is minimal. If, on the other hand, the musical situation is less predictable so that the antecedent-consequent relationship does *not* have a high degree of probability, then the information contained in the musical message will be high. Norbert Wiener has put the matter succinctly: ". . . the more probable the message, the less information it gives. Clichés, for example, are less illuminating than great poems." [5]

Since resistances, or more generally deviations, are by definition disturbances in the goal-oriented tendencies of a musical impulse, they lower the probability not only of a particular consequent but of the musical event as a whole. In so doing they create or increase information. And it does not seem a rash step to conclude that what creates or

---

[5] *The Human Use of Human Beings*, p. 21.

increases the information contained in a piece of music increases its value.[6]

Of course in either linguistic or musical communication a completely random series of stimuli will in all likelihood communicate nothing. For language and music depend upon the existence of an ordered probability system, a stochastic process, which serves to make the several stimuli or events mutually relevant to one another. Thus the probability of any particular musical event depends in part upon the probabilistic character of the style employed. Randomness of choice is limited by the fact of musical style.

The concepts of information theory suggest that the notion of resistance can be generalized by relating it through probability to uncertainty. For the lower the probability that any particular sequence of events will take place—that is, the lower the probability that the total message will be any particular one—the greater the uncertainty about what the events and the message will actually be. And also the greater the information contained in the total event. Thus greater uncertainty and greater information go hand in hand.[7]

The relationship between resistance and uncertainty is not difficult to discover. Whenever a tendency is inhibited—or, more generally, when deviation takes place—slight though perhaps unconscious uncertainty is experienced. What seemed perhaps so probable that alternative consequents were not considered now seems less so. For the mind, attempting

---

*[6] It is sometimes objected that analysis can never do full justice to the unique, ineffable beauty of a work of art and that, because it necessarily involves the use of conceptual categories, analysis always misrepresents and does violence to the unmediated quality of pure aesthetic experience. These points must, I think, be granted. The peculiar quality of a particular object, event, or experience—whether in art or in nature—can never be explained fully and without distortion. (These matters are discussed below, pp. 162–64 and pp. 215–16.) To insist upon an exhaustive and accurate account, however, is to give up all hope of rational explanation and communication. One can only assert that a work of art is beautiful or possesses "validity" (see, for instance, Albert Hofstadter, "Validity versus Value"). One cannot explain what validity *is*, or why one work has it and another does not. The judgment cannot be accounted for or disputed, for it is based upon immediate intuition or mystical insight.

While the achievement of analysis is no doubt imperfect and more debatable— precisely because it is open to public scrutiny and criticism—it is also potentially more fruitful and useful because it can be communicated and, at least modestly, documented.

[7] In part uncertainty is inherent in the nature of the probability process, in part it is intentionally introduced by the composer. See p. 15.

to account for and understand the import of the deviation, is made aware of the possibility of less probable, alternative consequents.

A distinction must be made between desirable and undesirable uncertainty. Desirable uncertainty is that which arises as a result of the structured probabilities of a musical style. Information is a function of such uncertainty. Undesirable uncertainty arises when the probabilities are not known, either because the listener's habit responses are not relevant to the style (which I have called "cultural noise") [8] or because external interference (acoustical noise) obscures the structure of the situation in question.

It seems further that uncertainty should be distinguished from vagueness, though the distinction is by no means clear-cut. Uncertainty evidently presumes a basic norm of clear probability patterns such that even the ambiguous is felt to be goal-oriented. Vagueness, on the other hand, involves a weakening of the transitive, kinetic character of syntactic relationships and as a result the sense of musical tendency is enervated. When this occurs, attention becomes focused upon the nuances and refinements of phrases, timbres, textures, and the like. And impressionism tends in this respect to be the sensitive projection of the sensuous. We shall return to another aspect of the relationship between value and uncertainty a bit later. Now we must briefly consider the nature of the unexpected or, more particularly, the surprising in relation to information theory.

All deviation involves the less probable. But because in most cases the less probable grows gradually out of the more probable or because in some cases the musical context is one in which deviation is more or less expected, listeners are as a rule aware of the possibility of deviation. They are set and ready for the less probable, though often unconsciously so. In the case of the unexpected, the probability of a given music event seems so high that the possibility of alternative consequents is not considered. It seems as though the message involves a minimum of uncertainty and that, when completed, it will have contained little information. But when at the last moment the improbable abruptly arrives, the listener discovers that his estimates of probability and uncertainty were wrong and that the event or message actually contained more information than it was presumed to contain.

Let us consider these matters in relation to an example from language and in relation to Geminiani's fugue subject. Take the phrase "she is as

---

[8] See pp. 16–17.

tall." First off, we can talk about the sequence of sounds in terms of probability, uncertainty, and information. The uncertainty of what will follow the sound "sh" is very high indeed, though clearly some sounds will be less probable than others, given the stylistic context we call English. Thus the sound or "word" *shvin* is highly improbable in an English sentence. But it is not impossible—witness the fact that it has just occurred in one.[9] The uncertainties are reduced and the probabilities increased when the sound "i" (e) arrives. But the pause which actually follows is only one of the possible sequels to the sound "she." The word might have become "sheep." Thus both the sound "i" and the pause add considerable information. And please note that silence is a part of information, musical as well as linguistic.

Now the same kind of analysis is possible for the first event in Geminiani's theme. Considering the notes B and E, for the sake of comparison, as equivalent to the sound "sh," it is clear that the number of possible consequents is very high. The event could have continued in many different ways, though again some (Example 3a) are more probable, given the stylistic context and the fact that this is the beginning of a work, than others (Example 3b). The high E, like the sound "i" (e), thus adds a great deal of information to the musical message (see Example 1).

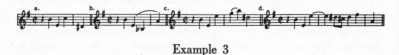

Example 3

The turning of the melodic line downward and the arrival of a clear downbeat—these complement each other—make it clear in retrospect that a musical event has been completed. Had the melodic line not been articulated by a change of motion or had the downbeat been suppressed, the musical event would have been different. That is, just as the sound "she" could have become part of the linguistic event "sheep," so the first three notes of this theme could have become part of the events presented in Example 3, parts *c* and *d*.

Of course these events, both the musical and the linguistic ones, exist only on the lowest architectonic level. They cannot stand alone, but are parts of larger wholes. That is, the musical event is part of a syntactical

---

[9] This "gimmick" is borrowed from Warren Weaver, "Recent Contributions . . . ," p. 267.

unit we call a theme, the linguistic event part of a syntactical unit we call a sentence or phrase. And these larger units, which are events on higher architectonic levels, are but parts of still larger musical sections or linguistic paragraphs or stanzas. These in turn are parts of whole pieces of music or works of literature.

Turning now to the partial phrase "she is as tall," it is evident that there is one highly probable syntactical consequent. That is, we expect that the phrase will be followed by the word "as" and then by a proper noun or a pronoun. And we would be surprised to find an adjective following either the word "tall" or the words "tall as." For instance, the phrases "she is as tall blue" or "she is as tall as blue" are rather improbable, though not impossible. The first of these alternatives might continue "she is as tall blue lilacs are," and the improbability of the simile increases the amount of information considerably.

If we take a more probable consequent, "she is as tall as Bill," we have acquired information, but syntactically speaking not very much. Notice incidentally that we actually leave out that part of the construction which is the most probable. That is, we omit the implicit "as Bill *is* tall" because in the context these words contribute no information and hence are unnecessary. Now if we look at the first part of the Geminiani theme we might say, by analogy, that the half-phrase up to the B corresponds to the part-phrase "she is as tall" and that the descent to the E corresponds to the most probable syntactical completion just as the words "as Bill is tall" do. Both completions are obvious and neither is very good. However, this does *not* assert that taken in the context of a larger whole, these phrases might not become part of a meaningful, valuable work.

Before we leave this comparison between musical and linguistic behavior, it might be amusing to construct examples involving the unexpected. Observe, first of all, that since the phrase "she is as tall" is syntactically incomplete, we are alert to the possibility of alternative consequents and that if the word "blue" follows (as in the phrase "she is as tall blue lilacs are"), it seems improbable but in a sense not unexpected. But if we take the phrase "she is as tall as Bill is," we assume our information is complete and are not ready for new information. And so if we add the word "wide" instead of the understood "tall," it is both improbable and unexpected. And the whole message contains more information than we presumed it to contain.

In a similar manner we can add to the Geminiani theme so that what at first seems to be a point of completion ceases to be so and becomes part of an unexpected twist of meaning (Example 4).

Notice that not only is information increased in this variant, but that the meaning of the descent from B is in retrospect *literally* different. For its obviousness now seems to have been a means of deception as to the ultimate intent of the theme.

Example 4

To summarize what we have learned from this excursion into the relationship of information theory to music and to value: first of all, we have found that resistance, or more broadly deviation, is a correlative of information. And since information is valuable—as tautology is not—our hypothesis as to the importance of deviation has received confirmation. Second, our inquiry has pointed to a relationship between information and deviation on the one hand, and uncertainty on the other. This implies that uncertainty is somehow related to value. This apparently paradoxical pairing will be considered presently.

Hypotheses gain in plausibility not only through the corroboration of other investigators and through correlation with other fields of inquiry but also by accounting for facts observed but hitherto unexplained theoretically. Our hypothesis can do this in explaining the difference between primitive music and art music. In so doing it is hoped that another aspect of the relationship between tendency inhibition and value will be revealed.

If we ask, "What is the fundamental difference between sophisticated art music and primitive music" (and I do not include under the term "primitive" the highly sophisticated music which so-called primitives often play), then we can point to the fact that primitive music generally employs a smaller repertory of tones, that the distance of these notes from the tonic is smaller, that there is a great deal of repetition, though often slightly varied repetition, and so forth. But these are the symptoms of primitivism in music, not its causes.

The differentia between art music and primitive music lies in speed of tendency gratification. The primitive seeks almost immediate gratification for his tendencies whether these be biological or musical. Nor can he tolerate uncertainty. And it is because distant departures from the certainty and repose of the tonic note and lengthy delays in gratification are insufferable to him that the tonal repertory of the primitive is limited, not because he cannot think of other tones. It is not his mentality that is limited, it is his maturity. Note, by the way, that popular music can be distinguished from real jazz on the same basis. For while "pop" music whether of the tin-pan alley or the Ethelbert Nevin variety makes use of a fairly large repertory of tones, it operates with such conventional clichés that gratification is almost immediate and uncertainty is minimized.

One aspect of maturity both of the individual and of the culture within which a style arises consists then in the willingness to forgo immediate, and perhaps lesser, gratification for the sake of future ultimate gratification. Understood generally, not with reference to any specific musical work, self-imposed tendency inhibition and the willingness to bear uncertainty are indications of maturity. They are signs, that is, that the animal is becoming a man. And this, I take it, is not without relevance to considerations of value.

"This is all very well and more or less plausible," someone will say, "but in the last analysis isn't music valuable for a variety of reasons rather than just for the rather puritanical ones which you have been hinting at? What of the sensuous pleasure of beautiful sound? What of the ability of music to move us through the deep-seated associations it is able to evoke? Are these without value?"

The problems raised by these questions—that of the relation of pleasure to value and that of the ordering of values—have concerned philosophy from its very beginnings, and I shall not presume to give definitive answers to them. What follows must therefore be taken as provisional.

At first it seems that we do in fact distinguish between what is *pleasurable* and what is *good*. Indeed the difference between them seems to parallel the distinction drawn above between immediate gratification and delayed gratification. But as we state it, the distinction breaks down, even linguistically. For delayed gratification too is pleasurable, not only in the sense that it does culminate in ultimate and increased satisfaction, but also in the sense that it involves pleasures related to the conquest of difficulties—to control and power.[10]

---

[10] This does not, of course, assert that all experience is either good or pleasurable. Total quiescence—the absence of any stimulation whatever—is both unpleasant and valueless; and so is its opposite, the complete frustration of a strong tendency which can find no substitute outlet. In connection with the former, it seems that patterned information is an important need of the human mind. For references, see chap. 3, n. 18.

Two points should be noted in this connection. In the first place, both immediate gratification and delayed gratification are pleasurable and both are valuable, though they are not necessarily equally valuable. Second, value refers to a quality of musical experience. It is inherent neither in the musical object per se nor in the mind of the listener per se. Rather, value arises as the result of a transaction which takes place within an objective tradition between the musical work and a listener. This being the case, the value of any particular musical experience is a function both of the listener's ability to respond—his having learned the style of the music—and of his mode of response.

Three aspects of musical enjoyment may be distinguished: the sensuous, the associative-characterizing, and the syntactical. And though every piece of music involves all three to some extent, some pieces tend to emphasize one aspect and minimize others. Thus at one end of what is obviously a continuum is the immediate gratification of the sensuous and the exclamatory outburst of uncontrolled, pent-up energy. At the other end of the continuum is the delayed gratification arising out of the perception of and response to the syntactical relationships which shape and mold musical experience, whether intellectual or emotional. The associative may function with either. It may color our sensuous pleasures with the satisfactions of wish-fulfillment. Or it may shape our expectations as to the probabilities of musical progress by characterizing musical events. For just as our estimate of the character of an individual influences our expectations about his probable behavior, so our estimate of the character of a theme or musical event shapes our expectations about how it will behave musically. And conversely, the way in which a musical event behaves—involves regular, deviant, or surprising progressions—influences our opinion of its character. Thus the syntactical and characterizing facets of musical communication are inextricably linked.

The question of the ordering of values still remains. Are the different aspects of musical enjoyment equally valuable? Is a piece of music which appeals primarily to sensuous-associative pleasure as good as one which appeals to syntactical-associative enjoyment? If we put the matter as crudely as possible—if we ask, "Is the best arrangement of the best pop-tune as good as Beethoven's Ninth Symphony?"—then the answer seems easy. But if we put a similar question using less polar works and ask, "Is Debussy's *Afternoon of a Faun* as good as the Ninth Symphony?" we have qualms about the answer.

At this point some of our social scientist friends, whose blood pressure has been steadily mounting, will throw up their hands in relativistic horror and cry: "You can't do this! You can't compare baked Alaska with roast beef. Each work is good of its kind and there's the end of it." Now granting both that we can enjoy a particular work for a variety of reasons and also that the enjoyment of one kind of music does not preclude the enjoyment of others—that we can enjoy both Debussy and Beethoven—this does not mean that they are equally good. Nor does it mean that all modes of musical enjoyment are equally valuable. In fact, when you come right down to it, the statement that "each is good of its kind" is an evasion of the problem, not a solution of it. And so we are still driven to ask: are all kinds equally good?

To begin the next stage of our inquiry, let us recall an idea brought out in our discussion of the difference between primitive music and sophisticated music. I refer to the observation that willingness to inhibit tendencies and tolerate uncertainties is a sign of maturity. Note, however, that the converse of this is also true. For maturation and individualization are themselves products of the resistances, problems, and uncertainties with which life confronts us. As George Herbert Mead has pointed out, it is only by coming to grips with these difficulties and overcoming them and by making the choices and decisions which each of us must make that the self becomes aware of itself, becomes a self.[11] Only through our encounters with the world, through what we suffer, do we achieve self-realization as particular men and women.

It is because the evaluation of alternative probabilities and the retrospective understanding of the relationships among musical events as they actually occurred leads to self-awareness and individualization that the syntactical response is more valuable than those responses in which the ego is dissolved, losing its identity in voluptuous sensation or in the reverie of daydreams. And for the same reasons works involving deviation and uncertainty are better than those offering more immediate satisfaction. I am not contending that other modes of enjoyment are without value, but rather that they are of a lesser order of value.

The difficulty is that, aside from the most primitive forms of musical-emotional outburst and the most blatant appeals to the sensuous such as one finds in the cheapest pop arrangements, there are no musical works of art in which syntactical relationships do not play a significant role. Nor will it do to try to arrange musical works in order of their syntactical versus their sensuous-associative appeals. For even a work such as Debussy's *Afternoon of a Faun*, which strongly emphasizes the

---

[11] *Mind, Self, and Society*, in particular Parts II and III.

sensuous, is syntactically complex—as complex, for instance, as the first movement of Mozart's famous Piano Sonata in C Major which is predominantly syntactical.[12]

Thus it seems that while the contrast between the sensuous-associative and the syntactical may provide a basis for evaluating the responses of listeners, it does not provide a basis for judging the value of most pieces of music. The sensuous-associative is of minor importance in the consideration of value.[13] Music must be evaluated syntactically. And indeed it is so. For who is to say which of two works has greater sensuous appeal or evokes more poignant associations? The matter is completely subjective. And if we ask, "Why is Debussy's music superior to that of Delius?" the answer lies in the syntactical organization of his music, not in its superior sensuousness.

What then are the determinants of value from the syntactical viewpoint? We noted earlier that complexity, size, and length are not in themselves virtues. For as we all know from sad experience, a large complex work can be pretentious and bombastic, dull and turgid, or a combination of these. Yet insofar as the intricate and subtle interconnections between musical events, whether simultaneous or successive, of a complex work involve considerable resistance and uncertainty—and presumably information—value is thereby created. This viewpoint seems more plausible when we consider that as we become more familiar with a complex work and are therefore better able to comprehend the permutations and interrelations among musical events, our enjoyment is increased. For the information we get out of the work is increased.

Obviously neither information nor complexity refers to the mere accumulation of a heterogeneous variety of events. If the events are to be meaningful, they must arise out of a set of probability relationships, a musical style. Moreover, the capacity of the human mind to perceive and relate patterns to one another and to remember them appears to limit complexity. For if a work is so complex that the musical events eclipse one another, then value will be diminished. Or, as mentioned earlier, if complexity and length are such that tendencies become dissipated in the course of over-elaborate deviations, then meanings will be lost as relationships become obscure. Of course if listeners are unable to remember the musical events, whether because of the magnitude of a

---

[12] In this connection it should be observed that instrumentation, texture, tempo, and dynamics, which are often thought of as contributing most to the sensuous-associative aspect of music, may, and in the work of fine composers do, function syntactically.

[13] The sensuous-associative may, however, be of importance in accounting for individual musical preferences.

work or because it involves stylistic innovations, then the piece of music may seem overcomplex when it is not so. This is why music at first found unintelligible and empty may later become understandable and rewarding.

We have been so conditioned by the nineteenth-century notion that great art is simple that the association of complexity with value is repugnant. Yet, while complexity is not the sufficient cause of value, the implication that the two are in no way related is simply not true. Can one seriously argue that the complexity of Bach's B Minor Mass has nothing to do with its excellence relative to the tune "Twinkle, twinkle little star"? Or think of some of the masterpieces of Western art: *The Last Judgment* by Michelangelo, Picasso's *Guernica*, *The Iliad*, Joyce's *Ulysses*, Mozart's *Jupiter Symphony*, Stravinsky's *Symphony of Psalms*.

Nevertheless one is reluctant. What of a relatively simple but touching work such as Schubert's song, "Das Wandern"? Is it not perfect of its kind? Is it not enchanting precisely *because* of its simplicity? Without arguing the point, it seems probable that the charm of simplicity as such is associative rather than syntactical; that is, its appeal is to childhood, remembered as untroubled and secure. However, a direct, one-to-one correspondence between complexity and value will not stand up. For we are all aware that relatively simple pieces such as some of Schubert's songs or Chopin's Preludes are better—more rewarding—than some large and complex works, such as, for instance, Strauss's *Don Quixote*.

This is the case because information is judged not in absolute, but in relative terms. For we evaluate not only the amount of information in a work but also the relationship between the stimulus "input" and the actual informational "output." Evidently the operation of some "principle of psychic economy" makes us compare the ratio of musical means invested to the informational income produced by this investment. Those works are judged good which yield a high return. Those works yielding a low return are found to be pretentious and bombastic.

Musical information is then evaluated both quantitatively and qualitatively. Hence two pieces might, so to speak, yield the same amount of information but not be equally good because one is less elegant and economical than the other. On the other hand, a piece which is somewhat deficient in elegance may be better than a more economical piece because it contains substantially more information and hence provides a richer musical experience.

Musical communication is qualitative not only in this syntactical sense. The content of musical experience is also an important aspect of its quality. With the introduction of "content" we not only leave the concepts of information theory, which is concerned only with the syntactical nature of music, but we also part company from those aestheticians who contend that musical experience is devoid of any content whatsoever. And we move from the consideration of value per se to the consideration of greatness.

For when we talk of greatness, we are dealing with a quality of experience which transcends the syntactical. We are considering another order of value in which self-awareness and individualization arise out of the cosmic uncertainties that pervade human existence: man's sense of the inadequacy of reason in a capricious and inscrutable universe; his feeling of terrible isolation in a callous and indifferent, if not hostile, nature; and his awareness of his own insignificance and impotence in the face of the magnitude and power of creation—all lead to those ultimate and inescapable questions which Pascal posed when he wrote:

> I see the formidable regions of the universe which enclose me, and I find myself penned in one corner of this vast expanse, without knowing why I am set in this spot rather than another, nor why the little span of life granted me is assigned to this point of time rather than another of the whole eternity which went before or which shall follow after. I see nothing but infinities on every hand, closing me in as if I were an atom or a shadow which lasts but a moment and returns no more. All I know is that I must shortly die, but what I know least of all about is this very death which I cannot escape.[14]

These ultimate uncertainties—and at the same time ultimate realities—of which great music makes us aware result not from syntactical relationships alone, but from the interaction of these with the associative aspect of music. This interaction, at once shaping and characterizing musical experience, gives rise to a profound wonderment—tender yet awful—at the mystery of existence.[15] And in the very act of sensing this mystery, we attain a new level of consciousness, of individualization. The nature of uncertainty too has changed. It has become a means to an end rather than an end to be suffered.

The reasons for contending that Beethoven's Ninth Symphony is a great work, while Debussy's *Afternoon of a Faun* is only excellent, should now be clear.[16] If we ask further about value per se, apart from

---

[14] *Pensées*, pp. 105–7.

[15] What I have been calling "greatness" is clearly related to what some philosophers have distinguished as the "sublime." * It is also related to what is later called "monumentality." See chap. 9, n. 92 and pp. 312–13.

[16] It seems possible that there is a correspondence between the several aspects of musical communication and the several levels of consciousness; that is, that the

Value and Greatness in Music

considerations of greatness, it seems that the Debussy may be the more elegant work, but the Beethoven is better. On the other hand, *The Afternoon of a Faun* is clearly a better work than the Mozart C Major Piano Sonata. And the greatest works would be those which embody value of the highest order with the most profound—and I use the word without hesitation—content.[17]

In *The Greek Way to Western Civilization,* Edith Hamilton finds that the essence of tragedy springs from the fact of human dignity and she goes on to say that "it is by our power to suffer, above all, that we are of more value than the sparrows." [18] This, I think, carries the insight only part way. Rather it is because tragic suffering, arising out of the ultimate uncertainties of human existence, is able to individualize and purify our wills that we are of more value than the sparrows.

But are not war, poverty, disease, old age, and all other forms of suffering evil? As a general rule they are. For in most cases they lead to the degradation and dissolution of the self. The individual will is lost in the primordial impulses of the group which, as Freud has pointed out, "cannot tolerate any delay between its desires and the fulfillment of what it desires." [19] In short, suffering is regarded as evil because, generally speaking, it brings about a regression toward the immaturity of primitivism.

In instances where the individual is able to master it through understanding, however, as Job did, suffering may ultimately be good. For though, like medical treatment, it is painful, suffering may lead to a higher level of consciousness and a more sensitive, realistic awareness of the nature and meaning of existence. Indeed all maturation, all self-discovery, is in the last analysis more or less painful. And the wonder of great art is this: that through it we can approach this highest level of consciousness and understanding without paying the painful price exacted in real life and without risking the dissolution of the self which real suffering might bring.[20]

---

sensuous-associative, the syntactical, and the "sublime" give rise to different levels of awareness and individualization.

[17] The distinction between *excellence* as syntactical and *greatness* which involves consideration of content makes it clear why we can speak of a "great work" that does not quite "come off." For there are works which seek to make us aware of ultimate uncertainties but which fail in execution. Furthermore, this distinction makes the difference between a masterpiece and a great work clear. Many of Bach's *Inventions* are masterpieces, but they are not great works.

[18] P. 168.

[19] *Group Psychology and the Analysis of the Ego,* p. 13.

*[20] The idea of self-realization through suffering is discussed in chapter 9, pp. 230–31.

One must therefore distinguish between moral values and individual values. Moral values deal with what will probably be good or bad for men taken as a group. Individual values are concerned with experience as it relates to particular men and women. The two should not be confused.[21] For a concern with moral values such as the social sciences exhibit (and their inductive-statistical method makes this all but inevitable) leads to a normative, relativistic view in which values change from culture to culture and from group to group within the culture. A concern with individual values such as one finds in the humanities leads, on the other hand, to a universal view of value, though recognizing that ultimate value goals may be reached by somewhat different means in different cultures. Indeed it is because the individual dimension of value is universal that, where translation is possible (as it is not in music), one is able to enjoy and value art works of another culture. Lastly, in contending that the ultimate value of art lies in its ability to individualize the self, I am conscious of my opposition to those who, like Plato, Tolstoy, and the Marxists, would make aesthetic value a part of moral value.

It is clear then that our hypothesis on the relation of resistance and uncertainty to value transcends the realm of aesthetics. For the choice to be made, the question to be asked, is in the final analysis metaphysical. It is this: What is the meaning and purpose of man's existence? And though one's answer can be rationalized and explained—though one can assert that it is through self-realization that man becomes differentiated from the beasts—it cannot be proved. Like an axiom, it must be self-evident.

In closing, I should like to quote from a letter written by a man who suffered greatly and who in so doing came to understand the meaning of suffering. The letter, dated February 14, 1819, two years before he died, is by John Keats.

---

*21 This was written before I formulated the general notion of hierarchic discontinuity (see chap. 6, pp. 96–97, and chap. 10, pp. 257–59) and before I discovered that similar distinctions had been made by other writers. The point is forcefully and explicitly stated by Bentley Glass: ". . . what is right enough for the individual may be wrong for him as a member of a social group, such as a family; . . . what is right for the family may be wrong for the nation; and . . . what is right for the nation may be wrong for the great brotherhood of man. Nor should one stop at that point. Man as a species is a member . . . of a terrestrial community and an even greater totality of life on earth. Ultimately, what is right for man is right for the entire community of life on earth" ("The Ethical Basis of Science," p. 1255).

Value and Greatness in Music

Man is originally a poor forked creature subject to the same mischances as the beasts of the forest, destined to hardships and disquietude of some kind or other. . . . The common cognomen of this world among the misguided and superstitious is "a vale of tears" from which we are to be redeemed by a certain arbitrary interposition of God and taken to heaven. What a little circumscribed straitened notion! Call the world if you please "the vale of Soul-making." Then you will find out the use of the world. . . . I say *"soul making"*—Soul as distinguished from Intelligence. There may be intelligences or sparks of the divinity in millions—but they are not souls till they acquire identities, till each one is personally itself. . . . How then are Souls made? . . . How but by the medium of a world like this? . . . I will call the *world* a School instituted for the purpose of teaching little children how to read—I will call the *human heart* the *horn book* read in that school—and I will call the *Child able to read,* the Soul made from that *School* and its *horn book.* Do you not see how necessary a World of Pains and troubles is to school an Intelligence and make it a soul? A place where the heart must feel and suffer in a thousand diverse ways. . . . As various as the Lives of Men are—so various become their souls, and thus does God make individual beings.[22]

---

[22] *Letters,* pp. 335–36.

CHAPTER
3

On Rehearing Music

Few musicians, listeners, or aestheticians have doubted that music is meaningful communication. But there have been frequent and sometimes heated disagreements as to the means, substance, and logical status of such communication. Depending upon what are viewed as the essential characteristics of musical signification, three basic positions may be distinguished: (1) the formal, (2) the kinetic-syntactic, and (3) the referential.[1]

1. The heirs of the time-honored Pythagorean mysteries have emphasized the central importance of the formal relationships existing among the structural units that constitute a musical event—whether that event be a phrase, a section, or a whole work. For them, musical understanding and enjoyment depend upon the comprehension of such factors as symmetry, balance, and perfection of proportion. Since a structural unit (a musical event) must be complete, or virtually so, before its formal design can be comprehended, this view of music tends to be retrospective, contemplative, and somewhat static. For such theorists, music is mobile architecture.

---

*[1] This view is modified in chapter 9. There, the three positions distinguished are: traditionalism, which considers content (referential meaning) and expression to be of central importance; formalism, which emphasizes the significance of form and process; and transcendentalism, which discounts the relevance of everything except the unmediated sense experience provided by the materials of the art work.

2. Those who adopt the kinetic-syntactic position contend that the cardinal characteristics of a musical event are functional rather than formal. Music is a dynamic process. Understanding and enjoyment depend upon the perception of and response to attributes such as tension and repose, instability and stability, and ambiguity and clarity. Because music is seen as a developing process, this viewpoint tends to be prospective, dramatic, and Faustian.

There are, however, differences of opinion within this group. Some, Hanslick [2] for instance, argue that the kinetic-syntactic process is purely and exclusively intra-musical. Others believe that the shape and form of the musical process symbolize the life of feeling [3] or directly evoke affective responses.

3. Though not generally esteemed by music theorists and academic critics, popular opinion—as well as a good number of practicing musicians and composers—has favored the referential position, which holds that music depicts or evokes the concepts, actions, and passions of "real," extra-musical experience. Because of their seeming similarities, this position must be distinguished from the one described above, in which kinetic-syntactic processes were said to symbolize or evoke feelings similar to those occurring in non-musical experience. The referential mode focuses attention not primarily upon the evolving, changing aspect of music, but upon the more or less constant, enduring moods and connotations delineated by tempo, timbre, dynamics, accentuation, and the other attributes of music that themselves tend to be relatively stable for considerable periods of time.

Whatever the relative merits of these different viewpoints may be, it seems safe to say that any account of musical communication that pretends to completeness must find a place for all three.[4] For the aspects of musical experience designated by these positions are inextricably linked. Thus the apprehension of the kinetic-syntactic process presupposes and is qualified by the inferences that listeners necessarily make about the kind of musical event that the process will probably produce when it is completed. Conversely, comprehension of a completed event necessarily includes and is qualified by the listener's awareness of the

---

[2] Eduard Hanslick, *The Beautiful in Music*; see particularly p. 135.

[3] Susanne K. Langer, *Philosophy in a New Key*.

[4] Perhaps those who would point out the importance of the sensuous enjoyment of music should be included in a separate category. However, while admitting that this aspect of music contributes to our pleasure, few theorists or aestheticians have seriously contended that it is of primary importance. * Until recently, that is (see chaps. 5, 8, and 9).

particular process by which the event came into being. In like manner, the referential character of an event influences our judgments (inferences) of how an event will progress kinetically. Conversely, the kinetic development of the music—whether it is continuous or interrupted, expected or surprising—performs an important function in characterizing gesture, mood, and connotation.

Musical communication, like that of literature and the plastic arts, depends upon the simultaneous interaction of all three modes of signification. This does not, however, mean that the modes play equally important roles in such communication.[5] And though the kinetic-syntactic position has always had champions, asserting that this mode is the central and crucial one for musical communication, their number and influence has been steadily growing since the end of the nineteenth century.[6]

As long as the kinetic position was stated in more or less general, philosophical terms it seemed unobjectionable. But in recent years there has been an increasing tendency for music theorists and aestheticians, using psychological concepts or those of information theory, to specify as precisely as possible the particular way in which the kinetic processes of music become significant communication. These specifications of the kinetic position have important implications for the problem of rehearing music.

The kinetic position, thus specified, can be crudely summarized as follows: the significance of a musical event—be it a tone, a motive, a phrase, or a section—lies in the fact that it leads the practiced listener to expect, consciously or unconsciously, the arrival of a subsequent event or one of a number of alternative subsequent events. Such expectations (or "subjective predictions") are entertained with varying degrees of certainty, depending upon what is *felt* to be the probability of any particu-

---

[5] Nor is the relative importance of the three modes of signification the same for all the arts. Moreover, within the stylistic history of one of the arts the amount of *relative* dependence upon any one of the modes may change. Debussy's style, for instance, places more emphasis upon referential significance and less upon syntactic process than does the style of the earlier Romantic composers.

[6] This is, of course, in part a reflection of the growing influence of this viewpoint in other disciplines. In philosophy, it is apparent in Whitehead's emphasis upon "process" and in Dewey's insistence upon the "dynamic" character of experience. In psychology, it appears in the Freudian notion of psychic "drives" and in the *Gestalt* analysis of perception in terms of "forces and tension." In literature, it has been implicit in the studies of Empson. In music theory, the work of Heinrich Schenker has perhaps been the most important single influence fostering the growth of the kinetic viewpoint.

lar event in a specific set of musical circumstances.[7] Or, viewed objectively, because of the way the human mind perceives patterns and because of the listener's learned stylistic habits, one musical event implies subsequent musical events with particular degrees of probability.

Musical significance is a function of the degree of probability that a particular musical event is felt to have; such probability depends not only upon the character of the event itself, but also upon the nature and probability of all the events that have gone before. Looked at in another way, the significance of an event is inseparable from the means employed in reaching it. The greater the probability of the relationship between an event and the means employed in reaching it, the less the significance of the event. Thus less expected routes toward "probable" events and less probable events reached in a more or less expected fashion (or some combination of these) will be more meaningful than predictable events that arrive in probable ways. Total probability of both means and ends amounts to tautology. Also, the more ambiguous the antecedent event (and hence the less certain our expectations as to what will follow), the greater the significance of the particular consequent that does arrive.

Stated in terms of information theory, which many of these writers have employed in their analyses: "It is the flux of information created by progression from event to event in a pattern of events that constitutes the reality of experience."[8] "The informedness of each new event in a pattern depends upon the predictions that the pattern of events has led us to formulate to the moment. The new event may confirm these predictions or it may fail to confirm them. . . . Information will be a measure of the degree to which a single prediction or an array of predictions is 'nonconfirmed' by the present event."[9]

A theory of communication in which the unexpected, the ambiguous,

---

[7] In part the listener's sense of *felt* probability is a product of the frequency with which a particular musical relationship has been experienced. In part, however, it is the result of the nature of human mental processes. See chap. 1 and also John Cohen, "Subjective Probability." * These matters are also discussed in chapter 11, particularly in the sections dealing with learning.

[8] Edgar Coons and David Kraehenbuehl, "Information as a Measure of Structure in Music," p. 145.

[9] *Ibid.*, p. 129. Also see Fred Attneave, "Stochastic Composition Processes"; Lejaren A. Hiller and Leonard M. Isaacson, *Experimental Music*; David Kraehenbuehl and Edgar Coons, "Information as a Measure of the Experience of Music"; A. Moles, "Informationstheorie der Musik"; and Joseph E. Youngblood, "Style as Information."

and the less probable are of crucial importance for the understanding of, and response to, music is apparently in direct conflict with the belief that good music can be reheard and re-enjoyed countless times. For if a work has been heard already, we will *know* what is going to happen and, in later hearings, the improbable will become probable, the unexpected will be expected, and all predictions will be confirmed. According to the kinetic-syntactic view, later hearings of a work should, therefore, yield less information—and consequently less enjoyment—than earlier ones.

But is not precisely the opposite the case? The better we know a work—the more often we have heard it—the more we enjoy it and the more meaningful it is. If this is so, then those who contend that the kinetic mode of signification is the crucial one for musical communication must be mistaken.

The matter is not, however, so simple. For without weakening the logical position of these theorists, cogent reasons can be advanced explaining not only why it is possible to enjoy a piece of music after repeated hearings, but also why later hearings of a work often yield more enjoyment than earlier ones.

1. Understanding music is not merely a matter of perceiving separate sounds. It involves relating sounds to one another in such a way that they form patterns (musical events). Furthermore, smaller patterns combine with one another to form larger, more extensive ones—patterns on higher architectonic levels. These in turn influence the further development of patterns on both lower and higher levels. Thus the implications of patterns on the several architectonic levels exist simultaneously and interact with one another.

Because listening to music is a complex art involving sensitivity of apprehension, intellect, and memory, many of the implications of an event are missed on first hearing. For to comprehend the implications of a musical event fully, it is necessary to understand the event itself clearly and to remember it accurately. Hence it is only *after* we come to know and remember the basic, axiomatic events of a work—its motives, themes, and so on—that we begin to appreciate the richness of their implications. It is partly for these reasons that a good piece of music can be reheard and that, at least at first, enjoyment increases with familiarity.

2. Memory is not a mechanical device for the immutable registration of stimuli. It is an active force which, obeying the psychological "law of good shape," organizes, modifies, and adjusts the impressions left by perception. In so doing, it tends either to "improve" (regularize) irregu-

lar but well-structured patterns or to "forget" poorly structured ones.[10] For instance, themes or parts of themes, which are strongly structured, are generally remembered quite accurately and easily, while transition sections and developments, which are weakly structured (less expected and predictable), are often forgotten, or are remembered as being more highly structured (more predictable) than they actually are. Because they tend to be forgotten or regularized in memory, the less well-structured parts of a work often remain unpredicted and unexpected through a number of hearings.[11] Consequently musical experience maintains its vitality longer than would otherwise be the case.

3. Though not wholly determined by the frequency with which a particular syntactic relationship has previously been heard,[12] prediction (expectation) is nonetheless significantly dependent upon the listener's learned habit responses, which are a product of his past musical experience. Hence each musical experience—whether of a work heard before or not—modifies, though perhaps only slightly, the internalized probability system (the habit responses) upon which prediction depends.[13]

As T. S. Eliot has pointed out, this process of modification is ahistorical.[14] Not only does hearing or rehearing a work, say, by Schubert, by modifying our internalized probability system, change our experience of the work of later composers (say, Stravinsky); it also changes our experience of the music of earlier composers—for instance, Bach.

The extent to which habit responses are altered by hearing a particular work depends both upon the breadth of the listener's musical experience and upon the stylistic novelty of the work. Generally speaking, the greater the number of works already experienced by a listener and the greater the number of styles with which he is familiar, the less hearing any particular work will modify his internalized probability system. Works in an unfamiliar style will effect more substantial modifications

---

[10] See Kurt Koffka, *Principles of Gestalt Psychology*, pp. 499–500, 507–8. The words "weak" or "strong," as used here, are terms of description, not valuation. Weak shapes perform an important function in molding kinetic process.

[11] The distinction between "recognition" and "recall" is important here. One may *recognize* that an unexpected consequent event is one experienced in a previous hearing without being able to *recall* (predict) it when one hears the antecedent event. In the former case, one frequently says, "Ah, now I remember."

[12] See n. 7, above.

[13] The formation of internalized probability systems is discussed in Meyer, *Emotion and Meaning in Music*, pp. 56–59, and in chap. 11, below.

[14] T. S. Eliot, *Selected Essays*, p. 15. Also see Max J. Friedländer, *On Art and Connoisseurship*, pp. 155–56. * Ahistoricism—the relationship of the past to the present—is discussed throughout Part II, but particularly in chapters 8 and 9.

in habit responses than works in a familiar idiom. Works already heard will influence internalized probability even less.

Insofar as a listener's internalized probability system and consequently his expectations have been modified by subsequent musical experiences, a work will tend to retain its interest and vitality upon rehearing. However, it is clear that the more music we know, the less our predictive habits will be changed by any particular musical experience.

4. A piece of music is more than a series of symbols in a score. It is their specific realization in sound or imagined sound. The performer, guided by traditional practice, interprets and articulates the composer's symbols, and in so doing both actualizes and particularizes the potential information contained in the score. He shapes and confirms (or nonconfirms) our expectations not about *what* events will take place (these have been more or less stipulated by the composer), but about *how* the events will take place—the manner and timing of their arrival. Insofar as each performance of a piece of music creates a unique work of art, to that extent the information contained in the performance is new. And by creating new information, the performer helps to make the rehearing of music rewarding and enjoyable.

5. Finally, the act of listening to a piece of music—whether for the first or the tenth time—tends to bring into play culturally conditioned beliefs and attitudes which facilitate and sustain aesthetic experience. Just as we are able to believe in—take seriously—the reality of a dramatic action, knowing at the same time that it is "make believe," [15] and are able to believe in that action (following its unfolding and responding to its surprises as if it were being revealed for the first time) even though we have seen it before and know what will take place, so too we are able to believe in the reality of a piece of music—to become involved in its syntactic structure—even though it has been heard before.

But our ability to enter into the aesthetic illusion is not constant. Rather it seems that the better we know a work, the more difficult it is to believe in, to be enchanted by, its action. Thus, although readiness to become vitally involved in a work of art always depends to some extent upon the charismatic power of the performance, the better the work is known the more difficult it is to be enthralled by it and, consequently, the more crucial becomes the power of the performance to make us believe again.

---

[15] See Ernst Kris, *Psychoanalytic Explorations in Art*, p. 42.

It may, at this point, be objected that while perhaps good reasons have been suggested for why it is possible to rehear music with enjoyment, it has not really been shown that a piece of music can be continually fresh and vital. The theoretical question has basically been begged. For suppose that a listener knows a work thoroughly, remembering the unexpected and the improbable as accurately as the expected and probable; suppose too that the listener's musical experience is so extensive that the modifications of his internalized probability system wrought by new experiences are so small as to be inconsequential; assume further that the work in question is recorded so that the performer's deviations have been learned and are predictable, and that the power of the particular performance has been attenuated by repeated listening. (And such a situation is not impossible.) Under these circumstances, will the listener find rehearing the work a rewarding experience?

The question put here is not one of theory. It is one of fact. If the answer is, "Yes, other things being equal, he will be able to enjoy the work as much as he ever did," then a theory asserting that kinetic process is the central and crucial fact of musical communication must be mistaken. For it is incompatible with experience.

The facts are not, however, as easily ascertained as one might suppose. Because they have generally had to depend upon the questionable reliability of introspection, empirical studies of musical enjoyment have been able to tell us very little about the nature and basis of musical experience. In addition to the reasons given above, rehearing may often be tolerated precisely because *listening* is not taking place—even though physiological responses are recorded and "something" is felt introspectively. In such a case, music might merely constitute a fortuitous stimulus to pleasurable daydreams of which each of us evidently has an inexhaustible supply.

Perhaps some day, when psychology has learned how to deal satisfactorily with higher mental and affective processes, we shall have empirically validated answers to our questions. For the present, however, we must turn to everyday experience. And ordinary observation indicates that composers, performers, and listeners do in fact tend to tire of music with which they become very familiar.

In the case of composers, the evidence is not direct. We know little about their listening habits. The evidence comes rather from a consideration of the nature of stylistic development.

It is frequently suggested that stylistic innovations are, directly or indirectly, the result of changes in the social, economic, and intellectual milieu in which the composer works. While such changes have undoubtedly influenced the development of musical styles, a view that attempts to trace all stylistic changes directly to social, economic, and intellectual forces is not tenable.[16] Even within a stable social-cultural continuum, composers develop and transform the tradition they inherit from the past, modifying modes of organization and enriching the syntax of style with innovation. The degree to which a particular composer transforms tradition depends both upon his particular personality and upon the cultural conditions of his time. Some composers make only modest modifications, others change style radically. But even a relatively "conservative" composer, such as Bach, transforms and develops the stylistic norms he inherits.

Why should such intra-musical changes occur? Let us look at a relatively simple instance of this process. It is frequently said that by the end of the classical period the dominant-tonic cadence had become a worn-out "formula." What does this mean? Does it imply that an emotion, a gesture, or a connotation became tiresome or that a beautiful proportion lost its perfection? Not at all. It asserts, as the word "formula" indicates, that the relationship became obvious and tautological—that the progression became so probable (predictable) that it furnished only minimal musical information.[17] The composer of the nineteenth century searched for and discovered new cadential progressions, not because new moods or emotions were better or more desirable than the old or because new proportions were more pleasing, but because the dominant-tonic cadence had become a cliché. The information potential of the style needed to be renewed.

The performer's behavior, too, indicates a need for novelty or, negatively, a distaste for rigid repetition.[18] He not only seeks new works to

---

[16] At times, of course, social-cultural developments play a major role in shaping style changes. The emergence of monody at the end of the Renaissance seems a case in point. * The relationship between cultural change and style change is discussed at considerable length in chapter 7.

[17] Though a growing emphasis upon artistic freedom and personal expression, nurtured by social revolution, undoubtedly quickened the rate of change, it did not determine or "cause" the change.

*[18] The importance of the need for patterned novelty as a basic human requirement is implicit or explicit in a large number of recent studies of creativity, developmental psychology, and stimulus privation. To cite but a few: Frank Barron, "The Psychology of Imagination"; D. W. Fiske and S. R. Maddi, *Functions of Varied Experience* (contains an extensive bibliography); J. W. Getzels and P. W. Jackson, "The Highly Intelligent and Highly Creative Adolescent"; Woodburn Heron, "The Pathology of Boredom"; John R. Platt, "The Fifth Need of Man"; and D. E. Berlyne, "Curiosity and Exploration."

play (though his choice is limited by his own stylistic taste and that of his audience) but also tends to change his interpretation of works he already knows well. In part such changes may be traced to maturation and artistic growth. But the mature artist—perhaps even more than the less experienced one—tends to vary his performance of familiar works. He does so partly because he is forever seeking the "ideal" performance of his imagination, which can never be realized because as his experience grows and changes, so does his imagined ideal. Partly, however, interpretations are changed because the performer delights in the challenge of creating—of making something new and fresh, not alone for the sake of the audience, but for himself. He reinterprets a work not because he could not play it as before but because through his discovery of new possibilities and implications in it, the work becomes revitalized for him.

Again it seems implausible to ascribe these changes primarily to a desire to depict different moods or connotations, though these will necessarily be somewhat modified by reinterpretation. And ordinary language corroborates this point. For we generally compare interpretations in terms of articulation and phrasing, which are syntactic, rather than in terms of moods or connotations.

It is even more difficult to see how the formalist position can explain changes in interpretation: does one performance create more perfect proportion than another? If so, why would the great performer, whose excellence presumably depends upon his having discovered such perfection, change his interpretation of a work?

Even allowing for the influence of economic factors, the preferences of performers, and passing musical fashions, the growth in the repertory of both live and recorded music seems to indicate that, within the limits of his particular taste and stylistic understanding, the listener too seeks new works to hear and new interpretations of familiar ones. But since the data available can be interpreted in a number of ways, a more theoretical approach must be sought.

Assuming that two works are generally of the same quality of excellence, it is, I think, clear that the more complex can be reheard with enjoyment more often than the simpler. But if the cardinal characteristic of musical experience lies in the ability of tones to depict moods or extra-musical associations, how is this to be explained? Why should one mood or association be more viable than another? Indeed, granting that a period of "psychic recovery" may be necessary between similar mood or connotative experiences, it is difficult, if one adopts the referential position, to see why enjoyment should be influenced by rehearing at all.

Similarly, if musical enjoyment arises out of the contemplation of ideal proportion and inevitable order, why should a complex work survive rehearing better than a simple one? Does a formal relationship increase in elegance when perceived for the second time and lose it when perceived for the fiftieth time? [19]

There are, however, two significant and instructive exceptions to the proposition that music cannot be reheard indefinitely. The first is the example of primitive music. Here apparently repetition is not only enjoyed, it is prescribed. The difference lies in the cultural situation. In primitive cultures music is not separated from other aspects of living—it is not placed in a special, "aesthetic" category. It is one with ritual and religion; and perhaps their inherent conservatism— particularly when their existence is threatened by alien cultures— accounts for the tendency toward exact repetition. Moreover, different cultures may have different attitudes toward repetition. In the West, for instance, exact repetition is felt to be wasteful and pointless, while, according to Whorf, the Hopi consider it efficacious and productive.[20]

The second exception is found in the tendencies of some recent experimental music. This music—whether employing chance operations in composition or in performance (e.g., requiring that the order of parts shall be decided by the capricious choice of the performer or even of the page turner)—is often purposefully and avowedly *anti*-kinetic. The music is without tendency or direction. Tones do not imply other tones; they simply exist. As Edward T. Cone has written: "The connections are mechanistic rather than teleological: no event has any purpose—each is there only because it has to be there." [21] Such music seems timeless not only in the sense that one experiences no awareness of motion through time in hearing it and in the sense that its temporal order is not fixed but also in the sense that our response to it is probably not affected by the number of times we hear it. The twentieth hearing is as meaningful (or meaningless) as the first.

---

[19] I do not intend to minimize the importance of the formal and referential modes of signification in shaping musical experience. But, as I have tried to show in chapter 2, these do not form the essential basis for musical judgment. Scriabin delineates moods and evokes connotations just as readily as—if not more readily than—Brahms; the phrase structure of Stamitz' music is more regular (perfectly proportioned?) than that of Haydn. * I would now want to be less absolute about these matters.

[20] Benjamin Lee Whorf, *Collected Papers on Metalinguistics*, p. 29. In Oriental music the kinetic process is evidenced in the changes that occur in quasi-improvised performance rather than in permanent changes in the style itself.

[21] "Analysis Today," p. 176.

On Rehearing Music

Looked at from the standpoint of information theory, the situation might be stated thus: the more "purely" random music is, the higher its information content, *but* the lower its utility as communication. For if communication is to take place, the symbols used must have the same significance (the same implications) for both the sender (composer) and the receiver (listener)—that is, they must evoke similar expectations. There must be a common universe of discourse. Randomness (the less- or un-predictable) must, if it is to play a part in human communication, arise within those finite and ordered systems of probability relationship that we call "style."

Since whatever order is heard in non-stylistic random works (and the human mind is such that it will discover patterns, if it can) is the order of the listener *only*, the question of rehearing such works is not a generic one, but is purely subjective and will vary from individual to individual.

Whatever the future of non-teleological music may be, the kinetic-syntactic mode has been the dominant one in the tradition of Western music, at least since the Renaissance. And it is at first disturbing and disheartening to face the fact that treasured masterpieces can, with repeated hearings, become exhausted and lose their savor. But two considerations may save us from despair. We can forget. And by forgetting we can, enchanted by a great performance, again experience the vitality which a familiar work once had for us. Such rediscovery of the beauty of, say, a Beethoven symphony once cherished and then too well known is not an uncommon experience. Second, and more important, it is partly because familiar works and accustomed styles become exhausted that new compositions are needed and new styles are developed. And these, by changing us—our ears, our minds, and our habit responses—are paradoxically able to redeem and revitalize the very works and styles they were created to replace.

CHAPTER
4

Forgery and the Anthropology of Art

In primitive cultures as a rule no special realm of experience is separated out as the aesthetic. Music, poetry, and the plastic arts are related—often through religion and ritual—to all other activities of the culture. And this was probably the situation in our own prehistory. Early in the course of Western civilization, however, Greek thought distinguished, though it did not radically separate, aesthetic experience from other fields of philosophical inquiry—from religion, politics, science, and so on. Indeed, Plato's insistence on the relevance of art for ethics and politics is an indication that the distinction was already generally recognized.

The distinction was necessary and justified. For, as philosophers and critics have pointed out, aesthetic behavior is different from ordinary behavior. We have certain distinctively aesthetic beliefs and attitudes which lead us to act in a special way in relation to works of art. This can be most clearly illustrated in the drama. We believe in the reality of dramatic action, empathizing with the characters and understanding their behavior; but at the same time we are aware that what is taking place is make-believe. The yokel who supposedly rushed up on the stage during a melodrama and shot the villain made his mistake precisely because he had not learned that in our culture aesthetic experience calls for inward action rather than overt behavior.

Yet the differentiation between aesthetic experience and other forms of experience can be carried too far. It began as a legitimate distinction, but over the years it has tended to become formalized as a categorical separation. One of the consequences of this separation is the view, explicitly asserted or implicitly held, that aesthetic criteria are a special kind of criteria unrelated to our other cultural beliefs and attitudes. The most obvious instance of this view is the common contention that we judge—or should judge—works of art on the basis of their intrinsic qualities alone, though what these qualities are is by no means always clear. The work of art, accordingly, is said to have its complete meaning within itself. Cultural history, style history, and the genesis of the art work itself do not enhance *true* understanding. According to Clive Bell, one of the most eloquent spokesmen for this view:

> Great art remains stable and unobscure because the feelings that it awakens are independent of time and place, because its kingdom is not of this world. To those who have and hold a sense of the significance of form what does it matter whether the forms that move them were created in Paris the day before yesterday or in Babylon fifty centuries ago? [1]

It is clear, however, that in actual practice we do not judge works of art in terms of their intrinsic qualities alone. Recently this fact was brought home forcefully once again when the prized Etruscan sculptures at the Metropolitan Museum of Art were discovered to be forgeries. As physical objects the statues were unaltered, but something had changed, and it is safe to predict that soon the works will be quietly consigned to the basement.

If the criteria of judgment are purely aesthetic, why should a work of art once found moving and valuable become a worthless curiosity when it is discovered to be a forgery? The purist is in a difficult position. He may argue that the original judgment was mistaken: that judged by its intrinsic qualities the work is in fact a poor one. But the coincidence between the discovery of forgery and the revision of judgment makes the objectivity of the criteria employed seem more than a little suspect. The courageous and consistent purist, however, will stick to his guns and contend that the work, though a forgery, is still beautiful and should be kept on exhibit. Thus Clive Bell asserts that if a work "were an absolutely exact copy, clearly it would be as moving as the original." [2] This also seems to be the position taken by Emily Genauer in an article on the Etruscan forgeries. Writing in the *Herald-Tribune* of

---

[1] *Art*, p. 37.
[2] *Ibid.*, pp. 59–60.

February 19, 1961, she wistfully hoped that "perhaps we are almost at the point of sophistication where we are able to enjoy a work of art for what it is." [3] In Miss Genauer's opinion, the trouble seems to be simply that museum directors and the general public are naïve.

Others would say that putting forgeries in the basement is nothing but a form of snobbism. This too is doubtful, but a consideration of what snobbism is may bring us closer to the issue involved. In a fascinating essay, "The Anatomy of Snobbery," Arthur Koestler defines snobbery as "the result of the psychological fusion of two independent value systems which are separate by origin and nature, but are inextricably mixed up in the subject's mind." [4] This focuses attention on the crucial point. If the value systems of aesthetics are independent of our cultural beliefs, as the purists like Clive Bell argue, then it *is* snobbish to banish forgeries. But in fact we are neither naïve nor childish when we banish them, because the effort to make a watertight separation between aesthetic criteria and cultural beliefs is mistaken and misguided.

Though the almost atomic differentiation of the surface of our culture tends to obscure them, a set of basic, encompassing beliefs and attitudes nevertheless underlies and conditions all our thinking and behavior. These beliefs, which are as a rule implicit and unconscious, have to do with our most fundamental assumptions about the nature of the universe and man's place and function in it, including the works of art that man creates.

Two interdependent aspects of belief may be distinguished. On the one hand, the term "belief" refers to convictions, consciously held or unconsciously accepted, that something is the case—an existing, enduring fact or principle. Belief in the existence of causation is an example of such a conviction. On the other hand, the term designates those modes of organization—e.g., language or mathematics—within which our convictions are embodied. As Michael Polanyi has put it: "Our most deeply ingrained convictions are determined by the idiom in which we interpret our experience and in terms of which we erect our articulate systems. Our formally declared beliefs can be held to be true in the last resort only because of our logically anterior acceptance of a particular set of terms, from which all our references to reality are constructed." [5]

---

[3] "Some Forgeries We Have Loved," p. 19.

[4] P. 19.

[5] *Personal Knowledge*, p. 287. In a similar vein, Edward Sapir writes that language is heuristic in the sense "that its forms predetermine for us certain modes of observation and interpretation" ("Language," p. 157).

Forgery and the Anthropology of Art

Beliefs are, then, deep-seated dispositional habits of mind and body and they constitute the fundamental framework within which we apprehend, interpret, and respond to the world.

It should be emphasized that the validity of the beliefs to be discussed is not at issue. I am not contending that causation, freedom, time, and so forth exist, but only that our culture believes that they exist and that its behavior, judgment, and understanding are subject to such beliefs. My role is that of the anthropologist studying the concepts and behavior of our culture rather than that of a philosopher examining the nature and truth of its concepts.

Cultural beliefs not only influence the way in which we perceive, think, and act, but they also condition and modify our emotional and physiological responses. It has become increasingly clear in recent years that mental attitudes, including cultural beliefs, have a direct and vital effect upon human physiology and felt sensation. For instance, Ronald Melzack points out that "the significance which pain has in the culture in which we have been brought up plays an essential role in how we feel and respond to it." [6]

Because our fundamental beliefs influence our sensations, feelings, and perceptions, *what* we know literally changes our responses to a work of art. Thus once we *know* that a work is a forgery our whole set of attitudes and resulting responses are profoundly and necessarily altered. It is pointless to say that it is all in the mind. Our beliefs are our beliefs and we can no more escape them once they have become part of our ingrained modes of thought and behavior than we can breathe in a vacuum.[7] Once we have them, such beliefs condition and qualify our responses just as surely as do physical forces or physiological processes. To pretend that this is not so—to continue to admire a proved forgery—is a pretentious form of inverted snobbery.

---

[6] "The Perception of Pain," p. 41; also see Joseph V. Brady, "Ulcers in 'Executive' Monkeys"; Eckhard Hess, "Attitude and Pupil Size"; and Philip G. Zimbardo *et al.*, "Control of Pain Motivation by Cognitive Dissonance," p. 217.

*[7] The analogy is more apt than I realized when this was written. For it is not a matter of having a particular set of beliefs or a conceptual framework versus *having none at all*. It is a matter of having these beliefs or this framework rather than some other one. Once the presence or existence of any object, attribute, or process is recognized by a culture or an individual as being separable from the rest of the universe—as *being* an object, attribute, or process—then it is by definition a conceptual category. And, particularly when it receives verbal recognition and sanction, the culture is obliged to adopt some attitude or set of beliefs toward it. After that, beliefs may change, but they cannot be nonexistent. There can be no ideological vacuum.

It may at this point be asked whether these observations do not lead to a completely subjective position vis-à-vis aesthetic criteria. Is not a work of art, then, great simply because we believe it to be so? This does not follow. For cultural beliefs are necessary causes for aesthetic apprehension and response; but they are not sufficient causes. All our cultural beliefs might be relevant to and involved in the apprehension of a particular work of art and we might still judge the work to be poor. But were they not pertinent, the work could not be seriously judged at all.

What are the cultural beliefs that underlie our aesthetic criteria? Probably one of the most important—one from which many of the others are directly or indirectly derived—is the belief in causation. This belief, which is evidently shared by most major cultures, is manifest in our language (the thesaurus, for instance, devotes a whole section to causation), our myths, our science, and our daily behavior.

Causation not only changes the quality, quantity, and relationships of things already in the world, but, from time to time, these are reordered in such a way that new entities and patterns come into existence. There is creation. And, for us, human creation is not just another ordered occurrence. It is a purposeful act of the individual human will.[8]

To create is to discover something new—to reveal in a timely and timeless *aperçu* some aspect of the world or some relationship of which we were previously unaware and, by so doing, to change forever our experience of the world and of ourselves. "When a great poet has lived," writes T. S. Eliot, "certain things have been done once and for all and cannot be achieved again." [9] The crucial word here is "achieved." They can perhaps be done again, but they cannot be achieved again. Beetho-

---

*8 This point is forcefully stated by John Dewey: "Suppose . . . that a finely wrought object, one whose texture and proportions are highly pleasing in perception, has been believed to be the product of some primitive people. Then there is discovered evidence that proves it to be an accidental natural product. As an external thing, it is now precisely what it was before. Yet at once it ceases to be a work of art and becomes a natural 'curiosity.' It now belongs in a museum of natural history, not in a museum of art. And the extraordinary thing is that the difference that is thus made is not one of just intellectual classification. A difference is made in appreciative perception and in a direct way. The aesthetic experience—in its limited sense—is thus seen to be inherently connected with the experience of making" (*Art as Experience*, pp. 48–49). One indication of the extent to which our basic cultural beliefs have changed (see chap. 8) is our willingness to accept "found objects" as art.

9 *Notes toward the Definition of Culture*, p. 118.

ven's late style is a discovery and an achievement. Someone coming later can only imitate it. And it is for this reason that forgers and copyists are considered to be artisans, not artists.

Creation is possible only if there is choice. And choice is possible only if there is freedom. Thus complementing our belief in causation is an equally basic belief in human freedom. An antecedent event is a necessary condition for the consequent event which follows, but it does not as a rule fully determine that consequent event. Consequent events are only probable, not inevitable.

In human affairs an event has more than a single implication. It generally has a host of implications, some of which may even be contradictory. Without the paintings of Cézanne the *Three Musicians* by Picasso might not even have been possible. Certainly it would have been different. But it might have been different anyhow. For the implications of the past are so abundant and so various that only a very few can be realized in any one work or discovered by any one artist. Creation is possible because within the limits of his artistic inheritance—his tradition—the artist is free to choose among the implications he can discover.

The central importance of this belief in freedom of choice is illustrated in our myths—from the story of Adam's fall on—in the disquisitions of philosophers, and in our everyday behavior. We act, and interpret the acts of others, on the assumption that there is personal freedom; and all our moral judgments depend upon our conviction that free choice is possible. (But it should at the same time be noted that we are able to choose effectively only because, like the artist, we act within a tradition which limits the range and probability of the choices available to us in a particular situation. Were all modes of behavior equally possible and probable we should be paralyzed in trembling indecision.)

Every achievement, every true discovery risks failure.[10] For a great work of art or a great scientific discovery is great precisely because the creator has dared to choose beyond the limits and bounds of the normal, the accepted, and the obvious. In so doing the creator—whether artist, scientist, scholar, or man of affairs—frees us from the determinism of

---

*[10] Risk-taking may, I think, be considered a special case of the general psychological need for patterned novelty—for information (see chap. 3, n. 18). It should be emphasized, however, that the ways in which the need for stimulation are satisfied will vary from one culture to another and even between different subcultures. Its realization as risk-taking has evidently been particularly important in Western culture.

the probable and the routine and makes significant changes in culture possible.[11] Of course, changes in our most basic beliefs—perhaps modifications would be a more accurate word—are very gradual indeed. But the accretion of minute changes does modify the character of such beliefs. Our conception of the universe is different, though not *very* different, from that of classical Greece.

We value—even revere—originality in art because the great artist, challenged by the unknown or the partially understood (by the ambiguities in and incompleteness of our vision of the world), has dared to risk failure in order to reveal a new aspect of the universe to us.[12] That such

---

[11] The forger takes no aesthetic risk—only the risk of being found out. Nor does the composer or painter who employs chance in a systematic way risk anything. Not merely because he is not, in any serious sense, responsible for the products produced—because he has not been involved in choosing—but because there is no way of judging whether the resulting work of art is a success or a failure (* see chaps. 5, 8, and 9).

*[12] The idea of risk-taking is related to the distinction made in chapter 2 between individual (ethical) values and social (moral) values. Except when it is dominated or controlled by a single leader—e.g., the conductor of an orchestra—for whom risk-taking may be a positive value, a group must act through consensus and compromise. Consequently, its behavior tends to be conservative and, adhering closely to established cultural beliefs and norms, to minimize risk. (Of course, there is the possibility of group hysteria—Nazi Germany being the obvious example.) The individual, on the other hand, not only *can* take risks but frequently finds positive pleasure in so doing. And the tendency toward hazard will be particularly powerful in a culture such as ours which has, at least until recently (see chap. 8), placed a premium upon individualism and originality. Looked at somewhat differently, because the enjoyment of *means* involves an appreciation of the values of skill and elegance (see chap. 9), its appeal tends to be individual. In group behavior, on the other hand, attention tends to be directed almost entirely toward goals to be reached. In general the larger the audience, the greater the tendency to emphasize obvious goals and patent content.

From this point of view, one of the distinctions between art-behavior and game-behavior may lie in the proportion of attention directed toward *means* as contrasted with *ends*. Insofar as behavior is guided primarily by the desire to reach a particular result—winning—in the most direct and certain way, a game is without an aesthetic component. Only as the enjoyment of means becomes a significant source of pleasure, making risk-taking behavior probable, does an activity become aesthetic. It is perhaps for this reason that we speak of a high-wire "artist" and think of bull-fighting as an *art* rather than as a game or sport. In a similar fashion, we speak about "playing" the stockmarket, when gambling is involved, but of "investing" when buying minimizes the possibility of risk. If these conjectures have merit, it appears that unless the positive attraction of novelty and risk-taking is taken into account, *individual* behavior as it actually occurs will remain less amenable to analysis—for instance, in terms of game theory—than group behavior.

originality has been prized since earliest times is shown by the fact that poets were thought to be divinely inspired and by the more mundane fact that even in ancient Egypt, as well as later in Rome, forgeries of works of the masters were not uncommon. If in the Middle Ages (and in some primitive societies) the individuality and originality of the artist were not considered very important, perhaps it was because his work was seen primarily as a religious symbol rather than as a work of art. Its revelation was generic rather than personal and individual.

The importance our culture attaches to originality is a corollary of our attitude toward repetition. In our culture—particularly since the Renaissance—repetition has been considered wasteful and unproductive. But this may not be the view of other cultures. According to Benjamin Lee Whorf, the Hopi, for instance, have a very different attitude toward repetition: "To us, for whom time is a motion on a space, unvarying repetition seems to scatter its force along a row of units of that space, and to be wasted. To the Hopi, for whom time is not a motion but a 'getting later' of everything that has ever been done, unvarying repetition is not wasted but accumulated. It is storing up an invisible change that holds over into later events." [13]

Though originality has probably always been considered an important attribute of art, the cult of the new, arising out of nineteenth-century notions of personal expression, has come to dominate our thinking about art to such an extent that it is well to remember that not all novelty is originality. Novelty, as Stravinsky has pointed out, is not difficult to come by—it is everywhere about us.[14] But true originality is rare indeed. As Max Friedländer, the art historian, has said:

> Something original is strange when first seen, shocking and unpleasant; something bizarre is striking and entertaining. The former is something enduring and permanent and only gains in impressiveness; the latter is a thing of fashion, is ephemeral, causes satiety and vanishes before long. . . . Whoever is creative in a truly original sense —especially if he be a man of genius—aims at being self-sufficient; whoever indulges in the bizarre, endeavours to impress his contemporaries or to amaze them.[15]

Here lies perhaps the most difficult problem of contemporary criticism: to distinguish the truly original from the bizarre.

From earliest childhood, we are taught by precept and example to

---

[13] *Collected Papers on Metalinguistics*, p. 39.
[14] Igor Stravinsky, *Poetics of Music*, p. 32.
[15] *On Art and Connoisseurship*, pp. 242–43.

believe in the cardinal importance of the creative act. Following the biblical account of creation come stories of Orpheus, Pygmalion, and David and Saul. Later we learn about the lives of the great artists of historical times. In hushed, reverent whispers our parents guide us through museums and point out masterpieces. In the concert hall and theater behavior is even more patently ritualized—as though it were a holdover from the distant past when art was a handmaiden of magic and religion. As adults we read biography and criticism and are today, perhaps more than ever before, concerned with the mysteries of the creative mind. Psychologists study creativity in scientists, artists, and children. Musicologists and art historians study sketches for large works and discuss problems of influence in an attempt to understand the creative process.

Our belief in the creative power of the great artist has about it an aura of primitive magic. His work of art is a kind of talisman, a fetish, through which we become identified with and participate in his magic power. Our willingness to become involved in aesthetic experience is partly a function of the relationship we feel with the artist's creative force. An original drawing, for instance, is more valuable than the finest reproduction, even one all but indistinguishable from it. This is true not merely in the economic sense that the original is scarce and hence costly. The original is also more valuable and more exciting aesthetically because our feeling of intimate contact with the magic power of the creative artist heightens awareness, sensitivity, and the disposition to respond. Once a work is known to be a forgery that magic is gone. All that remains is a cultural aberration, less valuable than a reproduction.

Belief in the importance of the individual creator is also indicated by the desire to know the name of the artist, composer, or writer who created the particular work we are enjoying. Some, of course, may want to know because they are afraid of appearing ignorant. But it must be emphasized that the desire to know who created a work is not necessarily a sign of snobbism. The pseudo-sophisticate who declares that he does not care who painted a picture or composed a quartet is just as mistaken as the snob who will venture no judgment until he is sure that the creator of the work is socially acceptable.

Our need to know the names of artists stems in part from an almost primordial dependence upon words. Without their magic we feel lost. We look at the stars at night and ask their names. Why? If the night enchants, what difference do names make? And yet we tend to ask. The reason is, I think, that from earliest childhood we learn to understand

and manipulate the world with words. To know the name is to exercise some control, however small—to be a bit less insecure.

But there is another, more important reason why we want to know who created a particular work of art—and when it was made. It is this. A work of art does not exist in isolated splendor. It is a part of history—the history of culture, the history of the art, and the history of the artist.[16]

We invariably understand an event or an object, partly at least, by understanding how it came to be what it is and, if it is an event in the present, by imagining its implications for the future or, if it is an event in the past, by being aware of its implications as realized in history.

Here, in fact, we arrive at the core of the problem. The great forgers have not been mere copyists. They have tried—and some have probably succeeded, for we know only their failures—to become so familiar with the style of the master, his way of thinking, that they can actually paint or compose as he did. Thus though their vision is not original, their works of art are, in a sense, creations. To state the case even more forcefully: suppose that, without any attempt to deceive and using his own name, a contemporary composer were to write a first-rate string quartet in, say, the style of Mozart. Would that work be judged to be as good as a work of comparable excellence by Mozart himself? To answer this question, let us return to the notion of causation.

In everyday affairs we tend to think of causation as involving two more or less independent and separable aspects of experience—a cause and an effect, a means and an end. And where the issues are unimportant this is probably an acceptable and practical way of looking at the matter. It does not as a general rule make much difference which of two routes we take to get to the supermarket. But in matters of moment, this is not the case. What a thing *is*—its significance—includes our knowledge and belief, whether these are correct or not, of how it came into being.

Music furnishes as clear an example of this point as one can find. In simple folk tunes as well as great symphonies a sequence of tones stated early in the piece sometimes returns toward the end. Yet when they recur, their significance is fundamentally changed. Think, for instance,

---

[16] Writing of the artist rather than the work of art, T. S. Eliot contends: "No poet, no artist of any art, has his complete meaning alone. His significance, his appreciation is the appreciation of his relation to the dead poets and artists. You cannot value him alone. . . . I mean this as a principle of aesthetic, not merely historical, criticism" (*Selected Essays*, p. 15).

of a simple folk tune such as "Au clair de la lune." The last four measures are exactly the same as the first four. But because their recurrence is the result (the effect) of what has gone before, they are truly different. This difference is easily tested. No matter how many times the first four measures are repeated, they will not end the piece satisfactorily. In order for this sequence of tones to end the tune, they must be the result of the means-ends relationship which brings about their repetition.

The significance and value of an idea, a human being, or a work of art do not exist in pristine isolation. Just as we judge an individual in the light of his past behavior and upon our expectation as to what he will do in the future, so we understand and evaluate works of art, artists, and artistic developments in terms of their genesis and their implications for the future. And just as we revise our opinion of the value of individuals depending upon what they become—noting that this one succeeded beyond our expectation or that one failed to fulfill his promise—so too it is with works of art and artists.

It is because we understand the early works of a master in terms of their implications (later works) and late works in terms of their genesis (the earlier works which led to them) that we emphasize the whole oeuvre of an artist with retrospective exhibits, concerts of one composer's music, and collected editions of a writer. And as Emily Genauer points out—rightly this time—one of the reasons why it is important to get rid of forgeries is that, by corrupting our vision of the artist's work as a whole, they lead to misunderstanding of his genuine works.[17] The Etruscan forgeries are a particularly clear illustration of this danger. It is for this reason, too, that historians of art, music, and literature are so intent upon ferreting out false attributions.

Another indication that in actual practice we evaluate particular works of an artist in terms of other works he has created is this: even the masters—a Mozart or a Shakespeare—have created works that fall short of greatness. And though these works are generally performed less often than their greatest works they are more often performed than

----

[17] "Some Forgeries We Have Loved," p. 19. * Also see Richard Harris, "The Forgery of Art," in which Sheldon Keck is quoted to the same effect: "When a person who lives in the twentieth century tries to fling himself back hundreds of years . . . he can't help injecting into that attempt part of his own times, his own style, his own personality, his own attitudes. And once a work of art of this sort finds its way into a museum, it wrenches the chronological and aesthetic framework out of joint. It falsifies history, and makes it much harder for us to go back to our roots" (pp. 142–43).

equally good or even better works of lesser artists. Partly, no doubt, this is because they will from time to time contain those brilliant insights, that sensitivity of phrase or line, which are the mark of the master. But partly they are performed more often because these lesser works are connected with and have implications for the greater ones. Each reveals and hence enhances the significance and value of the other.

Suppose, however, that our neo-Mozartian quartet, at first rejected as merely imitative of a past style, subsequently gave rise to new stylistic developments. Then, seen in retrospect as having been the beginning of a new movement, its implications would be different and, consequently, our understanding of its significance and value would be changed. It would no longer seem a bizarre anomaly. For it would now be judged not only in terms of its relationship to eighteenth-century music, but also in terms of its implications for twentieth-century music.[18]

Implicit in our belief in causation is a belief in time as a sequentially ordered series, articulated and made manifest by the chain of causally related events. For us time is not reversible. It seems to move in one direction only—toward the future.[19] We cannot, for instance, imagine that evolution or history will ever go backwards, that life could gradually return through the various stages of history and evolution to primordial protoplasm. Even if some catastrophic debacle were to return us, say, to the state of cavemen, we would not assert that time had reversed itself, but rather that the present resembled the past. This is also true of our interpretation of the history of the arts. The flat, two-dimensional representation preferred by many painters today is not that of ancient Egypt, though it resembles it. For today's emphasis upon the picture plane comes after, and is a deviation from, the three-dimensional perspective which dominated art from the Renaissance onward.

Because we experience the world in terms of past, present, and future, there is history. Our awareness of time—the causal chain of history— provides the framework within which we interpret and understand works of art. Without such a framework all works of art would coexist in a never-ending present and we would be unable to select and bring into play the attitudes, dispositions, and habit responses appropriate to a particular style, whether present or past.

It is because we believe in time and history that when we encounter a work written in the past—even if the past is only yesterday—we adjust

---

*18 The possibility of using the past is considered in chapter 9.
*19 In this connection, see chap. 10.

to its pastness, bringing into play modes of discrimination and patterns of expectation which are relevant to the style of the work. That is, we attune our minds to the viewpoints, conventions, and normative procedures which the artist had and which he presumed his audience to have. In so doing we exclude, as irrelevant, habits developed in connection with and appropriate to other styles—particularly later styles. Thus if we are to understand the significance of and experience the tensions created by the opening Adagio of Mozart's String Quartet in C Major, K. 465, we must attune our minds to, must be able to believe in, the reality and vitality of the harmonic norms of Mozart's style, even though we have experienced later music—say, that of Wagner or Bartók—in which these same harmonies might well represent repose. We are willing to believe in—to take seriously—the norms of a style only because of the prior belief that when the work was created its style was a vital, living universe of discourse with unexplored potentialities and undiscovered implications.

But if the work is discovered not to have been written in the past, such adjustments become irrelevant. Indeed, they become impossible. For we have no reason to believe in the norms of an eighteenth-century style if we know that a work was written last week. To say "it is all in the mind" is still no solution. The fact of the matter is that the mind cannot ignore what it knows and the body's physiological responses are not separable from the mind's cognition.

Though we relegate forgeries to the basement and will probably continue to do so, we feel somehow uneasy, almost dishonest, about it. Partly this is because in a world full of uncertainty, we would like to think that our judgments are wholly rational, objective, and absolute. Partly our uneasiness stems from the way in which we ordinarily verbalize and rationalize experience. We say "the painting is beautiful" and tend to think of beauty as an objective attribute of the work—an attribute independent of our act of perception. And if beauty is an objective attribute of a work of art, why should the discovery that the work is a forgery make any difference? It should still be beautiful. A tendency toward Platonic idealism is, so to speak, embedded in the way in which we ordinarily talk about and conceive of the world. This implicit Platonism, together with whatever we may have absorbed of the philosophic tradition itself, makes us uneasy.

But deep down we seem to be Aristotelians. For our behavior indicates that beauty is a quality of experience and that such experience is the result of an interaction which takes place within a cultural context, between an individual and a work of art. Our Platonic misgivings do not in the last analysis really disturb our behavior, but only our understanding of that behavior.

Whatever conflicts may arise on the level of philosophical ratiocination, it would seem that even a culture as differentiated and apparently fragmented as ours is really one. Our perception, apprehension, and understanding of the world arise within and are limited by an interrelated set of beliefs and attitudes. These are the most fundamental attributes of the style of our culture as a whole. They control, though they do not determine, the questions we ask of the world and the answers we discover in it. They provide the continuum of Western culture, which links Democritus to Einstein, Plato to Whitehead, and Praxiteles to Picasso. And because they establish a finite framework within which particular styles of art arise, develop, and change, it is these beliefs and attitudes which, in the final analysis, make creation and communication possible.

Our cultural beliefs condition and qualify our experience of the world. And art is just as much part of that world as philosophy, Ping-pong, or pandering. But this does not mean that aesthetic criteria are subjective—only that cultural beliefs are prior to them. Given genuine works of art within a vital stylistic tradition, objective understanding and evaluation are possible. Forgeries are banished to the basement because they are in conflict with our most fundamental beliefs about nature of human existence: beliefs about causation and time, creation and freedom.[20]

---

*[20] In chapters 8 and 9 I suggest that our cultural ideology is indeed undergoing significant modification which, were it not for the importance of scarcity and rarity, might make the "appreciation" of forgeries a real possibility.

CHAPTER
5

The End of the Renaissance?

No aspect of contemporary art has received so much publicity and so much attention from critics, professional and amateur, as the fact that it is often created by accidental or random means. Nor have the artists themselves discouraged such publicity—the storms of protest, the raillery, and the cries of outraged anguish. For, after all, notoriety, even when based on misunderstanding, is perhaps better than neglect.

While the use of random techniques in the plastic arts has received more publicity, the use of chance in music has been much clearer and more systematic. For though Jackson Pollock dripped his paint on a canvas from a considerable height and the French painter Mathieu hurls paint at his canvas from a safe distance, one cannot be sure how much was *really* accidental and how much was governed by an inspired spontaneity—an unconscious control of line, color, and texture arising out of the artist's past training and discipline.

In the composition of music no such doubts arise. For here chance procedures have been employed explicitly and systematically. This has been done in three basic ways: In the first, the composer uses a technique for randomization to create a fully written-out score. As John Cage put it:

> Those involved with the composition of experimental music find ways and means to remove themselves from the activities of the sounds they make. Some employ chance operations derived from sources as ancient

as the Chinese *Book of Changes* or as modern as tables of random numbers used also by physicists in research. Or, analogous to the Rorschach tests of psychology, the interpretation of imperfections in the paper upon which one is writing may provide a music free from one's memory and imagination.[1]

In the second way of randomizing music, the composer merely indicates, by means of a graph or schematic drawing, approximate pitches, time relationships, textures, dynamics, and so forth. The realization of this "score" is left to the performer or, if there is an ensemble, the performers. This method has been used by the Italian composer Sylvano Bussotti and the United States composers Morton Feldman and John Cage. Peter Gradenwitz describes the score of Bussotti's *Piano Piece for David Tudor* as consisting of "a line-drawing made up of straight and curved lines, arrows, vertical and diagonal signs of direction, ornaments, and so forth. This drawing is to inspire the pianist to whom the composer leaves every freedom to interpret the "signs of the 'score.' "[2] Where several players are involved in such a performance, the result may be random indeed. For not only are the particular pitches and the precise time relationships not stipulated in the parts played by the performers but, since these are indeterminate, their synchronization is also random. The coincidence of pitches is purely accidental. The third way of creating so-called indeterminate music is somewhat less random. In this case the composer writes down in detail several separate snippets of music, each lasting for only a few seconds. But the order in which these snippets is played is left to the whim of the performer. Karlheinz Stockhausen's *Piano Piece No. 11* is an example of such a work. Here are Stockhausen's instructions to the pianist:

> The performer looks at random at the sheet of music and begins with any group, the first that catches his eye; this he plays, choosing for himself tempo . . . dynamic level, and type of attack. At the end of the first group, he reads the tempo, dynamic, and attack indications that follow, and looks at random to any other group, which he then plays in accordance with the latter indications.
>
> "Looking at random to any other group" implies that the performer will never link up expressly-chosen groups or intentionally leave out others.
>
> Each group can be joined to any of the other 18: each can thus be played at any of the six tempi and dynamic levels and with any of the six types of attack. . . .

[1] *Silence*, p. 10.
[2] "The Performer's Role in the Newest Music," p. 62.

When a group is arrived at for the third time, one possible realization of the piece is completed. This being so, it may come about that certain groups are played once only or not at all.[3]

Random or indeterminate music must be distinguished from electronic music and from computer music. Electronic music is simply music composed *directly* on tape. That is, the composer begins with either natural sounds or those produced by a frequency oscillator, puts them on tape, and then by rerecording these sound fragments at faster or slower tempi, higher or lower pitches, louder or softer volumes, backwards or forwards, upside down, and so forth, constructs a piece of music. Such a work may involve chance elements or it may be completely pre-planned. In other cases a pre-planned set of time, pitch, volume, and tone-color relationships activated by an electronic mechanism may be put directly on tape. This kind of music has been written by Stockhausen, Boulez, Luciano Berio, Milton Babbitt, and others. Though the composition of "computer music" often *begins* with a series of random numbers corresponding to a series of pitches, the finished piece is not usually random. In computer music a set of rules or instructions—they might be the rules for writing a Bach fugue (if we really knew those well enough) or the rules for writing a popular tune—are fed into a computer which, following these instructions, selects appropriate notes from the random series and thus "composes" a piece of music. Depending upon the nature of the instructions fed into the computer, the compositions it produces can be either highly determined or completely random.

In discussing works of art, the critic can focus his attention upon the work itself—its organization, interrelationships, process of development, and so on, or he may concern himself with the *way* in which the work was created, or he may deal with the cultural beliefs and attitudes which led the artist to employ a particular means in a particular way. Since completely random or indeterminate music is avowedly and purposefully without any organization, it is impossible to analyze or discuss its form or process. I cannot, therefore, deal with the structure and organization of this music—with the music itself. Nor will I be concerned with the random procedures themselves. For while such procedures have received considerable publicity, they are more interesting as symptoms of a new aesthetic than as techniques for creating works of art. In other words, random procedures are a means to an end and their real signifi-

---

[3] *Klavierstüke XI.*

cance begins to appear when one asks *why*—for what purpose—they are employed. This distinction between means and ends is also important because in music, as well as in other arts, the same ends have been achieved in different ways. In fact, as George Rochberg has pointed out, the aesthetic effects produced by random methods of composition are, paradoxically, the same as those realized by totally ordered music.[4] Hence it is not surprising to find that sometimes the same composer writes both kinds.

It is easy, of course, to ridicule art created by accident—by asking "what does it represent?" or asserting that "my little child could have done that." And perhaps the child could. But for these artists that is not the point at all. If we take what they are doing seriously—and, as I shall try to show, their position is a consistent and tenable one—then precisely because the art and aesthetic of the avant-garde represents a radical break with our common cultural convictions, we shall be forced to examine and make explicit those fundamental assumptions about the nature of man, the universe and man's place in it, which are so much a part of our habitual modes of thought and perception that we unconsciously take them for granted.

What characterizes the music with which most of us are most familiar—the music of Bach or Haydn, Wagner or Bartók? Their compositions differ in many important ways: in melodic style, rhythmic organization, harmonic idiom, texture, and instrumental timbre. But they are alike in one fundamental respect. In this music, tones are related to and imply one another. Think, for instance, of the "Liebestod" of Wagner's *Tristan*, rising in cumulative sequences toward its powerful moment of climax; or of the kinetic intensity with which the slow introduction of Bartók's Sonata for Two Pianos and Percussion surges toward the Allegro which follows; or of the way in which the rondo-finale of a Haydn symphony plays with our expectations that the main theme will return—failing to appear just when everything seems ready for its return or arriving just when it is least expected.

Because of its marked, though not necessarily obvious, structure and pattern, as well as because of our past experience with its grammar and syntax, such music is perceived as having a purposeful direction and goal. As we listen, we make predictions—albeit unconscious ones—about where the music is going and how it will get there. Of course, our predictions may not be correct. What we expect may not occur or may

---

4 "Indeterminacy in the New Music," pp. 11–12.

do so at an unexpected time or in an unexpected way. But whether expected or not, what actually does take place is colored by the fact that predictions were made. That is, musical events are felt to be normal and regular, surprising, amusing, or even shocking, as they conform to, or deviate from, our predictions. Such goal-oriented music I shall call *teleological.* (Similarly, the converging lines of perspective in a painting by Raphael or David, the swirling kinetic curves in a Delacroix or Van Gogh, the directional "arrows" in a Tintoretto or Picasso, all focus the viewer's attention upon particular points of structural culmination—upon visual goals. And in literature the normal syntax of language, the delineation of human motivation, the explication of causal relationships among the sequential events of a narrative, and the presentation of dialectically structured thought processes—all combine to create a purposeful, goal-oriented art.)

But the music of the avant-garde directs us toward no points of culmination—establishes no goals toward which to move. It arouses no expectations, except presumably that it will stop. It is neither surprising nor, once you get used to its sounds, is it particularly startling. It is simply *there.* And this is the way it is supposed to be. Such directionless, unkinetic art, whether carefully contrived or created by chance, I shall call *anti-teleological* art. Here is what one young composer, Christian Wolfe, has to say about this music:

> The music has a static character. It goes in no particular direction. There is no necessary concern with time as a measure of distance from a point in the past to a point in the future. . . . It is not a question of getting anywhere, of making progress, or having come from any-where in particular. . . .[5]

What is involved here is not simply a new technique or method for realizing similar ends—as in the music of Haydn, Wagner, or Bartók where different means of creating goal-directed motion were employed. What is involved is a radically different set of ends, whether these ends be achieved by careful calculation as in the music of Stockhausen, the paintings of Tobey or Rothko, and the writings of Beckett and Alain Robbe-Grillet, or by random operations as in the music of Cage, the paintings of Mathieu, or the chance theater of MacLow's *The Marrying Maiden.* And underlying this new aesthetic is a conception of man and the universe, which is almost the opposite of the view that has dominated Western thought since its beginnings.

---

[5] Quoted in John Cage, *Silence,* p. 54.

The End of the Renaissance?

In spirit, practice, and general aesthetic outlook anti-teleological art has much in common with that inspired by existentialism. Nevertheless, on the philosophical level at least, these positions can be distinguished. Because the differences between these facets of avant-garde art may be important in the future, I shall, where it seems useful, attempt to describe them. Since both positions continue to change and evolve, however, the distinctions must be taken as only suggestive and provisional. The relationship of anti-teleological aesthetic to Oriental philosophy—and particularly to Zen Buddhism—is more direct and obvious. For many of these artists have read and been influenced by both Eastern and Western writings on Oriental philosophy. It is important to remember, however, that "influence" is not a one-way reaction. The artist's thinking and his creative attitudes must be *ready* to be influenced. It is said, for instance, that Debussy was "enthralled by the Javanese *gamelang* at the Exposition Universelle" of 1889.[6] He was able to be "enthralled" because the art of music, and his attitude toward it, had developed to a point where such an experience was possible. Had Beethoven heard the same music a hundred years earlier, he would probably have walked away muttering, "Barbarians!" It is because Western art had already developed ways of perception, modes of organization, and philosophical attitudes approximating those of the Orient that the avant-garde could be influenced by them.

In his book, *Silence,* John Cage urges the composer to "give up the desire to control sound, clear his mind of music [in the ordinary sense], and set about discovering means to let sounds be themselves rather than vehicles for man-made theories or expressions of human sentiments."[7]

Several important facets of the aesthetic of anti-teleological art are implicit in this quotation. In the first place, one is not listening to the relationships among the sounds presented, but just to the sounds as sounds—as individual, discrete, objective sensations. A syntax or grammar which would order these sounds and relate them to one another—creating goals, expectations, or a basis for prediction—is to be avoided at all costs. (And one way to make sure that you establish no syntactical-grammatical relationships is to employ the systematic use of chance as a technique of composition.)

Just as composers have sought, by chance or calculation, to destroy musical syntax by avoiding tonal relationships, repetitions, regular

---

[6] Edward Lockspeiser, *Debussy,* p. 240.

[7] *Silence,* p. 10.

rhythmic patterns, and the like, so painters have avoided symmetry, perspective, and the presence of recognizable objects or patterns because these tend to structure visual experience, creating goals and points of focus. Similarly in literature the elements of syntactical organization—plot, character, and conventions of grammar—have been progressively weakened until almost only words remain.

Why must one avoid the structured syntax of pattern and form? Cannot sounds be heard as sounds, or colors be seen as colors, and still be, so to speak, embedded in an order which relates the sounds or colors to each other? Perhaps. But it seems clear that the more one perceives the relationships among things, the less one tends to be aware of their existence as things in themselves—as pure sensation. You may, at some time, have had a radio or television set go haywire so that the sound was completely distorted. If so, you may recall that when the syntax and grammar became obscured and meaning was lost, you became very aware of sound *qua* sound—you became conscious of the bleeps, bloops, and squeaks. Or, if a color slide is so out of focus that the objects depicted cannot be recognized, one becomes intensely aware of the experience of color as color.

It is to the naïve and primitive enjoyment of sensations and things for their own sakes that these artists seek to return. We must, they urge, rediscover the reality and excitement of a sound as such, a color as such, and existence itself as such. But our habits of perception and apprehension—the accumulation of traditional preconceptions which we bring to aesthetic experience—prevent us from seeing and hearing what is really *there* to be perceived. The avant-garde novel aims, writes Bruce Morrissette, at "an art which creates a basically true and real image of man's situation among men and in the universe of neutral objects, without metaphysics, and scraped clean of the 'crust' of obsolete ideas." [8] Traditions, theories, systems are obstacles to be overcome by the artist as well as the writer. "As examples of such obstacles," the painter Mark Rothko cites "(among others) memory, history or geometry, which are swamps of generalization from which one might pull out parodies of ideas (which are ghosts) but never an idea in itself." [9]

The existentialists, too, seek to destroy our habitual modes of perception and thought. But for somewhat different reasons. The anti-teleological position holds that traditions, systems, and the like are evil because they limit our freedom of thought and action, deaden our

---

[8] "The New Novel in France," p. 19.
[9] Dorothy C. Miller (ed.), *Fifteen Americans*, p. 18.

sensitivity to sensation and feeling, and, in the end, alienate man from nature of which he should be a part. Art should, in Cage's words, be "an affirmation of life—not an attempt to bring order out of chaos nor to suggest improvements in creation, but simply a way of waking up to the very life we're living, which is so excellent once one gets one's mind and one's desires out of its way and lets it act of its own accord." [10] For the existentialists, on the other hand, man's alienation is part of the very nature of things. Nor is the revitalization of sensitivity of paramount importance. For them the accretion of traditional patterns of behavior and modes of thought must be stripped away, not only because they limit human freedom, but because, as noted later, they limit the individual's responsibility for the choices he makes.

Particularly when contrasted with the more somber outlook of existentialism, the anti-teleological position with its emphasis upon the value of naïve, direct experience and upon the natural goodness of man, seems characteristically American—despite clear overtones of romanticism a la Rousseau. Cage's words, quoted above, remind us of Thoreau's:

> If men would steadily observe the realities only, and not allow themselves to be deluded, life, to compare it with such things as we know, would be like a fairy tale and the Arabian Nights' Entertainments. . . . [However] by closing the eyes and slumbering, and consenting to be deceived by shows, men establish and confirm their daily life of routine and habit everywhere, which is still built on purely illusory foundations.[11]

On a somewhat less romantic level, the grammar and syntax of art—and their counterparts in the world of affairs: custom, law, and philosophy—are to be avoided because they continue to act as the vehicles for social and personal teleology. The anti-novel in which nothing happens because no event follows from any other, the directionless painting in which lines and colors lead to no points of culmination, and the anti-kinetic musical composition in which tones are without implications are perhaps at least in part a reaction to the mess that goals, purposes, and strivings have got us into.

The language of science, so full of words like force, tendency, and natural selection which imply purposes and goals, is, according to this viewpoint, misleading. Rightly understood these are purely descriptive terms. Nature has, in fact, no purpose or goal. It simply is. And like nature, art should simply present. Thus Rauschenberg contends that

---

[10] *Silence*, p. 12.
[11] Henry David Thoreau, *Walden and Other Writings*, p. 86.

"painting is always strongest when . . . it appears as a fact or an inevitability, as opposed to a souvenir or arrangement." [12] Alain Robbe-Grillet makes a similar point when he says of Beckett's *Waiting for Godot* that "the theatrical character is on *stage,* this is his primary quality—he is there." [13] Or, put negatively, the scenes in Robbe-Grillet's novel *Jealousy* are, Morrissette tells us, presented "without a word of analysis or commentary, in the pure domain of phenomenological semantics." [14] Similarly Cage, as we have seen, emphasizes that sounds should simply "be themselves rather than vehicles for man-made theories or expressions of human sentiments." [15]

Our relationship to art, like our relationship to nature, ought to be one of acceptance. This is true for both the artist and the audience. The artist, whether employing chance methods of composition or applying a predetermined arbitrary formula, should accept the unanticipated result without seeking to impose his personal will on the materials or making them conform to some syntactical preconception of what ought to take place. Similarly the audience should entertain no preconceptions, make no predictions about what will occur, and force no organization upon the series of individual sounds, colors, or words presented to it. A composer whose graphs are realized or whose notated fragments are ordered by a performer must accept what happens—and so should the audience, just as one accepts the sounds of a thunderstorm, a crying baby, a busy office, or silence.

Here another difference between the anti-teleological position and that of existentialism becomes apparent. In the anti-teleological view, existence is *one.* Being and non-being are not opposites, but merely different states which may happen to something. Death is a change in existence, not the negation of it. (Again one is struck by the kinship with a sort of pantheistic romanticism and thinks, perhaps, of Wordsworth's poem, "A slumber did my spirit seal.") Silence is just as real, just as much a part of existence as sound. As Rauschenberg has said, "A canvas is never empty." [16] For the existentialists, however, being and non-being are categorical opposites. Death is a horrible stupidity, making life absurd, yet at the same time making the human responsibility for individual choice the crucial fact of existence and the basis for whatever human dignity there is.

---

[12] Dorothy C. Miller (ed.), *Sixteen Americans,* p. 58.
[13] Quoted in Hugh Kenner, "Waiting for Godot To Begin," p. 49.
[14] "The New Novel in France," p. 18.
[15] *Silence,* p. 10.
[16] Miller, *Sixteen Americans,* p. 58.

The End of the Renaissance?

The denial of the reality of relationships and the relevance of purpose, the belief that only individual sensations and not the connections between them are real, and the assertion that predictions and goals depend not upon an order existing in nature, but upon the accumulated habits and preconceptions of man—all these rest upon a less explicit but even more fundamental denial: a denial of the reality of cause and effect. Once this is seen, the aesthetic of the avant-garde begins to make sense. For this is a position of uncompromising positivism [17]—or what I shall hereafter call *radical empiricism*.[18]

It may seem ridiculous to deny the reality of cause and effect—the existence of necessary connections between events. We should, however, remember the contentions of such philosophers as David Hume. And in the world of contemporary science—particularly in quantum mechanics, where events are not fully determined or predictable but only probable—the concept of cause and effect has again become problematical. After quoting from the second edition of Kant's *Critique of Pure Reason* to the effect that "all changes happen in accordance with the law of the connection of cause and effect," Henry Margenau states that "physics knows of no such law; as a matter of fact there is no plausible way of defining cause and effect." [19]

Actually this point requires some qualification. What is denied in quantum mechanics and in the aesthetic of radical empiricism is not the theoretical possibility of a principle of causation, but the theoretical possibility of isolating any particular event as being the cause of another particular event. This is the case because, since the world is seen as a single interrelated field or continuum in which everything interacts with—is the "cause" of—everything else, there are no separable causes and effects. Thus, discussing the emission of alpha-particles, Heisenberg writes:

> We know the forces in the atomic nucleus that are responsible for the emission of the *a*-particle. But this knowledge contains the uncertainty which is brought about by the interaction between the nucleus

---

[17] After writing the first draft of this article, I discovered that George Rochberg had also used the word "positivism" to characterize the tendency toward indeterminacy in contemporary music. See "Indeterminacy in the New Music," p. 11.

*[18] Because of its philosophical-scientific connotations, the term "radical empiricism" is evidently misleading. Consequently, when this set of beliefs and attitudes is discussed in Parts II and III, it is referred to as "transcendental particularism" or, in abbreviated form, as "transcendentalism."

[19] "Meaning and Scientific Status of Causality," p. 437.

and the rest of the world. If we wanted to know why the *a*-particle was emitted at that particular time we would have to know the microscopic structure of the whole world including ourselves, and that is impossible.[20]

This viewpoint, developed in connection with the *micro*scopic world of electromagnetic phenomena and quantum mechanics, has been applied with varying degrees of precision by the radical empiricists to *macro*scopic events.[21] Cage, for instance, writes that there is "an incalculable infinity of causes and effects . . . in fact each and every thing in all of time and space is related to each and every other thing in all of time and space." [22] Doré Ashton seems to echo this point when he tells us that Mark Tobey's paintings symbolize "his Heraclitan conviction that all things come out of one and one out of all things." [23] In a similar vein Robbe-Grillet asserts that chronological time distorts our experience because it "forces events into a pattern of causality and imposes an unjustifiable logic upon them." [24]

To deny causality is to deny the possibility of prediction. All notions of "if this occurs, then that must, or will probably, follow" disappear. Consequently (if I may be permitted so teleological a word), the music, art, and literature of the avant-garde is characteristically unkinetic and unfocused. In a novel by Robbe-Grillet, a composition by Cage, or a painting by Guston one does not, and should not, feel that one event follows *from* (is the result of) what went before. It simply "comes after." And since no event or action refers to or leads us to expect any other event or action, the sequence of events is, in any ordinary sense of the term, meaningless.

Again there is a difference in emphasis, if not in practice, between the existentialist wing of the avant-garde and the radical empiricist wing.

[20] Werner Heisenberg, *Physics and Philosophy*, pp. 89–90.

[21] Paradoxically, the aesthetic of the avant-garde at one and the same time accepts and rejects contemporary science. On the one hand, it employs the concepts and terminology of modern physics—indeterminacy, field theory, and the relativity of space-time—with freedom, if not always with accuracy, to rationalize and support its position. On the other hand, it represents a revolt against the world which science has revealed—a world which is an abstract, man-made construct of unseen particles governed by unknown forces. And the radical empiricists, reacting against the artificiality of this unreal world (as well as its fruits), have sought to reaffirm the existence, the poignancy, and the value of directly experienced sensation. * These matters are discussed further in chapters 8 and 10.

[22] *Silence*, p. 47.

[23] "Mark Tobey," p. 31.

[24] Quoted in Richard Gilman, "Total Revolution in the Novel," p. 99.

The End of the Renaissance?

For the radical empiricist, the isolated object freshly experienced is the chief source of value. The existentialist position, on the other hand, is apparently paradoxical: the meaning of the art work lies in its objectification of the meaninglessness of life itself. "What Sartre calls the 'anti-novels' of Nathalie Sarraute," writes Norman Podhoretz, "seem . . . to represent a total submission to the meaninglessness of existence." [25]

The denial of causality and the correlative denial of predictability have important consequences. In the first place, rational choice, which depends upon the possibility of envisaging the results of alternative courses of action, becomes a senseless fiction. (This being so, it makes no difference whether an art work is produced by the consistent use of chance, by a purely gratuitous act, or by the rigid application of a predetermined formula.) And attending to such a work of art, we, the audience, should not attempt to choose, even unconsciously, among alternative possibilities for continuation. We ought to remain detached, seeing, hearing, and observing the objective series of empirical events.

In their attitude toward choice the existentialists differ fundamentally from the radical empiricists. In the existentialist view, one performs a gratuitous act not because choice is meaningless but because only by such an act can the individual become fully responsible for his actions. In all other actions, responsibility can, in part at least, be attributed to the social order, traditional modes of thought and behavior, habit, and the like. Seen in this light, existentialism seems closer to the tradition of Western culture than does radical empiricism. For existentialism still seeks to solve the problems of the human condition—of man's despair in the face of death and his alienation from the world—within the basic framework of humanism, in which man is morally responsible for his own acts.

If predictability and choice are impossible, art cannot be a form of communication. For communication requires that the artist imagine or predict how others—the audience—will interpret and respond to the words, sounds, or visual designs he produces. As I write or speak, I choose my words by acting as my own audience; and I presume that you will respond to my words as I do. If I cannot imagine what your responses will be—and the systematic use of chance, for instance, precludes this possibility—then there can be no communication. Furthermore, in literature and music at least, communication depends to a considerable extent upon the use of a traditionally established, shared

---

[25] "The New Nihilism and the Novel," p. 585.

syntax and grammar. When these are destroyed, communication is substantially weakened. The artists and composers of radical empiricism are well aware of this. The painter Clyfford Still, for instance, asserts: "Demands for communication are both presumptuous and irrelevant. The observer usually sees what his fears and hopes and learning teach him to see." [26]

Furthermore, because aesthetic experience involves no predictions, no meanings, and no communication, the value of the work of art cannot be judged—any more than one can judge nature or natural objects in themselves. "Value judgments," writes Cage, "are not in the nature of this work as regards either composition, performance, or listening. The idea of relation . . . being absent anything . . . may happen. A 'mistake' is beside the point, for once anything happens it authentically is." [27] Since error depends upon having a preconceived idea of what should occur, this is indeed an art without error. As the painter Georges Mathieu has said, ". . . if we reduce the part played by conscious control in favor of spontaneity, we find ourselves in the position where *the very notion of error . . .* disappears." [28]

To deny the existence of causality is to deny the possibility of *form*. For implicit in relational concepts such as beginning, middle, and end, antecedent-consequent, or periodicity, is the belief that the events in question are causally connected. An end, or conclusion, is something *caused* by what went before. But in order to follow the form of a painting by Jackson Pollock, writes Allan Kaprow, "it is necessary to get rid of the usual idea of 'Form,' i.e. a beginning, middle, and end, or any variant of this principle—such as fragmentation." [29] Or, as Robert Goldwater has said, "In Mark Rothko's pictures the apparent end lies close to the apparent beginning—so close in fact, or in apparent fact, that they are almost indistinguishable." [30] In a similar vein the composer Stockhausen has spoken of "creating in each piece an individual, self-contained world like a crystal, which, when one turns it, is always different, but always the same. It should not matter whether the music is played from the beginning, middle, or end, so long as it goes full circle." [31] In literature, too, syntactical form has disappeared. Because the human mind—and the world as seen through it—is considered to be

---

[26] In Miller, *Fifteen Americans*, p. 22.
[27] *Silence*, p. 59.
[28] *From the Abstract to the Possible*, p. 21.
[29] "The Legacy of Jackson Pollock," p. 26.
[30] "Reflections on the Rothko Exhibition," p. 43.
[31] Quoted in Francis Burt, "An Antithesis," p. 69.

an unorganized conglomeration of sensations, thoughts, memories, and affects whose relationships (if such exist) we can never really know, the words and phrases describing the mind's activity have been divested of syntactical significance. The functional relationships among parts of speech tend to disappear. Similarly, sentences and paragraphs do not follow from one another. On the highest architectonic level—that of the succession of described events—expressed motivation and all rhetorical analysis of psychology are rejected. "Character and plot having disappeared from the novel," writes Jean Bloch-Michel, "what is left? The object, replies Robbe-Grillet. And an object without meaning." [32]

Because it presents a succession rather than a progression of events, this art is essentially static. There are no points of culmination or of focus. All events are equally important and time, as we ordinarily conceive of it, dissolves. There is only duration. For ordered time depends upon the existence and recognition of the beginnings and terminations of separable events or patterns. Stockhausen's image of music as a turning crystal which is always the same, yet always different, suggests Alfonso Ossario's description of a painting by Jackson Pollock: "The picture surface, with no depth of recognizable space or sequence of known time, gives us the never-ending present. We are presented with a visualization of that remorseless consolation—in the end is the beginning." [33] And writing of Samuel Beckett's novel *Malone*, Robert Hatch says that we "cannot possibly say whether we are with him [Malone] twenty minutes, two months, or ten years." [34]

These remarks suggest why radical empiricism probably finds its most idiosyncratic and convincing expression in the plastic arts. Since meaningful visual experience is, so to speak, directly and naturally presentational and objective, painting and sculpture can excite our interest and contemplation in the absence of explicit representation and an established vocabulary, grammar, and syntax. We can, that is, respond sensitively to fortuitous coincidences of line, color, space, and texture, delighting in the patterns and relationships which we discover, even as we do in looking at nature.

Even more important, the plastic arts are *de facto* static and timeless. Motions, goals, time, and syntax are not explicitly stated, but must be inferred by the viewer. Hence the order in which events are perceived is never fully determined in painting or sculpture. Even a teleological

---

[32] "The Avant-Garde in French Fiction," p. 469.
[33] In Miller, *Fifteen Americans*, p. 15.
[34] "Laughter at Your Own Risk," p. 113.

work in which our attention is directed toward definite focal points can be viewed in many different orders. Similarly it is possible to experience the structure of the visual world, whether ordered or disordered, without presuming that it communicates, has purposes, or even involves cause and effect.

In music and literature, on the other hand, a *de facto* chronology is *necessarily* established—even in a work whose order is the product of pure chance. And we tend, whether by nature or learning, to infer causal relationships from such a sequence of events. We attempt, that is, to relate earlier events to later ones, discovering implications and attributing a causal order to the series of stimuli. These tendencies are enforced by the fact that the sounds to which we attend most carefully are man-made, conventional events in which teleology and communication are almost invariably presumed.

If this analysis is correct, is it not possible that the arts will move in the coming years *not* toward a common, monolithic aesthetic as they seem to be doing today, but toward a plurality of aesthetics, each appropriate to its particular art? The aesthetics of the visual arts might, for instance, continue to develop the tendencies implicit in radical empiricism, reflecting the culture's conceptualization of the natural order of the material universe. And, since language is man's means of relating himself to the external world and to other men, literature might continue to be primarily concerned with the relationships of men to each other and to the universe—with the social-moral order or, if you will, disorder. And music, operating in the realm of pure syntax without reference to external objects or events would, then, develop an order reflecting and paralleling the structure and patterns of human mental processes.

Whatever one may think of the art of radical empiricism, the philosophical position of which it is the expression is, as I have tried to indicate, a consistent and tenable one. That this is so was pointed out by Alfred North Whitehead:

> Suppose that two occurrences may be in fact detached so that one of them is comprehensible without reference to the other. Then all notion of causation between them, or of conditioning, becomes unintelligible. There is—with this supposition—no reason why the possession of any quality by one of them should in any way influence the possession of that quality, or of any other quality, by the other. With such a doctrine the play and inter-play of qualitative succession in the world becomes a blank fact from which no conclusions can be drawn as to past, present, or future, beyond the range of direct observation. Such a positivis-

tic belief is quite self-consistent, provided that we do not include in it any hopes for the future or regrets for the past. Science is then without any importance. Also effort is foolish, because it determines nothing.[35]

New art has always been difficult to understand because it has always sought to replace old habits of thought and perception, old preconceptions and prejudices with new ways of looking at the world and fresh startling insights. But however drastically they may have modified the means of expression, the content, or the form of art, composers, artists, and writers of the West have, until now, had the same essential ends—the same essential philosophical orientation—as their predecessors. There is a clear line of development from Aeschylus to Shakespeare to Joyce, from Phidias to Michelangelo to Picasso, and from Monteverdi to Beethoven to Stravinsky.

Radical empiricism is not, however, an attempt to redefine goals and values within the long tradition of Western art and thought. Rather it seeks to break decisively with the most basic tenets of that tradition. "This new literature," says Robbe-Grillet, ". . . is going to represent—in its fulfillment—a revolution more total than those from which such movements as romanticism and naturalism were born." [36] And Cage, criticizing Edgar Varèse, the patron saint of experimental music, for injecting his personality—his teleology—into the music he writes, says that Varèse "is an artist of the past. Rather than dealing with sounds as sounds, he deals with them as Varèse." [37]

Man is no longer to be the measure of all things, the center of the universe. He has been measured and found to be an undistinguished bit of matter different in no essential way from bacteria, stones, and trees. His goals and purposes; his egocentric notions of past, present, and future; his faith in his power to predict and, through prediction, to control his destiny—all these are called into question, considered irrelevant, or deemed trivial. For these artists, writers, and composers—and, however influential they may be, it must be remembered that they represent only a small segment of the world of contemporary art—for these radical empiricists, *the Renaissance is over.*

Here is Georges Mathieu's description of the present situation:

> Our whole culture has allowed itself to be permeated, since the end of the Middle Ages, by Hellenistic thought patterns which aimed at bringing the cosmos down to human proportions and limited the

[35] *Modes of Thought,* p. 226.
[36] Quoted in Gilman, "Total Revolution in the Novel," p. 96.
[37] *Silence,* p. 84.

means of access to an understanding of the Universe to those provided by reason and the senses. . . . For the past ten years, painting . . . has been freeing itself from the yoke of this burdensome inheritance. After twenty-five centuries of a culture we had made our own, we are witnessing in certain aspects of lyrical non-configuration a new phenomenon in painting—and, one might add, in the arts in general—which calls into question the very foundations of 40,000 years of aesthetic activity.[38]

Whether the Renaissance is over for the rest of us—for our culture generally—only the future will tell. But whether it is over or not, the merit of considering the art and aesthetic of radical empiricism seriously is that it challenges us to discover and make explicit the grounds for beliefs and values which we unconsciously take for granted. If we are to defend our beliefs—our faith in a world of purpose and causality, time and prediction, choice and control, communication and morality, we must ask the most fundamental questions that can be asked: questions about the nature of man, his relationships to other men, and his place in the universe. Can we do more than simply assert our beliefs? Can we give empirically verifiable reasons for them? [39]

---

[38] *From the Abstract to the Possible*, p. 9.

*[39] Some of the difficulties with the "philosophy" of radical empiricism are considered below, in chapter 9.

PART II

As It Is, and Perhaps Will Be

INTRODUCTION

THE HISTORY of the arts in our time has been characterized by change. New styles and techniques, schools and movements, programs and philosophies, have succeeded one another with bewildering rapidity. And the old has not, as a rule, been displaced by the new. Earlier movements have persisted side by side with later ones, producing a profusion of alternative styles and schools—each with its attendant aesthetic outlook and theory.

Within the past two decades, for instance, abstract expressionism and action painting were followed by Pop art, hard-line painting and a return to representational art. These in turn have been followed by Op art. And today all these ways of painting coexist as competing and, in some instances, conflicting styles of art. In music the syntax of tonality continues to be used by some composers, while others have extended the serial techniques developed by Schönberg and his followers. Still other composers have employed the systematic use of chance in composition, performance, or both. Today all of these schools coexist as ways of composing, together with jazz, folk music, and popular music. Similar tendencies, though not so clearly defined, are to be found in literature.

Continual change resulting in a multiplicity of styles and techniques has created genuine problems for the public, because each style demands a somewhat different way of perceiving and understanding and, consequently, different criteria for judging. For example, the way of listening to a composition by Elliott Carter is radically different from the way of listening appropriate to a work by John Cage. Similarly, a novel by Beckett must in a significant sense be read differently from one by Bellow. A painting by Willem de Kooning and one by Andy Warhol require different perceptional-cognitive attitudes. And these differences, marked and major though they be, are slight when compared to the differences between such "elite" art and the popular art of everyday commercialism. A culture which includes James Bond and Robbe-Grillet, the Beatles and Milton Babbitt, Coca-Cola ads and action painting is indeed pluralistic and perplexing.

The perplexity and confusion of the public are certainly not the result of a dearth of discussion and polemic. Artists, as well as critics and historians, have described styles, developed theories, explained movements, and advocated philosophies. Partisans have praised, skeptics have scoffed, doubters have deplored. All this has produced some heat and considerable smoke, but very little light. The confusion engendered by multiplicity has persisted.

One wonders whether some order cannot be discerned in this tangle of tendencies; whether unity can be discovered in this rampant pluralism. Is there perhaps some common denominator? Some common direction of change? Or are we faced with a fragmented array of more or less independent and discrete styles, movements, and philosophies?

The easy, conventional non-answer is that "only the future can tell." And in this answer lies still another source of difficulty in our understanding of the current situation in the arts. Namely, it is hard to imagine what will follow the present pluralism. Will the burgeoning of styles and techniques continue? Will one of the various schools or movements in painting, music, or literature become dominant in years to come? Or will a group of different styles coexist as they seem to do today?

CHAPTER
6

History, Stasis, and Change

To speculate about the future is always hazardous. And, considering the present confusion in the arts, it is probably foolhardy. It is important to do so, however, not because one wishes to control or determine the future, but because our understanding of the meaning and significance of the present depends in part upon the implications which the present appears to have for the future. The point is really quite simple. What an event—in this case a cultural situation—*is*, what it means to us, is not merely a function of its existent present. Its meaning also depends in a very real way upon the events which have preceded and implied it, *and* upon the events which it in turn is thought, rightly or wrongly, to imply.[1]

So too it is with political events or with our understanding of the current situation in the arts. We must speculate—both in the philosophical and in the stock-market sense—about the future if we are to form any sort of coherent picture of the present. As A. N. Whitehead has said, "What we perceive as the present is the vivid fringe of memory tinged with anticipation." [2] Our understanding of the present always involves some notion, whether implicit or explicit, of what the future will be like—even if that future is imagined as being only a continuation of the present situation.[3]

---

[1] The only discussion of this point which I have come across is in William Dray's article, " 'Explaining What' in History": "We see the significance of historical events by noticing what they *lead to*, as well as what they arise out of" (p. 406).

[2] From *The Concept of Nature*, quoted in G. J. Whitrow, *The Natural Philosophy of Time*, p. 83.

[3] Since it is not the purpose of the speculations presented in this book to influence or control the future but rather to understand the present, the value of

It should be observed in passing that our guesses about the future are hazardous, not only because the behavior of future artists, writers, and composers is unpredictable, but because our guesses involve an element of methodological uncertainty analogous to that involved in quantum mechanics. This is because our predictions—our analysis of the present and hence our guesses about the future—necessarily modify and influence that future, just as the process of measurement in physics necessarily influences the future behavior of the system. Thus, for instance, Marx's predictions about the future overthrow of the bourgeoisie played a significant role in the future of the events predicted. And though this is a particularly striking example, more modest guesses about the future of painting, for instance, may also influence and modify the events that follow. Herbert J. Muller writes that "we cannot predict the future with certainty: prediction itself—that is, belief about the probable future—may make an incalculable difference in it." [4]

From this point of view, the distinction between the present and the past does not lie primarily in the areas of knowledge, understanding, clarity, or vividness. Often we know more about events in the past (e.g., the Civil War or Beethoven's symphonies), understand them better and feel them to be more vivid than ones in the present (say, the conflict between India and Pakistan or the music of Boulez). Sometimes, on the other hand, the reverse is true. Nor does it seem to me that the distinction lies, as L. Susan Stebbing argues, in *our* activity which "differs in relation to the present as contrasted with its relation to the past and its relation to the future." [5] For there are many events in the present in which our influence on the future is virtually nil; and, in a very real sense, we can and do alter the significance and meaning of the past, if not the literal events themselves. Thus André Malraux writes that "it is not research work that has led to the understanding of El Greco; it is modern art." [6]

Rather, the past is distinguished from the present in this: an event is

---

what follows depends more upon insights provided today than upon predictions confirmed tomorrow. Some sort of future must be envisaged if one is to comprehend and act in the present. Because the possible futures are plural, however, one may well be mistaken in one's envisaging. But this does not mean that one's judgments about the present were wrong. For because the envisaged future is always qualified and conditional—such and such will take place, *if* some particular set of conditions prevail—the envisaged future *might* have come to pass. Indeed, it might even have been the most probable one.

[4] "Misuses of the Past," p. 12.

[5] "Some Ambiguities in Discussions concerning Time," p. 118–19.

[6] "The Triumph of Art over History," p. 516.

considered to be past when, on a given hierarchic level of events, its implications appear to have been realized and its consequences on that level are known. It is through the realization of implications, through the completion of process, that patterns appear to have become closed and events are thought to be defined. It is because its consequences have not yet been realized—because it is, so to speak, still in process—that yesterday's news or work of art is felt to be in the present, to be contemporary, even though chronologically it is in the past.

HISTORY AS A HIERARCHIC CONSTRUCT

History is hierarchic. The length of time an event remains in some historical present depends upon the duration of the highest hierarchic level of which it forms a part—upon what might be called its historical "reverberation time." As a result, two events may be simultaneous and of roughly equal literal duration—say, a bridge game and the première of a new symphony. But the consequences of the bridge game (which is not part of a tournament or a series of games) are short-term; the event is closed-out after a few hours and it has no further consequences. The symphony, on the other hand, if it proves to be a significant achievement which becomes part of a larger pattern of events in the history of style, has implications extending over a considerable period of time. As a result, the symphony remains in a "present" longer than the bridge game.

If it be argued that the symphony remains longer in a present because it is important while the bridge game is trivial, the answer is that "importance" is, in fact, defined by the highest hierarchic level on which an event is thought to exist. Had the symphony been run-of-the-mill, its duration would have scarcely outlived its performance. To take another example, the assassination at Sarajevo was a major event, not because those murdered were noble or their lives of peculiar value, but because the event became part of a higher-order event—namely, World War I. Had this not been the case, the assassination would have long since been forgotten.

Thus it is not merely, or perhaps even primarily, because new facts are brought to light that each new generation to some extent rewrites history. Rather, insofar as recent events are conceived to be implications or consequences of earlier events, the significance of those earlier events is altered and the structuring of historical hierarchies is modified. It is this kind of thing which, I think, T. S. Eliot has in mind when he writes that what happens when a new work of art is created is something that happens simultaneously to all the works of art which preceded it. The existing monuments form an ideal order among themselves, which is modified by the introduction of the new (the really new) work of art among them. The existing order is complete before the new work arrives; for order to persist after the supervention of novelty, the *whole* existing order must be, if ever so slightly, altered. . . . Whoever has approved this idea of order, of the form of European, of English literature will not find it preposterous that the past should be altered by the present as much as the present is directed by the past.[7]

Eliot's own writing about the metaphysical poets, for instance, as well as their influence on his poetry has changed our evaluation of their place in history somewhat. From this a corollary of some importance follows: if a stasis of considerable duration became a fact, then the past too would be less fluid and changeable.

For a hierarchy to exist, some events or processes must be viewed as "closed out" on a given level, so that as events they can combine with one another to form a composite higher-level structure. Such higher-level structures similarly cohere to form still more extensive levels, and so on. Thus an event may be very brief—a few minutes, an hour, or a day. Or it may be more extensive—a life, a generation, a period (such as the Enlightenment), or a civilization. What constitutes such an event depends upon the patterning perceived on a given hierarchic level.

Such patterning makes it clear that history is a construct. But, as L. Susan Stebbing points out, although "the past and the future are constructs . . . we must be careful to notice that *being a construction* does not entail *being unreal*." [8] Nor does it involve being arbitrary. Historical constructs, like scientific ones, are derived from an order existing in the real world of historical fact; but the patterning discovered in that world will depend in part upon the interests and goals of the investigator. For this reason, historians with different interests, who are studying different kinds of events, will tend to structure history in different ways. For the student of European political history, for instance, the French Revolution is an event of momentous significance, a point of hierarchic articulation; but for the historian of European music, it is a minor ripple in a style period which runs roughly from 1750 to 1827—or perhaps even to 1914. One cannot assume that history moves in a monolithic fashion. Hence, it is a mistake to insist upon

---

[7] *Selected Essays*, p. 15.

[8] "Some Ambiguities in Discussions concerning Time," p. 119.

coordinating style periods among the several arts, or upon relating style periods to political or social history. Events may coincide or they may not. Whether they do is something to be demonstrated, not something to be assumed.

Periodization is not, then, merely a convenient way of dividing up the past. It follows from the hierarchic character of history. Periodization is a necessity, if the succession of particular events in the past is to be understood as being something more than chronicle—that is, as being more than a series of events strung like beads upon the slender thread of sequence.[9] Were it not hierarchically articulated into reigns, epochs, style periods, movements, and the like, the past would lose immeasurably both in understandability and in richness. As Herbert A. Simon has pointed out, "The fact that many complex systems have a . . . hierarchic structure is a major facilitating factor enabling us to understand, to describe, and even to 'see' such systems and their parts." [10] Periodization is also important because it makes possible the identification of historical movements. According to William Dray, such identification is an important and often neglected aspect of historical explanation: ". . . explaining what a thing is, i.e., how it should be regarded, is just not the same enterprise at all as explaining why it . . . happened." [11] Our conceptual classification of an event influences the way in which we perceive and understand it. A period of disturbance and turmoil in which everything seems confused becomes understandable when we subsume it under the category "revolution," just as a section of music without patent melodic structures and characterized by marked and rapidly shifting harmonic motion is more understandable when conceived of as a "development section." And our ability to analyze the interactions within such a "what" depends upon our concep-

---

[9] In other words, history is distinguished from chronicle in terms of the kind of structural relationships each creates, not on the grounds that the latter fails to inquire into reasons and causes. Chronicles do consider causes, though they tend to be those—for instance, the psychology of individual human motivation—which explain particular actions and incidents rather than large-scale movements and processes. Because his purview is confined to the events he has witnessed or has heard about from other witnesses, the chronicler cannot concern himself with long-range implications. Consequently he cannot construct those complex "arched" hierarchies which we call histories. Nor can he inquire into those large-scale causes which are often referred to as the "forces of history." A chronicle is, from this point of view, a type of "flat" hierarchy. For a discussion of different kinds of hierarchies, see chapter 12.

[10] "The Architecture of Complexity," p. 477.

[11] " 'Explaining What' in History," p. 405.

tualization of the kind of event being studied. This observation is akin to Michael Polanyi's idea that "the study of an organ must begin with an attempt to guess what it is for and how it works." [12] Thus, to extend Dray's interesting idea, what perhaps really is happening is that such classifications are a way of describing the "functions" of large-scale, high-level historical events. In a sense they are both formal entities within the large-scale processes of history (the revolution is such only in the context of preceding and following events, just as the development section is so only in the context of the preceding exposition and the ensuing recapitulation) as well as classifications which serve to call attention to features within their own structure (on lower hierarchic levels) and which lead us to compare them with both wholes and parts of other events so classified.[13] Finally, by suggesting, as I shall, that we are in, or are about to enter, a period of extended stasis, I am in part explaining *what* a thing (the present) is by bringing various seemingly diverse and disparate events under a single general concept.

In the construction of successive hierarchic systems, there is a strong temptation to discover recurrent cycles and patterns of repetition. This is partly because events appear to be more clearly defined and separated from one another when such recurrence is present. The more exact the repetition of a pattern—whether audible, visual, or conceptual—the more certain we are about the limits of the events. (This phenomenon is very clear in music: one of the most effective ways to articulate the structure of a musical motive, phrase, or section is to begin to restate it.) Hence historians, seeking to delimit events as unambiguously as possible, tend to look diligently for patterns of repetition, discovering cycles which frequently are not supported by the facts.

Another way of delimiting an event, period, or movement is to discover significant differences between the event and what precedes or follows it. In this case, the attempt to define periods unambiguously may lead to an overemphasis on the element of novelty and change.

Both kinds of distortion—the search for cycles and the exaggeration of novelty—arise because the limits of a style or movement, particularly its beginnings, are difficult to define precisely. Styles do not come into existence clearly and fully articulated, but tend to change in a processive way from barely noticeable beginnings. Here an analogy with the syntactic processes of music may help to illustrate what I have in mind.

---

[12] *Personal Knowledge*, p. 360.

[13] In this connection, see the distinction between form, process and hierarchic structure in music, in chap. 12.

As with a style (or any relatively complex historical event), a musical motive, theme, or even section takes shape gradually. At first the implications of tones are ambiguous. Even within the context of a familiar style, the implications of one or two tones are very numerous. As more tones and rhythmic relationships are added, the possible continuations become more limited and a pattern begins to emerge. As the phrase continues to unfold, both its consequential implications and its hierarchic organization become clear: what the probable structure of the total event—the closed-out pattern on the level of theme—will be, becomes evident, though even at the very end surprises may occur. Only when the theme is clearly complete—when some new event has begun—can we fully and securely comprehend its hierarchic structure. And at this point it has become part of a section whose structure has still to evolve.

Moreover, the divisions between elements and parts of a musical hierarchy are not always decisively articulated. Sometimes there are elisions and overlappings of events or processes on a given level. In other cases, elements which appeared to be ambiguous while in process become clear and unequivocal in retrospect. Several events may exist simultaneously and be "closed out" either together or at different times. Always, there is an interaction and interconnection among simultaneous events and among the several hierarchic levels. But the ambiguities of beginnings and the complexities of simultaneous or overlapping events, though they make analysis a subtle and challenging art, do not negate the fact of hierarchic organization.

So too it is, I think, with history. What makes historical events more difficult to describe, analyze, and explain is not merely the wealth of potentially pertinent data but the fact that, while the beginning and end of a musical work are decisively marked—by silence—historical events flow into one another, overlap, and coincide without any definitely defining articulation. There is no pause, no silence, in the flow of historical events. Though history is in this respect more difficult to analyze than music, it does not follow that historical events are not hierarchic and that the delineation of periods is unimportant. We may agree with James Ackerman in accepting "a theory of confluent, overlapping and interacting styles in place of a cyclic-evolutionary one" without concluding, as he does, that then "the problem of fixing limits becomes much less urgent." [14] The task does not become less urgent, but it does become more difficult, requiring a heightened sensitivity to

---

[14] "A Theory of Style," p. 236.

complexity, increased subtlety, and, above all, an ability to live with ambiguity.

A hierarchic view of processive events—whether in history, biology, physics, or music—has frequently led to still another, more serious, error, a methodological mistake which I shall call the *fallacy of hierarchic uniformity*. This error arises from the tacit and usually unconscious assumption that the same forces and processes which order and articulate one hierarchic level are operative, are equally effective, and function in the same fashion in the structuring of all levels. For instance, until recently there was a tendency to suppose that the same forces—the law of supply and demand, the principle of the free market, and so forth—functioned equally effectively and in the same fashion on all levels of economic activity, from household to international finance. This view, shared by Marxists and conservative economists alike, is becoming more and more doubtful. Just as the forces governing the behavior of physical processes seem to be different or to function differently as one moves from the indeterminacy of the microcosmic world of quantum mechanics to the predictability of the macrocosmic world of planetary motion, so too the forces and principles governing behavior in the historical-cultural realm seem to change or function differently as one moves from the behavior of individuals and small groups to that of nations and cultures. Herbert A. Simon points to this disjunction of hierarchic forces when he says that "in hierarchic systems, we can distinguish between the interactions *among* subsystems, on the one hand, and the interactions *within* subsystems—i.e., among the parts of those subsystems—on the other. The interactions at different levels may be, and often will be, of very different orders of magnitude." [15]

In the area of cultural evolution, Robert Adams evidently has a similar sort of process in mind when, according to Julian H. Stewart, he insists upon "a rejection of any orthogenic, teleological, or other hypothetical built-in tendency of a culture to evolve in certain ways and of the possibility that any single principle can explain all stages of evolution. Adams' assumption that new principles—qualitatively new causal factors and processes—account for each stage is very fundamental." [16]

To put the matter positively: hierarchic structures are necessarily

---

[15] "The Architecture of Complexity," p. 473. These matters are discussed further in chapters 10 and 12.

[16] "Toward Understanding Cultural Evolution," p. 729; also see Maurice Mandelbaum, "Societal Facts."

discontinuous and non-uniform. It is only because the forces, laws, or principles that structure processes and organization—whether in the worlds of physical, biological, or social events—are *non-uniform* that hierarchic structures can develop at all. Were such forces uniform and homogeneous, the world would be so too. This discontinuity of hierarchic structures has been clearly recognized in biology. Thus Ernest Nagel observes:

> There is no serious dispute among biologists over the thesis that the parts and processes into which living organisms are analyzable can be classified in terms of their respective loci into hierarchies of different types. . . . Nor is there disagreement over the contention that the parts of an organism belonging to one level of a hierarchy frequently exhibit forms of relatedness and of activity not manifested by organic parts belonging to another level.[17]

(The concept of hierarchic discontinuity may perhaps provide a new way of looking at the determinism versus free-will problem. Without presuming to settle the question, might it not be that the problem stems from a failure to distinguish between the relatively undetermined, non-statistical processes characteristic of the level of individual choice and those forces which, more determined and quasi-statistical, are operative on the higher levels of sociocultural history? If it could be shown that the forces functioning on these different hierarchic levels were fundamentally different—and in what ways—then the higher-level processes leading, for instance, to the simultaneous discovery of the calculus might not *in principle* be in conflict with our belief in Newton's and Leibnitz' freedom of choice. In other words, it may be that the problem of determinism versus free will stems from a confusion of hierarchic levels of analysis.)

If, as I have tried to show, history is hierarchic, then what constitutes the present will depend in part at least upon the problem which the historian has set himself. As William James has written, "The practically cognized present is no knife-edge, but a saddle-back, with a certain breadth of its own on which we sit perched, and from which we look in two directions in time." [18] The breadth of the saddle-back is a function of the hierarchic level with which we are concerned. For the geologist the present may extend for thousands of years in either direction, while for the gossip columnist it is perhaps no more than a few hours.

---

[17] *The Structure of Science*, p. 435.
[18] *Principles of Psychology*, p. 609.

STASIS AND CHANGE

Since understanding requires it and curiosity makes it enticing let us put the question bluntly: in what ways may we expect the arts to change in the coming years? I should like to suggest—and, considering the rapidity and frequency with which styles have followed one another in recent years, the suggestion will probably seem a rash one—that the coming epoch (if, indeed, we are not already in it) will be a period of stylistic stasis, a period characterized not by the linear, cumulative development of a single fundamental style, but by the coexistence of a multiplicity of quite different styles in a fluctuating and dynamic steady-state.

If this suggestion seems bizarre, it is in large part because the history of Western civilization has, for the past five hundred years or more, been characterized by almost continual, cumulative change. Recognition of this fact led in the eighteenth and nineteenth centuries to the tacit assumption that change—often formulated as a kind of cultural Darwinism (Spencer), as a theory of progress (Hegel), or as a pattern of cyclic movement (Vico and Spengler)—was an essential condition of life and, by extension, of history in general and history of style in particular.

As we shall presently have occasion to observe, such categorical and often quasi-teleological formulations no longer seem very convincing. In part this change of attitude is the result of the work of the historians themselves. For their studies of ancient cultures and of non-Western civilizations has made it clear that cumulative, long-range change has by no means been the rule in most cultures. Thus Robert L. Heilbroner points out:

> For most of the world's people, who have known the changelessness of history, such stress upon the difficulty of change would not be necessary. But for ourselves, whose outlook is conditioned by the extraordinary dynamism of our unique historic experience, it is a needed caution. Contrary to the accepted belief, change is not the rule but the exception in life.[19]

And this has been the case in the history of the arts in many cultures. Eric Schroeder, for instance, observes: "In general, Persian art since the eleventh century, has been characterized, as production of both literary and visual form, by extraordinary intricacy and extraordinary adequacy of convention. Theme and composition were used again and again." [20] In China, according to Clay Lancaster, "It was for Hsieh Ho

---

[19] *The Future as History*, p. 195.
[20] "The Wild Deer Mathnawi," p. 119.

during the late fifth century to set down in writing the Six Principles which were to remain the basis of most subsequent Chinese criticism and practice of painting down to the present day." [21] A similar stability appears to have prevailed in the arts in India: "Between the third and the seventh centuries A.D., and particularly during the Gupta imperial age (320 to 570), the culture of India achieved an elegant and complete expression which remained ideally normative for later generations." [22] Likewise, Japanese *gagaku* (court) music of the Heian period (A.D. 794–1185) has, says William P. Malm, "managed to survive to the present day, apparently with little distortion. Such a continuous line of patronage has no parallel in the history of Western instrumental music, though in all fairness we must add that the Western emphasis has been more on evolution than on preservation." [23] And Ackerman tells us that "in ancient Egypt stability predominated to the point that barely perceptible innovations were sufficient to secure the vitality of a style for three millennia." [24]

Change is, of course, a fact of existence.[25] We are born, mature, grow old, and die. In this case the potential inherent in a limiting set of preconditions is realized as an essentially invariable pattern which is finite and sequential, lawlike and conjunct. In such *developmental change* both the rate and the extent of change are generally specified by the preconditions of the process itself. In other cases—for instance, the tendency of the climate to become warmer during a particular geological age or for cultures to become more differentiated in the course of their histories—change takes place within a limiting set of preconditions, but the potential inherent in the established relationships may be realized in a number of different ways and the order of the realization may be variable. Change is successive and gradual, but not necessarily sequential; and its rate and extent are variable, depending more upon external circumstances than upon internal preconditions. Moreover, the process may reach a stable steady-state or may even reverse itself. Such changes, which are probable rather than invariable, will be called *trends* or *trended changes.*[26]

There are, however, changes which involve permanent and fundamen-

---

[21] "Keys to the Understanding of Indian and Chinese Painting," p. 99.

[22] William H. McNeill, *The Rise of the West*, p. 363.

[23] *Japanese Music and Musical Instruments*, p. 30.

[24] "A Theory of Style," p. 228; also see A. L. Kroeber, *Style and Civilizations*, pp. 37–9.

[25] As is permanence, since we can know one only in terms of the other.

[26] For the distinction between laws and trends, see Karl R. Popper, *The Poverty of Historicism*, pp. 115–16.

tal alteration in the natural world, in human culture, or in man's conceptualization of the universe—whether natural or cultural. The advent of truly novel technological means (e.g., the Neolithic discovery of agriculture, or the invention of radio), a basic shift of scientific concept or paradigm (e.g., the Copernican revolution,[27] or a radical biogenetic restructuring) are examples of *mutational change*. Such changes are disjunctive and, at times, capricious. On a higher hierarchic level, *evolution* might be defined as a series of successful and consequential mutational changes.

In the arts, mutational change takes place when some aspect of the material, formal, syntactic, or other preconditions of a style are altered. Examples would be the discovery of linear perspective, the invention of serial techniques, or the creation of a new set of basic aesthetic goals. The fundamental presuppositions of a style will from time to time be referred to as the "premises" of the style. The term should not, however, be understood to imply that a style is in any sense a logical deductive system.

Observe that a mutational change does not necessarily involve the displacement of the earlier by the later. A genetic mutation, for instance, may lead to the development of a new species, but the original species may continue to flourish. Similarly, in mathematics the discovery of Riemannian geometry did not invalidate Euclidean.[28] Nor, as we shall see, does the invention of a new art style necessarily eclipse previously existing ones.

It should be emphasized that a series of developmental or of trended changes, no matter how extensive and prolonged, will not in themselves produce a mutational change. Such a series may lead, however, to a situation in which an organism, a scientific theory, or a set of stylistic norms ceases to be consonant with its environment. For instance, a series of scientific discoveries may produce new information which cannot, despite all attempts at adjustment, be harmonized or reconciled with the paradigm that originally led to the discoveries. Or, a style may accumulate such a wealth of deviations and use them with such abandon that the norms of the style become obscured or even threatened. In both cases, a kind of "cultural dissonance" arises between an existing set of premises or presuppositions and the larger cultural situation, with the result that a mutation is likely to occur and to endure—to be consequen-

---

[27] See Thomas S. Kuhn, *The Structure of Scientific Revolutions*.

[28] Scientific paradigms evidently do, however, generally replace one another. See *ibid*.

tial. Or, in the reverse situation, internal changes may have been minimal, but a significant alteration in the external environment—for example, a marked change in climate or the conquest of one nation by another—makes a mutational change probable, perhaps even necessary, if the species or the culture is to survive.

Some changes—for example, the seasonal changes in a particular landscape, changes of personnel in a government bureau, or those which occur in the various different versions of a folksong—are neither developmental nor mutational. Nor do they necessarily exhibit any discernible trend. Rather they involve the *varied transformation* of an essentially stable set of relationships or the *interpretive* realization of a constant, enduring tradition. Such varied transformation has been characteristic of the arts in a number of different cultures.

Still other changes, such as the oscillating equilibrium among species in a balanced ecological environment or the non-relational, yet persistent, undulation of ocean waves, may best be described as *fluctuating*. (Fluctuating change will be considered in more detail later.) And, last of all, some changes—perhaps the weather from day to day—are without any apparent order or pattern whatsoever.

Change, then, is not *one* thing. There are many different kinds of change—and at least as many different causes as there are kinds. Although an adequate, let alone exhaustive, account of change and its causes is beyond both the scope of this study and the competence of this writer, it seems clear that the rate and extent of change, as well as the kind of change, depend upon the interaction of three main variables: (*a*) the inherent characteristics of the process or relationship being considered; (*b*) the physical, biological, and cultural environment in which the events take place; and (*c*) the hierarchic level of the changes being observed. This being so, attempts to employ a single model—whether evolutionary, developmental, cyclic, or the like—to account for changes in different types of phenomena or on different hierarchic levels of the "same" phenomenon are, at the very least, suspect.

These comments are pertinent to the problem of style change in the several arts. If any works at all are being produced, some sort of change will be present. But the rate and extent of change, as well as the kind of change, will depend upon the art and the style being considered, the sociocultural environment, and the hierarchic level on which the events take place. In Western culture, where innovation and novelty have tended to be positive values, change has been rapid and extensive, taking the forms of dynamic trends or of marked mutation. And, as long as neither determinism nor teleology is thought to be implied, the series of such changes may in some sense be regarded as evolutionary. In other cultures—those of ancient Egypt, India, the Hopi Indians, and so forth—stability has been highly valued, and change has taken the form of a varied transformation within traditionally established cultural norms.

The distinctions among different kinds of change are important because they call attention to the fact that there may be significant differences between the works of different artists in the same or successive generations—or, even within the work of a single artist (Picasso is perhaps a case in point)—without there being a linear trend, much less a development or an evolution. This is so not only in cultures where varied transformational change has been the rule. The variety resulting from a rivalry among several more or less independent styles, movements, and experiments may produce a great deal of activity, as one style and then another becomes the focus of artistic-cultural attention, but the cumulative and linear character necessary for a development, trend, or mutational series may be lacking.

This means that change and variety are not incompatible with stasis. For stasis, as I intend the term, is not an absence of novelty and change—a total quiescence—but rather the absence of ordered sequential change. Like molecules rushing about haphazardly in a Brownian movement, a culture bustling with activity and change may nevertheless be static. Indeed, insofar as an active, conscious search for new techniques, new forms and materials, and new modes of sensibility (such as have marked our time) precludes the gradual accumulation of changes capable of producing a trend or a series of connected mutations, it tends to create a steady-state, though perhaps one that is both vigorous and variegated. In short—and this is what I hope to show—a multiplicity of styles in each of the arts, coexisting in a balanced, yet competitive, cultural environment is producing a fluctuating stasis in contemporary culture.

The kind of style change observed depends, as noted earlier, not only upon the structural-syntactic premises of the style itself and upon its cultural environment but also upon the hierarchic level being considered. Thus in contemplating the possibility of stasis, the span of time involved is important. A single generation is clearly inadequate. For aside from the fact that the work of a single artist generally, but not invariably, exhibits some sort of trend (perhaps in the direction of increased control of materials and refinement of means), the kind of change usually intended by the term "stylistic development" (with

102

which "stasis" would be contrasted) necessarily transcends the individual and the generation.

Nor are we considering what have customarily been designated as "style periods"—Renaissance or Baroque, for example. For if there is a stasis in which a number of relatively discrete and independent styles coexist without cumulative trends or developments, there would be no periods having definable stages, such as a beginning, middle, and end. There would instead be a succession of changes in which first one and then another of the existing styles in one or another of the arts became the focus of aesthetic interest and creative activity.

In short, in contemplating the possibility of stasis, one is considering the most encompassing hierarchic level within Western culture, and perhaps even within cosmopolitan world culture. Although in the course of events a stasis, like any other kind of activity, will end, giving way to some other manner of change, it is impossible to guess its duration precisely because fluctuation lacks the definition of pattern upon which such a prediction might be based. A stasis might last for three or four generations (it has, I think, already lasted for two), or for as many as ten or more.

In chapters 8 and 9, I hope to indicate why it seems probable that the arts today can best be characterized as being in a fluctuating steady-state. But before suggesting why this seems probable, I must show that it is even possible. For it is often explicitly argued or tacitly assumed that the "forces of history" dictate that styles develop or evolve, or that, if they do not do so, they necessarily decline, become decadent, or die. To show that stasis is possible and that it does not necessarily entail decadence and decline, the general nature of stylistic change must be explored. And, in the course of such exploration, we will come across evidence that makes the probability of stasis seem less unlikely.

CHAPTER

7

Varieties of Style Change

Many theories of style change have been proposed. Often these contain suggestive and illuminating ideas. But few will stand careful scrutiny. Some shortcomings may be charged to the ethno- and chronocentric tendency to derive laws and principles of cultural-stylistic change from relatively recent events in Western civilization. Western patterns of style change, however, constitute only a small part of the sample available; and, as mentioned earlier, they are perhaps the exception rather than the rule. Certainly any viable theory of the nature and causes of such change will have to consider evidence from other cultures—cultures in which change has taken other forms and other directions.

Even more serious has been the failure of most theories and descriptions of style change to appreciate and reckon with the highly complex nature of styles, of cultures, and of their interaction. In the face of such complexity it would be imprudent and presumptuous even to sketch something pretending to be a theory. I hope only to show that the unconscious assumptions and explicitly stated axioms which have been thought to preclude the possibility of stasis are untenable and that our current cultural posture is, in fact, characterized by features which make stasis seem probable.

CHANGE AND STYLISTIC VITALITY

Though "all the major theories of style have," in James Ackerman's words, "been determinist in the sense that they define a preordained pattern of 'evolution,' " [1] evidence from the history of our own as well as other cultures makes it very doubtful that there are inexorable or invariable laws of style change. Statements to the effect that a style "tends first to develop and progress, later to degenerate and die. An art or a philosophy moves on; it cannot continue to spin on a pivot" [2] are suspect not only because words like "progress" contain hints of a hidden and unwarranted teleology (the implication that styles have a destiny toward which they move), but also because they fail to specify what time span (hierarchic level) is being considered. Kroeber himself points out elsewhere [3] that Egyptian art did *not* evolve, but remained "substantially identical" for two thousand years. If this is not "to spin on a pivot," what is? How long is "continue"?

The thesis that if a style does not develop and change, it necessarily decays and dies, is also of interest because it requires that we examine the concept—frequently bandied about, but seldom adequately explained—of stylistic "vitality." Surprisingly, Ackerman himself writes that "art has never been static; when it is not vital, it degenerates." [4] The trouble with such absolute statements is that the crucial terms—such as "static," "vital," and "degeneration"—are left undefined.

What does "static" mean? If it means literally without *any change whatsoever*, then stasis would entail not merely degeneration but the cessation of *all* artistic activity. For as long as any works of art are being produced, there are bound to be differences among them. Some sort of change will, of necessity, be present. Even in the most tradition-bound styles there are changes, however modest, when any works of art are created. And even "degeneration" is a kind of change. The term "static" must, therefore, refer to a particular sort of change—one that does not involve the cumulative innovation characteristic of trended, developmental, or evolutionary change. But what evidence is there that cumulative innovation is a prerequisite for stylistic vitality, or, conversely, that its absence necessarily leads to degeneration? [5]

Indeed, what are the characteristics of "vitality" and "degenera-

---

[1] "A Theory of Style," p. 230.

[2] A. L. Kroeber, *An Anthropologist Looks at History*, p. 41.

[3] *Style and Civilizations*, p. 38.

[4] "A Theory of Style," p. 228.

[5] It is possible that Western historians and ethnologists, assuming on the basis of their own cultural experience that style development is a *law*, search for and consequently "discover" similar developments in other cultures, even though none actually took place, where change took the form of a varied transformation or even of a fluctuating stasis.

tion"? Do the terms refer to definable, objective stylistic traits, or are they essentially culturally loaded, valuative terms? The latter is, I suspect, often the case, and when it is, the position is ethnocentric and the line of reasoning circular. The argument assumes what it purports to prove. That is, based upon relatively recent Western ideology which disparages repetition [6] and places a premium upon innovation (together with personal expression which tends to foster novelty),[7] this position equates cumulative, linear change with vitality and, not surprisingly, concludes that whatever does not change in this way necessarily is or becomes decadent.[8]

How might degeneration and vitality be objectively defined? Certainly a style would be considered moribund if no composer, artist, or writer used it or if no audience could understand it or find works employing it significant and satisfying. Consider, however, the positive version of this definition: If works of art are being created in a style and if experienced audiences find them significant and satisfying, then the style is vital.[9]

---

[6] See the quotation from Whorf, p. 61.

[7] See chap. 8.

[8] This account of style change was probably affected by the analogical model chosen. Since the nineteenth century, many cultural historians and anthropologists have used the biological processes or the behavioral patterns of the individual organism as a model for culture. The model provides the terms and categories for describing and characterizing cultures which are, accordingly, said to be "born," to "mature" or "die," to be "healthy" and "vital," to be "masculine," "Apollonian," and so forth. The model, together with the conceptual categories it establishes, predisposes the scholar to select and organize data in particular ways and, in so doing, influences the kinds of change (or other processes) he looks for and, consequently, the kinds he finds.

A model may, of course, be heuristically and methodologically useful. The danger arises when the metaphor is taken to be the real thing—when it is understood so literally that new insights and formulations become difficult. Because man is obviously and intimately involved in culture, the danger is specially acute in this case. Not only is there a strong tendency toward reification, but there is also a correlative temptation to ignore the hierarchic discontinuity between the level of the individual organism and the various levels of cultural activity.

[9] It follows from this that the post-Romantic tonal style of composers such as Britten, which has not been undergoing marked change, is potentially as vital as the experimental styles of composers like Cage, Berio, and Stockhausen. Both groups of styles have produced a considerable literature and each has a reasonably large body of appreciative listeners. If it be urged that, say, Berio is a more "original," "creative" composer than Britten, then (aside from demanding definitions of creative and original) the answer is that the question is not one of stylistic vitality but of the ability and talent of the particular composer. Of course,

Varieties of Style Change

But if this definition is allowed, non-cumulative change (in the form either of varied transformation or of a fluctuating stasis) is not necessarily incompatible with stylistic vigor. For artistic activity and audience appreciation do not require—logically or psychologically [10]—that innovation take place or that successive changes be cumulative, let alone "progressive." Quite the contrary. As we have seen, evidence from other cultures indicates that works of art can proliferate and audiences can appreciate them in the absence of cumulative, long-range change. Few historians or art connoisseurs would, I imagine, wish to contend that Chinese landscape painting, which remained relatively stable in style for generations, was less "vital" than Western figure painting, which, since the Middle Ages, has undergone almost continual style change.

It might be argued that a style is vital when it is developing new techniques, forms, and materials. From this point of view, one might contend that the style of recent experimental music (for instance, that of Boulez) is more vital than the style of "neo-tonal" music (for instance, that of Britten). But the same line of reasoning would lead to the conclusion that the style of the eighteenth-century preclassists (Sammartini, Monn, and others), which was developing new syntactic and formal relationships, was vital, while the more stable style of late Baroque music (Bach, Handel, and others) was not. Indeed, Burney held essentially this view. But from our vantage point, it seems preposterous to contend that the style of the *Saint Matthew Passion* and *Messiah* was moribund—though it was certainly not undergoing substantial changes in syntax, form, or aesthetic outlook.[11]

Finally, it has at times been suggested that a style is vital when artists can still discover unrealized conceptual-expressive potential in it. Or, conversely, that the potential of a style can be so thoroughly exploited that the style becomes exhausted or used up. Two comments seem relevant. First, from this point of view, continued, cumulative change

---

one might contend that the vitality of a style is indicated by its ability to attract inventive composers. But then no style would *necessarily* ever become moribund or decadent.

[10] This statement clearly involves a modification of the views expressed in chapter 3. I now suggest that, though change is psychologically necessary, it may take any one of a number of different forms; and that the extent and rate of change needed to ensure stylistic "vitality" depends upon the character of the culture. The psychological need for novelty may well be fundamental, but it can be satisfied in many different ways (see pp. 127–28).

[11] It is beside the point to argue that Bach's own style was "developing" and hence vital. This statement is true of any artist who learns his craft at all; it is true of Britten as well as of Boulez.

would probably produce such exhaustion. Where varied transformation or non-cumulative fluctuation creates a dynamic steady-state, the vitality of a style should be prolonged. Second, the notion of "exhausting" a style is largely a culture-bound concept, stemming from beliefs in the importance of originality and in the value of individual expression—beliefs important in Western ideology but by no means so in all cultures or in all epochs.

DIRECT CAUSATION THEORIES

The relationship between art and culture is one of reciprocity. Artists shape and, at the same time, are shaped by culture. Like all other human activities and products, the arts are both manifestations of culture and a basis for its delineation. Consequently, no one will doubt that there is a continual and intimate interaction between styles of art and the cultures of which they form a part. But what is continual is not necessarily simple; and what is intimate is not necessarily direct.

Yet probably the most prevalent theory of style change is that which explicitly asserts or tacitly assumes that changes in style are a direct and necessary result—are caused by—specific changes in other areas and facets of culture. Social, political, or economic changes; scientific and technological discoveries; changes in physical environment; shifts in population; and so forth—all are used, either singly or in combination, to "explain" or account for changes in style.

More often than not, it is assumed that one such factor is the *prime* cause of change. Thus the metaphysics of dialectical materialism is, according to Bertrand Russell, "translated, where human affairs are concerned, into the doctrine that the prime cause of all social phenomena is the method of production and exchange prevailing at any given period." [12] These phenomena, in turn, create changes in intellectual concepts and styles of art. Other theories attribute changes in style directly to social changes, changes in cultural ethos, and the like. But whatever the cause or complex of causes chosen, such a "billiard-ball" theory of style change is too simplistic and naïve. As Curt Sachs has observed, "Very little in music can be fully traced to social and technical changes." [13]

---

[12] "Dialectical Materialism," p. 286.

[13] *The Wellsprings of Music*, p. 133; also see Alfred Einstein: ". . . this fluctuation [of musical styles] does not by any means always correspond to the ebb and flow of the cultural, political, and general currents of the age" (*Essays on Music*, p. 7).

Historical facts do not support a theory of "direct" causation. Extra-stylistic "forces" do not in themselves appear to be either necessary or sufficient causes for style change. As I shall try to show a bit later, a considerable amount of evidence indicates that, once its material, syntactical, and ideological premises have been established, a style, if it is going to change at all, tends to change in its own way and may conceivably do so even at a time when other aspects of the culture are quite stable. More important at this point is the fact that the course of stylistic change is not invariably and directly affected by changes—even major ones—in other facets in the cultural environment. To cite but two examples: The style of Viennese classical music (*ca.* 1750–1827) was not essentially influenced by either the French Revolution or the Napoleonic Wars, both of which must surely be counted as major social, economic, and political events in the history of western Europe. And "from 2600 to 600 B.C. the totality of life and culture altered at hundreds of points, while Egyptian art stood almost still." [14]

Or, to take another tack, if changes in the arts are a direct and immediate reflection of cultural changes, how are we to explain the tendency of an "art language" (in music or literature) to develop independent of changes in the casual or vernacular language. They should parallel one another or develop together. But what seems to happen is that changes in the vernacular language *do* follow cultural changes very closely—indeed, we probably cannot know about cultural changes apart from changes in the vernacular. But this is not necessarily true of "art language," which tends at times to follow its own course of development, rejuvenating itself periodically at the fountain of ordinary speech. [15] This is what seems to have happened in poetry at the beginning of the Romantic period and to music somewhat earlier—at the beginning of the classical period. And it has happened in our own time in literature. The constant interaction between "high" and "popular" culture would not be possible if changes in the former were a direct reflection of changes in culture generally.

The proponents of direct causation theories have at times suggested that it is unrealistic to expect a cause to produce an immediate style change; perhaps the effect follows at a temporal distance. But if this argument is allowed, it is difficult to see how, out of the myriad changes and modifications constantly taking place in both style and culture, one could isolate any specific characteristic (or group of characteristics) as

---

[14] Kroeber, *Style and Civilizations*, p. 38.
[15] See T. S. Eliot, *Selected Prose*, p. 63.

being a sufficient cause of style change—let alone *the* sufficient cause. It is one thing to show a correspondence—to match traits or point to seemingly correlative changes—and quite another to demonstrate the existence of a necessary connection. Thus Meyer Schapiro says that "common traits in the art of a culture or nation can be matched with some features of social life, ideas, customs, general dispositions. But such correlations have been of single elements or aspects of a style with single traits of a people; it is rarely a question of wholes." [16] Cultures are as a rule so rich, various, and changeable that, if one admits the possibility of action at a distance, then almost any hypothesis can be made to seem plausible through the discovery of correspondences.

It has been possible for proponents of such theories to gloss over and disregard negative evidence such as this because they have not always been careful to distinguish between change of style and change of subject matter. It is obvious that those arts which are explicitly representational—literature, painting, and sculpture—frequently reflect (direct or indirectly) the outstanding events of a culture in their choice of subject matter. What Jacques Louis David paints is obviously influenced by the French Revolution, republican ideals, the rise of Napoleon, and so forth. Similarly, the poetry of Shelley reflects the ideals of liberty and freedom prevalent at the beginning of the nineteenth century. But the problem of style change is not primarily one of what is represented,[17] but one of how the representation is realized. Delacroix also represented events inspired by the French Revolution, but he did so in a style very different from that of David. Byron too reflects prevalent ideals of liberty, but in a style different from that of Shelley. The same subject matter may be presented in very different ways: compare, for instance, an "Assumption of the Virgin" by Fra Angelico with one by Titian or a "carpe diem" sonnet by Shakespeare with one by e. e. cummings. The history of style asks questions about the use of language—the choice of words, syntax, forms; about the use of paint—the kind of colors and color relationships the artist uses, the way he organizes objects on a canvas, the sort of brush stroke he uses, and so on; and about the way in which tones are combined, melodies are built, and forms are articulated.

Furthermore, most theories of "direct causation," and in fact most

---

[16] "Style," p. 301.

[17] Of course, this may be relevant for other purposes—e.g., where the work of art is being considered as a social-historical document.

theories of style development, make a number of important assumptions—often unstated—which are at the very least questionable.

The first of these is that styles are successive. The reason for this assumption seems to be that if economic, political, and social events, which on any particular hierarchic level are necessarily successive, are assumed to be direct causes, then their effects (on style) must also be successive. But, as we have already noted, this is simply not the case. Ackerman summarizes the situation clearly: "Since the extinction of one style is neither the prerequisite for nor, necessarily, the result of the initiation of another, old and new styles may exist side by side and mutually influence one another; and several new ones may coexist even in the same locale: in Paris of the early twentieth century: Cubism, the Fauves, Futurism, etc." [18]

Cultures, particularly complex ones, are not monolithic. They are made up of a number of interacting and interdependent subcultures each of which may have its own style of music, art, and literature. Our culture, for instance, supports jazz, tin-pan alley music, classical symphonic music, and electronic music. In literature it supports Beckett, *Peyton Place*, and Pogo.[19] Nor, us a rule, are cultures internally consistent. Not only may different subcultures be characterized by diverse modes of behavior and conflicting convictions, but inconsistencies may exist within a single subculture. This is particularly evident in the area which I shall call cultural ideology (see below pp. 128–30). Our culture, for instance, has in the past maintained the following pairs of beliefs at one and the same time: there are necessary (determinist) laws of historical development, but men have free will; [20] great works of art are the unique expression of the soul of the individual artist, yet such works are universal; and "nothing is explicable except in terms of its history

---

[18] "A Theory of Style," p. 236.

[19] Though each subculture and its audience may be distinguished from others in terms of behavior patterns, beliefs, linguistic habits, aesthetic attitudes, and so on, it is important to remember that most people belong to a number of different subcultures.

[20] "Alfred North Whitehead once underscored the dilemma by saying that the radical inconsistency in modern thought is our firm belief in man as a self-determining organism and our equally firm belief in the validity of deterministic laws" (Wylie Sypher, *Loss of the Self* . . . , p. 28). This is paralleled, according to Sypher, by an equally "disastrous clash between the Ideals of individual liberty and social well-being" (*ibid.*, p. 17). As noted earlier, it is possible that some of these clashes are the result of a confusion among separable hierarchic levels.

and . . . the value of anything is independent of its history."[21] It is difficult to see how a single "cause" or set of causes could be responsible for this sort of diverse multiplicity. More specifically, the direct causation theory fails to account for the fact that within one culture and at one time not only may styles overlap and exist side by side but also the styles of different subcultures may exhibit different patterns of change.

Second, though it is difficult to doubt that there is an intimate interaction between the arts and all other aspects of culture, it cannot be assumed that the many variables—economic, social, technological, ideological, and so forth—are equally influential and interact in the same way in all cultures or in all epochs of a particular culture. Nor can it be assumed that the roles played by the several variables involved in style change remain constant from one cultural hierarchic level to another. What the variables are, their relative effectiveness, and the manner and extent of their interaction (whether producing cumulative development, varied transformation, fluctuating stasis, or some other sort of change) is precisely what must be studied and analyzed for each particular culture and style.

But whatever the course and character of stylistic change, a priori value judgments between different kinds of style change are irrelevant and unilluminating. A stable style which over many years produces a rich harvest of works within a continuing tradition—as in Java or south India—is not less vital and valuable than a style which develops cumulatively and changes radically.

Finally, direct causation theories are questionable because fundamental differences among the several arts may create important differences in the way in which each changes. Though these are evidently matters of emphasis, they are nonetheless noteworthy.

Music is by nature—because of its materials—expressly and explicitly both syntactical and formal. It does not, except through the addition of a text or a written program, denote. References to the extra-musical world of objects, qualities, and actions which are discovered in a piece of music are the result of inferences (and they may be completely legitimate ones) made by listeners.[22] As a result, communication—intelligibility or affective experience—depends heavily upon the ability of the audience to perceive and comprehend the syntactical and formal implications which melodic-rhythmic patterns, harmonic progressions, and the like have for one another, *and* on all

[21] Morris R. Cohen, *Reason and Nature*, p. 269.
[22] See Donald N. Ferguson, *Music as Metaphor*, p. 55.

112

hierarchic levels. Such ability is acquired through experience in performing [23] and listening to music in the style(s) of the culture. This being the case, composers, almost by necessity, build upon the musical vocabulary, grammar, and syntax developed by their predecessors. It should be noted that the syntactical processes of a style depend more upon acquired habit responses—modes of perception and cognition—than do the formal means employed. For this reason, composers can more easily be influenced by remote formal models than remote syntactical relationships. To put the matter in another way: three-part structures (e.g., A–B–A) are possible in a wide variety of styles, but the harmonic implications of tonal music cannot easily be introduced into, say, atonal or serial music.

The visual arts, on the other hand, have (at least until recently) been both formal and representational. Because they are non-temporal and hence literally static,[24] syntax or kinetic process in the plastic arts must be inferred by the observer. Thus, though statements about rhythm, direction of motion, and implication in the visual arts may be suggestive, useful metaphors based upon valid inferences, they refer to no syntactical processes actually taking place in the art work. Because formal relationships (such as symmetry, radiality, and arborescence) and subjects to be represented are, unlike grammatical-syntactical processes, neither necessarily nor essentially man-made and man-modified, the plastic arts are in principle less tradition-bound than music and literature.[25] But though the plastic artist can discover afresh in nature or can borrow from remote cultures and epochs more easily than the composer, it is important to realize that the specific use he makes of such forms or subjects will depend significantly upon his cultural milieu.

Literature is explicitly both referential and syntactical. Like music it tends to emphasize intra-stylistic syntactical continuity. Because reference is less dependent upon syntax than is formal organization (the case in music), literature can, like the plastic arts, range widely in cultural time and space in its search for subject matter. Particularly when it is narrative or depicts sequential thought processes, literature tends to lack marked formal structure: patent repetition, obvious symmetry, clear

---

[23] Stylistic learning is considered in more detail in Chap. 11.

[24] Mobiles and kinetic art are not exceptions, since their motion is neither syntactic nor implicative.

[25] "In principle," but not usually in practice—as iconography shows. See E. H. Gombrich, *Art and Illusion*.

periodicity, and the like. When highly structural formal relationships are present in literature, they are often derived from or closely associated with musical processes—for instance, poetic forms such as the villanelle, ballad, or sonnet. Repetitive or periodic structures in recent prose literature are often avowedly derived from music.

These differences make it clear that though the "arts" (like Wittgenstein's "games") have a family resemblance, there are important differences between them which affect not only our perception and understanding of them but also the ways in which they tend to develop. This being true, there is no compelling reason for assuming that the several arts necessarily develop at the same rate or in the same way (or, that their developments reflect that of the culture generally) ; [26] their patterns of change may be congruent at some times and not at others. Certainly it seems doubtful that they always develop in a parallel fashion. Perhaps they are comparable only at times of major cultural-ideological change—for instance, at the beginning of the Renaissance—and then, so to speak, go their own separate ways. In any case, this is precisely what must be not assumed but proved.

These observations are not intended to suggest that there is no connection between cultural change and stylistic change. Rather the merit of the "direct causation" hypothesis has been considered—and its lack of finesse perhaps unfairly exaggerated—in order to indicate something of the diversity and complexity of cultures, styles, and their modes of interaction; to emphasize, consequently, that no simple, unconditional explanation of style change is likely to be tenable; and to show that the evidence thus far examined does not preclude the possibility of a stylistic stasis.

THE INTERNAL-DYNAMIC HYPOTHESIS

Let us now consider the thesis that, once its fundamental material, formal, and syntactic premises have been established, a style tends to change or develop in its own way, according to its own internal and inherent dynamic process. Though this hypothesis has considerable

---

[26] Thus, in attempting to relate the arts to one another and to their cultural context, it seems prudent to base comparisons upon those aspects of each art which are explictly specified, rather than upon those which are subject to the uncertainties of inference. That is, music and visual arts should be compared in terms of formal structure which is explicitly specified in both; music and literature should be compared in terms of syntactic processes; and literature and the visual arts in terms of subject matter.

merit—particularly because it directs attention to stylistic changes rather than similarities of subject matter—most statements of it, including my own,[27] have been too absolute and unconditional. For instance, Kroeber is curiously ethnocentric when he writes:

> Unless goals can now be set further ahead or widened, and the style be reconstituted on a new basis, there is nothing left for its practitioners but maintenance of the status reached; which is in its nature —by implied definition, as it were—incompatible with the play of creative activity. In other words, styles are produced by forces that are inherently dynamic.[28]

As we have already observed, however, some styles have remained virtually static over long periods of time; and whether styles *must* deteriorate (indeed, whether the term can be objectively defined) is open to serious question.

The internal-dynamic hypothesis, then, must be qualified to read something like this: Once its fundamental premises have been established, a style tends to change—*if it is to do so at all*—in its own way, according to its own inherent dynamic process. Two further reservations must be made.

1. It is unlikely that the internal-dynamic hypothesis is an absolute, universal principle of style change. Rather it is probably one which depends for its operation upon the presence of other complementary cultural conditions. Consequently it will shape the process of stylistic change in some cultures and cultural circumstances but not in others. Because of the ideological and technological complexion of Western culture since the Renaissance, the internal dynamic hypothesis does appear useful in the analysis and understanding of the process of style change in the West. Recent changes in Western culture (described in chapters 8 and 9), however, make it seem doubtful that this hypothesis will continue to provide fruitful explanations for style change.

2. The hypothesis does not stipulate or imply that sociocultural forces—extra-stylistic events and conditions—play no part in specifying the ways in which the potential of a style, its inherent developmental tendencies, will be realized. It is clear, for example, that nineteenth-century nationalism had an important influence upon the music of the Russian Five. But these composers employed folk tunes and reacted against the "formalism" of German symphonic music in a manner which,

---

[27] See pp. 49–51.
[28] *Style and Civilizations,* p. 37.

though unique and special, was nonetheless in accord with the developing potential of the style. Other composers of the period responded to nationalism in other ways, developing their own characteristic idioms and means.

Because our understanding of its intra-stylistic change is not as a rule clouded by distracting changes in subject matter (as is often true with literature and the visual arts) and because, being a primarily syntactic art, its development relies heavily upon continuity of tradition, music furnishes the clearest exemplar of this sort of inherent, internal change.

A musical style is a finite array of interdependent melodic, rhythmic, harmonic, timbral, textural, and formal relationships and processes. When these are internalized as learned habits, listeners (including performers and composers) are able to perceive and understand a composition in the style as an intricate network of implicative relationships, or to experience the work as a complex of felt probabilities. Because styles do not come into existence fully articulated and defined but emerge gradually, it is usually impossible to describe precisely how and when new styles come into being. For reasons that are only generally apparent, a mutational change takes place. But, though it is not possible to specify why, or even exactly when, a new style comes into being, the pattern of trended, internal style change which it subsequently follows is clear—at least in broad outline.

A style is *learned*, even by the composers who "invent" it. As with the early learning of a language, a new style tends to involve a considerable amount of redundancy.[29] Such redundancy not only results from the repetition of works and of patterns and processes within works but is an important characteristic of the structures themselves; that is, the patterns and processes employed in the early stages of a style tend to possess a clear, even obvious, order, regularity, and coherence so that they reinforce, sustain, and affirm one another. (Such reinforcement is also hierarchic, though complex and extended compositions are not common during the early stages of style development.) Moreover, the rate of change within such style-establishing compositions tends to be relatively slow.

As the musical community (composers, performers, and listeners) becomes familiar with the typical processes, procedures, and schemata of a style, syntax and structure tend to become more involved and complex. Less probable progressions are used with greater frequency,

---

[29] The terms "redundancy" and "information" as used in this book are defined below, pp. 277–79.

schemata become more intricate and less obvious, and hierarchic structures become more extended. Because the musical community has internalized its "norms," compositions in the style can be, and usually are, less literally redundant. To put the matter in another way: the amount of musical "information" that the community can comprehend and the speed with which it can do so is a function *both* of the extent of *internalized (cultural) redundancy,* that is, the depth and strength of stylistic learning; *and* of the amount of *compositional (structural) redundancy* presented by a particular work, that is, its objective order and regularity.

The lower internalized redundancy is, the higher compositional redundancy must be, if the work is to be intelligently understood and sensitively experienced. Conversely, the higher the rate of internalized redundancy, the lower may be the rate of compositional redundancy and, correlatively, the higher the rate of compositional information. Assuming that the amount of musical information demanded by the community tends toward the maximum compatible with sensitive understanding,[30] then it should be the case that, as internalized redundancy increases with stylistic learning, compositional redundancy should decrease. Or, looked at from the standpoint of information, the amount of musical information actually comprehended tends to remain constant (toward the maximum possible), but, as internalized redundancy rises, the amount of compositional information will also tend to increase.

Some such sort of change in the direction of reduced redundancy and of increased information seems to have taken place in the history of particular musical styles in the West. For instance, the music of the Florentine Camerata (*ca.* 1600), and of the early Baroque in general, is compositionally considerably more redundant than the music which preceded it—the music of Lassus, Byrd, and Gesualdo. As the norms of the new style became part of the audience's habit responses—as the level of cultural redundancy rose—the level of compositional redundancy declined. On the whole, Bach's music is much less redundant than Cesti's or Scheidt's. Similarly, the music of the early classicists—for instance, that of Monn or Sammartini—presents the listener with much more compositional redundancy (less information) than does the music of the late Baroque. And, once again, as the stylistic behavior of the "dramatic" style became familiar, redundancy was progressively

---

[30] For experimental evidence supporting this hypothesis, see Colin Cherry's discussion (*On Human Communication,* pp. 281–82) of experiments by Miller, Bruner, and Postman.

reduced: first in the works of Haydn, Mozart, and Beethoven; then in the music of the Romantic composers; until, in the early compositions of Schönberg and in the music of Strauss, Hindemith, Bartók, and Stravinsky, the compositional redundancy rate is really quite low.[31]

It is because particular styles have generally moved in the direction of reduced redundancy that their histories tend to be asymmetrical with respect to time, that stylistic history cannot, so to speak, be played "backwards." [32] For instance, if we were told that two groups of works of the same type belonged to a single style period, we could in most cases tell which came earlier. But, it seems quite doubtful whether one could, without prior knowledge of the over-all history of Western musical styles, do this for works from different style periods. In other words, though one could, I think, on these grounds alone decide that Frescobaldi preceded Bach, one could not—in the absence of other information—guess that Machaut preceded Frescobaldi.[33]

Perhaps it is in terms of the relationship between internalized and compositional redundancy that the phases of intra-stylistic change are to be distinguished. Early stages of a style tend to be characterized by an excessive amount of compositional redundancy—so much so that they often appear to later generations to be somewhat naïve and even tedious. In the history of Western art music since the Renaissance, this "preclassical" phase has as a rule been quite brief. In the mature or "classic" phase of style change, an equilibrium between internalized and compositional redundancy is typical. The audience must be experienced, but prodigious feats of integrative memory are not required. Theoretically, there is no reason why this equilibrium could not continue indefinitely; and one of our interests will be to see why this has not been so in the West. The later stages of a style—often referred to as "mannerism"—tend to be marked by an active and often explicit pursuit of the less common and probable facets of syntax and structure. Schemata are elliptically suggested rather than explicitly presented, or are disguised in luxuriant decoration. Compositional redundancy is drastically re-

---

[31] That such a reduction in redundancy has in fact taken place in Western art music since the eighteenth century is indicated by the studies of Robert Allen Baker ("A Statistical Analysis . . .") and Lejaren A. Hiller ("Research in Music with Electronics").

[32] One cannot help noting a parallelism between the tendency of styles to become less redundant (more "shuffled") and the operation of the law of entropy.

[33] Obviously there are exceptions: the "sports" (Satie) and the geniuses (Beethoven).

duced. Sensitive, accurate appreciation demands considerable experience and training.

These matters might be diagrammed as follows:

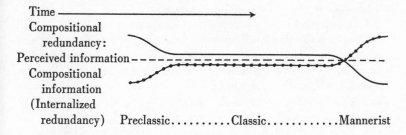

Time ⟶

Compositional
redundancy:

Perceived information

Compositional
information
(Internalized
redundancy)   Preclassic..........Classic...........Mannerist

A number of further reservations and observations must be made in connection with this account of inherently dynamic style change.[34]

1. The pattern of change described is neither necessary nor invariable. Other kinds of intra-stylistic change—for instance, interpretive transformational change—are possible. Indeed, it may well be that, as noted earlier, the internal dynamic hypothesis is relevant only to the history of music, and perhaps the other arts, in the West; and perhaps only from the Middle Ages until the early part of the twentieth century. Nor is there any "law" which dictates that the process must in every case run its full course from an archaic preclassicism through mannerism.

2. The account stipulates nothing about changes from one set of stylistic "premises" to another. How and why style mutations take place is an even more complex, subtle, and perplexing matter. The characteristics and conditions of existing styles, internal and external influences upon the ideology and sociopolitical structure of the culture, the decisions and personalities of individual composers, and probably just plain chance—all these play a part in such fundamental, but initially often veiled, mutational changes. Adequate explanations of mutational change are difficult, then, not only because the beginnings of styles are often hard to identify, but also because an *over*abundance of potential or actual causes makes it nearly impossible to isolate and assess the

---

[34] In general, this account is admittedly highly speculative. Indeed, it may well be downright mistaken. Perhaps, as Curt Sachs suggests (*The Wellsprings of Music*, pp. 214–15), there are no common patterns of style change. Such a conclusion would not, however, invalidate the basic point being made in this chapter: that a fluctuating style stasis is possible, and that it would not necessarily lead to decadence.

influence and action of any particular cause. And the problem is further complicated by the fact that the relative importance of the various causes of change may be different for different cultures and different hierarchic levels of change within each culture; and they may also vary from epoch to epoch within a single culture.

3. A reduction in redundancy may take the form of deleting, as well as of adding, information. That is, by telescoping or leaving out parts of schemata and processes which have become normative and predictable, the relative level of compositional information may be raised. For this reason, the "simplification" often found to be characteristic of the late work of an artist—one thinks of Beethoven, Verdi, or Matisse—may not be incompatible with the tendency toward increased information.

4. Because intra-stylistic change does not involve a modification of the premises of a style, but rather a realization of the possibilities inherent in such premises, intra-stylistic changes are not necessarily linear and cumulative. Consequently, some works coming late in the chronology of a style may be actually less complex (more redundant) than those which preceded them.

More specifically, because the change in the direction of increased information is a tendency—a statistical trend rather than an invariable law—exceptions may occur both among works of a single composer and within the series of "styles" created by the oeuvre of all the composers in a particular style period. Such exceptions are the result of the action and interaction of a number of different factors, such as:

a) The compositional type being employed. Bach's inventions are, as a rule, more redundant than his fugues.

b) The presence of other kinds of information. The level of purely musical information is generally lower when music is combined with verbal or visual information (see chap. 11).

c) The occasion or purpose for which a particular work was written may affect the level of information. Schumann's *Album for the Young* is a case in point.

d) The presence of special aesthetic or cultural-historical circumstances. Partly because their strongly felt nationalism found expression in the extensive use of folk idioms, which tend to be simple and regular, the music of the Russian Five (Borodin, Moussorgsky, *et al.*) is, on the whole, much more redundant than that of Wagner, though Wagner's music precedes theirs.

e) A reaction against a particular stylistic tendency and the search for a new direction within the basic norms of the style. The music of

Milhaud or the later works of Hindemith are perhaps examples of this sort of tendency.

f) The disposition and taste, however formed, of the individual composer. This is all but impossible to isolate and document, but it almost invariably impinges upon points *d* and *e*, above, as well as upon individual psychology, teachers, and the like.

5. Since the hypothesis that styles tend to change in the direction of increased compositional information is a "statistical" one, it cannot in the absence of other documentation (type of work, occasion for composition, etc.) be used even in a broad and general way to date works within the history of a style. Nor, conversely, can the hypothesis be confirmed or disconfirmed by reference to individual examples from the literature of a style period.

6. Were this hypothesis adopted, it would probably be necessary to revise some of the periodizations traditionally employed in music history. Such revision would not necessarily be bad. Our present criteria for establishing the limits of style periods are by no means unambiguous. Both musical and extra-musical criteria are usually employed and are frequently confused with one another. If a viable measure of stylistic information-redundancy rates could be devised—one which took account of innate modes of perceptual structuring, as well as purely statistical frequencies (see chap. 1)—the hypothesis might provide a useful, objective way of defining the limits of particular styles and periods.

Its use as a heuristic device would be especially pertinent if it were the case that, as suggested above: (a) the course of style change is not necessarily congruent either with changes occurring in the intellectual and sociopolitical areas of culture, or with those taking place in the other arts; and (*b*) the account of stylistic learning presented in chapter 11 (and elsewhere in this book) has merit. It should be emphasized, however, that the use of the hypothesis would not preclude the use of other supplementary data in the definition and periodization of styles.

7. The fact that styles often appear to follow a common pattern of change does not imply a teleological viewpoint. Like the growth of crystals or the development of biological structures, the nature of the processes and procedures discovered by composers and the kinds and forms of structures they invent are implicit in the basic premises of the style. There is no *goal* toward which a style—or even a series of styles—moves. The internal dynamic hypothesis is consonant with Ackerman's observation:

> What is called "evolution" in the arts should not be described as a succession of steps toward the solution of a given problem, but as a succession of steps away from one or more original statements of a problem. . . . The pattern of style change, then, is not determined by any destiny nor by a common goal, but by a succession of complex decisions as numerous as the works by which we have defined the style.[35]

What is constant is the tendency of a style to change, if it is to do so at all, in the direction of increased syntactic and structural information. The particular realizations of this tendency depend upon the characteristics of the style at a specific stage in its "career," upon extra-stylistic circumstances that influence the composer, and, by no means least, upon the composer's own capacity for invention and discovery. No particular realization of the tendency toward higher levels of information is either necessary or inevitable.

Moreover, just as the growth of crystals or of biological organisms depends upon their physical environment, so too the kind, rate, and extent of style change is a function of the cultural-ideological environment in which it exists. In some cultures intra-stylistic changes have been slow or, after a particular level of complexity is reached, virtually nonexistent: there is stasis. In others, notably in Western culture, changes have been abundant and fairly rapid. It is the reasons for such changes in the arts—music in particular—that we must now consider.

MUSICAL MEANS AND STYLISTIC STASIS

The first thing to notice is that the often rapid and fairly radical changes, both within and between styles, which have characterized the history of music in the West, were made possible by the invention and rapid improvement of an adequate symbolic notation. Without such notation, traditions and techniques can be preserved and passed on only orally, and cumulative development is, consequently, severely restricted. The composer-performer who works in an essentially oral tradition where notation, if it exists at all, is mnemonic rather than symbolic, must learn directly from his master. He cannot study or know the works of his more remote predecessors or, in the absence of easy communication, even those of his contemporaries in other locales. Where an adequate symbolic notation exists, on the other hand, compositional techniques, procedures, schemata, and formal structures can be pre-

---

[35] "A Theory of Style," p. 232. Also see chap. 12, n. 32.

served with considerable accuracy.[36] Once a student has learned the notation and the inflections proper to its realization, he can study, learn, and build upon the written scores not only of his own teachers but of his predecessors and distant contemporaries.

Notation makes possible not only the preservation and availability of works such as these but their very existence. The tendency of styles to develop in the direction of increased complexity and more extended hierarchic structure can be fully realized only if durations, pitches, and so forth of the several instruments or voices can be specified with considerable precision. Such specification is crucial for performance and also for enabling the composer to relate parts, sections, and procedures throughout the work to one another. By thus relying on notation rather than pure memory he can construct complex, arched hierarchic structures. These, serving as models and sources of technical-musical "advances," can lead to new kinds of organizations and novel syntactical means. In complementary fashion, notation permits audiences to hear such complex structures often enough that they can learn to understand them.

In an oral tradition, however, an unavoidable reliance upon memory limits the kinds, extent, and complexity of hierarchic structures.[37] In the absence of notation, complexity tends to be local—that is, to involve nuances of melodic inflection, subtleties of metric crossing, refinements of tone color and expressive inflection. Because these arise within some sort of relatively short cyclic or repetitive formal plan, hierarchic structures tend to be "flat." Such works, although freely and imaginatively reinvented by each generation of composer-performers, do not as a rule develop cumulatively beyond a certain point.[38] That is, without a system of notation intra-stylistic change is limited by the capacity of memory. A style cannot develop beyond a certain point—perhaps that of the early "classic" phase. At this point stasis will tend to take place.

This is relevant to the present inquiry because the notation system

---

[36] But never with perfect accuracy. For an absolutely precise and detailed system of notation would contain so much information to be scanned that it could be read only very slowly. Any notation, whether musical or linguistic, must depend to a considerable extent upon an oral tradition within which symbols and signs are interpreted and realized.

[37] Thus Curt Sachs writes that "practically all the forms that we meet in primitive, oriental, and western folk music are surprisingly short-winded" (*The Wellsprings of Music,* p. 123; also see *ibid.,* p. 175).

[38] The distinction between composer and performer also depends upon the existence of an adequate notational system.

which has heretofore served the West so well is no longer adequate to the needs of those contemporary composers who are attempting to develop new materials and techniques. Novel graphic and diagrammatic methods have been invented to represent pitch, time, timbre, and other aspects of sound; elaborate, and often cumbersome, ways of specifying complex metrical and temporal relationships have been devised; and new ways of notating expanded pitch systems have been suggested. All these, together with a rash of writings on the subject, are evidence of a crisis in notation. Some composers, on the other hand, have avoided the problem of notation altogether by composing directly on tape, and others have achieved substantially the same result by allowing the desired intricacies of pitch-time relationship to arise out of more or less free improvisation. It should be noted that some of these attempts to solve notational problems represent a kind of return to an oral tradition; that is, the composer must give the performer detailed instructions about how to realize his graphs or in what "style" to improvise.

Though an existing symbolic system can be modified—as a rule by adding new symbols—it is extremely difficult really to change systems (to substitute one for another), particularly in a mass-producing technology in which radical change is expensive and where the demand for change is confined to a minute fraction (however influential they may be in some circles) of the total musical activity of the culture. To put this matter more forcefully, it is probably in principle more difficult to substitute a new notational system for an existing one than it was to promote and promulgate the existing one in the first place—when *no* notation existed.

In the area of tonal relationships, an aspect of music which has heretofore been central in major changes in style, the possibility of significant change also seems doubtful. For not only will new or radically modified notation schemes have to be both devised *and* accepted if a new tonal system is to replace the present equal-tempered chromatic scale, but new instruments will have to be invented, manufactured, and sold and a new performance tradition developed, taught, and mastered. Moreover, as I have suggested elsewhere,[39] change in the tonal structure of styles has generally moved in the direction of filling in gaps in the repertory of tones in the system—a tendency toward equidistant scale steps. Since the equal-tempered scale is *already* uniform, however, change, if it is to come at all, must be invented and imposed from outside the tonal system. In view of the fact that a real change in the

---

[39] *Emotion and Meaning in Music*, pp. 131–34.

structure of a tonal system would necessarily involve major changes in every aspect of musical life—the construction of instruments, the printing of scores and educational materials, not to mention the techniques of performers and the perceptual responses of listeners—it is difficult to believe that anything but a compelling internal need can change tonal systems.[40] But there appear to be no such internal pressures; the equal-tempered scale, far from encouraging change, tends to promote stasis.

This perhaps suggests that attempts to devise new methods of notation and to extend old ones are indications that major style changes, rather than stasis, are in prospect. But there are, I believe, strong reasons for doubting that this is the case. In the first place, for reasons already mentioned, it appears unlikely that a really new symbolic notation, even if invented, would be accepted and flourish. Hence, insofar as a genuine notational impasse exists, it will tend to limit and discourage change. That is, it will be a "force" contributing to stasis. Second, in many—perhaps most—instances the need for new means of notation has been created by extensions, particularly in the realm of durational relationships of already existing formal and syntactical procedures. Change has been in the direction of further complexity *within* the archetypal style. There are few signs of the sort of shift of premises and of the concomitant simplification of means that have generally characterized new stylistic starts. Third, because the new notational schemes are graphic and diagrammatic, they are strongly dependent upon an oral tradition; and such oral-dependent traditions tend to be conservative—to encourage deviation within an essential stasis. Certainly it would be difficult for the sorts of cumulative changes which have characterized the history of Western music to take place in the context of a diagrammatic or graphic notation. Finally, the fact that there seems to be little inclination to change the fundamental repertory of pitches makes it at least doubtful that major style changes are in prospect.[41]

---

[40] Perhaps it is because such change is all but impossible that composers, searching for new means and methods, for the most part have turned their attention to the areas of meter, rhythm, and tempo.

[41] In a somewhat similar fashion, technology may also limit the direction and, to some extent, the scope of change in the other arts. For instance, before the invention of the Gothic arch or, more recently, of reinforced concrete, certain kinds of structures were simply not possible; before the discovery of oil paint and canvas particular kinds of textures, color mixtures, and overpainting were not possible; before the invention of motion pictures (and later the television camera) many sorts of dramatic theatrical effects could not be achieved; and before the invention of electronic tape a wide variety of sounds and sound sequences could not be employed in music. [Note continued next page.]

But even if a notational impasse were not to limit the character and scope of change, stasis may nevertheless be possible. For notation, both today and in the past, is at most an implementing condition for a particular kind of stylistic development. It is perhaps a necessary condition for cumulative change, but it is not a sufficient condition. As evidence of this, one need only cite the fact that in the plastic arts, where symbolic notation is not involved, stasis has been possible in many non-Western cultures, or that in cultures with an adequate written language, stasis has often been the rule.[42] In short, while notation limitations may confine change, notation per se does not promote change. Thus the question of what "forces" promote intra-stylistic development remains.

STYLE CHANGE AND THE INDIVIDUAL

Recent research in human, as well as animal, psychology [43] has shown that there is a fundamental human need for varied stimulation. Without such stimulation, the psychological and even physical development of the child is often abnormal; and, when stimulation is absent, the behavior of the normal adult is frequently disturbed. Deprived of varied and patterned perceptual experience man becomes neurotic, tense, and prone to hallucinations—as though the psyche were attempting to supply its own stimulation. If the need for patterned stimulation is indeed a basic requirement for psychic well-being, then it does not seem unrea-

---

Of course, the use, if any, made of a discovery depends most importantly upon the cultural situation in which it takes place. For instance, theories of equal-tempered tuning were proposed in the West long before such temperament was actually used; and inventions and thories have been discovered which were never used by the culture (see, p. 138). On the other hand, though technology only allows —does not force—change to take place, it seems evident that a slowing down of technological change would tend to limit the speed and direction of change in other cultural areas. This is of importance because, as we shall see, it is possible that Western technology may not continue to change at the rapid pace that has been characteristic of it for the past hundred years or so.

[42] It might be inferred from this that the invention of music notation in the West was a consequence of the "desire" for change. While this is plausible, it seems to me that it was quite possibly a fortuitous discovery—one which happened to have enormously important consequences. For if one assumes that the discovery of music notation resulted from some cultural necessity, then one must explain why no satisfactory notational scheme has been developed for the dance. In any case, the nature of invention is a highly complex subject; and simple explanations are almost always suspect. In this connection, see A. L. Kroeber, *Anthropology*, chap. 9, particularly pp. 352–57.

[43] The literature is considerable. See chap. 3, n. 18.

sonable that this need should play a significant role in creative activity and, consequently, in the style changes which result from that activity. The need for variety, though generally stated in other terms—such as creativity, expression, and individualization—has in fact been posited as one of the causes for style change. Thomas Munro, for instance, suggests that styles may change because "after varying and developing one style for a time, people eventually tire of it and want to try a different one." [44] And Ackerman writes that

> the pattern of [style] change is a product of the tension in society and in the artist between the instinct for stability and security of established schemes and the human capacity . . . for creating something unique and individualized. Change is slow when the former is stronger, rapid when the latter prevails. As a rule the factor of stability gets more support from society and its institutions, and the factor of change from the individual imagination. [45]

Though this thesis, which I have also espoused, [46] has much to recommend it, it requires comment and qualification.

1. To state this view in terms of uniqueness and individualization tends, I think, to be misleading. Not only are the terms ambiguous—in a literal sense every work of art (perhaps even a forgery or copy of an existing work) is both unique and individual—but more important, though Ackerman is careful not to say this, the words might be thought to imply that the artist "strives" for uniqueness and individualization. This need not be the case. The artist, elaborating upon established themes and models or inventing new manners of realizing stylistic schemata, creates variety without consciously intending to make something individual and personal or unique and novel. Quite the opposite. Often his conscious goal is that of faithful, though not rigid, adherence to traditional forms and procedures.

In short, the way in which the need for varied experience is fulfilled depends upon the way in which a particular culture views change and novelty, personal expression and aesthetic experience, and, in fact, upon the total complex of beliefs, attitudes, and dispositions which may be called its *ideology*. Consequently, it does not follow, as Munro seems to suggest, that the need for variety necessarily produces cumulative

---

[44] "What Causes Creative Epochs in the Arts?" p. 39.

[45] "A Theory of Style," p. 232. Also see Alan P. Merriam, *The Anthropology of Music,* p. 305.

[46] See pp. 49–51.

change. Variety can be and has been realized in cultures where varied transformation or fluctuating change produces stasis.

2. While society and its institutions generally support stability, because (among other reasons) the public, the patrons, and the purveyors of the arts generally prefer what is familiar and easily understood, this is by no means always so. In the plastic arts today, for example, novelty and change are encouraged by patrons, dealers, and museum curators. In music, universities and foundations frequently support and thereby encourage the composition of experimental works. On the other hand, when an art is used and supported by a group or social institution that is opposed to change, then what might be called the "inherent inertia" of society is particularly marked. It is important to emphasize again that complex cultures are markedly diverse and pluralistic. Hence, while some subgroups—or even the large mass of people—within a culture may resist change in the arts, other groups, perhaps a small but influential minority, may encourage and promote it.

Furthermore, one must distinguish between the behavior of society (social groups) and the ideologies which are an aspect of, yet feed back into, that behavior. For example, in the late nineteenth century, society (public and patrons) and institutions (museums and academies) strongly favored and supported the stability of established traditions in the plastic arts. But the ideology of the high subculture with which both the artist and society were associated emphasized the importance of individualism, self-expression, progress, and development; and change and novelty were thereby encouraged.

As I have sketched it, the pattern, extent, and rate of intra-stylistic change is, then, the result of a complex interaction among the premises of a particular style, the idiosyncrasies of specific composers, the human need for variety, the technological resources of the art, its relation to cultural institutions and social groups, and the cultural ideologies of both the artist and his public. In this picture, the premises of the style provide internal, systemic limits for the pattern of change. The extra-stylistic forces, constituting the environment within which the inner potential is realized, act to limit the extent, the rate, and the specific manner of realization. Though always present, change can take many forms—among them may be that of a fluctuating, yet dynamic, steady-state.

IDEOLOGY AND STYLE CHANGE

Because it has already been used, most recently in connection with the discussion of changes within a style, and will be of even more importance in what is to follow, the term "cultural ideology" should be defined as specifically as possible.

A cultural ideology is a complex network of interrelated beliefs and attitudes consciously or unconsciously held by members of the culture as a whole and by groups within the culture. As José Ortega y Gasset has put it:

> It follows that man must ever be grounded on some belief, and that the structure of his life will depend primordially on the beliefs on which he is grounded; and further that the most decisive changes in humanity are changes of belief, the intensifying or weakening of beliefs. The diagnosis of any human existence, whether of an individual, a people or an age, must begin by establishing the repertory of its convictions. . . . I have spoken of them as a repertory to indicate that the plurality of beliefs on which an individual, a people or an age is grounded never possesses a completely logical articulation, that is to say, does not form a system of ideas such as, for example, a philosophy constitutes or aims at constituting. The beliefs that coexist in any human life, sustaining, impelling, and directing it, are on occasion incongruous, contradictory, at the least confused.[47]

The most deep-seated beliefs, attitudes, and dispositions which form the fundamental basis of an ideology are not as a rule rationally arrived at, or are they usually consciously held. Rather they are the unconscious premises, the basic categories, which channel and direct our perceptions, our responses, our cognitions—in short, our understanding of ourselves and the world.[48] Examples of such basic strands in an ideological network would be beliefs about the nature of causation, time, order, and the like. Shading into these fundamental ways of interpreting experience, and perhaps more easily changed, are the culture's more consciously held beliefs about the world. As examples which have been important in recent Western ideology one may cite the culture's beliefs about social progress, originality, the dignity of labor, the differentiation between mind and body, the value of aesthetic experience, and so forth.

Like both culture and language, an ideological network is "a composite of elements of very different age, some of its features reaching back into the mists of an impenetrable past, others being the product of a develop-

---

[47] "History as a System," pp. 283–84.

[48] More and more evidence from psychology and anthropology indicates that our physiological responses are not separable from our mental-psychological attitudes. What we "know" and believe has a profound effect upon what we perceive and how we respond. See chap. 4.

ment yesterday." [49] Thus, while its most fundamental premises may be difficult to modify, an ideology is not "prohibitive of variation and change; it is not a closed logical system of beliefs and premises but rather a historically derived psychological system open to change." [50] In other words, though the strands of the network tend to support, reinforce, and complement one another, discrepancies and contradictions may arise within an ideology without destroying it. [51] For example, aspects of the larger cultural ideology may be modified, omitted, or contradicted in one or more of the particular subcultures. Or two subcultures may differ even on some fundamental issue. Often such discrepancies within and between subcultures are not apparent even to members of the group(s) because no direct confrontation of premises takes place. But when differences between subcultural ideologies are marked or when there is a direct clash of incompatible tenets within an ideology, some sort of accommodation or modification will, as a rule, take place within the total network.

The fact that ideologies change, are not necessarily consistent, and may be pluralistic makes it doubtful that some sort of abstract spirit—a *Zeitgeist*—guides or determines the destiny of a culture in a mystical and necessary way. Nor is a cultural ideology the expression of a group personality which is somehow independent of the behavior and beliefs of the individuals involved. [52] Rather, it is a set of specific and identifiable attitudes, convictions, and dispositions which are invented, modified, and communicated by particular men and women whether in the present or in the distant past.

Finally, it is important to note that the relationship between ideology and the culture from which it arises and which it influences is not a one-way affair. There is a continual interplay between an ideology and other aspects of culture including the arts. (It is a kind of "chicken and egg" situation; for instance, one cannot really say whether the political-social-economic situation is antecedent to [the cause of] a particular ideology or whether it is the other way around. Both are

---

[49] Edward Sapir quoted in Harry Hoijer, "The Relation of Language to Culture," p. 261. Hoijer uses the term "cultural metaphysics" to designate what I am calling "ideology." I prefer the latter term because it carries fewer implications of explicit, conscious systematization.

[50] *Ibid.*, p. 265.

[51] Here I disagree with Kenneth Boulding, who believes that "in an ideology each part will reinforce the other with an internal logic and consistency" (*The Meaning of the 20th Century*, p. 163).

[52] This view is carefully criticized by Meyer Schapiro, "Style," pp. 299–300.

facets of a single complex cultural process.) Of course, some aspects of culture may play a more important role in influencing ideology—and through it other facets of culture—than others; and, conversely, some aspects of culture may be more easily altered by changes in ideology than others. In Western culture, since the Renaissance, science and natural philosophy have had an important influence on ideological changes—partly, of course, because the ideology itself considered science to be an important source of "truth" and knowledge. Thus scientific discoveries—those of Galileo, Newton, Darwin, and Einstein— nurtured by the ideology of the West, have been fed back into that ideology creating important modifications not only in beliefs about the nature of the universe, but in other realms (religion, philosophy, art, etc.) as well. These in turn have influenced other facets of cultural behavior. In other cultures ideas and ideals different from those held in the West have been dominant in the prevailing ideology. For instance, the ancient Egyptians were not historically oriented and had little sense of the past and future. According to Henri Frankfort,

> they conceived of the world as essentially static and unchanging. It had gone forth complete from the hands of the Creator. Historical incidents were, consequently, no more than superficial disturbances of the established order, or recurring events of never-changing significance. The past and the future—far from being a matter of concern— were wholly implicit in the present; and [their whole civilization] . . . can all be understood as a result of a basic conviction that only the changeless is truly significant.[53]

To put the matter briefly, an ideology acts both as the climate within which cultural and stylistic changes take place and, to mix the metaphor, as the meeting ground on which changes in separate and noncontiguous facets of culture can interact with and influence one another.

The role of cultural ideologies in intra-stylistic change has already been touched upon. Their importance in changes between styles is probably at least as great, if not greater. And it is to a consideration of such changes that we briefly turn.

Though "direct causation" theories are, as we have seen, too monistic, mechanistic, and absolute to account for the multiplicity of styles within a culture, the relative independence of intra-stylistic change and the diversity of kinds of stylistic change, it is impossible to deny that some sort of connection exists between general cultural change and style change in the arts. For it is obvious that the almost continual change in

---

[53] Quoted in G. J. Whitrow, *The Natural Philosophy of Time*, p. 56.

our culture generally—in social organization, intellectual concepts, technology, and the like—has been accompanied by more or less constant changes of style in the arts, while in those cultures in which style changes have been minimal, the culture as a whole has tended to be stable and relatively unchanging. And it would appear that though the political, social, intellectual, and technological facts of a culture do not *cause*, and are not necessarily directly connected with, stylistic events, the same ideological climate which fosters change in one aspect of culture tends to do so in others. Precisely what is affected—whether the bald fact of change, the direction of change, or only the rate of change—will depend upon the particular circumstances of the total fabric of the culture at the time in question. It is, however, important to notice that there is a distinction between fostering and determining; the ideological climate can foster stylistic change without determining or specifying its pattern of development. Indeed it can do so without necessarily influencing the direction of change.

But this account does not stipulate what role cultural ideologies play in changes between styles. It does not do so because no general account is, I think, possible. Viable generalizations or laws which attempt to explain why and how styles are initiated are difficult—perhaps impossible—to arrive at, not only because the beginnings of styles are, as noted earlier, extremely hard to identify, but because the process of change is itself culture-dependent. Probably the most one can do by way of generalization is to list the possible variables upon which, at any particular moment, a specific change of stylistic premises may depend: the characteristics of existing styles and of past styles upon which the artist might have drawn, the technological state of the art, the relationship of the artist to socioeconomic conditions, the individuality of the artist, the prevailing ideology of the culture, and last, but perhaps not least, the fact of the fortuitous. How these variables interact with one another and with the cultural ideology which serves as a meeting ground and what the influence of one variable is in relation to others—these will change from culture to culture and from epoch to epoch within a culture.

The preceding discussion of what might be called the "cultural ecology" of style change makes no pretense to final answers. It is, I hope, suggestive rather than systematic or conclusive. Yet this much does seem to me both clear and certain: neither factual evidence nor theoretical considerations preclude the possibility of stasis. If the suggestion that the West faces the prospect of stasis in the arts appears remarkable and perhaps even bizarre, it is because we have become so accustomed to change that it seems almost to be a law of cultural life.[54] Indeed the most recent changes, which are partly still in process, are perhaps the most momentous in five centuries. They are, in fact, so momentous that they have brought about important alterations in the ideology of Western culture and have affected even the tendency-toward-change itself. What these ideological revisions are and how they may affect the character of stylistic change will be the subject of the next chapter.

---

[54] It may appear inconsistent, as well as rash, after having just admitted that I am unable to explain precisely how styles originate, to propose to explain changes that are still in process. But this misses a crucial point, namely, that I am not proposing to explain the genesis of a new style, but rather why presently existing styles will probably not undergo fundamental change in the foreseeable future.

CHAPTER
8

The Probability of Stasis

The presumption that social-cultural development is a necessary condition of human existence is not tenable. The history of China up to the nineteenth century, the stasis in ancient Egypt, and the lack of cumulative change in countless other civilizations and cultures make it apparent that stability and conservation, not change, have been the rule in the history of mankind generally. Once this is recognized, theories which postulate necessary cycles, developments, dialectics, or progressions become suspect. If the history of Western civilization has been conspicuously characterized by change, then one must look to the peculiarities of the culture and its ideologies for reasons and explanations.

TOWARD STABILITY

At the end of the previous chapter, it was pointed out that in general cultural changes and stylistic changes have tended to go together and that, conversely, stasis in the arts has often been accompanied by relative stability in other areas of a culture. Though a general cultural stasis is probably not a necessary condition for stasis in the arts, it would nevertheless lend weight to the thesis that the arts are about to enter a period of relative stability if it appeared that other areas of culture—particularly Western culture—were also moving in the direction of stability and non-cumulative change.

That this is in fact the case has been suggested by several scholars in other fields. Discussing the socioeconomic conditions of today's world and the prospects for the future, Robert L. Heilbroner concludes that "it is certain enough that the tenor of world history will remain much as it is for a long while to come." [1] Looking at the future of the twentieth century, Kenneth Boulding finds it necessary to make two assumptions, which we too must make: that there will be no major nuclear conflict and that the population explosion will somehow be controlled.[2] Granting these two assumptions, Boulding finds that the future of what he calls "post-civilized society" will take the form of "a stable, closed cycle, high-level technology." [3] Similarly, William H. McNeill, having reviewed the history of world cultures, suggests:

> The globe is finite and if the rival political-social-economic power systems of our time coalesce under an overarching world sovereignty, the impetus now impelling men to develop new sources of power will largely cease. Naturally, great tasks of social and economic betterment will remain. . . . But for this, application of already familiar methods on sufficient scale and with a store of resolution and intelligence already well within human reach should suffice. And once these initial adjustments have successsfully been made, a stalwart, more than Chinese bureaucratic immobility would, in all probability, soon define the daily life of cosmopolitan world society.
>
> . . . .
>
> What such a vision of the future anticipates . . . is the eventual establishment of a world-wide cosmopolitanism, which, compared with the confusions and haste of our time, would enjoy vastly greater stability.[4]

More specifically, it is clear that some of the conditions which have heretofore fostered change in the West no longer exist. One of these is the possibility of revolutionary discovery. The discovery of new lands and exotic cultures, which has in the past frequently stimulated the imagination of Western man and influenced his customs and beliefs, is no longer possible.[5] Thus, discussing the changes in communication which took place in the West at the beginning of the modern era (*ca.*

---

[1] *The Future as History*, p. 205.

[2] The conflict between capitalism and communism seems to be resolving itself, as the capitalist nations solve more and more problems in the public sector through planning, and the socialist nations introduce the profit motive—or at least the free market—and greater intellectual freedom in the private sector.

[3] *The Meaning of the 20th Century*, p. 149.

[4] *The Rise of the West*, p. 806.

[5] The likelihood of the existence of anything comparable to human life within communication distance—within our solar system—seems very remote.

1500), McNeill writes: "Western Europe . . . was the principal gainer from this extraordinary revolution in world relationships, both materially and in a larger sense, for it now became the pre-eminent meeting place for novelties of every kind. This allowed Europeans to adopt whatever pleased them in the tool kits of other peoples and stimulated them to reconsider, recombine, and invent anew within their own enlarged cultural heritage." [6] But today this situation no longer obtains. What we face is "global cosmopolitanism" in which novelty is no longer readily at hand.[7]

Nor is the study of the past—whether geological, biological, or cultural—likely to change our knowledge of that past substantially. New facts will, of course, be brought to light,[8] and each new generation of historians will reinterpret the significance of these facts—though if cultural stability is achieved, the necessity for such reinterpretation will diminish. The information explosion in history [9] has led, however, to the discovery of most of the major pieces of the historical puzzle and sketched in broad outline how to fit them together. Future scholars will undoubtedly fill in missing pieces, but it seems very doubtful that the basic picture will be fundamentally changed.[10]

The closing of the geographical-cultural frontier and the substantial completion of our picture of the past have been complemented by revolutionary changes in communication and a staggering increase in our knowledge of other cultures—and theirs about us. We not only know that other cultures exist, but we have a great deal of information about them. Consequently, as the possibility of discovering cultural novelty in other lands and in other epochs diminishes, one significant source of ideological-cultural change is eliminated. More specifically, with reference to the arts, discovery is no longer a real possibility. By and large the arts of other cultures, past and present, are available on phonograph records, in translations of literature and philosophy, and in museums or in reproductions. The artist need only choose his source of influence. Both the cultural present and the cultural past are from this point of view timeless and static.

---

[6] *The Rise of the West*, p. 565.

[7] *Ibid.*, p. 764, and the conclusion of the book.

[8] One area in which substantial changes of viewpoint are possible is cosmological history, including the early history of the earth. But the influence of new discoveries in this field upon cultural history are not likely to be significant.

[9] See Boyd C. Shafer, "The Study of History in the United States."

[10] Though the accumulation of information continues at a staggering pace, whatever is discovered is bound to have less and less impact upon the vast sea of historical data.

But what of those areas of discovery and innovation which have probably been most responsible for the recent revolutionary changes in our culture and its ideology—the areas of science and technology? Will not changes in these areas continue? Certainly. But there are strong reasons for believing that, although technology and science will continue to flourish in the years ahead, the changes which occur will not affect established, fundamental premises and methods. The changes will be in degree (more efficient computers, faster means of communication, larger nuclear reactors) rather than in kind (a new theory of genetic change, novel means of transportation, etc.). Moreover, even the rate of change is probably slowing down. An examination of possible future developments in fields such as transportation, the improvement of computers, the construction of high-energy accelerators, the limiting of disease and of population, and the exploration of our physical world leads John R. Platt to believe that the rate of technological and scientific change is leveling off and that

> most of the dramatic changes that have characterized the 20th century . . . cannot possibly continue at the present rates. . . . It becomes obvious that many of them must converge rather soon to various kinds of limits, so that these aspects of society must begin to take on much more stable forms.
>
> . . . I think it can be shown that many of our present changes are already rushing rapidly toward such limits. And many of our social adjustments to change are well on their way to what might be called "steady-state forms" that could accommodate orders of magnitude of further technical development without much additional restructuring.[11]

This is not to assert that, as Platt points out, "marvelous developments" do not lie ahead, particularly in biology, where we have much to learn about the nature of human mental processes. But at this point in time it does not appear likely that these possible discoveries will effect such revolutionary changes in society and in cultural ideology as have occurred during the past hundred, or perhaps even five hundred, years.

IDEOLOGY AND CHANGE

Though novelty, either from contact with alien cultures or from technological innovation within the culture, has fostered change in the West, it does not necessarily do so. To foster change, novelty and discovery must occur in a favorable ideological-cultural environment.

---

[11] "The Step to Man," p. 607.

The tremendous importance of the environment is dramatically illustrated in the differences between the uses made of technological discoveries and cultural contacts by China and the West. Technological and
scientific discoveries made in China had little effect upon Chinese life;
but when brought to the West, these same inventions had momentous
consequences.

> The real importance of the denser communications across Asia
> . . . lay not in any effects upon China, but in the penetration into
> Moslem and Christian lands of certain key elements of Chinese tech-
> nology, notably gunpowder, the compass, and printing. The impor-
> tance of these devices for western European history can scarcely be
> overestimated; yet in China their impact was comparatively modest.[12]

The ideological network which has for the past four centuries nurtured such momentous changes in Western culture was formed during
the Renaissance and Reformation out of a composite of concepts and
beliefs some of which dated back to ancient Greece and some of which
were essentially new. Partly because of its own internal inconsistencies
and partly because the changes which it helped to engender in the
political-economic-social sphere fed back into it, the ideology has, since
the seventeenth century, undergone considerable modification. Some
strands of the initial network were strengthened by events in the culture
as a whole; for instance, the success of the sciences reinforced the belief
that nature consistently obeys laws and that human reason has the power
to discover these. Other strands were weakened—for instance, the belief
in the role played by divine intervention in human affairs. And still
others were reinterpreted in the light of the development of culture and its
ideology—for instance, the view of history as a goal-directed progress.

It is beyond the scope of this study to outline the development of
Western ideology and its relation to the culture from which it sprang.
Such an account would involve writing an intellectual-social history of
Europe from 1600 to 1950. Nor will any attempt be made to discuss all
tenets of the ideology or to trace their interconnections. I plan instead to
consider the ideology as it existed in the late nineteenth and early
twentieth centuries and, more specifically, those tenets which indicate
that our view of the world is becoming consonant with an impending
stasis. Hence important strands in the network will be discussed only in
passing and others will perhaps be neglected altogether. Moreover,
though Western ideology is undergoing revolutionary changes, it is
important to emphasize that not all tenets of post-Renaissance ideology

---

[12] McNeill, *The Rise of the West*, pp. 530–31.

are being altered, replaced, or scrapped. Some of its fundamental tenets are not only preserved in the new ideology but are considered more certain and pervasive than when first promulgated. To cite three important instances: an essentially secular approach to an understanding of the nature of man and the universe; a correlative belief in the power of the human mind to discover truth without appeals to supernatural or other authority; and a tolerance for the diversity and differences of viewpoint and method produced by intellectual pluralism. In some cases only one facet of a particular tenet is called into question or modified. For instance, while the naturalism of Greek origin is preserved, the teleology with which it tended to be coupled is not; or, though human creativity is still a cultural value, its particular realization as personal expression is not. The change in ideology which is in process does not, in other words, constitute a total break with the past; but it does call into question many basic premises of the preceding network. Finally, because the tenets of an ideology do not constitute a system in which one or two ideas act as axioms from which other concepts or beliefs are deduced, the order in which the tenets are discussed implies no priority of any kind.

THE VIEWPOINT OF ANALYTIC FORMALISM

From the seventeenth century on, physics became the prime model for conceptualizing the universe and man's place in it.[13] Its cumulative successes in prediction and in fostering technological discovery led to a belief that absolute, unchanging, and deterministic laws of nature could be discovered in all areas of knowledge. It was also supposed that the causal connections of which the laws were a realization were direct and simple, necessary and sufficient. Similar laws were sought in history, economics, and the newly developing social sciences. Up to the end of the nineteenth century, there were good grounds for feeling that the enterprise would succeed. Advances in chemistry, geology, and biology seemed to indicate that regular laws and final, fundamental truths could be found in those sciences. A chrono- and ethnocentric view of history made it appear that there were also constant and absolute laws of social evolution and change.

But toward the end of the nineteenth century, new discoveries in the

---

[13] "As the Principia won over the physicists' thinking . . . it became a model for every other field of inquiry. . . . This attitude was expressed by Helmholtz: 'To understand a phenomenon means nothing else than to reduce it to the Newtonian laws'" (Norwood R. Hanson, *Patterns of Discovery*, p. 91).

physical sciences led to questions about the nature of matter and, subsequently, the concepts of absolute time and space were called into question. In the social sciences, the development of Freudian theory made eighteenth- and nineteenth-century notions of human behavior, based upon rational and enlightened self-interest, seem very doubtful; World War I, too, made bourgeois pride in progress seem somewhat premature. The antirational reactions of the 1920's—Dadaism, futurism, and surrealism—were symptoms of changes of attitude which were intensified by the depression of the 1930's, by World War II, and, above all, by the changes in scientific theory that occurred after 1900.

By the early 1940's, three fundamental axioms of the "age of rational faith" no longer seemed tenable: (*a*) the existence of simple, one-to-one causation; (*b*) the discoverability of a single set of absolute and eternal truths or laws; and (*c*) the deterministic character of physical laws, biological processes, and social development. The universe could no longer be viewed as an enormously complex mechanism which, once set in motion by "God," would run its inevitable course in a predictable way. Uncertainty entered into the conceptualization of the world, not only as part of physical and social theory, but metaphysically and epistemologically: "laws" became *hypotheses,* which were expected to be revised; "causal certainties" became *statistical probabilities;* and the possibility of an embracing unity through a reduction to physics or some other single set of premises came to seem more and more remote. Pluralism, nurtured by permissive secularism, thus produced not a group of interconnected disciplines united under a single set of axioms and postulates—and an all-embracing world view—but rather a multiplicity of sets of axioms (of coexisting, and at times even conflicting, constructs) both within and between disciplines. Truth and reality turned out to be pluralistic. And, be it noted, pluralism allows, perhaps paradoxically, for the possibility of monistic models.

The concept of truth as a single, unchanging picture of reality no longer seems tenable. In mathematics, for instance, new geometries have been developed which, employing different axioms and postulates, coexist as alternative "truths" alongside Euclidean geometry which had seemed absolute and empirically validated for two thousand years. New counting systems were devised; binary and octal systems became "valid" and useful alternatives to the decimal system. There is no longer a *single* mathematical "truth." Similarly, in science, different hypotheses are used to explain different types of phenomena—even within the same discipline.

Moreover, the succession of scientific paradigms which have followed one another are no longer seen as more and more accurate pictures of some "ultimate" reality. That this is an attitude shared by scientists is made clear by Henry Eyring in his presidential address to the American Association for the Advancement of Science:

> "What is truth?" After 19 centuries, we are still getting new answers to this question posed by Pontius Pilate. The reason for this lack of definition is clear enough. The universe is so complex that even the widest-ranging vision is at best partial and tentative. Each generation sets itself the task of re-evaluation and reinterpretation and so the quest for Truth is unending.[14]

The history of science may be viewed as a "process of evolution *from* primitive beginnings—a process whose successive steps are characterized by an increasingly detailed and refined understanding of nature"; but such progressive refinement does not necessarily entail "the notion, explicit or implicit, that changes of paradigm carry scientists and those who learn from them closer and closer to the truth." [15] It should be noted that Thomas S. Kuhn's conception of scientific development is explicitly non-teleological. Describing the history of scientific research, he says that "the entire process may have occurred, as we now suppose biological evolution did, without benefit of a set goal, a permanent fixed scientific truth of which each stage in the development of scientific knowledge is a better exemplar." [16]

Once it is accepted that alternative sets of axioms and alternative hypotheses may, in a given context, be valid and tenable, the history of scientific theories should become a subject for serious study. And this, indeed, appears to be happening. "Interest in history [of science]," writes Jane Oppenheimer, "has become respectable for those . . . who choose to think of their work in broad perspective. . . . The history of science is now a scientific discipline in its own right, even to the extent that the National Science Foundation and National Institutes of Health give financial support for historical studies, considering them as advancing scientific welfare." [17]

Mathematical and scientific theories are conditional, not only in the

---

[14] "This Changing World," p. 1.
[15] *The Structure of Scientific Revolutions*, p. 169.
[16] *Ibid.*, pp. 171–72.
[17] "Perspectives in Biology," p. 7.

sense that they are artificial—*but by no means arbitrary*—constructs,[18] but also because the constructs developed can neither logically nor empirically establish total and absolute truths. Gödel's famous paper, for instance, "confronted mathematicians with proof that the axiomatic method has certain inherent limitations which rule out any possibility that even the ordinary arithmetic of whole numbers can ever be fully systemized by its means. What is more, his proofs brought the astounding and melancholy revelation that it is impossible to establish the logical consistency of any complex deductive system except by assuming principles of reasoning whose own internal consistency is as open to question as that of the system itself." [19] In microphysics a somewhat different situation obtains. The discovery of certain and ultimate truths are impossible because the observer is himself part of the measuring system.

> We can no longer speak of the behavior of the particle independently of the processes of observation. As a final consequence, the natural laws formulated mathematically in quantum theory no longer deal with the particles themselves but with our knowledge of them. Nor is it any longer possible to ask whether on not these particles exist in space and time objectively, since the only processes that we can refer to as taking place are those which represent the interplay of particles with some other physical system, e.g., a measuring instrument.[20]

Causation is no longer to be understood as an objective, observable connection—an empirical fact whose existence is independent of man's conceptualization of the world. Nor is it, *à la* Hume, considered to be merely the result of a constant contiguity of sequential events. Rather, as Norwood Hanson puts it:

> Causes are certainly connected with effects; but this is because our theories connect them, not because the world is held together by cosmic glue. . . . The notions behind "the cause x" and "the effect y" are intelligible only against a pattern of theory, namely one which puts guarantees on inferences from x to y.[21]

In the social sciences, where the possibility of discovering fixed, objective laws had essentially been a hope rather than a conviction,

---

[18] In this connection Norwood R. Hanson, for instance, observes: "The neutrino idea, like those of other atomic particles, is a retroductive *conceptual construction*. . . . This does not make the subject matter of atomic physics less real. Elementary particles are not logical fictions . . ." (*Patterns of Discovery*, pp. 124–25; italics mine).

[19] Ernest Nagel and James R. Newman, "Gödel's Proof," p. 71.

[20] Werner Heisenberg, "Non-Objective Science and Uncertainty," p. 446.

[21] *Patterns of Discovery*, p. 64.

scholars became increasingly doubtful about the existence of a single ultimate and immutable truth. The careful study of other cultures and past civilizations made it more and more apparent that many of the axioms thought to govern individual and social behavior were in fact ethnocentric extrapolations from recent Western cultural norms. Hence, though there may be, say, general cross-cultural laws of individual mental behavior,[22] these are realized in different ways—as different objective facts—in different cultures. More important, the hierarchic character of human behavior—ranging from that of the individual, through that of the group, to that of the culture as a whole and its institutions—led to the development of different disciplines each of which considered somewhat different facts and proposed somewhat different axioms and postulates.

(The picture has been confused. A failure to recognize that hierarchies are in principle discontinuous led to attempts at reductionism or unification of *all* the social sciences. The result has been a blurring of the distinctions between disciplines. Few have seen, as Maurice Mandelbaum points out, that "one cannot understand the actions of human beings as members of society unless one assumes that there is a group of facts which I shall term 'societal facts' which are as ultimate as are those facts which are 'psychological' in character"; [23] and further, that though any model or set of facts must take account of the interaction among the levels of the hierarchy, attempts to reduce social behavior to individual behavior or to integrate all social science into a single discipline "is a mistaken goal for sociologists and psychologists to pursue." [24])

Many historians and philosophers of history have of late espoused the view that history is a construct. Thus, Johan Huizinga believes that "history is always an imposition of form upon the past, and cannot claim to be more." [25] History is a construct, so it is often argued, because it is always written from a present viewpoint and hence is

---

[22] See Leonard B. Meyer, "Universalism and Relativism in the Study of Ethnic Music."

[23] "Societal Facts," p. 478.

[24] *Ibid.*, p. 477; also see Ernest Gellner, "Holism versus Individualism in History and Sociology."

[25] "A Definition of the Concept of History," p. 5. This does not mean that history cannot be objective and true. One could make a similar statement about science— science is always the imposition of form upon natural events—though I would prefer to say "the discovery of form" in history and science. Also see n. 18, above; W. H. Walsh, "'Meaning' in History," p. 297; and L. Susan Stebbing, quoted on p. 92, above.

necessarily interpretive and selective. Thus, Philip Bagby writes that the historian "presents the past in the light of the present, illuminated by the tastes and preoccupations of his contemporaries. It is primarily for this reason that 'history' must constantly be rewritten. Each generation must find its own interpreters, the historians who will show how the past can be related to the new needs and problems of the day." [26] In a similar vein, George Herbert Mead notes: "If we had every possible document and every possible monument from the period of Julius Caesar, we should unquestionably have a truer picture of the man and of what occurred in his life time, but it would be a truth which belongs to this present, and a later present would reconstruct it from the standpoint of its own emergent nature." [27] It should be observed, however, that should the future prove to be generally static and stable, as this study is suggesting, then the accounts given of the past would have less reason for changing —that is, they would become stable too.

Though the constructivist character of historical studies allows for a plurality of interpretations even of the same event, it does not follow that historical accounts cannot be objective and valid. Charles Frankel's discussion of this problem seems particularly clear and persuasive:

> . . . the question of whether a given sequence of events did or did not have certain results is an objective, factual question. Accordingly, while two historians may legitimately choose different terminal consequences in interpreting the same general period of history, this does not mean that any terminal consequences at all may be chosen. Further, two interpretations of a given period may in fact not be offering two accounts of the same facts, but accounts of different facts. The first begins with an event, E, and traces its consequences, C_1, C_2, C_3 . . . to terminal consequence T_1. The second begins with the same event E, but traces *other* consequences, C_x, C_y, C_z . . . to terminal consequence T_2.

Frankel's analysis leads him to point out that

> although it is obvious that historians with different social habitats will view the stream of events from different perspectives, it does not follow that the past, or our beliefs about the past, must necessarily be recreated in each generation. Sometimes new evidence about what has happened turns up, or new and more reliable theories of human

[26] *Culture and History*, p. 49. This is an extreme and socially "activist" expression of a common thesis. It is not the position of those who believe that history must "get inside" historical figures and events in order to explain or to understand them.

[27] "The Test of the Accepted Past," p. 74.

nature or social structure. When this happens, the historians of later ages do rewrite the histories of their predecessors: they disagree about the facts. But when the historians of a later age write history in terms of terminal consequences that are different from those with which their predecessors were concerned, they are not rewriting history, they are writing another history. The old history can be true, and true not only for the earlier age in which it was written but for the later age as well.[28]

More generally still, after examining the reasons given for supposing that the social sciences are necessarily subjective, Ernest Nagel concludes that "the various reasons . . . for the intrinsic impossibility of securing objective . . . conclusions in the social sciences do not establish what they purport to establish, even though in some instances they direct attention to undoubtedly important practical difficulties frequently encountered in these disciplines." [29]

The pervasiveness and persuasiveness of these new attitudes toward the nature of knowledge and the validity of theories reflect, and are reflected in, the philosopher's conception of his task. For if knowledge is a construct, then it makes little sense for philosophy to ask what ultimate reality or truth really are; and the task of unifying all knowledge within a single comprehensive system or set of premises becomes less urgent (if not less attractive), since such an all-embracing system would itself be a metaconstruct not essentially different with respect to validity or epistomological status from other lower-order constructs. Rather, philosophy has more and more concerned itself with the development and analysis of logical systems and theories in different disciplines, with the nature of induction and scientific method, with the validity of arguments and assertions, and with the categories within which experience is conceptualized and communicated. Part II of Patrick Gardiner's *Theories of History* provides a number of representative examples of this new attitude; and Gardiner himself points to these concerns, writing that "it is one thing . . . to argue in favor of the acceptability of a particular hypothesis in physics or biology—to do this is to argue as a physicist or a biologist: it is another to examine the form such arguments take, the sorts of consideration that are adduced in their support, the terms in which they are stated—matters that may be of philosophical interest and importance." [30]

---

[28] "Explanation and Interpretation in History," p. 421.

[29] *The Structure of Science*, p. 502 and, in general, chaps. 13 and 14.

[30] P. 265. Similarly, Norwood R. Hanson writes that "philosophers can but record, compare and analyze the positions of mechanical law statements in the concept-system that is classical mechanics" (*Patterns of Discovery*, p. 113).

THE DEMISE OF THE IDEA OF PROGRESS

These changes in the epistemological beliefs of Western culture have been complemented by correlative changes in the culture's conception of the nature of change itself. The Idea of Progress, born in the seventeenth century and nourished on the successes of science and technology, became an article of faith in the eighteenth and nineteenth centuries.[31]

> It was not doubted that the laws of Nature, like those of Louis XIV, were designed with reference to predetermined ends. Hence the laws of Nature came to be thought of as the orderly provisions which Nature makes for the realization of certain specific purposes, these purposes, discernible by the exercise of reason, being nothing other than the promotion of the progress and happiness of mankind.[32]

The amalgamation of a dubious scientism and a naïve optimism with an unwarranted faith in historical necessity and an imprudent teleology has come to seem badly mistaken.

The assumption, which had a deep and pervasive influence upon nineteenth-century philosophy (e.g., Hegel), social science (Karl Marx), and literature (Tolstoy and Zola),[33] that deterministic laws, like those of Newtonian mechanics, are universal (pervading the realms of biology, psychology, and history) has not proved tenable. Not only have no universal, necessary laws of human behavior been discovered, but even in the physical and biological sciences strictly deterministic systems appear to be the exception rather than the rule.

The idea of historical progress was more difficult to countenance in the humanities. Few were prepared seriously to contend that there had been "progress" in literature or art from Greek times. Even in music, where there was some feeling that the art had "advanced" since the Middle Ages,[34] the case was seldom stated in terms of necessary prog-

---

[31] As J. B. Bury put it, "Belief in [progress] is an act of faith" (*The Idea of Progress*, p. 4).

[32] Frederick J. Teggart, *Theory and Processes of History*, p. 90.

[33] Thus Tolstoy tells us that "in historic events, the so-called great men are labels giving names to events. . . . Every act of theirs, which appears to them an act of their own will, is in an historical sense involuntary and is related to the whole course of history and predestined from eternity" ("Man as the Creature of History," p. 267) ; for Zola, see "The Novel as Social Science," p. 276.

[34] The eighteenth- and nineteenth-century view that music had progressed from "primitive" beginnings is discussed by Curt Sachs in *The Wellsprings of Music*, pp. 5–8.

ress. With the development of historical musicology and ethnomusicology, the notion of stylistic progress has to all intents been given up. But though the idea of stylistic progress never gained much currency in the discussion of the arts, the idea of determinism did. It took the form not of a necessary progress between works or styles but of a belief in aesthetic inevitability within works. Every note in a good work of music, every word in a good poem, so it was argued, was necessary and unalterable. Inevitability became an aesthetic criterion, a test of value.[35] The doctrine of inevitability in art, though still with us even in some of the most advanced theoretical formulations, is nevertheless being questioned not only in the theory and practice of arts, which are allowing considerable scope for aleatoric or chance events, but also in philosophical aesthetics.[36]

Belief in the existence of a natural teleology—arising perhaps from a need to reconcile scientific secularism with a faith in some sort of divine concern in human affairs—has never been important in modern physical science. It is generally now discredited in biology.[37] In the field of evolution, once the exemplar of purposeful progress, it is becoming evident that "natural evolution selects on the basis of relatively short-time decisions and that most species become extinct. The process is unable to foretell the future, hence today the inevitability of progress and the existence of a master plan must be questioned."[38]

In the social sciences, teleology seems a more plausible form of explanation. But two world wars, the inhumanity of twentieth-century dictatorships, and the great depression dealt severe blows to man's confidence in the inevitability of progress. The development and growth of the social sciences, given impetus partly by the desire to demonstrate that society had progressed, ultimately cast doubt upon the notion of progress. For the attempt of anthropologists and cultural historians to understand exotic and earlier cultures in their own terms (through empathetic identification) led to the realization that the "superiority" of

---

[35] Historical determinism also involved value judgments. For a criticism of this position, see Morris R. Cohen, *Reason and Nature*, pp. 377–79. It is suggestive, and perhaps not mere happenstance, that those composers who emphasize the importance of aesthetic inevitability are often also those who use the idea of historical necessity to justify their practice. See chap. 10; "The Argument from Historical Necessity."

[36] See Catherine Lord, "Organic Unity Reconsidered"; and Susan Sontag, *Against Interpretation,* p. 33.

[37] For example, Erwin Schrödinger says, "Nature does not act according to purpose" (*What Is Life?* . . . , p. 22).

[38] Van Rensselaer Potter, "Society and Science," p. 1018.

western European culture could not be taken for granted—that, rightly understood, other cultural ideologies and modes of behavior were reasonable, defensible, and valuable. These changes interacted with the philosophical ones mentioned above. A growing tendency toward cultural relativism encouraged the view that reality was a construct and truth was pluralistic. The development of such views in turn hastened the demise of the belief in a natural and necessary progress.

The upshot of these changes, then, has been a growing skepticism about and disenchantment with the idea of natural and necessary social-historical progress. What contemporary thought lacks, according to Robert Heilbroner, "is not *personal* optimism. It is *historic* optimism—that is, a belief in the imminence and immanence of change for the better in man's estate, the advent of which can be left to the quiet work of history." [39]

While the Idea of Progress did not actually create change, its fundamentally optimistic view of the historical process provided an atmosphere which welcomed and encouraged change. As Charles Beard put it, ". . . if the idea of progress is not a stubborn outcome of true history, it may, as a faith in possibilities, actually *make* history." [40] Such in-principle optimism no longer convinces. Change is losing its charm. The future no longer winks seductively. We are willing to abide; stasis is possible. But neither does the past offer nostalgic security. Time's arrow is no longer value-laden.

A final, if somewhat speculative, point—related because it concerns general cultural attitudes toward change, and complementary because it involves changes in religious, rather than secular, belief: I should like to suggest that one source encouraging change in the West, particularly after the seventeenth century, lay in the religious dogma of man's native sinfulness. For if man is believed to be born flawed—inheriting Adam's sin, and perhaps guilt for Christ's death as well—then he must strive to change, seeking redemption and salvation whether in this world or the next. Particularly for Protestants—and the Idea of Progress was strongest and technological change most marked in Protestant countries—change was evidently an important value.

The growth and successes of natural science, however, have led to an increasingly secular view of man and the universe. Especially during the last fifty years, the effective confutation of the mind-body dualism (see chap. 9), one of the crucial supports for the doctrine of spiritual

---

[39] *The Future as History*, pp. 47–48.
[40] In his Introduction to J. B. Bury's *The Idea of Progress*, p. xxviii.

immortality, has seriously weakened religious faith and, along with this, belief in the innate sinfulness of man. To the extent that this belief has heretofore fostered change in our culture, that force for change is no longer really effective.

THE NEUTRALITY OF HISTORY

Doubts about the existence of a natural and necessary law of progress coupled with a correlative skepticism about the possibility of discovering ultimate reality and final truth have radically altered man's attitude toward and relationship to both the past and the future. The present is no longer seen as the glorious culmination of a progression from the primitive and misguided to the refined and the enlightened. If, in the seventeenth century, "the past had changed from a source of inspiration to a collection of mistakes and the future, hitherto so featureless, had risen up like a Promised Land," [41] in the twentieth century the past has once again become a relevant source of insight and, like both the present and the future, of provisional truth. But the new ideology has not returned to earlier views in which the past—usually one particular past—was specially favored as a source of insight and inspiration. The emerging ideology is, so to speak, "neutral" with respect to both history and ethnology. It is neither chrono- nor ethnocentric. "Our civilization," writes Huizinga, "is the first to have for its past the past of the world, our history is the first to be world-history." [42]

The potential relevance of the past has also been enhanced by the development and growth of scholarship in the humanities and social sciences. The vast burgeoning of knowledge about our own history and the histories of other cultures that has taken place over the past century has profoundly affected the ideology which originally gave rise to these disciplines. Just as improved communication has "contracted" physical space, bringing peoples and cultures into a single world and eroding cultural differences, so increased knowledge has "compacted" historical time and diminished the differences between the past and the present. Today we know virtually as much about ancient Greece as about eighteenth-century France, and as much about eighteenth-century France as about twentieth-century America. The past, whether recent or remote, has become as available as the present. Moreover, the differences will diminish still further because the now recent past (since the 1940's) will

---

[41] Heilbroner, *The Future as History,* p. 22.
[42] "A Definition of the Concept of History," p. 8.

be preserved on photographs, film, videotape, phonograph records, tape recordings, and the like. When the world history of music can be purchased in any record shop, what does it mean to say that Beethoven is in the past? His music is just as readily heard as that of Boulez— more so! In art, "all styles become wholly present and simultaneous." [43] In literature the past is not only readily at hand in new inexpensive editions, but it is vividly re-presented on film and recordings. Though he may exaggerate somewhat, Marshall McLuhan states the case clearly: "Since new, empathic methods of art and cultural analysis give us easy access to all the modalities of human sensibility we are no longer limited to a perspective of past societies. We recreate them." [44] The experiential difference between past and present will probably seem less striking in the future. For though the events of the mid-twentieth century will become chronologically remote, our great-grandchildren's experience of our times will perhaps not be experientially very different from their experience of their own in, say, the year, 2065: they will be able to hear and see Lyndon B. Johnson, even as they do their own President; watch civil rights demonstrations, even as they watch their own social action groups; listen to Stravinsky conduct his music, just as they do their own composers.

The events of history become more relevant and more available as the intellectual and psychological distinction between past and present becomes attenuated. Until the twentieth century, one of the important differences between the two was that the past seemed more orderly (even when in turmoil, since this was understood teleologically), more understandable, and even more meaningful than the present. This was partly due to faith in the Idea of Progress. For if one believed in progress, then the myriad of alternative consequences which might have followed a past event could, in effect, be ignored: only the realized and supposedly necessary consequences needed to figure in explanation and understanding. The meaning of history was blatantly chronocentric: the past was used not merely to explain, but to justify, the present. But our enormous wealth of information about the past, coupled with a disenchantment with the idea of necessary, teleological processes in history, now makes the past seem just as intricate and perplexing (if not quite as uncertain) as the present. The day in which historical distance lent idyllic enchantment is over. The motivation of Oedipus was complex. The noble savage is no more.

---

[43] Ellman and Feidelson, *The Modern Tradition,* p. 456.
[44] *The Gutenberg Galaxy,* p. 60.

The Probability of Stasis

The change is not merely one of degree of relevance; it is also a change in kind of relevance. The demise of the Idea of Progress and of the belief in final truths has changed the roles of past and present. As long as history was thought to be inevitable and purposeful, the past had only an ancillary relevance—that of preparation. Its childish and faltering ideas were but naïve steps on the way to present truth. But once development is viewed *from* the past *to* the present and yesterday's truths are given sympathetic respect and understanding, the past is no longer radically different, at least in this respect. Past and present are chronologically separate but epistemologically equal.

History is no longer a picture in receding perspective with a vanishing point in the past—a perspective, which the artist uses only to focus attention upon some central figure or event in the foreground. Rather it is like a Chinese scroll painting which, though it can be scanned as a whole, is usually studied in sections, the limits of the sections—the patterns discovered—depending in part on the structure of the historical content and in part upon the interest of the viewer. But the picture is such that each part is an equally important and detailed configuration of events.

FORMALISM IN THE ARTS AND CRITICISM

The tendency to minimize the distinction between past and present is also evident in the prevalence of formalism in the arts and in criticism. According to this view, a work of art has its complete meaning within itself.

> Basic for contemporary practice and for knowledge of past art is the theoretical view that what counts in all art are the elementary aesthetic components, the qualities and relationships of the fabricated lines, spots, colors, and surfaces. These have two characteristics: they are intrinsically expressive, and they tend to constitute a coherent whole. The same tendencies to coherent and expressive structure are found in the arts of all cultures. . . . Such ideas are accepted by most students of art today, although not applied with uniform conviction.[45]

Subject matter is accorded merely "plastic," not representational, significance, and the importance of that aspect of the plastic arts which would most obviously distinguish the past from the present is minimized.

---

[45] Meyer Schapiro, "Style," p. 282.

History is irrelevant.[46] A corollary of this view is the contention that the genesis of the art work—the history of the artist and his tradition—are of no importance in the appreciation and understanding of the art work itself. Thus Harold Rosenberg writes:

> Everyone knows that the label Modern Art no longer has any relation to the words that compose it. To be Modern Art a work need not be either modern nor art; it need not even be a work. A three thousand-year-old mask from the South Pacific qualifies as Modern and a piece of wood found on a beach becomes Art.[47]

Formalism has, of course, not been confined to criticism. Rather, it happened the other way around: formalist criticism was developed to explain—indeed, to justify—developments in the plastic arts. The tendency to emphasize the central importance of purely plastic values, as distinguished from representational ones, is obvious in cubism, geometric abstract art, abstract expressionism, and, more recently, in Op art. Where representation is present, it is assumed, by artists as well as critics, to be the vehicle for the presentation of the *real* stuff of painting—color, line, texture, and their organization.

In music, composers have tended to embrace formalism with greater ardor than have critics, though academic criticism and that of composers have in general discussed music in technical, formal terms. Emulating the development of abstract formal systems in logic and mathematics, a number of composers have sought to develop more or less formal systematic procedures for limiting choices; and some have evidenced formalist proclivities in the use of conceptual terms borrowed from the sciences—particularly from quantum mechanics.[48] Still other critics have, as we have seen, attempted to create a formal model based upon ideas suggested by the mathematical theory of information.

In literature, the trend toward formalism has been less in evidence. Perhaps this is partly because, as noted earlier, formal organization is not a primary mode of structuring in literature, and partly because one can never escape from reference in literature—language is necessarily a

---

[46] See Clive Bell, quoted on p. 55, above.

[47] *The Tradition of the New*, p. 36; also see Munro Beardsley, "On the Creation of Art," pp. 301–2. I cannot forbear calling attention to the paradoxical conjunction of the idea that history is irrelevant with the idea that novelty is a value. For if chronological context is beside the point, how can one know what is novel at all? In a thoroughgoing formalist position, novelty is not merely irrelevant, it is unknowable. Conversely, if novelty is a basis for value, then history must become the foundation of criticism.

[48] See below, chap. 10.

way of referring to events in the "real" world. Nevertheless, an ahistoricism, which deprecates the significance of ethical, social, and time-bound historical, cultural values while stressing the importance of internal, structural values, has been of some importance. Thus, for instance, Ellmann and Feidelson observe that "the main bent of symbolist theory, whether in relation to nature or to abstract thought, is to preserve the autonomy of art. . . . With reckless single-mindedness, art expresses nothing but itself." [49]

If art expresses nothing but itself, if it is self-contained with respect to meaning, then who made it or when it was created makes no difference. The constructivist-formalist doctrine is neither chronocentric nor ethnocentric. If the present is not seen as the result of an inevitable goal-directed process and if earlier events are differentiated from later ones historically, but not psychologically or epistemologically, then the past can be as meaningful, relevant, and valuable as the present. Indeed, as I hope to show in chapter 9, this doctrine makes possible, at least in principle, the use of past styles.

The constructivist world is pluralistic within, as well as between, disciplines. Not only will different contemporary styles be able to grow side by side—Boulez and Cage as well as Barber; Warhol and de Kooning as well as Wyeth; Robbe-Grillet as well as Beckett or Bellow—but past styles will be able to coexist with these as valid, viable, and potentially vital constructs. Similarly, it will in principle be possible for the West to borrow from other cultures.

Change will be possible. But the invention of new constructs or the revival of earlier ones will not necessarily, or even probably, produce cumulative development. Rather, because the constructs are considered to be formal entities theoretically independent of one another, change will tend to take the form of a fluctuating stasis. Thus, even while asserting that novelty is a central value, Rosenberg implies that change will probably not be cumulative: ". . . a supreme Value has emerged in our time, the Value of the *new*. . . . This Value is a completely fluid one. . . . Modern Art does not have to be actually new, it only has to be new to *somebody*." [50] Formalism neither precludes change and novelty, nor does it foster them. For if one construct is as valuable and viable as another, then there is no need actively to search for, or to create, novelty. Since the new is not "better" or more pertinent than the old, stylistic change should not in itself be a desideratum.

---

[49] *The Modern Tradition*, p. 12.
[50] *The Tradition of the New*, p. 37.

TOWARD IMPERSONALITY AND OBJECTIVITY

Like the Idea of Progress, the idea of individual genius and the correlative concept of art as personal expression—both of which evolved during the seventeenth century and developed until the end of the nineteenth century—tended to encourage cumulative change. Tracing the origins of the concept of musical genius to ideological changes which began in the Renaissance, Professor Edward E. Lowinsky shows that the concept of genius was intimately associated with correlative ideas of creativity, personal expression, and originality. In the post-Renaissance world, "Invention and originality distinguish genius from talent. Talent imitates: genius creates. . . . [Creation is] making something new, something that the world had not seen or heard before, something fresh, original, personal." [51] Since they can be known only in terms of an existing common practice, the emphasis placed upon individual expression and originality led to departures from traditional norms and established rules. "In transcending the rules, genius opens new vistas and music gains new dimensions of expressiveness. Any musical device, to reach the sphere of emphatic expression, must border on the limits of the permissible or, indeed, cross over them. Any work of genius must exceed the limitations of the ordinary." [52]

These ideas about the nature of artistic creativity appeared to be amply confirmed by experience in other areas of the culture. Science had triumphed by overthrowing the "rules"—scholastic philosophy. Its striking successes, together with those of technology, made it seem obvious that creativity was equivalent to the discovery of novelty. To progress was to change.

The prestige accorded to originality and individual expression strongly encouraged change.[53] But the idea of expression through deviation presupposes the existence and viability of traditional norms. Consequently, this sort of change must be permutational and evolutionary

---

[51] "Musical Genius—Evolution and Origins of a Concept," pp. 493–94.

[52] *Ibid.*, p. 493. I suggested in *Emotion and Meaning in Music* that composers "by their very nature as creators and makers" tend to change styles (pp. 69–71). I would now want to limit the relevance of this suggestion to the development of Western music from about 1450 to 1950.

[53] This also appears to be the case in other cultures. According to Alan P. Merriam, "change and receptivity to change will be more frequent in those cultures which stress the importance of the individual composer" (*The Anthropology of Music*, p. 305).

rather than combinational and revolutionary. That is, change must be cumulative and developmental.

Belief in the power of the individual and in the significance of personal expression which had been a central tenet of Western thought since the beginning of the seventeenth century has been fading rapidly in recent years. Henley's lines:

> I am the master of my fate:
> I am the captain of my soul

have come to seem somewhat pompous—a bit arrogant. The genius, the brilliant creator struggling alone with momentous discoveries or decisive decisions, has given way to the research group, the managerial team, and the governing committee. The arts, particularly the arts of mass media, also involve group activity in which the final *product* (a more precise word than creation)—a motion picture, television show, or Broadway musical—is the result of conference and compromise among script writer, director, actors, producer, and so forth. Impersonality characterizes human relationships: the master-pupil relationship has given way to the class of 500 and the television lecture; the physician-patient relationship has been replaced by the clinic of efficient but detached specialists; the intimacy of the personal has yielded to the impersonal mass.

In the arts, impersonality has taken different forms. In general, it has meant that "we must no longer confuse humanism with romantic individuality or with an anthropomorphic view that put the self at the center of things." [54] An artist's, poet's, or composer's chief aim is not to express his individual personality but to present an impersonal objective view of the world or general principles of order. Thus, T. S. Eliot maintains that "Poetry is not a turning loose of emotion, but an escape from emotion; it is not the expression of personality, but an escape from personality." [55] A new objectivity is called for in which the writer describes and depicts the particularity and concreteness of things. "Instead of [a] universe of 'signification' (psychological, social, functional) we must try to construct a world both more solid and more immediate." [56] Thus those writers who emphasize the abstract and the formal are related to those who seek to be absolutely literal, to deal only

---

[54] Wylie Sypher, *Loss of the Self* . . . , p. 14.

[55] *Selected Essays*, p. 21.

[56] Alain Robbe-Grillet, "Dehumanizing Nature," p. 364.

with concrete particulars; for both seek to be objective and impersonal.

In the plastic arts, impersonal objectivity is clearly shown in Pop art and *objets trouvés* in which the artist bases his work on someone else's "creation." It is not *his*—nor perhaps does it even belong to the man who "made" it, but to the culture at large. And the people depicted are not as a rule individuals but stock characters in stock situations.[57] Similarly, constructions—a series of spoons, campaign buttons, or what-not embedded in plastic, or parts of an automobile welded together, or the play of geometric shapes—are not personal expressions or even commentaries on the "vulgarity" of the culture. They are simple presentational objects—facts. Op art, too, is a kind of objective formalism. "The establishment of abstract painting has made it permissible for color, tone, line and shape to operate autonomously. . . . Stripped of conceptual associations, habits, and references to previous experience, perceptual responses would appear to follow innate laws." [58]

In music, impersonality and objectivity take other forms. The composer who works with predetermined formulas for the pitch, time, timbre, and dynamic series of his piece, and then merely follows these, is not involved in the configurations and combinations which result. Thus, "Anton Webern conceived the row non-subjectively, so that to a certain extent it functioned externally," [59] and Boulez's composition *Structures Ia* "proceeds logically from the selected elements, and he wants to leave it pure, to let it 'be itself,' so to speak." [60] Similarly, the composer who allows random events to choose for him is being objective and impersonal. [61] And, of course, the final stage of impersonality takes place where the musician programs rules for a computer and allows the computer to do the composing. The case is clearly stated by Ernst Krenek:

> One of the most antitraditional features common to all of these new endeavors is a tendency toward depersonalization of the act of composing. Whether the composer subjects his creative activity to a set of self-chosen rules preordering every phase of the work-in-progress,

---

[57] Despite its obviously representational character, Pop art is, I think, anti-illusionist. By "blowing up" the comic strip or repeating the photographic image through a silk screen process, it emphasizes the artificiality and spuriousness of the illusion; and, by extension, the aesthetic illusion in general. See below, pp. 212–13.

[58] William C. Seitz, *The Responsive Eye*, p. 7.

[59] Herbert Eimert, "What Is Electronic Music?" p. 6.

[60] György Ligeti, "Pierre Boulez," p. 41.

[61] See John Cage quoted on pp. 68–69, above.

or whether he limits his action to registering the results of chance operations that by definition are beyond his control, in any event he does not present any longer the image (established by tradition of long standing) of the sovereign master who, under the uplifting power of free inspiration, creates at will new and original musical shapes that will transmit the message of his heart to properly attuned audiences.[62]

The concept of art as objective and impersonal is obviously related to the current tendency toward formalism. The artist, like the scientist, "discovers"; and he no longer "creates" by expressing himself; he constructs. Music becomes allied to formal logic or mathematics. The novel becomes a kind of research or a species of problem-solving.

If the individuality and personal will of the artist is no longer considered significant and central, if making an art work is a discovery rather than a creation, then it becomes more or less irrelevant who created a given art work or when it was created. Art becomes anonymous. Thus, according to von Hoffmansthal, "Our time is unredeemed. . . . And do you know what it wants to be redeemed from? The individual. . . . We are anonymous. . . . Individuality is an arabesque we have discarded." [63] Similarly, Pierre Boulez writes, "If it were necessary to find a profound motive for the work I have tried to describe, it would be the search for . . . 'anonymity,' " [64] And Hans Arp tells us that "the works of concrete art should not be signed by their creators; these paintings, these sculptures, these objects, should remain anonymous in the great studio of nature like clouds, mountains, seas, animals, men." [65] The personality and even the identity of the artist are irrelevant for criticism. The value of a work of art "is independent of the manner of production, even of whether the work was produced by an animal or by a computer or by a volcano or by a falling slop bucket." [66]

Insofar as the belief in individualism and self-expression encouraged developmental change in the arts, that cause of change is virtually nonexistent today. Though the search for novelty still seems to persist, it is in most cases (see p. 220) an anachronistic, paradoxical one—

<hr>

[62] "Tradition in Perspective," p. 36. In a similar vein, Boulez is quoted as having said, "Our problem is to make a new musical language . . . to annihilate the will of the composer in favor of a predetermining system" (Harold C. Schonberg, "Very Big Man of Avant-Garde," p. 11).

[63] Quoted in Sypher, *Loss of the Self* . . . , p. 16.

[64] "Sonate, que me veux-tu?" p. 44.

[65] "Concrete Art," p. 52.

[66] Beardsley, "On the Creation of Art," p. 301.

incongruous with the ahistorical constructivism and the objective impersonality which characterize the new ideology.[67]

TRANSCENDENTAL PARTICULARISM

In order to describe and comprehend the complexity of things and
events, formalists analyze the world into sets of interrelated, but nonetheless theoretically discrete, hierarchic systems; and it explains these
constructs in terms of relatively simple, isolated, specifiable, and time-
directed causal processes. As knowledge has grown through improved
methods of analysis and experiment, as well as more refined techniques
of observation, large hierarchic systems have been found to be composed of subsystems. With each further division of experiential wholes
into subhierarchies, this picture of the world has come to seem more
abstract and artificial. Though new disciplines such as the mathematical
theory of communication and the theory of games may provide bridges
between different areas of inquiry by relating them to a single model or
set of hypotheses, it appears unlikely that analytic formalism will develop a high-level theory capable of synthesizing the multiplicity and
diversity which it has produced into a single, encompassing view of the
universe.[68]

Reacting against this abstract and fragmented picture of the world, as

---

[67] It is relevant to observe that the history of the arts in other cultures suggests a
more than incidental connection beween impersonality and stasis. Thus in China
from the Han to the Sung period, art was, according to Max Loehr, essentially based
upon a single ideological set: "for about twelve hundred years the representational trend continued without serious disruption" ("Some Fundamental Issues in
the History of Chinese Painting," p. 42). This stasis was coupled with an objectivity in which the nature of the artist was revealed, but without willfulness—the explicit, conscious goal of self-expression (see *ibid.*, and James F. Cahill, "Confucian Elements in the Theory of Painting." There appears to have been a similar
coupling of stasis and impersonality in the art of India, which, as we have already
noted, remained stable for generations. Pravas Jivan Chaudhury writes of the mind
of the Indian poet that "all self-interest or eccentricity or individual predilection are
shed away; the mind gets disinterested, yet not indifferent to objects, rather it is absorbed in them" ("Indian Poetics," p. 291). And elsewhere Chaudhury observes
that *rasa*, one of the central concepts of Hindu poetry, "is realized when . . . the
self loses its egoistic, pragmatic aspect and assumes an impersonal contemplative
attitude" ("The Theory of Rasa," p. 148).

[68] Contemporary philosophy "unites" by considering kinds of arguments, the
structure of theories, and the nature of knowledge, rather than by discovering previously unnoticed facts, relationships, or causal connections between separate hierarchic systems or different levels of the same system.

well as against nineteenth-century beliefs about individualism, progress, and teleology, already discussed, one significant current in contemporary thought, which I previously called "radical empiricism" [69] but would now prefer to call "transcendental particularism," has in one way or another sought to emphasize the interrelatedness of the world and the concreteness of our experience of it. Partly because of its emphasis on the significance and reality of immediate sense experience, transcendentalism has appealed more to artists, writers, and composers than to scholars, philosophers, or scientists. And because it is essentially an attitude toward experience rather than a method for studying and organizing experience, it appears in a number of somewhat different variants—though all are agreed on fundamental beliefs. Despite basic and deep differences of views on some issues, however, analytic formalism and transcendental particularism complement each other and, as we shall have occasion to point out, agree about several very important ideological tenets.

According to transcendentalism, the constructs of analytic formalism—whether in the arts or in the sciences—misrepresent and distort our understanding of the world. What are truly real, and really true, are concrete, particular sense experiences. These are what we know. The rest is inference. Theories and hypotheses, hierarchies and relationships, are abstract, artificial extrapolations which come between man and the unique, existent facts of the universe. When perception is ordered in terms of such abstract conceptual categories, the primordial, concrete immediacy of things is obscured. We see a circle rather than *this* incomparable red roundness; we hear this chord as, say, a dominant-seventh, functionally related to the chord which follows, rather than as a singular combination of sounds valuable in themselves; and we feel emotions in terms of the classificatory arrangements institutionalized by our culture rather than as unique, incomparable responses. "At every instant," writes Robbe-Grillet, "a continuous fringe of culture (psychology, ethics, metaphysics, etc.) is being added to things, disguising their real strangeness, making them more comprehensible, more reassuring." [70] To experience the poignant, deep-down freshness of things, we must get rid of preconceived categories, including those arising from personal goals and private desires. The world should be perceived and experienced, not in terms of self-interest, but objectively and disinterestedly; and art should be created in the same way. On this

---

[69] In chap. 5.

[70] "Dehumanizing Nature," p. 363.

point, analytic formalism and transcendental particularism are in essential agreement, though for very different reasons. Consequently, insofar as objectivity weakens the tendency toward cumulative change, transcendentalism also favors stasis.

NON-TELEOLOGY

Metaphysical frameworks, metaphoric language, and psychological theories are also rejected because, since they are the source for prediction and expectation, desire and hope, they are the cause of disappointment, frustration, and anxiety. Thus Herbert Kohl writes: "Robbe-Grillet feels that Sartre is anguished over objects *because he expects answers from them. . . . Ultimately, it is human expectations, and not the world of objects, that gives rise to despair.*" [71] In order to perceive and understand the world as it really is, man must give up purpose, strivings, and goal-directed behavior. Teleological explanations are misleading and anthropomorphic. Man is part of nature. And just as nature has no purpose—it simply is, it *exists*—so it should be with man and with the art he invents.[72]

Though there are differences of degree among those taking the transcendentalist position, transcendentalists are in general more emphatic in their rejection of teleology than are analytic formalists. For the former altogether reject the teleological view—the functional view of the universe in terms of separable, specifiable causes; the latter tend to argue that while it is best to avoid teleological explanations, the difference between teleological and non-teleological statements has to do with the way in which theories are formulated. As Ernest Nagel points out, "despite the *prima facie* distinctive character of teleological (or functional) explanations . . . they can be reformulated, without loss of asserted content, to take the form of non-teleological ones, so that in an important sense, teleological and non-teleological explanations are equivalent." [73] Once again—though again for different reasons—analytic formalism and transcendental particularism are essentially agreed. And again both positions suggest the probability of stasis. For,

[71] *The Age of Complexity*, p. 222.

[72] Moreover, if, as G. J. Whitrow suggests, "The psychological origin of the concept of time is . . . to be found in the conscious realization of the distinction between desire and satisfaction" (*The Natural Philosophy of Time*, p. 52), then such an anti-teleological attitude is consonant with a timeless view of the world which, as we shall see, is an important tenet of transcendental particularism.

[73] *The Structure of Science*, p. 403; and in general see pp. 401–28.

insofar as goal-directed attitudes and beliefs have in the past encouraged change, an explicitly antiteleological posture removes that cause and permits, perhaps even favors, stasis.

A paradox is evidently latent in some versions of the transcendentalist position. On the one hand, by disparaging purposeful behavior, it tends to discourage (or is at least neutral with respect to) change; on the other hand, the belief that traditional constructs and categories distort human experience tends to encourage change—because novelty is always becoming "traditional" and established: today's innovation becomes tomorrow's norm. Observe, however, that the novelty nurtured by such a view will consciously eschew continuity—that is, basing the new upon the old. Whatever change takes place would be explicitly noncumulative, producing not style development but fluctuating stasis.

ART AND NATURE

Among the traditional categories and distinctions which transcendentalism would discard is the bifurcation of the world into art versus nature or art versus life. Says Hans Arp:

> I became more and more removed from aesthetics. I wanted to find another order, another value for man in nature. He was no longer to be the measure of all things, no longer to reduce everything to his own measure, but on the contrary, all things and man were to be like nature, without measure.[74]

And Harold Rosenberg tells us that "the new painting has broken down every distinction between art and life." [75] Art and nature are one. Only our traditional metaphysical "baggage" makes us separate them. As art ceases (which it should) to be teleological, it will become more like nature—and, like nature, it will become objective and impersonal.

If the distinction between art and nature is mistaken, aesthetic valuation is irrelevant. One should no more judge the value of a piano sonata than one should judge the value of a stone, a thunderstorm, or a starfish. "Categorical statements, such as right and wrong, beautiful or ugly, typical of the rationalistic thinking of tonal aesthetics," writes Luciano Berio, "are no longer useful in understanding why and how a composer today works on audible forms and musical action." [76]

This view is evidently quite different from that of analytic formalism,

---

[74] "Concrete Art," p. 49.
[75] *The Tradition of the New*, p. 28.
[76] "Form," p. 140.

which seems to encourage such distinctions. The positions approach one another, however, in that analytic formalism also tends to minimize the distinction between art and nature. According to analytic formalism we know what nature is only in terms of the constructs which science or myth provides to explain and order the world. Such constructs are conditioned truths, not absolute knowledge. The validation and valuation of constructs is, at least partly, an aesthetic consideration, having to do with the artistry with which the artifice, the theory, is made and justified. "I now have the conviction," writes Freeman Tilden, "that pure science is pure art." [77] Teggart observes that "the academic historian, no less than his predecessor, is engaged in the construction of a work of art." [78] The difference—and it is a real difference—between transcendental particularism and analytic formalism is that the former minimizes the art-nature distinction by absorbing art into nature, while the latter tends toward a similar result by absorbing nature (the constructs of science) into art.

CAUSATION AND EXPLANATION

If, as most transcendentalists emphasize, only specific, concrete facts, not the relationships between them, are real, then causation becomes a fiction and casual explanation a delusion. Thus, Wylie Sypher points out that Nathalie Sarraute "has learned what the nineteenth-century scientists never learned—observation is more revealing than explanation. She is not at pains to account for her findings, but prefers a true phenomenalism, asserting nothing beyond the data"; [79] and "Ionesco discards the laws of cause and effect on which both theater and science had been built." [80] To understand the world, including the arts, in terms of organic processes and abstract causes is a mistake. As Henri Pousseur, a leading French composer, says, "if the deep significance of Webern's mission lies in the fragmentation of musical shape, the immanent concretizing of everything momentary; then is it not precisely this criterion of organic quality that is called into question?" [81]

Causal explanation is called into question not merely because it is "abstract" but because it cannot adequately account for the unique

---

[77] "Not by Truth Alone," p. 1416.

[78] *Theory and Processes of History*, p. 35.

[79] *Loss of the Self* . . . , p. 89.

[80] *Ibid.*, p. 99. Sypher is mistaken if he intends to suggest that science has in fact given up causal explanation. See Nagel, *The Structure of Science*, chap. 10.

[81] "Outline of a Method," p. 80.

individuality of the particular, which is what is really important and significantly real. Even in the physical world, where there appears to be a high degree of order and regularity, science does not attempt or claim to explain every particular attribute of an object or event—for instance, the specific colors and cloud formations of *this* sunset, every detail of the circulatory system of this organism at this moment, and so on. In human affairs, where the variables are much more numerous and more intricately intertwined, the possibility of explaining the uniqueness of an event seems remote indeed. The discoveries of Freud and his co-workers made simplistic explanations of human behavior impossible. H. Stuart Hughes observes that

> it was apparent to Freud that at the unconscious level the deter-mination of choice was by no means a simple affair. It was custo-marily a question of plural causation; most psychic events were "over-determined." Hence it was usually impossible to ascribe to them a mechanical one-to-one relationship of cause to effect.[82]

Causal explanation in the social sciences tends to avoid explaining the particular altogether. It is concerned with general trends, statistical frequencies, and normative behavior patterns. Thus, we can predict approximately how many people will die in automobile accidents over a Labor Day weekend—but not who they will be. And one can scarcely blame the artist, who is by nature and training sensitively concerned with the concrete and the particular, for being offended by the callous-ness of such abstract information.

It is not necessary, on this view, to deny the existence of cause and effect. If, because only particulars are real, one wishes to account for every single attribute of an object or an event—whatever makes it the unique thing it is—then every possible cause is a necessary cause and all necessary causes are equally important. Since there is "an incalculable infinity" of such causes,[83] the unique individuality of things can never be fully explained. Causal explanation is not *in principle* impossible, but it is so in actual fact.

Though analytic formalism and transcendental particularism are clearly in conflict regarding the efficacy of causal explanation, it should be emphasized that they do not necessarily disagree about either the existence or the nature of causation. The conflict has to do not with *how* something is to be explained but rather with *what* is to be explained: whether an archetypal process or an unique event, whether a general

---

[82] *Consciousness and Society,* pp. 133–34.
[83] See John Cage, quoted on p. 78, above.

class or a specific fact. It is important to observe that if the possibility of definitive causal explanation (the only kind that will adequately explain the uniqueness of events) is denied, the future cannot be intelligently predicted. And to preclude the possibility of intelligent prediction is to deny the possibility of rational choice—since the latter necessarily depends upon the former. If choice is willfully arbitrary, capriciously anti-traditional, or just plain random, the changes to which it leads will tend to be non-cumulative—to produce stasis.

TIME, ORDER, AND HIERARCHIC STRUCTURES

If only unique particulars, not the causal connections between them, are real, then no event either presumes or implies the existence of any other event. If events are without implication, it makes no difference in what temporal arrangement they are experienced or described. The world is, to all intents and purposes, without directed time. Moreover, even though the existence of causation be admitted, human time is without direction when attention is focused exclusively on the uniqueness of particulars. Let us see why this is so.

To be perceived and understood hierarchically, an event-system must be what Herbert A. Simon has called "decomposable." That is, the strengths of interactions within and between hierarchic levels and systems must be of different orders of magnitude. The "forces" holding some parts of a hierarchy together must be different in strength and in kind from others. Simon writes:

> We have seen that hierarchies have the property of near-decomposability. Intra-component linkages are generally stronger than inter-component linkages. This fact has the effect of separating the high-frequency dynamics of a hierarchy—involving the internal structure of the components—from the low frequency dynamics—involving interaction among components.[84]

When, however, attention is directed only to the uniqueness of things, then each and every attribute of an object or event is equally significant and necessary. There can be no degrees of connectedness within or between events. But if each and every cause of any event is equally important and relevant, the world cannot be perceived or understood hierarchically. To look at the matter somewhat differently, hierarchic

---

[84] "The Architecture of Complexity," p. 477, and in general the section on "Nearly Decomposable Systems," pp. 473–77.

systems are possible because there is redundancy within and between systems. An event which is without any redundancy whatsoever is its own simplest description.[85] To concern oneself only with the uniqueness of events is to picture a non-redundant and, consequently, a non-hierarchic universe. Many of the artists of transcendentalism have recognized this connection between emphasis on the concrete particular and the creation of non-hierarchic succession. Henri Pousseur, for instance, tells us that in the new music, "even very closely related shapes will be grasped as specific events, not to be identified with each other; . . . any impression of repetition . . . will be excluded, and one will no longer be conscious, neither between the various structures nor between the elements, of a flavorising, periodic and polarized hierarchy of events. This in fact appears to be the essential condition for a correct attitude to the new musical sensibility." [86]

There are, no doubt, many reasons why, as Norbert Wiener put it, "we are directed in time, and our relation to the future is different from our relation to the past." [87] One reason why human time appears to have direction is, I suspect, because we perceive and understand the world in terms of hierarchic systems.[88] A hierarchic structure is functionally unidirectional. It necessarily moves from relatively simple elements to more complex, composite structures. A non-hierarchic change existing in time—for instance, a crescendo of sound or a progressive increase in illumination—can be reversed without loss of meaning. But a hierarchic process cannot be reversed without loss of meaning and pattern unless, of course, the hierarchy itself is reversible—has the form of a symmetri-

---

[85] See *ibid.*, p. 478. Because in such a non-redundant world works of art cannot be described in simpler terms, criticism necessarily consists of: (*a*) an itemized list of the attributes of the art work, (*b*) a "translation" of such a list into a poetic-verbal analogue, (*c*) an account of the "rules" involved in the construction of the work, or (*d*) a discussion (such as is being presented here) of the cultural-ideological significance of the art work, rather than an analysis of its internal relationships and meanings. And these have in fact been the modes of criticism employed in dealing with the art of transcendentalism. (These matters are discussed in more detail in chapters 11 and 12.)

[86] "Outline of a Method," p. 66.

[87] *Cybernetics*, p. 44. Also see Martin Gardner, "Can Time Go Backward?"

[88] It is not enough to argue, as G. J. Whitrow does, that "whatever the laws of nature, the direction of time in our personal experience is the direction of increasing knowledge of events" (*The Natural Philosophy of Time*, p. 270). For "events" are themselves defined by the existence of some degree of closure—of patterned decomposability. In a world without hierarchies—a world of unique particulars—there would be no separable events to "know." And, consequently, perhaps no sense of temporal order and direction.

cally shaped time event: A–O–W–O–A. A Beethoven symphony cannot be played backwards; nor can the order of its parts, which are functionally implicative, be changed. In the non-functional, non-hierarchic music of transcendental particularism, however, temporal direction and order are, appropriately, variable. Thus, Karlheinz Stockhausen writes of his music that "the structure of the piece is not presented as a sequence of development in time, but rather as a *directionless time-field* in which the individual groups also have no particular direction in time." [89] Similarly, it is perhaps because the microscopic events of quantum mechanics are described in statistical rather than functional-hierarchic terms that "on the sub-atomic level, there may be no consistent direction of time." [90] From this point of view, it is neither surprising nor preposterous that the artists of transcendentalism should find the model provided by microphysics particularly attractive.

For other artists and writers, the model of mental behavior provided by Bergson, Freud, and Jung led to a breaking up of temporal direction. ". . . the notion of the unconscious as the storehouse of imperishable memory recurs again and again in the early twentieth-century novel. An obsession with *duration* . . . is forever returning. A sense of time as it is actually lived, of the work of the unconscious in lengthening and foreshortening it, of its twists and deceptions gives its special flavor to Alain-Fournier's *Le Grand Meaulnes*, to Mann's *The Magic Mountain*, and, most characteristically, to Proust's *Remembrance of Things Past*." [91]

Like analytic formalism, transcendental particularism repudiates the Idea of Progress—but for different reasons. The former denies the possibility of progress on what are essentially empirical grounds. The latter, on the other hand, rejects the *idea* of progress per se—not only because teleology is misguided and rational choice an illusion but because in a world without definite and consistent temporal order the very idea of moving toward or away from anything is an impossible

---

[89] "How Time Passes," p. 36.

[90] Whitrow, *The Natural Philosophy of Time*, p. 312. Whitrow's statement apparently contradicts the view that because the behavior of microstates is governed by the law of entropy, they are necessarily uni-directional with respect to time. It is possible, however, that the directionality of time depends upon the hierarchic level being considered: the action of individual particles may be "without temporal direction," but the collection of particles may, as a statistical aggregate, obey the law of entropy and therefore be directed in time.

[91] Hughes, *Consciousness and Society*, p. 366.

absurdity. And if progress is impossible, it is pointless to encourage change.

Not only is time without consistent direction but its segmentation into past, present, and future is open to serious question. To see why this is so, it must be recalled that transcendentalism has two related branches. One contends that only particulars are real. Causation is a fiction; implication, an illusion. Since the past is related to the present, and the present to the future, in terms of the implications which earlier events are presumed to have for later ones, in a world without causation or implication there can be no temporal divisions. Past and future coexist in an all-encompassing, but fluctuating, present.

The other branch of transcendentalism reaches the same conclusion but for somewhat different reasons. While admitting the reality of causation, it insists that all things in all of time and space are inextricably connected with one another. Any divisions, classifications, or organizations discovered in the universe are arbitrary. The world is a complex, continuous, single event. Or, to look at the matter somewhat differently, if one is to escape from disappointment and frustration, one must, as Robbe-Grillet points out, give up expecting answers from the world. One can give up expecting answers only if one moves from the level of being *in* the universe, where choices and hence goals are unavoidable, to being *out* of it—on the transcendental level where time, and hence purpose, no longer obtain. That is, one must move to a hierarchic level in which the universe is seen as eternal and static. In which there is neither sin nor redemption, sadness or joy, wisdom or folly, love or hate, but merely quiescent existence: position and magnitude, color and shape. To divide temporal duration into past, present, and future is to distort and misrepresent both experience and reality. Everything persists in a timeless present.

The world of transcendental particularism is not only timeless in principle, it is experientially timeless as well. Whether pictured as a vast array of unrelated, unique particulars or as a complex network of inseparable, intersecting relationships, the world, if it is to be truly comprehended, must be experienced as an integral whole. To know and understand the world—in all its transcendent diversity and intricate actuality—as a single indivisible whole, our experience of it must be immediate, intuitive—almost mystic. And it must then be timeless.

That this is the attitude of many transcendentalists is indicated by their attraction to Zen Buddhism and to *some* forms of existentialism. In Zen Buddhism true understanding comes through *satori*—a kind of en-

167

lightenment in which the ultimate oneness of things is revealed.[92] Existentialists, beginning with a concern for the particularity of the concrete —and a concomitant distaste for the abstract and analytical—also move toward a view which is transcendental and timeless. Thus, Hans Meyerhoff writes: "All existentialist thinkers assign to the category of time a central place in their metaphysical systems. . . . The point of departure is . . . temporality, or historicity . . . ; the point of arrival is usually an attempt . . . to . . . 'transcend' this temporally situated mode of man's existence." [93] The interest in hallucinatory states and psychedelic drugs —LSD, for example—is also a sign of the search for a transcendental view in which the complexity and diversity of existence is made coherent and cohesive. A patient under the influence of LSD evidently experienced this sort of view when she reported: "For once I can see the order upon order. What looked like a mess, a confusion, is just the vast complexity of it all, towering layers of interweaving movement. Once you see the pattern of the vortex, it all fits." [94]

Such a vision of an encompassing oneness, a cohesive connectedness, has led artists to picture a static universe in which ordered, sequential time disappears, leaving only a timeless duration. Discussing the sense of time in Alain Resnais's film *Hiroshima, Mon Amour*, Wolfgang A. Luchtung says:

> The phenomenon mentioned above might be described as the prevalence in so much "time-art" of a *perpetual present*. We find it in Lawrence Durrell, in Proust, in Robert Musil's *Der Mann ohne Eigenschaften*, in the new French school of the *antiroman* . . . and, of course, in Alain Resnais himself. . . . The method by which this effect of a perceptual present is achieved may best be circumscribed as a "flattening" of past and future into an even present.[95]

In experimental music "duration in the sense of a process incorporating a human past, present, and future in its stream of movement is," according to George Rochberg, "no longer possible." [96]

If the world of transcendentalism is explicitly and in principle time-

---

[92] "For in Taoism and Zen," writes Alan Watts, "the world is seen as an inseparably interrelated field or continuum, no part of which can actually be separated from the rest or valued above or below the rest" ("Beat Zen, Square Zen, and Zen," p. 7) ; also see D. T. Suzuki, *Zen Buddhism*, chap. 4.

[93] Quoted in Hughes, *Consciousness and Society*, pp. 396–97.

[94] Sidney Cohen, "LSD and the Anguish of Dying," p. 72.

[95] " 'Hiroshima, Mon Amour,' Time, and Proust," p. 308.

[96] "Duration in Music," p. 61. Similarly in painting, visual directionality (from which temporality might be inferred) disappears.

less and static, the world of analytic formalism tends to be so in effect. For if, as formalist criticism contends, all values inhere in the work of art itself so that it makes no difference when or where it was made—or even if it was man-made at all—then from the standpoint of appreciation and perception, all art works coexist equally in the present. Furthermore, since reality and truth are conditional constructs, all pasts are potentially equally relevant for the present. Though this viewpoint does not deny the fact of temporal sequence, it does mean that one may discover relationships with, and find useful models in, epochs which are not chronologically contiguous. Finally it should be observed that in the world of analytic formalism, the chronological distinction between past, present, and even future is itself a function of the constructs being employed. For some purposes an hour ago is the past; for other purposes the present includes Greek culture; and for still others the present is a geological age. For the extent and duration of any specious present depends upon the hierarchic level on which the events being considered take place.

A timeless world, or one in which the distinction among past, present, and future becomes obscured, is static. Quite properly, it is a world without goals, without progress. However actively it may fluctuate, it does not move *toward* anything. And this is perhaps the ultimate paradox: that the philosophy of the avant-garde precludes the possibility of there being an avant-garde. For if the world is static and directionless—a perpetual present—how can the forces of art move toward an objective? [97] The very concept of an avant-garde implies goal-directed motion—the conquest of some new territory. It depends upon the teleological beliefs which both transcendental particularism and analytic formalism call into question. If the Renaissance is over, then the avant-garde is ended.

---

[97] Ackerman writes that the artist cannot move "toward the future. In his terms the future is void—how can he move toward it? If he dreams of its wonders, the dreams themselves, like his art, are creations of the present" ("A Theory of Style," p. 231).

CHAPTER

9

The Aesthetics of Stability

> And therefore I have sailed and come
> To the holy city of Byzantium.
> —W. B. YEATS

Introduction

In the preceding chapters I have tried to show, first, that stasis is possible, both theoretically, because theories that posit necessary evolutions and inevitable developments are not tenable, and empirically, because there have been civilizations in which the arts and other aspects of culture have remained stable for relatively long periods of time. Second, I have argued that recent changes in Western thought and ideology indicate that it is not unreasonable to suppose that our culture—and perhaps a world-wide cosmopolitanism as well—is entering a period of fluctuating stasis, a sort of dynamic steady-state. In this chapter, I shall attempt to sketch in broad outline what the characteristics of such a statis might be and, more specifically, how it may affect the arts.

Before so doing, I should like to emphasize once again that the attempt to understand the present by imagining what might follow it is not unique to this particular endeavor. Any picturing of a historical present entails implicit, if not explicit, predictions and expectations about the future. I am advocating not that we should now predict where we have not previously done so but that we consider the possibility of adopting a different picture of the process of historical style change and, consequently, of the existing cultural situation including its possible future. I am suggesting that, whatever its usefulness may heretofore have been, the paradigm of style history and cultural change which has dominated Western thought since the seventeenth century does not seem able to illuminate or make understandable the situation in the arts today.

The present seems to be aberrant, uncertain, and baffling because the prevalent view of style change—involving notions of progress and teleology, *Zeitgeist* and cultural coherence, necessity and organic development, or some combination of these—posits the eventual establishment of a single common style in each, or even in all, of the arts. As a result, composers as well as critics and historians have come to expect that one dominant style would emerge in the arts—whether as the result of radically new developments, an accommodation of prevailing styles to one another, or the "triumph" of some existing style. Thus Winthrop Sargeant, commenting upon the works of composers who employ quite different styles, says, "The astonishing thing is that these composers all exist at the same time, and the inference to be drawn from this fact is that none of the revolutions has been definitive." [1] And, though composing in an idiom anathema to Mr. Sargeant, Boulez also tacitly assumes a monolithic model of style development, asserting, "Anyone who has not felt . . . the necessity of the 12-tone language is SUPERFLUOUS. For everything he writes will fall short of the imperatives of our time." [2]

But suppose that the paradigm which posits cumulative change and the discovery of a common style is no longer pertinent and viable? Perhaps none of the "revolutions" will be definitive; then astonishment would disappear. Suppose, too, that there are no "imperatives" of the sort that Boulez assumes (Whose imperatives? What is "our time" but the totality of actions, including art works, that take place in it?), and, consequently, that no style is necessarily superfluous. Suppose, in short, that the present pluralism of coexisting styles (each with its particular premises and even its attendant ideology) represents not an anomalous, transient state of affairs, but a relatively stable and enduring one.

I am suggesting not only that such a hypothesis is neither theoretically absurd nor empirically impossible but that, once it is adopted, seemingly incompatible pieces of the puzzling present begin to form an

---

[1] "Twin Bill," p. 88.
[2] Harold Schonberg, "Very Big Man of Avant-Garde," p. 11.

intelligible pattern. If our time appears to be one of "crisis," it does so largely because we have misunderstood the present situation and its possible consequences. Because a past paradigm has led us to expect a monolithic, all-encompassing style, the cultural situation has seemed bizarre and perplexing. The "crisis" dissolves when the possibility of a continuing stylistic coexistence is recognized and the delights of diversity are admitted. The question then becomes not is this style going to be THE STYLE, but is this particular work well-made, challenging, and enjoyable.

The Profile of Pluralism

THE DYNAMICS OF FLUCTUATION

What the proposed hypothesis, then, envisages is the persistence over a considerable period of time of a fluctuating stasis—a steady-state in which an indefinite number of styles and idioms, techniques and movements, will coexist in each of the arts.[3] There will be no central, common practice in the arts, no stylistic "victory." In music, for instance, tonal and non-tonal styles, aleatoric and serialized techniques, electronic and improvised means will all continue to be employed. Similarly in the visual arts, current styles and movements—abstract expressionism and surrealism, representational and Op art, kinetic sculpture and magic realism, Pop and non-objective art—will all find partisans and supporters. Though schools and techniques are less clearly defined in literature, present attitudes and tendencies—the "objective" novel, the theater of the absurd, as well as more traditional manners and means—will, I suspect, persist.

Though new methods and directions may be developed in any or in all of the arts, these will not displace existing styles. The new will simply be additions to the already existing spectrum of styles. Interaction and accommodation among different traditions of music, art, or literature may from time to time produce hybrid combinations or composites, but the possibility of radical innovation seems very remote. As will be suggested, however, the abrupt juxtaposition of markedly unlike styles—perhaps from different epochs and traditions—within a single work may not be uncommon.

---

[3] Pluralism is by no means confined to the arts. Diversity and heterogeneity characterize most disciplines and subjects. Often disparate paradigms or conceptual schemes coexist within a single field. See below.

The Aesthetics of Stability

Though a spectrum of styles will coexist in what is essentially a steady-state, this does not mean that in a given art all methods and idioms will be equally favored at a particular time. In music, for example, one or possibly two of the stylistic options available to composers may for a number of years prove especially attractive; and activity will be most intense in those parts of the stylistic spectrum. But this will not indicate that other traditions and idioms are no longer viable or are declining. For subsequently, fascinated by different problems or swayed by different attitudes, composers will, by and large, turn to other traditions and other styles.

Such a succession of wavelike fluctuations may make it appear as though one style has followed or replaced another. But what will in fact have happened is that one style—or perhaps a group of related styles—will, so to speak, have "crested," becoming for a time particularly conspicuous. And at the very time most composers are riding the crest of the stylistic wave, others will have continued to follow ways and procedures temporarily less popular.

Fluctuation of this sort has, it seems to me, been characteristic of the history of the arts during the past fifty years. Various musical styles have appeared to succeed one another—late romanticism (serial as well as tonal), primitivism, neo-classicism, aleatoric and totally ordered music; but almost all have continued, in one form or another, as ways of making music. Some—for instance, serialism—have already "crested" more than once; none has really disappeared or been replaced. In the plastic arts, where learning a syntax is not involved and the resistance of performers to novelty is not a consideration, fluctuation has been both more rapid and more patent. After a long sequence of styles and movements, beginning with those that followed World War I and continuing through abstract expressionism, action-painting, Pop, Op, and so on, many painters are "returning" to more or less traditional forms of representation, to surrealism and the like. Not that the latter styles were ever really abandoned—only that for a time the majority of artists found them less provocative and exciting than other means and modes.

Though a fluctuating stasis may well be characteristic of present and future changes in the arts, I do not wish to suggest that the rate, direction, or kind of changes exhibited by them will be concurrent or congruent. Sometimes style changes in two or more arts may be simultaneous. In such a case, if the arts in question move in a similar direction—say, toward greater freedom from traditional norms or toward a more meticulous control of means—some common ideological-aesthetic tendency may be involved. At other times, such concurrent changes may simply happen by chance. More often than not, however, each of the arts will probably exhibit its own peculiar pattern of style fluctuation.

The continuing existence of a spectrum of styles is also indicated by the fact that a number of composers, artists, and writers have found it possible to move easily from one practice or tradition to another— according to their interest, taste, or humor. Thus, after developing and writing a number of works in the twelve-tone method, Schönberg found it interesting and not inconsistent occasionally to compose in the idiom of tonal music. In like manner, Picasso has from time to time returned to a neo-classicism which he first employed quite early in his career. If the repertory of available styles grows, as I believe it will, to include many of the styles of earlier Western art [4] and even some from non-Western civilizations, such shifts in style from one work to another will become more common.

This does not imply that all artists, or even a majority of them, will be stylistically polylingual. Many will cultivate only one of the many styles available. (Generally these will, I suspect, be the "Traditionalists" for whom art is a form of personal expression, and whose motto must, accordingly, be: One Man, One Style.) Frequently, too, there will be deep and irreconcilable differences between artists working in different traditions or espousing different ideologies.[5]

Which styles or traditions are preferred by any considerable number of artists at a particular time—and for how long—will depend upon a number of different factors. The ability of one outstanding composer—or perhaps even a group of composers—to write convincing, effective, and interesting music in a particular idiom will be important in attracting others to the style. The challenge and fascination of particular compositional methods and problems may also serve to stimulate a wave of activity in a particular part of the stylistic spectrum. Related to this is the real possibility that one style may be abandoned and another adopted simply because the composer no longer finds the problems and procedures of the first style interesting. At times a conceptual model of order (or disorder), developed in connection with some other art or one of the sciences, may also influence the direction of style change. Nor, as recent history indicates, should one underestimate the role played by theory and criticism in shaping stylistic interests and tendencies. Fi-

---

[4] When the term "art" or "work of art" is used, it will generally mean all the arts. Similarly, when the term "artists" is used alone, it will refer to plastic artists, musicians, writers, and so on.

[5] See Harold Rosenberg, *The Tradition of the New*, pp. 54–55.

nally, the power of patrons, particularly institutional ones—foundations, universities, symphony orchestras, museums, and the like—to encourage or discourage stylistic movements and tendencies may be of considerable importance.

Because they may not necessarily exhibit any consistent direction or pattern, such successive waves of stylistic activity may seem little more than a series of fashions. Possibly so; but the implied value judgment is not warranted. For since in the coming years the criteria of aesthetic value will, according to the present hypothesis, be those of skill and elegance, rather than those of imitation, expression, or social relevance as they have been in the past, style fluctuations occasioned by problems to be solved would not be capricious or merely modish. Just as the scientists, for instance, tend to direct their energies toward sets of problems where developments in one field have made exciting advances and elegant solutions possible (perhaps in a different field)—yesterday in nuclear physics, today in genetics and molecular biology—so, for the composers, musical problems broached or solutions proposed in one segment of the stylistic spectrum may make elegant and fruitful activity in some other segment possible and attractive.

PLURALISM, FLUCTUATION, AND THE AUDIENCE

The role and influence of the audience in the ebb and flow of fluctuation and its relationship to stylistic pluralism are more difficult to assess. One crucial characteristic of the present situation, however, does seem clear and certain: there is not now, and probably will not be, a single cohesive audience for serious art, music, and literature as, broadly speaking, there was until about 1914. Rather, there are and will continue to be a number of different audiences corresponding roughly to broad areas of the spectrum of coexisting styles. Just as some artists, writers, and composers will be stylistically polylingual—changing styles for whatever reason—so one individual may belong to several audiences within the same art.

For music, by far the largest audience will no doubt continue to be that which supports and attends concerts devoted to the standard repertory of eighteenth- and nineteenth-century music. One segment of this audience will also find contemporary tonal music—the music of Barber, Britten, Poulenc, Shostakovich, and others—appealing and moving; another, and different, segment will consist of those who are attracted to somewhat more adventurous music in the modern idiom—say, the music of Bartók, Berg, Hindemith, and Schönberg. Still another subdivision of the standard repertory audience, but distinctly separate from the preceding two, will be made up of the many enthusiasts for Baroque music. Related to this group, but not as a rule to the standard repertory audience, is the growing and appreciative audience for the music of the Middle Ages and the Renaissance. The audience for highly complex experimental music, whether serially organized or not, will remain, as it is now, a distinct and devoted, but very small group. Aleatoric music, particularly in its more theatrical forms, will probably attract a somewhat different group, though members of the audience for experimental music will be part of it. Finally, crossing and overlapping the last three, will be the audience attracted to electronic music of various kinds.

Audience divisions in the other arts seem quite similar. Readers of literature are generally divided in terms of their ability or willingness to cope with syntactic complexity, subtlety of subject, intricacy of narrative and of thought development. Because the continuum of complexity—from the explicitly popular (Irving Stone, S. N. Behrman) through the serious (Faulkner, Shaw, Eliot) to the avant-garde (Beckett, Robbe-Grillet)—is not marked by striking changes in style premises as in music, audiences for literature are less distinct and separate than those for music. Nevertheless, it seems evident that, generally speaking, the readers of Irving Stone are not those of Faulkner or of Ionesco. Nor are they likely to become so—adult education classes or no. Unlike those for music or the visual arts, audiences for literature are sometimes organized in terms of preferred genres—theatergoers, readers of poetry, readers of novels. Once again, one individual may belong to more than one group.

Whatever the antagonisms among contemporary schools and movements in the plastic arts may be,[6] the audience for and patrons of modern art are, on the whole, catholic in their taste, delighting in abstract expressionism and surrealism as well as in Pop, Op, and kinetic art. Individuals will, of course, have preferences within these styles, but the salient division within the art audience is probably drawn along historical lines—art up to and including impressionism versus art after impressionism. Or, to put the matter in other terms, those for whom aesthetic pleasure is closely tied to the expressive and mimetic qualities of the subject represented as against those for whom the plastic qualities of significant form are the primary source of aesthetic value.

Audiences have, of course, always been divided into progressive and conservative, popular and serious. But today the extent of fragmentation

---

[6] *Ibid.*, pp. 60–61.

is considerably greater, the divisions noticeably deeper—and, in music and literature, they have persisted for half a century. Moreover, the situation today is quite different in three other respects from that which has been characteristic in the past.

In the first place, the various audiences for the several arts are neither cohesive with respect to class nor consistent with respect to taste and style. As Harold Rosenberg has pointed out:

> The radical twist in the art situation begins in earnest when the typi-
> cal art audience is no longer recognizable by the insignia of its social
> function. The turnout at a current art show . . . is by comparison
> with the elites of former days a very odd group; not only does it fail
> to represent social authority, it does not even represent its own social
> function as a professional group, since other artists and members of
> the same professions as those present, with an education, income,
> prestige, equivalent to theirs, despise this art.[7]

Not only may members of the same economic, social, and educational group have radically different tastes, but one individual's preferences need show no consistency. Someone fascinated by aleatoric, experimental music may prefer science fiction to the "new" novel. Collectors of expressionist and surrealist painting listen to Schubert, rather than to Schönberg. And readers of avant-garde novels may, at the same time, have a predilection for Baroque sculpture and for the music of India.

This calls attention to the second point, namely, that today's taste is ahistorical and acultural both within and between arts. In the past, Western art audiences have tended to ignore or to denigrate the art which preceded theirs—as well as the art of other cultures. It would not have occurred to a patron of the arts in the seventeenth century to listen to Machaut's music, look at Cimabue's paintings, or read Chaucer's poetry (though he would probably have read the works of Greek and Latin authors). Moreover, if he had chanced upon the work of those earlier masters, he would almost certainly have found the music odious, the paintings primitive, and the poetry coarse. Without doubt he would have found the art of other civilizations beyond the pale. Though there have been times when the art of other cultures and of past epochs was admired and cultivated in the West—for instance, the taste for *chino-iserie* in the eighteenth century and the Pre-Raphaelite movement at the end of the nineteenth—the allure always depended heavily upon the enchantment of the exotic and the supposed superiority of the past. But

---

[7] *Ibid.*, pp. 61–62.

for a twentieth-century audience this appeal is irrelevant: the past is no longer distant, and the distant is no longer mysterious. Today, when the same person may delight in modern jazz and Renaissance polyphony, read Haiku poetry and Berthold Brecht, collect action painting and pre-Columbian art, the attraction of past or foreign art lies neither in the romance of the remote nor the charm of the unusual, but in significance of form and perfection of craft. And though we may discover some thread of consistency, individual preferences are often fortuitous and arbitrary.

Third, because there has, in the past, generally been one common practice—or, if more than one, then the later was destined to replace the earlier—and a single, cohesive audience, artists tended, though perhaps unconsciously, to create for that audience, accommodating their materials and means to its abilities and taste. Today's stylistic pluralism, however, makes it more appropriate for the individual to discover and follow the styles of music, art, and literature which appeal to him, whether because of education or social position, temperament or chance.

As foreseen here, the future, like the present, will hold both a spectrum of styles and a plurality of audiences in each of the arts. There will be no convergence, no stylistic consensus. Nor will there be a single unified audience.

I find nothing shocking or deplorable in this. Though countless conferences and symposia are held each year at which the lack of a large audience for serious and experimental art, music, and literature is regularly and ritually lamented, I do not think that our culture is ailing or degenerate because *Ulysses* is not a best-seller and *Wozzek* is not on the hit parade. They never will be. Expectations based on the premise that art is, or should be, egalitarian are not only doomed to disappointment but misleading because they create false aims for education and mistaken goals for foundation and government patronage. Democracy does not entail that everyone should like the same art, but that each person should have the opportunity to enjoy the art he likes.[8] Contemporary art should be supported not because it will produce a "golden age"

---

[8] It does not follow from this that all works of art are equally good or that all tastes are equally refined. The clichés of a soap opera are undoubtedly less valuable than the subtle complexities of a serious drama. And one should certainly endeavor to improve the taste and sensitivity of individuals. But it is pointless, if not downright snobbish, to bemoan the fact that many, who lack either the leisure and education or the inclination and maturity, do not enjoy such works. Respect and esteem for the dignity of other human beings—which I take to be central to the democratic ethos—does not, fortunately, depend upon aesthetic taste and sensitivity.

in which everyone will delight in the experimental and complex but because some few today find it exciting and valuable.

Meyer Schapiro's remarks are, I think, very much to the point:

> While some critics judge this heterogeneity to be a sign of an unstable, unintegrated culture, it may be regarded as a necessary and valuable consequence of the individual's freedom of choice and of the world scope of modern culture. . . . The present diversity continues and intensifies a diversity already noticed in the preceding stages of our culture, including the Middle Ages and the Renaissance, which are held up as models of close integration. The unity of style that is contrasted with the present diversity is one type of style formation, appropriate to particular aims and conditions; to achieve it today would be impossible without destroying the most cherished values of our culture.[9]

PLURALISM, PAST AND PRESENT

As Schapiro observes, the present diversity is by no means new. Differences of class and occupation, tradition and education, taste and temperament, have always been reflected in diverse philosophical, ideological, and aesthetic viewpoints. And with the Age of Reason, observes William H. McNeill, "the modern pluralistic age of intellect began. . . . Never since has the Western world as a whole seriously tried to establish a single all-embracing truth and doctrine." [10] What *are* new, however, are the scope and intensity of heterogeneity and, more important, our bald, explicit, and inescapable confrontation with it.

Although diversity had been growing since the seventeenth century, the fact was seldom squarely faced. The very ideology that nurtured pluralism tended, until recently, to eclipse its presence and obscure its significance. To believe in progress, a dialectic of history, or a divine plan was to acknowledge, at least tacitly, the existence of a single force or principle to which all the seeming diversity would one day be related. To accept the Newtonian world view, or later the theory of evolution, was almost inevitably to subscribe to monism and to look forward to a time when all phenomena would be reduced to, or subsumed under, one basic, encompassing set of laws. The notable achievements of science were taken as proof that Truth was One. Behind the manifest variety of phenomena and events lay, it was supposed, the latent unity of the universe which would eventually be discovered and embodied in a

---

[9] "Style," pp. 285–86.
[10] *The Rise of the West*, pp. 685–86.

single, all-embracing model. Because the oneness of things was what was *real*, surface diversity and incongruity could be disregarded.

But this picture of the world is, as we have seen, no longer entirely convincing. The inevitability of progress, the reality of either a divine or natural purpose in things, the existence of a single set of categorical cultural norms, and, above all, the possibility of discovering some single fixed and final truth—all these beliefs have been questioned and found wanting. Not only has no unified conceptual model of the universe been forthcoming, but diversity within as well as between fields has increased enormously during the past fifty years. And our awareness of this diversity has been intensified by the remarkable revolution in communication.

In an ideological climate in which determinism is doubted and teleology is suspect, in which causation is complex and laws are provisional, and in which reality is a construct and truths are multiple—in such a climate it is increasingly difficult to escape and ignore the pervasive presence of pluralism. Impelled by the human desire for simplicity, economy, and elegance, the search for an overarching unity will unquestionably continue. But at the same time it is necessary to recognize that the "dissonance" of intellectual and cultural diversity will probably not be resolved, in the foreseeable future, into a single, consonant "chord of nature." [11]

Because pluralism is a salient and characteristic feature of our culture, and will probably continue to be so for many years, it is of some interest to examine its development in the sciences as well as the arts somewhat more closely. The more so for this reason: Diversity was strongly encouraged by the ideology which flourished from the seventeenth to the twentieth centuries. As it burgeoned, producing revolutions in both the arts and sciences, diversity contributed significantly to the dissolution of the ideology that nurtured it. And the new ideology brought about important changes in the sources and character of pluralism itself—changes which have played an important part in fostering experimentation in the arts.

In the sciences the ideal of a single, final truth was self-defeating. For the more intense the pursuit of unity, the more fragmented the picture of the world became. In the search for first principles, new facts and phenomena kept turning up. To study them, new disciplines were devel-

---

[11] I should like to suggest that, if a unifying principle is discovered, it may well be not a causal "law" but a general principle such as that governing the structuring of hierarchic systems.

oped; to explain them, new theories were proposed. These in turn led to the discovery of further novelty—and so on.

The development of new disciplines was, partly at least, a result and reflection of the hierarchic structure of the complex systems being studied. That is, as the analysis of physical, biological, and social systems progressed, further hierarchic levels were differentiated and new methods and models were devised for their study.[12] At the same time, the accumulation of information in the several fields of investigation became so vast that large fields had to be divided and then subdivided. For example, on the level of individual behavior, it has been found useful to divide psychology into a myriad of small areas: child psychology, learning theory, abnormal psychology, and so on.

The proliferation of subjects and disciplines, theories and models, gradually turned a difference in degree into a difference in kind. For it came to seem increasingly doubtful that unity and coherence were just around the next theoretical corner. If pluralism was going to be a continuing condition, then the coexistence of diverse theories and models could be better supported and comprehended if the status of the former were changed from one of asserted proof to one of conditional truth, and the status of the latter from one of substantive reality to one of man-made construct.

This shift in significance was complemented and corroborated by a second set of circumstances: the search for definitive truth had generated major changes in physical, biological, and social theory, as well as in mathematics. What had been thought to be established fact proved to be provisional and had to be revised. The sciences, abetted by philosophy, began to reflect upon their own history and to consider the nature and status of their methods and theories—with the results noted just above.

In the arts the sources of pluralism were different; yet its development was in many ways similar. During the late eighteenth and nineteenth centuries, an ever growing emphasis on the importance of personal expression and a correlative concern for the creation of distinctive national idioms, produced a considerable amount of stylistic variety within the traditional norms. In music, for example, the last decade of

---

[12] At times, models developed in connection with different levels appeared to conflict. But while the coexistence of different paradigms within a single field of inquiry *may* involve "competition" and disagreement over fundamentals (see Thomas S. Kuhn, *The Structure of Science, passim*), such discrepancies may, I suspect, also be reflections of discontinuities inherent in the structure of the system itself.

the nineteenth century held works as diverse in spirit and inflection as Debussy's *L'Après-midi d'un faune,* Strauss's *Ein Heldenleben,* and Rimsky-Korsakov's *Czar Saltan*—though all were rooted in the style of traditional tonality. In the visual arts, diversity was, if anything, more marked and more personal. Artists as different in manner and outlook as Cézanne, Monet, and Klimt, for instance, all painted during the first decade of the twentieth century. Similarly in literature, striking differences mark the work of men such as Yeats and Kipling, Proust and Galsworthy—all of whom were active during the first years of this century. The studies of historians and ethnologists—calling attention to the integrity and validity of earlier Western art and to the arts of other cultures and civilizations—contributed significantly to the magnitude and scope of stylistic diversity.

Faced with clearly compelling works in a wide variety of styles, artists and critics alike found it impossible to escape the conclusion that the forms and features of artistic truth and beauty were not one, but many. On the other hand, they found it equally difficult not to believe that beneath this manifest diversity common, unifying principles operated. These were found to reside not in the surface of representation—in cultural symbols and idioms, materials and techniques—but in the significance and expressive power inherent in the structure and organization of the particular work. Each work of art exhibited its own principles of order and was to be understood "in its own terms." There was, in brief, a movement in the direction of formalism.

At the same time that these shifts in attitude were taking place, a more radical change was in progress—one which was to encourage the development of experimentalism, whether under the aegis of analytic formalism or transcendental particularism.

Since the Renaissance—and before that, in the ancient world—it had been virtually an article of aesthetic faith that art, though different from nature, was nevertheless based upon natural, and hence necessary, principles or laws. In music, for example, it was supposed that the diatonic and chromatic scales, the major-minor modes, functional harmony, and tonal syntax could ultimately be traced back to the natural properties of sound. Similarly in the visual arts, it was believed that the proper use of color, line, perspective, form, and the like depended upon natural and universal principles. And although languages were obviously not universal, it was felt that behind this manifest diversity some common, fundamental laws would eventually be discovered.

But the inescapable presence of a multiplicity of styles—Western and non-Western, old and new—raised serious doubts about the intrinsic naturalness of particular materials, procedures, and forms. The doubts were intensified, even confirmed, by the invention of the twelve-tone system in music and the development of cubism in painting. The tremendous impact of these revolutions lay not so much in the use of new syntactic-formal means—for Schönberg and Berg, at least, used the new method to realize traditional expressive goals—but in the fact that they demonstrated in a dramatic and seemingly unequivocal way that *art was literally artificial.*[13]

That styles of art are artificial, man-made constructs; that traditions and solutions, far from being sacrosanct, need to be questioned and revised; that creation consists of the impersonal invention of means and relational systems and the discovery of their implications—all these ideas prompted a number of artists to identify themselves with and to emulate the methods and procedures of science. (In part, they were encouraged to do so by the apparently correlative changes taking place in the conceptual status of scientific theories.) The work of art was no longer to be thought of as an expression of feelings or ideas, or as a representation of reality, but rather as the solution of a problem that was unique and intra-artistic. Art, like science, was to be experimental; or, like logic or mathematics, a contextually isolated, self-contained system. The possibilities and implications of existing stylistic systems were to be thoroughly explored and carried through to logically, if not psychologically, necessary conclusions. Or, if desired, new systems could be devised and their consequences derived and exhibited.

Though present during the 1920's and 1930's, experimentation was consciously and systematically employed only after World War II. Its method—rigorous and uncompromising, yet, at the same time, self-indulgent—is trenchantly described by Harold Rosenberg:

> Pure art, physics, politics, is nothing else than art, physics, politics that develops its procedures in terms of its own possibilities without reference to the needs of any other profession or of society as a whole. . . .
>
>   It is pushing these possibilities to their logical extreme, rather than the penetration of new areas of experience or understanding, that results in the recognition of the work as "vanguard." [14]

Experimentation has, particularly in music, tended to promote both a high order of complexity and a marked contextuality. Where the perception of relationships and the understanding of syntactic implications are

---

[13] The anger and resentment aroused by these movements was due, I suspect, in no small measure to the fact that by implication they threatened a whole system of beliefs and attitudes.

[14] *The Tradition of the New*, pp. 68–69.

neither expected nor appropriate—for instance, in the music of transcendentalism, whether random or totally organized—complexity and
contextualism should not constitute a serious problem for listeners who
hear the succession of sound-combinations, objectively observing fluctuations and variations in density, timbre, speed, and so on. The problem is rather one of developing a proper aesthetic attitude toward
discrete sound sensations. On the other hand, where patterns, syntactic
implications, and structural relationships are relevant, indeed essential,
for perception and understanding—as they are in the music of analytic
formalism—then, as we shall see, complexity and contextualism tend to
constitute formidable obstacles for the listener.[15] If there were a relatively prolonged stasis, however, and if, as I suspect, few technical-
stylistic possibilities in the serial method remain to be explored, then
listeners might be able to learn the repertory of technical permutations;
and, if this proved to be the case, higher levels of cultural redundancy
would make understanding and appreciation by a somewhat larger
audience possible.

One final, and perhaps peripheral, observation: Though efficient communication and easy, rapid travel are making what were distinct and
separate national and ethnic cultures more and more alike, I doubt that,
as some have suggested,[16] culture as a whole is becoming more homogeneous and uniform. For within this cross-cultural uniformity, occupational and ideological differences have tended to become more, not less,
marked. An increase in diversity of models, ideologies, and disciplines
coupled with an increase in specialization (a casual glance at a list of
learned journals or of trade publications in almost any field will show
how far such intellectual fission has gone) has produced a large number
of distinct and divergent subcultures. Engineers and businessmen, scholars, scientists, and artists can as a rule communicate more effectively
with their counterparts thousands of miles away than with their neigh-
bors down the block or their colleagues down the hall. The situation in

---

[15] See chaps. 11 and 12. Advanced experimentalists have been able to continue
to compose complex, contextual music, remaining more or less indifferent to the
limitations of the laity and the demands of the market place, partly because they
have been supported—and in that sense also encouraged—by various institutional
patrons: universities, foundations, museums, and government. Were they not thus
nurtured, they would have had to simplify their music, sell insurance, or starve—
for the audience for such music has been very small indeed.

[16] See A. L. Kroeber, *An Anthropologist Looks at History, passim*; Marshall
MacLuhan, *The Gutenberg Galaxy*, pp. 214–15; and Kenneth Boulding, *The Meaning of the 20th Century*, p. 18.

the sciences, described by I. Bernard Cohen, holds in varying degrees for almost all fields: "Today all scientists are generally reduced to the status of laymen with respect to any branch of scientific endeavor that does not border on their own narrow specialty." [17] In the arts, styles, and the techniques and ideologies that accompany them, have also become cross-, but *not* intra-cultural. The composer of chance music at an American university generally has more to say to his opposite number in Poland or Japan than to the composer of traditional tonal music who occupies the office next door. In short, the sum of homogeneity has not increased, rather diversity has taken other forms. What is developing is a world culture divided into occupational "tribes."

Nor do I share Kenneth Boulding's concern that a stable, high-level technology will lack the "trouble, difficulty, challenge or even pain" that man requires "in order to stimulate him to that constructive activity which is necessary to prevent him from going to pieces." [18] For the tension and challenge of understanding—of ordering the growing pluralism—will present plenty of problems. Rather, I think, the danger is that increased specialization will force a decline in the level of general cultural communication—the level of "popular" culture. For communication is a matter not merely of a common language but of shared experience and knowledge, beliefs and attitudes. In general, the more heterogeneous a group is (size being constant), the less "sharing" there is, and, consequently, the lower the common denominator of discourse will be. (In the army or "in the field" at a large cocktail party, conversation is by and large reduced to gossip—banal observations about food or the movies, the weather or sex.) As occupational tribes become more sharply differentiated, the level of cultural discourse will tend to decline: stock subjects will be scanned superficially, banal questions will receive platitudinous answers, and, saddest of all, humor will become increasingly broad, crude, and cliché-ridden.

The Presence of the Past

This study has from time to time suggested that changes in ideology may lead to more frequent and more explicit use of past idioms and materials than has been the case since, say, the seventeenth century.

---

[17] "Science and the Nonscientist," p. 2; also see Freeman Tilden, "Not by Truth Alone," p. 1415, and Rosenberg, *The Tradition of the New*, p. 65.
[18] *The Meaning of the 20th Century*, p. 147.

Because they would constitute a significant addition to the pluralism of the present, it is of some interest to consider both the circumstances making such "revivals" possible and some of the characteristic ways in which the past might be used. Though music will be the central focus of attention in this inquiry, the same considerations are, I believe, relevant to the other arts and examples from them will be cited as much as my imperfect knowledge will allow.

It is generally accepted as a self-evident fact—indeed, as a truism—that it is impossible to employ a style developed during some earlier epoch in the composition of a contemporary work. It is not entirely clear what this statement really asserts. Several different interpretations are possible.

One meaning of the statement might be that if a composer writing in the twentieth century employs the syntax and forms and procedures that were in use at some earlier time, the music should not be considered "contemporary." This position involves a whole group of assumptions, which we have already touched upon and will consider again, about the existence of a cultural "spirit" and its relationship to the arts of the time. But for the present, it is enough to point out that, taken at face value—in the absence of metaphysical-dialectic accouterments—the assertion is patently false. For if a composer living today writers a piece of music, that piece of music is *by definition* a contemporary work, regardless of whether the idiom employed was invented yesterday or five centuries ago and regardless of whether the work is good, bad, or indifferent. Of course, seen in this light, the statement is really a truism: that is, if a past idiom is used in the present, it is not a past idiom with respect to that use.

If, on another interpretation, the statement is taken to assert that the use of the past cannot be authentic and convincing, then the question hinges, at least initially, upon the degree of rigor and precision required of the *re*-presentation. Clearly nothing prevents a composer who is sensitive to and knowledgeable about the style of some earlier epoch from employing the norms, forms, and procedures of that epoch with considerable accuracy and propriety. It is probably impossible, however, both logically and psychologically, for a contemporary composer (or artist of any kind) to write in *exactly* the same style as that current, say, in Italy during the 1720's. Logically it is impossible because any addition to the repertory of Italian Baroque music—whether composed in the eighteenth or the twentieth century—changes that repertory and, consequently, our judgment of style based upon it, if only ever so slightly. More important, psychologically it appears to be virtually impossible for someone living in the twentieth century fully and successfully to adopt the outlook of some earlier time, partly because he knows what the stylistic implications of the past in fact were, and partly because his view of the past is necessarily colored and modified, albeit unconsciously, by present interests and concerns.[19]

What is probably really intended by this statement is that a composer living today cannot write compelling, vital, worthwhile music in some earlier style. Granting that complete stylistic accuracy is an unattainable goal—if, indeed, it should be a goal at all—is this really the case? Since value judgments are involved, the question of "fact" is difficult, perhaps impossible, to determine. But I know of no theoretical or practical reason why a talented, well-trained contemporary composer could not write, say, an excellent concerto grosso in the manner of the late Baroque. And though, unless he were a man of genius, the composition would surely fall far short of the work of Bach, it might easily compare favorably in interest and quality with the countless works of lesser Baroque composers whose compositions our tedium-tolerant audiences evidently find a source of unfailing delight.

But once such a work was known to have been composed in the present, it would, at least up to now, have been rejected by both audience and critics as being corrupt, contemptible, and dishonest. It would have been thus rejected, not because of its inherent qualities, but, as we have seen (chap. 4), because of our cultural beliefs about originality and creation, causation and history. The radical changes in Western ideology described in the preceding section and in chapter 8, however, now make it conceivable that composers will find it possible to employ—either relatively strictly or with considerable interpretive freedom—models, styles, and even particular musical ideas developed or written in earlier epochs; and, as the ideals and beliefs of the audience and critics change, they, too, may come to understand the relevance of the past.

In order to show why the past may again become a source of models and materials, syntax and procedures, let us consider how the ideas and beliefs, which have hitherto precluded such "borrowing," have changed.

THE IDEOLOGICAL ACCESSIBILITY OF THE PAST

Until recently it was, as we have seen, an article of cultural faith that one of the chief aims of an artist was to express his innermost thoughts,

---

[19] This is indicated, for example, by the fact that forgers can deceive only their contempories, not later generations (see Max J. Friedländer, *On Art and Connoisseurship*, chap. 36). It is possible, however, that if there were a lasting stasis, then the culture's view of the past might well be become more stable.

feelings, and emotions. To create was to embody these unique and personal insights and affects in pigment, in words, or in tones. If this embodiment truly reflected the inner being of the artist, his work would be original and idiosyncratic. Since the artist's thoughts and feelings were partly a result of his interaction with and response to his own cultural milieu, his peculiar individuality could not possibly find its true and proper expression in the idiom and style of another epoch or an alien culture.

The ideal of individualism and the goal of intense personal expression have now been repudiated by two of the important ideologies of our time and have been derogated by some traditional artists. In their place has been substitued the concept of the work of art as an objective construct. Originality is no longer tied to the discovery of means expressive of the artist's inner experience, but to the ordering of materials; and creativity is seen not as an act of self-revelation, but as a species of problem-solving. Since any style can constitute a basis for objective construction and for the presentation of principles of order, such views are not incompatible with the use of past art works as sources for materials, relational patterns, and syntactic procedures and norms. Form and technique have thus superseded inspiration and expression. Logically, all modes of organization and all styles become equally available and viable.

Related to the doctrine that the artist expresses himself and his milieu in his work is the proposition that the style, techniques, and forms which arise in a particular culture are manifestations of the unique exigencies of that culture and that, consequently, their use under other cultural conditions is somehow illicit and reprehensible.

If this thesis is to be more than a redundant truism—"the art of a culture is the art of a culture" [20]—then, as noted above, further assumptions must be required. Perhaps the most important of these is that each culture is characterized by a single encompassing spirit or *Geist* which prevades and unifies all its activities and products. Whatever fails to conform to this fundamental pattern is rejected as alien or ignored as inconsequential.

Though one may legitimately discover common trends, movements, and viewpoints within a culture, as I have been trying to do, this does not warrant ignoring other competing or contradictory tendencies and

---

[20] See Alfred Einstein, *Essays on Music*, pp. 3–4. Moreover, because we often rely heavily upon the art of a culture in characterizing its general outlook and values (its "spirit"), the whole enterprise tends to become more or less circular.

ideas.[21] For instance, though the mystical tradition was not the dominant one during the high Middle Ages, it cannot on that account be slighted and swept under the carpet of cultural uniformity. If, as I argued in chapter 7, it is true that direct causation theories are not tenable and if styles have a tendency to develop in their own fashion, then the whole idea of a monolithic, homogeneous culture becomes only one possibility among many.

Of course, some cultures, usually relatively simple ones, do exhibit a high degree of coherence.[22] But it does not follow from this that all, or even most, cultures do so. Complex cultures, such as ours, are as a rule not only highly diversified and heterogeneous; they are not even self-consistent. Competing styles, ideologies, and modes of cultural behavior may coexist; and no law of history has, as far as I can discover, been proposed and validated which asserts that accommodation between divergent tendencies *must* take place—that cultures necessarily become more homogeneous and uniform. Indeed, not only is it difficult to find reliable grounds for deciding which tendencies and movements in a complex, multifarious culture should be considered the prime manifestations of its SPIRIT, but even if one adopts some sort of *Zeitgeist* position—or, perhaps more plausibly, contends that particular cultures generally exhibit predominant styles of behavior, belief, and artistic "expression"—there seem to be no compelling reasons why the spirit of a culture should not be characterized by a tendency toward diversity, a tolerance for pluralism, and a taste for incongruity.

Whatever may be the objective validity of these beliefs, the crucial point is this: once they were accepted as cultural "dogma," they had the effect of making it psychologically all but impossible for an artist to employ the ideas of other artists or the styles developed in earlier epochs. As long as it was believed that the artist's primary task was to express his inner, unique self and his times, or that a particular style was the necessary and inimitable product of a specific culture, it was very difficult for an artist to use the ideas and materials of his

[21] Einstein's notion that "art is more rarely a mirror image of culture than is generally supposed" (*ibid.*, p. 4) is, I believe, logically mistaken precisely because it tacitly assumes that cultures are homogeneous and consistent. The point is that, since any work of art is by definition a manifestation of the culture from which it arises, it must necessarily "reflect" that culture. What can happen is that art may react against the dominant values and attitudes of a culture, but it will nevertheless at the same time be reflecting some of the values which exist in the culture.

[22] It is because such cultures tend to be homogeneous that Einstein is able to suggest that the art of archaic epochs tends to mirror the spirit of the age—not simply because "art still has the function of worship" (*ibid.*, p. 6).

predecessors or the norms and techniques of earlier epochs with a sense of integrity and conviction.[23]

Almost all these views have in one way or another been called into question during the past fifty years. For a great many artists, expression is no longer the goal of composition; styles are no longer the unique expressions of an epoch, but are man-made constructions; history is no longer a dialectic succession of necessary stages, but an objective ordering of recorded evidence; and truth is no longer single and ultimate, but provisional and pluralistic. Thus the ideological and psychological conditions which have hitherto precluded the free and open use of past means and materials no longer prevail. The present may now incorporate the past.

It should, moreover, be pointed out that the same ideological beliefs which precluded the use of past idioms and materials also made stylistic eclecticism seem a serious defect—a threatening impropriety. For if a work of art is the unique expression of an individual whose personality is presumably consistent and unified, then the work of art he makes should be so too. For the same reasons, the artist was expected to be essentially consistent between works as well as within them—though a gradual development was to be expected. In parallel fashion, if each style reflects the ethos of the culture out of which it arises and if each ethos is, so it was believed, homogeneous and consistent, then the resulting style should be so as well.

Other facets of the ideology also tended to make eclecticism seem illicit and reprehensible. For example, the Idea of Progress and the related views of evolution, even when not explicitly applied to style change, involved a belief in an ordered, consistent succession of stages—a notion incompatible with a mixture of past and present. Similarly, the model of organic unity often employed to account for the internal structure of the work of art and, at times, the history of cultures—and hence of styles—called for a single, unified, self-consistent process.

But with the change in ideology, eclecticism again becomes possible. If a work of art is an impersonal construct, and creation a kind of problem-solving, then experiments with mixtures of means and materials, either within or between works, need not constitute an imperfection. On the contrary, the skillful and elegant combinations of disparate

---

[23] There were, of course, important exceptions. In music, for instance, it was possible to use the theme of another composer as the basis for a set of variations; and in the visual arts it was common to copy the works of the masters—often in a medium other than that of the original—primarily for the sake of study but also for plain enjoyment.

styles (or of ideas borrowed from different works and different composers) within a single work may become a challenging and attractive
problem. As Meyer Schapiro has observed: ". . . the notion of style has
lost . . . the crystalline uniformity and simple correspondence of part to
whole. . . . The integration may be of a looser, more complex kind,
operating with unlike parts." [24]

This analysis suggests that if earlier styles and materials are employed in contemporary art, music, and literature, it will most likely be
done by those inclined toward formalism, rather than by those who still
consider works of art to be vehicles for personal expression. One cannot
"use" the expressive quality of a Bach, a Rembrandt, or a Donne. It *is* a
unique, personal fact. As Wylie Sypher has said of the last stage in the
development of the doctrine of individual expression, Romantic art "has
the logic of private experience, not of style." [25] In like manner, it will
probably be the formalist rather than the expressionist who delights in
the possibilities of mixing styles and materials from different epochs
within a work or in employing different stylistic models in successive
works.

> To be objective is to be detached, to be capable of, perhaps im-
> pelled to, wit and irony. The romantic cannot allow the intrusion of
> comedy upon a serious passage, and cries out against the mingling of
> the noble with the trivial, the elegant with the burlesque.[26]

That this is indeed the case is shown by the fact that it has been avowed
and explicit formalists, such as Eliot and Stravinsky, who have employed past procedures, models, and materials most patently and most
extensively.[27] And we are thus confronted with an amusing paradox:
the end of the Renaissance—of belief in teleology, individualism, expression, and so forth—has made possible a return to the styles and materials originally fostered by those beliefs.

THE PSYCHOLOGICAL ACCESSIBILITY OF THE PAST

Should earlier styles and art works become viable sources of ideas
and procedures, idioms and models, then not only will the pluralism of

[24] "Style," p. 284.

[25] *Loss of the Self* . . . , p. 52.

[26] Babette Deutsch, *Poetry in Our Time*, p. 167.

[27] Traditionalists such as Shostakovich, Thomas Wolfe, or Marc Chagall seldom
make use of past idioms or ideas. Occasional returns, such as Prokofiev's *Classical
Symphony* are clearly sports within an essentially neo-Romantic oeuvre.

the present be enriched, but the character and significance of the past will be substantially modified. There are two reasons for this. First, present interests and insights tend to illuminate and color the art works of earlier epochs or of other cultures with which contemporary artists feel a special kinship. Thus, as noted earlier, contemporary art, rather than research, has led to a renewed appreciation of El Greco's painting; Eliot's interest in the metaphysical poets has affected our reading of their work; and the concern of contemporary composers with metric relationships has enhanced our understanding of the music of the fourteenth and fifteenth centuries. If the use of the past becomes characteristic of our time, comprehension and appreciation of the art of other epochs will continually be brought into focus through its reworking in the present.

Second, and more important, not only will the past be illuminated by the present, but it may, in a significant sense, become part of the present. If the suggestion that "an event is considered to be past when . . . its implications appear to have been realized and its consequences . . . are known" [28] has merit, then it follows that, once an earlier idiom becomes a viable means of creating in the present, its "pastness" tends to become irrelevant—merely chronological. Its implications are no longer "closed out"; and, as the past becomes relevant and consequential, its "pastness" disolves. It is literally then a part of the present. Should not only most past styles, but those of other cultures, eventually become facets of contemporary art, then all styles would come to coexist in an encompassing present. The ahistoricism of formalism would thus prove to be compatible with the timelessness of transcendentalism.

As our relationship to the past has changed, so, too, have the sources of our interest in it. Until the beginning of the twentieth century, past epochs and alien cultures attracted artists more because of empathy with the dominant ideals and outlook of the culture than for specifically stylistic reasons. It was the ideas and ideals of Greece which, through humanism, influenced the Renaissance artists, not primarily its stylistic-compositional concerns. Similarly, Jacques Louis David uses Roman subjects and classic sculpture in the *Oath of the Horatii* in order to symbolize and refer to the republican virtues of the French Revolution, not because of an interest in Roman art as such.

This sort of "ideological nostalgia" was possible partly because, until recently, the more remote in time or place another culture was, the less complete and detailed was our knowledge about it and, consequently,

----

[28] Pp. 90–91.

the more easily it could be pictured and colored in terms of current interests and attitudes. Chronological distance was able to lend enchantment because, in the somewhat clouded mirror of history, the past could be seen as a reflection of the present. Conversely, cultures have often reacted against their immediate predecessors because they knew their idiosyncrasies too well and thus found it impossible to remake the past in the image of the present.

But the vast increase in our knowledge of the past and of alien cultures has brilliantly burnished the mirror of history, making all pasts essentially comparable in both completeness and complexity. Because it has become more difficult to make a particular past conform to and confirm current beliefs and attitudes, ideological empathy becomes less important in deciding which epochs or cultures engage the interest of contemporary artists.

There is another important reason why ideology may no longer provide the basis for choosing among possible pasts: any specific ideology, at least for the formalist, represents not a final solution or an ultimate truth but only one among a number of potentially viable constructs.

If this analysis is correct, it should follow that in the future a particular past will be favored and explored because of the specifically artistic problems it poses rather than because of the ideological position it represents.

In short—and this cannot be too much emphasized—the contemporary use of the past does not involve an attempt to reverse time's arrow, to return to the untroubled virtue of an idealized past or to escape into the piquant pleasures of the exotic. To be vital and significant, productive and convincing, the use of the past must arise out of pressing artistic problems and compelling compositional concerns. Mere imitations of past manners are discredited and forgeries are relegated to the basement (see chap. 4), because they are monolinear with respect to time. Because they point only backwards, they are, both figuratively and literally, inconsequential. Today the past is neither the exemplar of ancestral virtue, nor a miscellany of blind blunders. Rather it is the repository of countless potentially absorbing problems and possibilities—challenges to the imagination and skill of the contemporary artist.

THE USES OF PAST ART

If all pasts—remote as well as recent ones—coexist as ever present possibilities upon which the artist, writer, or composer may draw, in what specific ways will this potential be realized? Though the evidence is still fragmentary, reason, together with what data there are, suggests that a thoroughgoing and literal copying of all the attributes of a past idiom or manner is out of the question, at least in the near future. That is to say, it is highly unlikely that madrigals will be composed in the manner of Monteverdi, that poetry will be attempted in the style of Spenser, or paintings done in the idiom of Perugino. There are two main reasons for this: (1) the past is relevant for the present not primarily for the solutions it proffers but, as noted above, for the problems it raises; and (2) the emphasis placed upon individuality and originality is still so strong and prevalent that a straight forward, unqualified use of an earlier style—even an adventurous one, creatively concerned with compositional problems—would probably be misconstrued, by critics and audiences alike, as being no more than a servile imitation.

It should be stressed that the uses of the past being considered here are *intra-artistic*. What is involved is not merely the use of an idea, character, or event taken from history or mythology. Such representation has been the stuff of literature and painting—and to a lesser degree of music—since the beginnings of art. Rather what is meant is the use of specific phrases or themes, structural plans or syntactic procedures, taken from a particular work, or a group of works of art in the same medium. For instance, Lucas Cranach the Elder's painting *Venus and Amor* would not in this sense constitute a use of the past; but Picasso's lithograph (1949) based upon Cranach's painting would. This sort of "use of the past" is, so to speak, aesthetically self-reflective, as Richard Poirier indicates in his review of John Barth's *Giles Goat-Boy*:

> One explanation is that these American novelists . . . have discovered a new mass of fictional material. They have discovered this material in the novel itself—its history, its conventions, its structures and styles, all weighted with presumptions about the nature of reality— and in the various philosophical and psychological theories by which contemporary experience has been analyzed. Novelists have of course always parodied one another; but the novel of self-parody, which takes pleasure in exposing the limits of its own procedures, has had up to now very few exponents except Sterne and Joyce.[29]

This calls attention to a point of some interest: the ways in which existing art works are often used today are related to the tendency of the evolving ideology to minimize the distinction between art and nature.

---

[29] "Wescac and the Messiah," p. 1.

This is particularly clear in painting. Heretofore when painters have used particular art works from the past, whether recent or remote, they have usually done so in order to learn from the earlier work, to have a facsimile for study, or because a patron wanted a copy of a work that he particularly admired.[30] Though his own way of seeing would almost inevitably make the copy different from the original,[31] the artist tried to re-present the original as faithfully as possible. From the point of view of, say, a Renaissance artist, copying someone else's work was a very different enterprise from "painting from nature." For the contemporary artist, however, the earlier work may be considered just another existent fact; and he deals with it in the same fashion as he would any other visual stimulus—as he would a "real" landscape, figure, and so on. Thus, for example, one could not tell merely from its style and organization that Picasso's panel of 1950 was based upon Courbet's *Les Demoiselles des Bords de la Seine*—though once the model is known the pleasure derived from the paraphrase is somehow colored and even heightened. Or, when an artist uses all or part of a photograph or reproduction of an art work in a montage, often it is given no special status, but is just like any of the other "found" objects included in the work. In short, if the distinction between art and nature is irrelevant—partly because both are constructs—then "nature" is no longer a special or preferred source for ideas and knowledge, forms and relationships.

It seems possible to distinguish among four different, though in some instances overlapping, ways in which the art of other epochs has been used in the present. They will be called *paraphrase, borrowing, simulation,* and *modeling.*

1. In *paraphrase* very nearly all the essential formative features of an existing work—its subject matter, themes, structures, and stylistic procedures—are used in a relatively sustained and rigorous way as the basis for all or part of a new work whose spirit and significance are clearly contemporary. Through a reordering of parts or materials, a modification of syntax, a change of inflection or vocabulary, an alternation in manner of representation—or some combination of these—a stylistic modification takes place.

Stravinksy's *Pulcinella Suite,* based upon the music of Pergolesi, is an unequivocal example of paraphrase in music. Artful nuances of melodic-

---

[30] This is very clear from the copies presented in K. E. Maison, *Art Themes and Variations.*

[31] Particularly since the copy was frequently in a different medium—e.g., a drawing or engraving of an oil painting or a sculpture.

rhythmic emphasis, harmonic idiom, instrumentation, and so forth transform the past into the present. And, what is more, the piquant paraphrase is more vital and vibrant than the original.[32] The nature of paraphrase is also indicated by Stravinsky's account of how he "completed" Gesualdo's motet:

> When I had written out the five existing parts in score, the desire to complete Gesualdo's harmony, to soften certain of his *malheurs* became irresistible to me. One has to play the piece without any additions to understand me, and "additions" is not an exact description; the existing material was only my starting point: from it I recomposed the whole. The existing parts impose definite limits in some cases, and very indefinite ones in others. . . . I have not tried to guess "what Gesualdo would have done," however—though I would like to see the original; I have even chosen solutions that I am sure are not Gesualdo's. . . . My parts are not an attempt at reconstruction. I am in it as well as Gesualdo.[33]

Paraphrase in music must be distinguished from both *transcription* and *arrangement*. In transcription, means different from those of the original work are used to re-present it as accurately as possible. Examples would be Brahms's orchestration of his own *Variations on a Theme by Haydn* or Bach's keyboard concerti based upon orchestral concerti by Vivaldi and others. An arrangement generally involves significant additions to, deletions from, or changes of order in the original. Haydn's *Scottish Songs* or suites taken from some larger work—for instance, Ravel's suites from *Daphnis et Chloé*—would be examples of arrangements. Though the distinctions seem clear enough in these examples, transcription and arrangement often blend into paraphrase. For instance, Webern's transcription of Bach's ricercar and Vaughan Williams' arrangement of "Greensleeves" shade into paraphrase. But despite overlappings, the difference between paraphrase and other forms of "imitation" of existing work is, at least theoretically, decisive: the merit of a transcription or of an arrangement is measured by its ability

---

[32] Speaking of Pergolesi's music, Stravinsky has said: "*Pulcinella* is the only work of 'his' I like" (*Stravinsky in Conversation with Robert Craft*, p. 90). Perhaps it is generally the case that, when an entire work is a paraphrase, the paraphrase must be based on an incomplete work or one that is not quite of first quality. A paraphrase of, say, the first movement of Beethoven's String Quartet in C-sharp Minor, Op. 131, is all but inconceivable because the coherence of structure and the impress of character are so powerful that the paraphraser is left little scope for his art.

[33] *Ibid.*, p. 47.

to reproduce the character and "tone" of the original; the merit of a paraphrase, on the other hand, depends not upon its faithfulness to a model but upon its inherent interest as a work in its own right.

A recent example of paraphrase in literature is Robert Lowell's *The Old Glory*, a set of three plays based upon stories by Hawthorne and a short novel by Melville. Robert Brustein observes that "while Mr. Lowell has managed to adapt these tales with relative fidelity to the original texts, he has made them wholly and uniquely his own. . . . . And it is his subtle achievement not only to have evoked the past, but also to have superimposed the present upon it, so that the plays manage to look forward and backward at the same time." [34]

Translations whose goal is re-presentation rather than facsimile may also attain the status of paraphrase. This is the case with Pound's *Homage to Sextus Propertius*—as R. P. Blackmur makes clear by placing the original text, Pound's paraphrase, and H. E. Butler's Loeb Library word-for-word rendering side by side. [35] Pound bases his *Homage* on passages from the elegies of the first century (B.C.) Roman poet, rearranging "them freely, playing on sound and association from his own standpoint as well as from that of the original text. His aim was to make an original modern poem out of the light that Propertius's sensibility and his own seemed to cast on one another." [36] Pound himself observed: "There was never any question of translation, let alone literal translation. My job was to bring a dead man to life, to present a living figure." [37] As Blackmur's description of Pound's *Cantos* indicates, paraphrase may be combined with other ways of using the past—for instance, borrowing (see below)—and with "original," freely invented materials:

> The first thing to notice is that the classical material is literary—translation and paraphrase; the Renaissance material is almost wholly historical; and the modern material is a composition of the pseudo-autobiographical, the journalistic, and the anecdotal. Excepting the two Cantos—the first and third—which are longish translations, the narrative structure is everywhere anecdotal—and the special technique within the anecdote is that of the anecdote begun in one place, taken up in one or more other places, and finished, if at all, in still another. [38]

---

[34] Introduction to Robert Lowell, *The Old Glory*, p. xi.
[35] *Form and Value in Modern Poetry*, pp. 87–89.
[36] M. L. Rosenthal, *The Modern Poets*, p. 55.
[37] Quoted, *ibid.*, p. 56.
[38] *Form and Value in Modern Poetry*, pp. 95–96.

As transcription often borders on paraphrase in music so adaptation—as well as translation—often borders on paraphrase in literature. The play based on Melville's *Billy Budd,* the movie *Tom Jones,* and the musical *My Fair Lady* are adaptations—though the last of these is close to paraphrase. In general, an adaptation differs from its model in means and medium; a paraphrase differs from its model in significance as well. An opera—for instance, Debussy's *Pelléas et Mélisande*—should evidently be regarded as an adaptation with respect to text, but, taken as a whole, it must be counted as an essentially original creation. A selective reordering of existing materials literally employed—for example *The Seven Ages of Man,* based on excerpts from Shakespeare—would be an *arrangement.*

In the visual arts, paraphrase generally involves a varied, but basically congruent, re-presentation of the subject matter (indeed, it is difficult to imagine a paraphrase of a non-objective work), formal structure, linear quality, and sometimes the basic palette of an existing art work, but done in such a way that the plastic significance of the original is either subtly or radically altered. In addition to those already mentioned, the following are recent examples of paraphrase in painting: Picasso's paraphrases of Velasquez' *Las Meninas* (forty-five variants), or Delacroix's *Les Femmes d'Algers* (fourteen variants), and of El Greco's *Self Portrait* (?); Matisse's paraphrase of De Heem's *Still Life Arrangement;* Francis Bacon's of Diego Velasquez' portrait of Pope Innocent X; and Derain's paintings based on Ghirlandaio's *Christ Carrying the Cross* and Breughel's *Massacre of the Innocents.*[39]

Some paraphrases—for instance, Derain's—are quite close to their models; others are almost unrecognizably different. Thus, according to Michael Aytron:

> Joan Miro . . . has probably taken the paraphrase further than any other contemporary. The sense-nonsense relationship which he has established with the works of the past is utterly without Picasso's ruthlessness, or Bacon's morbidity or Buffet's wearisome impoverishment. Using curiously chosen pictures, as apparently irrelevant to himself as to each other, such as Raphael's *La Fornarina,* Jan Steen's *The Cat's Dancing Lesson,* and Engleheart's *Portrait of Mrs. Mills,* he has made cheerful game of the old masters and in doing so he has translated the initial image into a language far more remote from the original than Picasso's.[40]

---

[39] All of these examples are reproduced in Maison, *Art Themes and Variations.*
[40] Introduction to *ibid.*, p. 28.

In the visual arts, too, paraphrase must be distinguished from more literal forms of re-presentation, that is, from the *copy*—though again the distinction is not an absolute one. Because paintings and sculptures are one-of-a-kind art works—cannot be reproduced as can a book, a drama, or a piece of music—copying had been common since earliest times. Partly because the artist's goal was to make an existing masterpiece available to himself and to others, and partly because in the past there tended to be greater communality of style, such re-presentations, though always slightly different for their models, were—and were intended to be—essentially faithful facsimiles. More recently, however, as printed reproductions have replaced the artist's copy and as aesthetic attitudes have changed, artists have tended to use existing works as points of departure for the formulation of contemporary statements of visual order. Thus, as in music and literature, one may distinguish between a copy and a paraphrase by suggesting that the merit of the former depends to a significant degree upon the fidelity with which it captures the spirit and character of its model, while the merit of the latter depends importantly upon the pertinence and quality of its own unique plastic presentation.

2. In *borrowing*, existing materials—usually fairly brief excerpts (a melody, a line or stanza of verse, or part of a painting), but sometimes larger sections or even whole works of modest size—are quoted, copied, or reproduced exactly, or almost exactly. When, as is frequently the case, the force and import of the borrowed material depends upon the audience's familiarity with the tone and significance that it had in its original context, the excerpts are generally taken from works which an educated Westerner might be expected to know. In any one work, borrowed elements may be drawn from a wide variety of sources—from the works of different artists and from works created in different style periods or even in different civilizations. These elements are juxtaposed, integrated, and combined both with one another and with newly invented material in such a way that past and present, transcending surface disparities and manifest eclecticism, inform and illuminate one another, creating a new conceptual order—a new work of art.

Though borrowing necessarily involves *allusion*, the two can, nevertheless, be distinguished. In "pure" allusion—for instance Tchaikowsky's use of the "Marseillaise" in his overture, *The year 1812*, or Berg's quotation for *Tristan and Isolda* at the end of his *Lyric Suite*—pre-existing material, rather than performing a significant syntactic or structural function in the work, is presented as a passing reference—a reminiscence.

Although basing a set of variations upon a pre-existing theme has been common since the Baroque period, this sort of use of the past does not really constitute "borrowing" in the sense in which I am using the term. First, there is usually no stylistic cross-over between the old material and the variations based upon it—both belong to the same fundamental style system. Second, and more important, neither the constructive procedure of the work nor its character as a whole is affected by the fact of borrowing—the existing material is a source for invention rather than a part of the invention. The many works from the eighteenth to the twentieth century which employ folk music in some form are closer to borrowing in the modern sense, though here again the pre-existing material is often merely adapted to the prevalent compositional practice—as, for example, in the fourth movement of Beethoven's String Quartet in F, Op. 59, No. 1.

Charles Ives's Fourth Symphony is, as Kurt Stone's description makes clear, a mixture of borrowing and allusion: ". . . the texture abounds with bits of familiar hymns and other simple tunes. This labyrinth of allusions and quotations . . . may be likened to a whirling microcosm of independent musical particles, each on its own path, *yet all governed by a central magnetic force.*" [41] The fact of borrowing and the characteristics of the compositional procedures employed are inextricably linked. The kind of experience which the "whirling microcosm of independent musical particles" is supposed to produce, is made clear by Ives himself: "As the eye, in looking at a view, may focus on the sky, clouds, or distant outlines, yet sense the color and form of the foreground, and then, by bringing the eye to the foreground, sense the distant outlines and color, so, in some similar way, can the listener choose to arrange in his mind the relation of the rhythmic, harmonic and other material." [42]

A recent and very clear example of borrowing in music—which I cannot resist mentioning both because it was commissioned by the Fromm Music Foundation for the Seventy-fifth Anniversary of the University of Chicago and because the manuscript was received while I was

---

[41] "Ives's Fourth Symphony: A Review," p. 4. Italics mine.

[42] Quoted, *ibid.*, p. 11. Stone's criticism of Ives's work on the grounds that "musically speaking any other tunes would have done just as well" (p. 14) is objectionable on three counts. First, because it misses the importance of the stylistic incongruity between the tunes and their setting. Clearly jazz tunes or completely unfamiliar tunes would *not* have done as well. Second, and related to this point, the criticism discounts the significance of character, not only per se but as it operates to qualify the understanding of syntax (see chap. 2). And finally it is a sign of Stone's implicit acceptance of the doubtful dogma of "inevitability" in music as a criterion of value.

writing this chapter—is George Rochberg's *Music for the Magic Theater*, a work which makes skillful and interesting use of materials taken from Mahler's Ninth Symphony and Mozart's Divertimento, K. 287.

Describing what is perhaps the most famous example of borrowing technique in English literature, T. S. Eliot's *The Waste Land*, M. L. Rosenthal writes:

> Its artful manipulation of these traditional elements illustrates the modern poet's increased consciousness of his sources. Eliot sometimes quotes these sources directly, as in the lines from Dante and others at the close of the poem which suggest his own (and our) spiritual state. Sometimes he parodies them, as in his echo of Goldsmith's lines on womanly chastity. . . .
>
> Also Eliot often reworks his sources. This happens with brilliant effect in Part II of *The Waste Land*, in a passage grounded on a famous description in Anthony and Cleopatra. . . . Eliot follows Shakespeare's lines with exact parallelism at first, and retains throughout the passage enough of the latter's tone to keep the implied contrast between the passionate and heroic Cleopatra and the hysterically neurotic woman who is Eliot's subject clearly in view.[43]

It is important to emphasize that, even when existing materials are quoted exactly, their significance is altered by their new context and special use. R. P. Blackmur's discussion of the "psychology of borrowing" applies, I think, to music and painting as well as to literature; and it is relevant to both varied and strict borrowing:

> Even if a text is wholly quotation, the condition of quotation itself qualifies the text and makes it so far unique. Thus a quotation made from Marvell by Eliot has a force slightly different from what it had when Marvell wrote it. Though the combination of words is unique it is read, if the reader knows his words either by usage or dictionary, with a shock like that of recognition. The recognition is not limited, however, to what was already known in the words; there is a perception of something previously unknown, something new which is a result of the combination of the words, something which is literally an access of knowledge. *Upon the poet's skill in combining words as much as upon his private feelings, depends the importance or the value of the knowledge.*[44]

---

[43] *The Modern Poets*, p. 16. Another work which makes extensive use of borrowing is Pound's *Cantos*. Also see R. P. Blackmur's discussion of borrowing in the poetry of Marianne Moore (*Form and Value in Modern Poetry*, p. 240 and *passim*).

[44] *Form and Value in Modern Poetry*, p. 184. Italics mine—to emphasize the ideals of objectivity and skill.

In the visual arts borrowing has, as far as I have been able to discover, been less common. No doubt this is partly because there is no reproducible symbolic text to quote; and, until recently "re-presentation" was not a matter of including part of an existing work in a new one, but of copying the whole work. Where borrowing has occurred—for instance, in Manet's portrait of Zola which includes a copy of his own *Olympia*—its function has been primarily that of allusion rather than that of compositional structuring. Recently, however, there have been some striking instances of borrowing—instances in which the use of existing materials is of central importance in the formal and representation organization of the art work.

Larry Rivers' *Dutch Masters and Cigars, 1964* is a case in point. In his interesting discussion of the painting, J. A. Richardson observes that the television commercial for Dutch Masters cigars

> entailing animation of a Rembrandt is—as is using his *The Syndics* for a trademark—clearly an instance of honoring greatness with levity. Rivers reverses this direction by memorializing the trivial and making the cigar box into a cultural monument *that synthesizes past and present.* The coupling of his adumbrate drawing style with Rembrandt's figure dispositions produces an extraordinary effect of renewed vitality. There is a kind of Baroque counterpoint occurring between the two new compositions in the rhythmic play of angular blotches that move through the figures, helping to articulate them at one point, seeming to erase them at another.[45]

Two other instances of borrowing which might be mentioned are Marisol's *Mona Lisa, 1961–62* based on Leonardo's painting; and Joseph Cornell's *Medici Slot Machine,* in which reproductions of Medici portraits are combined with a map of Rome, a compass, and other symbols of the Renaissance.

3. *Simulation,* to distinguish it from paraphrase and borrowing, involves neither literal nor varied use of materials—melodies, verses, or pictorial elements—taken from a particular work of art. Rather, salient features of a past style—melodic-rhythmic idiom, harmonic process, and formal structuring in music; vocabulary, grammar, modes of organization, and narrative method in literature; qualities of line, texture, and color, and sense of shape and plastic organization in the visual arts—are combined with and modified by inflections, techniques, and concerns which are characteristically contemporary. (In music, for instance, these

---

[45] "Dada, Camp, and the Mode Called Pop," p. 552. Italics mine. Richardson mentions another example of Rivers' borrowing: *The Second Greatest Homosexual,* a construction based upon Jacques Louis David's famous painting *Napoleon.*

concerns take the form of preferences for rhythmic-metric variety and asymmetry, for pungent rather than saccharine sonorities, and so forth.) Since no deception—no counterfeit of yesterday—is intended, not all features of the earlier style are, as a rule, employed. The resulting work is neither nostalgic nor complacent, not primarily because elements taken from contemporary practice are usually employed, but because when it is really *revived*, not merely reproduced, the past style becomes a means for the definition and elucidation of present circumstances, artistic problems, and aesthetic attitudes.

During his so-called neo-classical period, Stravinsky made extensive use of simulation techniques. For instance, the Mass employs sonorities, melodic-rhythmic inflections and formal procedures derived from the style of the late Middle Ages; *The Rake's Progress* is based on the idiom and organization of eighteenth-century opera; the *Dumbarton Oaks Concerto* reverts to the manner and form of the Baroque concerto grosso; and the list could be easily extended. But however scrupulous his use of the past, the resulting synthesis is always of Stravinsky and of today. For, as is clear from his description of the composition of his Piano Concerto, Stravinsky's goal is not imitation, but re-creation: "I attempted to build a new music on eighteenth-century classicism using the constructive principles of that classicism . . . and even evoking it stylistically by such means as dotted rhythms." [46]

A considerable number and variety of composers have employed simulation techniques in recent years. Ravel uses the rhythm and melodic character of seventeenth-century dance music in *Le Tombeau de Couperin*; Richard Strauss juxtaposes Lullian restraint and nineteenth-century Viennese schmaltz—though the former is not uninfluenced by the latter—in his suite from *Le Bourgeois Gentilhomme*; and Benjamin Britten, as Henry Leland Clarke's review indicates, combines a number of different simulated pasts in one work, the *War Requiem*:

> Of course the music is eclectic. It is historically full-blooded. It draws on the open-fifth organum of the Romanesque; on the rhythmically differentiated lines of the Gothic; on the otherworldly *a cappella* sounds of the Renaissance; and the pompous dotted rhythms of the Baroque. . . . The vocabulary, like that of Coventry Cathedral, comes from every part of the Western story, but what is said is the artist's own. [47]

---

[46] *Stravinsky in Conversation* . . . , p. 35.
[47] P. 958.

Similarly, Hans Werner Henze's opera, *The Bassarids*, is described as "mixing styles that rang of Rameau, Smetana, Wagner, Schönberg, Stravinsky, Puccini, Offenbach—even Gilbert and Sullivan. . . . Henze would not describe the score as derivative, despite the familiar touches. He is merely an eclectic, he suggests, paraphrasing Goethe: 'An eclectic is one who, out of what surrounds him, out of what goes on about him, applies to himself that which conforms to his own nature.' " [48] Other composers have, with varying results, turned not to the past of Western art music but to quite different traditions—to folk music, jazz, and Oriental music. Sometimes—perhaps Bartók is a case in point—what may have begun as a kind of simulation becomes so much an ingredient of the composer's own idiom that it can no longer be counted as a use of the remote.

Simulation has not, to the best of my knowlege, been common in literature. Though it is said that Pound "sometimes . . . assumes another poet's tone or method as in the Dantean 'Hell Cantos,' " [49] modern writers have in general depended much more heavily upon paraphrase, borrowing, or modeling than upon simulation. Perhaps this is because the particularity of the present is most vividly delineated when the connotations and meanings evoked by reference to a specific work from the past are reflected back upon it. Perhaps, too, this is because it is difficult for literature, which is technically in one dimension—like a single melodic line, without the resources of harmony, counterpoint, and instrumental timbre—to simulate without crudely imitating.

I should, however, like to mention a marvelously amusing, and for present purposes, interesting instance of simulation. John Barth's novel *The Sot-Weed Factor* employs a vocabulary and diction, idiom and structure, subject and setting, which, at least to this untutored reader, seem characteristic of the eighteenth-century novel. Yet an exaggeration of typical traits—a more extravagant use of coincidence, a more outlandish collection of lurid characters, and a more wanton recourse to Rabelaisian humor—tell us that it goes beyond the bounds of its prototypes. Nevertheless, we believe, as we read it, that its diction and style, as well as its action and setting are of the past. But when we come to the "philosophical" disquisitions of the protagonists and the "erudite" observations of the narrator (both very much a part of the style being simulated), we tend to read and understand them in terms of twentieth-century problems—metaphysical, ethical, and aesthetic. I am

---

[48] *Time*, August 12, 1966, p. 50.
[49] Rosenthal, *The Modern Poets*, p. 70.

The Aesthetics of Stability

uncertain to what extent this is the result of the nature of the problems themselves and the way they are stated, and to what extent it is due to our knowledge that the work is contemporary. Probably both play a part. Finally, the propriety of the style is not merely a function of its seventeenth-century setting, but also of intent; as *Joseph Andrews* was to the pious moralism of *Pamela,* so *The Sot-Weed Factor* is to the spurious heroism of the contemporary historical romance.

Although a number of painters and sculptors have, with varying degrees of fidelity, simulated both earlier styles of Western art and styles of non-Western art—Etruscan painting, Chinese calligraphy, medieval painting, and so on—none has simulated so wide a variety of styles and manners as the protean Picasso, who has drawn upon Greek vase painting, Roman sculpture, and primitive African art, to name but three of his most obvious sources. He is, according to Michael Aytron, "the most eclectic artist ever to achieve the reputation of greatness, and he has done so during a period when eclecticism and indeed any tendency toward imitation is condemned. . . . Picasso is essentially the inhabitant if not the curator, of Malraux's 'Museum without Walls.' " [50]

4. *Modeling* involves neither taking specific materials from an existing work (paraphrase or borrowing) nor adopting the syntax or manner characteristic of another style (simulation). Rather, following the basic structure and process of a particular work, yet at the same time reshaping its manifest content and its significance, the new work is constructed as a fairly rigorous analogue of the old. It is not enough that both works employ the same traditional forms or procedures—that is, that both be sonata forms or Italian sonnets. Thus Schönberg's Suite, Op. 25, though it "reverts" to a genre more common in the Baroque than in the early twentieth century, is not an example of modeling. Nor is Dylan Thomas' villanelle, "Do Not Go Gentle into That Good Night."

If modeling is to occur, the artistic means must be such that the elements and events in the new work can, though radically transformed, still act as analogues for those in the old. This requires the existence of a functional syntax which is either common or isomorphic to both works.

Because they employ no explicit syntax, analogical modeling is not possible in the plastic arts. If a painting or sculpture is to be recognizably based upon some earlier work, the new must not only follow the basic formal organization of the old, but it must represent enough of its subject matter to make the relationship between them apparent. But were this the case, then the new work would be an example of para-

[50] Introduction to Maison, *Art Themes and Variations,* p. 22.

phrase rather than one of modeling. For instance, Manet's painting *Le Déjeuner sur l'Herb* is based upon part of Marcantonio Raimondi's engraving *The Judgment of Paris*.[51] But the figures and their composition are clearly *variants*, not analogues, of those in the original. The work is a paraphrase. Had Manet substituted, say, abstract forms or rocks or vegetation for the figures, it would have been impossible in the absence of other information—letters, reported conversations, or sketches of the artist—to know that his work was based upon Raimondi's.

In music the difficulties are practical rather than systemic. Because music is not denotative, and also perhaps because its formal plans tend to be highly schematic, there would be no way of establishing the existence of modeling on musical grounds alone, unless the parallels between the earlier and later works were very precise. (For instance, it would probably be impossible in the absence of extra-musical information—or patent thematic similarity, in which case the later work would be a paraphrase—to know whether, say, one sonata-form movement was based on another, even though both followed the same tonal scheme and had roughly the same proportions.) But the radical changes in style which have occurred during the past seventy-five years have tended to move music away from functionalism and hence from the possibility of modeling. Even those tonal idioms still in use have lost much of their functional definition. Consequently it is almost impossible to construct analogues sufficiently precise for successful modeling.

I have introduced the concept of modeling—and perhaps belabored a minor point—not only because it is a distinguishable "use of the past," but also because if, in the future, it became ideologically and psychologically possible to return to past styles in a fairly fundamental and sustained fashion, then the kind of modeling I have described might well become a mode of musical composition. It might, that is, be possible to compose an analogue of a particular Josquin motet or a specific Haydn sonata.

Even in literature unequivocal cases of modeling are not common. Only where the source is explicitly specified by the subject matter—as, for instance, in O'Neill's *Mourning Becomes Electra*, or, most recently, John Barth's parody in rhymed couplets of *Oedipus* in *Giles Goat-Boy*—does the fact of modeling become certain; and then it approaches paraphrase. James Joyce's *Ulysses* is an interesting instance of modeling. T. S. Eliot's remarks about the work are worth quoting because

---

[51] Which is, in turn, based on a lost cartoon by Raphael.

they constitute a concise formulation of the attitude of many contemporary artists toward the uses of the past:

> In using the myth, in manipulating a continuous parallel between contemporaneity and antiquity, Mr. Joyce is pursuing a method which others must pursue after him. They will not be imitators, any more than the scientist who uses the discoveries of an Einstein in pursuing his own, independent, further investigations. It is simply a way of controlling, of ordering, or giving shape and significance to the immense panorama of futility and anarchy which is contemporary history.[52]

Eliot's statement calls attention once again—as have many of the examples cited—to the fact that it is those artists, writers, and composers for whom creation is an act of impersonal discovery, a skillful ordering of objective materials rather than an expression of personal feeling, who have found the substance, forms, and procedures of the past most fruitful and who have used them frequently and freely. They have also often used them eclectically, some combining various pasts together with the present in a single work, others paraphrasing or simulating different pasts in different works, but always with a sense of the press of the present rather than a yearning for yesterday. And it is perhaps not irrelevant to observe that among those who have found the past a source of creative vitality are the greatest and most original—not bizarre—artists of the twentieth century: Stravinsky, Picasso, Eliot, and Joyce.

In closing this section, it should be emphasized that I am by no means suggesting that the past is a discovery of the twentieth century. Obviously it is not. Other epochs have found earlier and alien cultures a source of insight and inspiration. And other epochs have used the past in ways similar to those described above. During the late Middle Ages and Renaissance, for instance, this was notably the case in literature: writers made extensive and often quite literal use of both earlier and contemporary sources—Roman comedy, historical chronicles, and current narratives. Though the painters and sculptors of the period found ideals in the art of the ancient world, the work of their contemporaries and immediate predecessors provided the main models. In music, parody—a kind of combination of paraphrase and borrowing—was common. But

---

[52] "Myth and Literary Classicism," p. 681. Eliot employed modeling himself. *The Cocktail Party* was based on Euripides' *Alcestis:* "I was still inclined to go to a Greek dramatist for my theme . . . and to conceal the origins so well that nobody would identify them until I pointed them out myself" (*Selected Prose,* p. 83).

materials were taken largely from current sources, even if, like Gregorian chant, they had had a long history. Despite important and patent differences, the aesthetic attitude toward composition had something in common with that prevailing today. According to Alfred Einstein,

> this music is based on the principle of musical construction, on a principle that forces together more or less heterogeneous ingredients. . . . To call such music expressive in the modern sense just because of some mistaken notions about its artfulness would amount to a gross lack of insight. . . . Subjective expression not only remains forbidden, it is not possible at all.[53]

Marshall McLuhan has strongly emphasized the parallels between medieval and modern culture: "Whereas the Elizabethans were poised between medieval corporate experience and modern individualism, we reverse their patterns by confronting an electronic technology which would seem to render individualism obsolete." [54] But there are also marked—indeed, decisive—differences. After three centuries during which the past became less and less available as a source of creativity, changes in ideology—moving, as McLuhan rightly observes, in the direction of detached objectivity—have made it possible for artists, writers, and composers once again to paraphrase, borrow, and simulate past models, materials, and manners. As I pointed out at the beginning of this section, however, their, and our, relationship to and experience of the past has changed radically. And so has the complexion of culture. Whatever the similarities, a generally homogeneous culture like that of the Middle Ages cannot be equated with or serve as a prototype of a radically pluralistic, heterogeneous civilization such as ours.

The Values of Stability

Our culture—cosmopolitan world culture—is, and will continue to be, diverse and pluralistic. A multiplicity of styles, techniques, and movements, ranging from the cautiously conservative to the rampantly experimental, will exist side by side: tonality and serialism, improvised and aleatoric music, as well as jazz with its many idioms, and popular music; abstract expressionism and hard-line painting, constructs and kinetic art, Pop art and surrealism, as well as figure and landscape

---

[53] *Essays on Music*, pp. 106–7.
[54] *The Gutenberg Galaxy*, p. 1.

painting; the objective novel, theater of the absurd, poetry of formalism and of social protest, as well as more traditional styles of prose and verse. Through paraphrase, borrowing, style simulation, and modeling, past and present will, modifying one another, come together not only within culture, but within the oeuvre of a single artist and even within a single work of art.

Though new idioms and methods may be developed, they will not displace existing ones. The gamut of possibilities—from completely pre-planned order to total chance, from teleological structuring to goalless meandering, from syntactic formalism to subjective psychologism, from the explicitly analytic to the essentially mystic—has all but reached its limit.[55] New idioms and methods will involve the combination, mixture, and modification of existing means rather than the development of radically new ones—for instance, a new pitch system or a new grammar and syntax. As mentioned earlier, not all styles and means will be equally attractive at any given time. Changes will tend to occur in waves, some styles or methods cresting at one period, others at another.

Complementing this stylistic diversity and these patterns of fluctuation will be a spectum of ideologies ranging from teleological traditionalism, through analytic formalism, to transcendental particularism. The spectum will encompass a myriad of philosophical-aesthetic positions, old and new: idealism and naturalism, pragmatism and existentialism, analytic philosophy and phenomenology, as well as various sorts of mysticism. These, combining with one another, will produce a host of particular positions and attitudes shading into one another.

The fabric of culture will be colorfully heterogeneous and intricately patterned. Some strands of the stylistic-ideological weft will be woven together tightly for a considerable distance; others will never touch. Some combinations and configurations will return as the fabric unfolds through time; others will be present only once and then be modified or abandoned. Some threads—those of the warp (to continue the metaphor)—will run almost throughout the entire length of the cultural epoch, impinging upon, positioning, and, as it were, coloring all the strands of the weft. One of these, formalism, has already been described and will be further discussed in what follows. A parallel and correlative strand, pervading and tingeing the fabric of contemporary aesthetic

---

[55] I realize that, given the history of past pronouncements of this sort, such an assertion will seem wildly extravagant; but I see no alternative to the *logic* of the situation. After all, the wolf *did* finally appear!

thought is that which emphasizes the values of elegance and ingenuity, skill and refinement. It is with contemporary art and culture as seen from the vantage point of these values that this section will be chiefly concerned.

THE EMPHASIS ON MEANS AS AGAINST ENDS

Changes in aesthetic attitudes are matters of emphasis, having to do with what is considered to be the main focus of appreciative attention—the locus of artistic significance and value. In the past, the materials and form of an art work—language and syntax, color and line, pitch and rhythm—were in general regarded as necessary but nonetheless secondary aspects of art. They were, so to speak, the accidents of an art work, not its essence. They constituted the *means* by which the goal of communication of subject matter was to be achieved. Whether art was viewed as an imitation of actions, passions, or objects, as a way of representing ideas or of expressing emotions, or as a mode of social criticism, the central concern of appreciation and understanding was with subject matter.

Aesthetics and criticism were dualistic. On the one hand were the materials and form of a work of art, the *means*; on the other hand were subject matter, expression and meaning, the *end* or goal. The former were significant because they made the latter possible.[56] If one asked what a work of art was "about," the answer was almost always in terms of subject matter or whatever it was thought to express, symbolize, or signify.

The dualism in aesthetics and criticism was analogous and, as we shall see, not unrelated to the Cartesian mind-body dualism, form and materials being comparable to the body, subject matter and meaning being comparable to the mind. And just as the mind-body dichotomy has come to seem less and less tenable, so differentiation of materials and form from subject matter and meaning has come to seem less and less convincing. It is not that art no longer represents, it often does; or that it is no longer expressive, it frequently is; or that it has ceased to be socially relevant, at times it may well be so. Rather it is that, for most contemporary artists, critics, and aestheticians, content and meaning are no longer considered to be definable and explicable apart from the

---

[56] Or the division was tripartite, and the separation between material and form, on the one hand, and meaning on the other was even greater; that is, materials and form communicated content, and content in turn expressed or symbolized emotions or meanings.

specific materials of a work of art and their formal structuring in that work. This, I take it, is the essential import of Archibald MacLeish's famous dictum:

> A poem should not mean
> But be.

As the dualism in criticism has disappeared, serious artists and critics have tended to direct a major part of their attention to the materials and form of art works. This is partly the result of a general movement in the direction of formalism and constructivism, not only in the arts but in the sciences and philosophy as well,[57] and partly the "rediscovery" that materials, form and process can themselves be sources of aesthetic significance and delight. For instance, discussing the poetry of James Dickey, Marc R. Cogan observes that Dickey "creates a kind of poetry which has very little to do with the imitation of objects and almost nothing to do with the imitation of process. The poetic process is itself the subject of the poem. . . . The process belongs, in a degree, to all men and operates, in a degree, in all times."[58] An even more exclusive preoccupation with language per se is evident in M. Barthes's statement, "Le langage n'est pas prédicat d'un sujet, inexprimable ou qu'il servirait à exprimer, il est le sujet."[59] A similar emphasis upon structure as against expressive content is evident in Ligeti's description of the essential values of Boulez's *Structures Ia:*

> Webern's interval objects . . . still contain a trace of the (discretely) "expressive," and although the satisfaction derived from his music is the result of quite different qualities, the traces of "expression" present at times do provide crutches for the struggling listener. All this has vanished in our example from Boulez' "Structures"; they

[57] Skepticism about the possibility of separating ends from means has not been confined to those concerned with the arts. Scientists and social scientists have emphasized that choices are made as ways of moving *away* from problems and perplexities, not of moving toward clearly envisaged goals. And, reviewing Charles E. Lindblom's book, *The Intelligence of Democracy: Decision Making through Adjustment,* Amitai Etzioni writes: "Man cannot neatly separate goals from means . . . ; he cannot gain—in the realistic limits of time and cost—the needed information to judge rationally among alternatives. The world is an "open" system in which there is no end to the consequences" ("On the Process of Making Decisions," p. 746). From this point of view, depreciation of the ends-means dualism is related to the general tendency, mentioned earlier, to avoid teleological formulations and explanations.

[58] "Homo Faber: The Process of Poetry," p. 2. Also see the statement by Richard Poirier, above.

[59] Quoted in "Crisis in Criticism," p. 546.

expose to view something that in Webern already formed the nucleus: beauty in the erection of pure structures.[60]

The emphasis upon means as against content has also been encouraged by the desire of artists and critics for objectivity and rigor; or, looked at the other way around, by their consciousness of the abuses of inept and willful interpretation.[61] That is, given a knowledge of the practice and tradition of a style, materials and formal structures can be analyzed as presentational facts; but the significance of content—often symbolic—is subject to the hazards and vagaries of subjective interpretation.

The parallel to the mind-body relationship is again suggestive: understanding a work of art in terms of its materials and form is analogous to understanding mind in terms of physiological processes, instead of attempting to "interpret" the meaning of—the motivation or purpose behind—behavior. From the viewpoint of art and criticism, if one directs attention to the materials and their organizations, meanings—expressive, representational, or social—will, as it were, take care of themselves.

Of course, some artists and critics still preserve the dichotomy, stressing the primal importance of content, whether manifest or symbolic, as against materials and form. Significantly, these are most often men who use—"interpret"—works of art to support, or exhibit the relevance of, some extra-aesthetic theory or dogma: for instance, the Freudians or the Marxists.

The need to label and stereotype through the interpretation of subject matter, however, is by no means confined to those committed to an orthodoxy. Whenever a work of art seems strange or eludes easy understanding, there is a temptation to discover that the work represents or symbolizes the artist's beliefs about decadence, war, religion, sex, and so forth. Much contemporary art has, without warrant, been subjected to this sort of blatant and flatulent criticism. For example, as mentioned earlier (see chap. 8, n. 57), Pop art is *not,* as often suggested, a commentary on the vulgarity of American civilization, or the spiritual emptiness of our culture. Rather it emphasizes the distinction between expressive,

---

[60] "Pierre Boulez," p. 62.

[61] Both these points are forcefully, and often brilliantly, developed in Susan Sontag's book of essays, *Against Interpretation,* which, unfortunately, I did not read until I had written all but this final section of chapter 9. I mention this partly by way of apology, but mostly because my views and Miss Sontag's are at many points remarkably similar and, since they were arrived at independently, serve in a sense to confirm one another.

socially pertinent values and those of skill and elegance. For what the Pop artist does is to take the socially useful, the communicative, and the content-filled—for instance, the Campbell soup can or the comic strip—and make it into an essentially formal kind of art, an art of skill and elegance. As Susan Sontag points out, the content of Pop art is so blatant that it is uninterpretable.[62] That this is the attitude of artists as well as critics is made clear by Robert Rauchenberg: "I was busy trying to find ways where the imagery, the materials and the meaning of the painting would be, not an illustration of my will, but more like an unbiased documentation of what I observed, letting the area of feeling and meaning take care of itself." [63] The trouble with much Pop art—at least from a formalist point of view—is not that it is, so to speak, ideologically unsound but that it lacks the inventive skill and formal elegance which would make it aesthetically interesting. Consequently, it is often considered a kind of representation; and, as representation, it is at best trivial.

To cite a similar instance of overinterpretation in literature: it has frequently been said that Ionesco's early plays are "about" meaninglessness or "about" non-communication. But as Susan Sontag observes,

> this misses the important fact that in much of modern art one can no longer really speak of subject-matter in the old sense. Rather, the subject-matter is the technique. What Ionesco did . . . was to appropriate for the theater one of the great technical discoveries of modern poetry: that all language can be considered from the outside, as by a stranger. . . . His early plays are not "about" meaninglessness. They are attempts to use meaninglessness theatrically.[64]

In the pluralistic present, different styles, movements, and kinds of art will place greatest emphasis upon different segments of the continuum which runs from *ends* to *means*. As the diagram given below indicates, at one end of the continuum are popular novels and Hollywood movies, tin-pan alley music and illustrative painting. In these kinds of art, content—representational significance—is the almost exclusive focus of interest.[65] Moving toward the center, traditionalism shades into formal-

---

[62] *Ibid.*, p. 10.

[63] Quoted by Dorothy Gees Seckler, "The Artist Speaks: *Robert Rauchenberg*," p. 76.

[64] *Against Interpretation*, p. 119.

[65] One interesting indication of this emphasis upon content is the tendency of popular commercial art to "abstract from" and condense—as in *Reader's Digest* reductions of novels to plot—or to arrange as in popular (for instance, hit-parade) music. Either condensing a lyric poem, where materials, process, and form are one

ism, in which materials and structure are inextricably linked to content. Particularly when, in its more experimental phases, it underlines the importance of materials, formalism, in turn, shades into transcendentalism. At the extreme side of the "means" segment of the continuum are the assemblages and happenings—whether contrived or accidental—of transcendentalism. Here the materials are everything, but they have no significance beyond themselves, beyond the fact of their existence.

ENDS .... MEANS
  Content   *Form and Process*   *Materials*
(Commercial and
 popular art)
.... Traditionalism .... Transcendentalism ....
   .... Formalism ....

The dichotomy, discussed above, can also, then, be analyzed as tripartite. This is of some importance because it indicates that the present stylistic pluralism exhausts the *logical* possibilities of kinds of aesthetic emphasis. New ways may perhaps be found to represent content, to embody form and process, or to present sensation; but no new *kinds* of emphasis are possible.[66]

Despite the possibility of a tripartite analysis, however, the analogy to the mind-body dualism is still pertinent. There are two reasons for this. First, the mind-body problem can itself be viewed as tripartite: mind as subjective content (introspective psychology), as structure and process

---

with content in the creation of meaning, or arranging a jazz composition is patently impossible.

[66] Though styles of art and their attendant ideologies will be distributed throughout the entire length of the ends-means continuum, it does not follow that the distribution will be the same for all the arts. Because of differences in their materials and modes of structuring (see pp. 112–14, above), different arts will tend to gravitate toward a particular segment of the continuum. Literature, for instance, will probably operate toward the "ends-content" part, though it will also be attracted to the processive portion of the central segment. To put it the other way around, because it is by nature representational and syntactic, it is inconceivable that literature could ever become merely materials. Music will tend to emphasize the central segment of the continuum, deviating from this more in the direction of materials than in the direction of ends and content. And the visual arts will tend toward the materials segment, while at the same time shading into the formal emphasis of the central part of the continuum.

Nor will the distribution remain constant from wave to wave within the anticipated stasis. At one period, one part of the continuum will tend to attract a number of artists from all the arts; at another time, they will be attracted by the possibilities offered by a different segment of the continuum.

(neurophysiology), and as material substance (biochemistry). Second, the crucial question involves the resolution of a dualism. For the relationship—the continuity—of form and materials in aesthetics, and of neurophysiology and biochemistry in the analysis of mind, is much less problematic and difficult than the relationship of these to content. To put the matter in a different way: materials and form are evidently hierarchically quite continuous; but between these and content there seems to be a significant hierarchic disjunction.

Another dualism—the distinction between art and nature—is also resolved as one moves along the ends-means continuum from content, through form and process, to materials. This is the case because nature is not *about* anything. It has no "content"; nor has it any goal or purpose. Consequently, the greater the emphasis placed upon ends—upon content as an aesthetic component—the more decisive the distinction between art and nature. Conversely, the further one moves toward the means part of the continuum, the less significant the art-nature distinction becomes.

When transcendentalism focuses exclusive attention upon the materials of art—when aesthetic experience derives from and depends upon no man-made or traditional syntax or form—a work of art is not different from a natural object; indeed, it may *be* a natural object, as in "found" art. According to the aesthetic of transcendentalism, art has no content, no structure, and no purpose. Like nature, it simply exists. The traditional distinction is irrelevant and misleading.

For the formalist, as I pointed out earlier, art and nature are distinguishable, but equivalent, in that both are understood as abstract constructs which organize a reality in order to comprehend and communicate a picture of the world. This view is admirably stated by Jacob Horner, the hero of John Barth's novel *End of the Road:*

> Articulation! There, by Joe, was *my* absolute, if I could be said to have one. . . . To turn experience into speech—that is, to classify, to categorize, to conceptualize, to grammarize, to syntactify it—is always a betrayal of experience, a falsification of it; but only so betrayed can it be dealt with at all, and only in so dealing with it did I ever feel a man, alive and kicking. . . . I responded to this precise falsification, this adriot, careful myth-making, with all the upsetting exhilaration of any artist at his work. When my mythoplastic razors were sharply honed, it was unparalleled sport to lay about with them, to have at reality.[67]

---

[67] P. 96. I have included the last two sentences because of their obvious reference to the values of formalism—skill and refinement—which will be discussed later.

As It Is, and Perhaps Will Be

(Here the objections of the transcendentalists to the structuring of experience are met head-on. In the act of capturing and presenting a reality, art necessarily distorts it, as criticism in its turn distorts the work of art. But only in this way—by abstracting, selecting, emphasizing, and so on—can reality, whether in perception, in art, or in science, be understood at all. The transcendentalist may not violate the world, but neither can he understand it, save perhaps through mystical experience—and then he cannot communicate it to anyone else. As Bentley Glass put it, "knowledge is a social construct." [68] Any particular reality—whether intuited by common sense, symbolized in a mythology, or formalized by empirical science—is a construct; for there can be no perception without conceptualization, and every conceptualization entails abstraction from the particularity of concreteness, entails, that is, becoming a construct.)

For the formalist, then, art and nature are comparable, not because we are able, after twenty centuries of trying, to reduce art to natural or scientific principles, for we are not; nor because both can be comprehended within a single inclusive theory such as systems analysis, information theory, or mathematical logic, for this goal has by no means been realized. Rather art and nature are comparable because they are assigned the same epistemological status and because, further, of a common aesthetic component—a delight in, and admiration for, structural elegance and rhetorical skill. The importance of this component in the arts will be considered presently. Its importance in science is unequivocally affirmed by Joel H. Hildebrand:

> . . . we are building fragments of information into structures of great beauty, comparable as achievements of the human mind and spirit with the greatest works of art and literature. These structures are a major part of humanism. To define science as technology, or as "classified information," as in a certain dictionary, is as misleading as it would be to characterize the Parthenon as calcium carbonate.[69]

Once again, the ends-means continuum may be divided into either two or three parts. The tripartite division has been implicit in the preceding discussion: if content is the focus of aesthetic attention and of value, the result is a decisive separation between art and nature; if the emphasis is upon form and process in relation to both content and materials, art and nature are seen as comparable, but not identical; and if materials are made the exclusive focus of interest, art and nature are

[68] "The Ethical Basis of Science," p. 1256.
[69] "Order from Chaos," p. 441.

essentially indistinguishable. Observe, however, that here too the decisive disjunction articulates the continuum into two parts rather than three. That is, in *both* transcendentalism (since it would no more analyze and conceptualize nature than it would art) and in formalism, art and nature are epistemologically equivalent. But, when there is an aesthetic emphasis upon content, an *in principle* dichotomy between art and nature is unavoidable.

This analysis, coupled with Hildebrand's statement, calls attention to the fact that the fundamental division in the contemporary search for truth and knowledge is not that between the sciences and the humanities, but one which corresponds to the basic disjunction in the ends-means continuum—the distinction between ends and content, on the one hand, and form, process, and materials, on the other. That is, the division between science (the form, process, and materials segment) and technology (the content-goals segment); or, in Harold Rosenberg's words, the division of the professions into "pure and applied, theoretical and practical, 'for its own sake' versus profit and social utility." [70]

NOVELTY AS A VALUE (A PARENTHESIS)

In our century, the new has not merely been accepted by artists and critics; it has, particularly in recent years, been pursued and cultivated. This active search for novelty had its roots in the ideology which dominated Western culture from the seventeenth to the twentieth century. As we saw in chapter 8, trust in the inevitability of Progress and dialectic development (beneficent, cumulative change), belief in the value and importance of personal-cultural expression (originality and uniqueness), and faith in the existence and ultimate discoverability of a single encompassing truth—all encouraged change and eventually produced such a rapid succession of styles, techniques, and movements that relevant habits of perception and discrimination and adequate critical criteria (based upon such habits) had virtually no time to develop. In our time, as Susan Sontag points out: ". . . styles do not develop slowly and succeed each other gradually, over long periods of time which allow the audience for art to assimilate fully the principles of repetition on which the work of art is built; but instead succeed one another so rapidly as to seem to give their audiences no breathing space to prepare." [71] In the absence of viable critical criteria, the one thing that

---

[70] *The Tradition of the New*, p. 68; also see below, pp. 224–25.
[71] *Against Interpretation*, pp. 34–35.

could be assessed was whether the artist's method, style, or "idea" was new. Novelty, often mistakenly confused with "originality" from which it sprang, gradually became a criterion for judging works of art. And this gave further impetus to the search for the new—for novelty for its own sake.

But the radical changes in ideology which have occurred in the twentieth century have made the pursuit of novelty somewhat incongruous—at least for formalists and traditionalists. For, generally speaking, self-expression and subjectivity have been superseded by impersonality and objectivity, the Idea of Progress and of dialectical development have given way to a neutral ahistoricism; and constructivism and relativism have replaced the quest for a single and comprehensive truth. Moreover, if, as I am suggesting, we are in, or entering, a period of fluctuating stasis, the continued existence of a relatively stable set of styles would allow time for audiences to assimilate principles of stylistic order and to develop viable critical criteria. Then the crutch of novelty as value could be thrown away and criticism could again stand upon its own feet.

Though the pursuit of the new is, in these respects at least, outmoded, it nevertheless seems to continue, particularly among the more radical transcendentalists. And the question arises of how this pursuit is to be understood: Is novelty really a value? If so, of what sort? What is the relationship, if any, of the search for the new to aesthetic beliefs and attitudes? Will the search continue in the years ahead? In attempting to answer these questions, my point of departure will be Harold Rosenberg's suggestion that the new is valuable because it enlarges the sensibilities and awareness of the art audience:

> Form predominates in a work of art after it has become familiar to us; when the surprise, or shock, of novelty has passed, we prize it for its beauty. It is, however, in their disquieting phase—when their strangeness causes them to seem outside of art—that innovating paintings work to expand our consciousness and sensibilities. . . . Thus to appreciate the new *as the new* involves considerations beyond the aesthetic. The key is content. . . . New art is valued for the novel state it induces in the spectator and for what it reveals to him about himself, the physical world, or simply his way of reacting to paintings.[72]

It should be observed, first, that in a literal, yet significant sense, every work of art is unique and therefore in some degree novel. Conse-

---

[72] "The New as Value," p. 142; also see Susan Sontag, *Against Interpretation*, p. 296.

quently, every work of art evokes a specific awareness in, and extends the sensibilities of, those who perceive it. This is true of works in the same style system—for instance Stravinsky's Octet and his Symphony in Three Movements—as well as of works in very different styles. Indeed, it is also true of different performances of the same work.

Clearly Rosenberg has in mind a more radical sort of novelty—a *generic* newness in which sensibility is not merely heightened and refined, but in which innovation creates a shift in aesthetic outlook, a change in aesthetic categories. It is the "idea" or movement—whether of Pop art or kinetic art, aleatoric theater or theater of the absurd, the objective novel or random music—which is novel in this sense. This is indicated by the fact that Rosenberg bases novelty upon "content" and, elsewhere, equates the painter's "idea" with categorical concepts such as "No more black; or, No straight lines." [73] Such generic novelty— emphasizing the "what" of a work of art to the exclusion of the "how"—provides no criteria for judging individual works of art.[74] Thus as Rosenberg himself indicates (when he notes that after a work "has become familiar to us . . . we prize it for its beauty" and "to appreciate the new *as the new* involves considerations beyond the aesthetic"), novelty is not an aesthetic value, but an instrumental one. Its function is to expand consciousness and awareness.

It is, of course, tempting to suppose that the more modes of experience an individual can respond to, or the broader his aesthetic horizons, the better. Or, to state it as a truism, a wide range of sensibility is preferable to a narrow one, a rich response to the world is better than an impoverished one. But it is by no means self-evident that a broadening of categorical sensibility is per se valuable, particularly if it is achieved at the expense of nuance and refinement of perception and response. And it is not unreasonable to suppose that a succession of radical innovations tends to preclude subtle and precise understanding. What is gained in breadth may well be lost in depth.[75]

---

[73] *The Tradition of the New*, p. 67.

[74] But particularly in a situation of fluctuating pluralism, this is, in all senses of the phrase, *the* critical question.

[75] In addition, it is at the very least doubtful that all experiences, whether in life or in art, which are novel and consequently expand consciousness are *necessarily* valuable. If one wants to maintain an essentially ethical-utilitarian view of aesthetic value, as Rosenberg seems to do, then it seems more reasonable to emphasize, as I did in chapter 2, the ability of aesthetic experience to shape and refine the human will and to satisfy the human need for patterned information. Such goals, however, can be most effectively realized, not through the introduction of generic novelty, but through the experiencing of deviation as it occurs within the context of an established tradition. [Note continued next page.]

But the crucial difficulty with this view of the significance of novelty is that it attempts to account in traditional terms for a non-traditional phenomenon. The account is traditional in its emphasis upon content, in the implicit separation of art and nature, and indeed in the very notion that the expanded sensibility of the individual is an important value. Yet the search for generic novelty is itself antitraditional in a number of important respects: for instance, it precludes gradual stylistic development upon which expressive deviation depends; it rules out the possibility of arriving at a single, ultimate truth (style); and by placing no limits upon the category of art, it effectively destroys the art-nature distinction. For the traditionalist, and for the formalist as well, innovation is neither a means nor an end. It is a by-product of aesthetic acitivity and creativity, an unsought result either of the search for self-expression or of the desire to construct with elegance and ingenuity.

Rosenberg's observation is accurate, but his explanation is, I believe, mistaken. Insofar as it is pursued by traditionalists and formalists, novelty is a misguided goal. Novelty is the value—or, more accurately, the method or technique—of transcendentalism. It will continue as the "value" of transcendentalism neither because it expands sensibility nor because rapid stylistic change does not allow sufficient time for appropriate habits of perception and relevant critical criteria to evolve,[76] but because only by avoiding established methods and normative procedures can the artist emphasize and present the concrete particularity of sense experience, unstructured by habit and unguided by known schemata. Though ever more difficult in a situation of fluctuating stasis and therefore perhaps employing ever more radical innovation, the transcendentalists' search for novelty will continue. For the transcendentalist, then, novelty is not a value any more than counterpoint, heroic couplets, or linear perspective are values for the traditionalist or the formalist. It is a method or technique, perhaps the *only* method or technique of transcendentalism. And novelty is cultivated not because it expands the

---

Moreover, just as a continuous stream of surprises eventually makes surprise impossible because we come to expect the unexpected or stop predicting altogether, so a prolonged series of innovations leads us to hold all categories and norms in abeyance. Once we conclude that anything is possible, or that all eventualities are equi-probable, novelty is no longer knowable. The new, if it can be said to exist at all, no longer shocks and cannot expand sensibility.

[76] And *not* because of the economics of the market for the visual arts. For were this an important "cause" of innovation, then innovation and experimentation would not have taken place in music and literature, where economic considerations by no means favor change.

categorical sensibilities of the audience but because it destroys them altogether.

Indeed, as pointed out earlier (chap. 8), the very concept of value is neither appropriate to, nor helpful in, the appreciation of the art of transcendentalism. And Harold Rosenberg points out that the spontaneous impersonality of action-painting leads to a freedom from value: "The gesture on the canvas was a gesture of liberation from Value— political, esthetic, moral." [77] Though one should not, indeed one cannot, evaluate this art—any more than one judges the "value" of a paramecium, a rock, or the motion of the sea—one can respond to it, expressing likes and dislikes as one does about natural objects or events. But such preferences cannot be justified or explained—merely asserted. In the art of transcendentalism, there is literally and *in principle* "no accounting for taste." This being so, the discussion in the following section is relevant to the art of transcendentalism only as it approaches that of formalism.

At the opposite end of the ends-means continuum, the art of commercial traditionalism so blatantly emphasizes subject matter that to know what something represents is to know its "essential" meaning. Value tends to be utilitarian: didactic (novels of social significance), hortative (advertising art), wish-fulfilling (soap operas), or conducive (music to "flunk" by). Since the serious art of traditionalism is largely concerned with the representation of content—as, for instance, in the plays of Arthur Miller, the painting of Magritte, and the music of Menotti— criticism is, for the most part, concerned with explanation: psychological, symbolic, iconographic, and historical. And the criteria of value have, by and large, been derived from the disciplines involved in such explanation.

Content-art—and formal art viewed in terms of content—has been the subject of a vast amount of criticism, some wise, some unwise. It is neither necessary nor possible to discuss this literature here. The more so, because many of the scrupulous artists of our time, even those inclined toward traditionalism, are moving in the direction of formalism. Similarly, though some will doubtless continue to adopt an extreme position, there are, I think, signs that many artists and composers hitherto associated with "pure" transcendentalism are becoming more concerned with structure and process in art.

Though considerable evidence indicates that formalism will be the dominant aesthetic ideology in the coming stasis, neither the values of

---

[77] *The Tradition of the New,* p. 30.

traditionalism nor those of transcendentalism will be eclipsed. Subject matter will be a central value for those continuing to work within the "ends" segment of the ends-means continuum. Skill and elegance, ingenuity and refinement, will be the chief values for those working in the central segment. And novelty will be the method (the "value") of those who continue to espouse the transcendentalist position. These relationships—coupled, perhaps rashly, with what seem to me to be related modes of criticism and correlative philosophical positions—are diagrammed below.

	ENDS .... MEANS		
Aesthetic emphasis:	*Content*	*Form and Process*	*Materials*
Aesthetic position: {	....Traditionalism.... ....Form	....Transcendentalism.... alism..........	
Basis of valuation:	Subject Matter	Skill and Elegance	(Novelty)
Mode of criticism:	Interpretive	Analytic-formal	Descriptive
Correlative philosophies:	Social Action (Marx and Freud) Naturalism Existentialism Pragmatism	Analytic Philosophy Linguistic Philosophy	Mysticism Phenomenology

THE VALUES AND THE PREVALENCE OF FORMALISM

Formalist art neither presents reality, as transcendentalist art does; nor does it represent reality, as traditionalist content-art does. It constructs *a* reality. As their relationships to reality differ, so, too, do the means employed by each of these aesthetic ideologies to compel belief in, and validate the authenticity of, their respective realities. In a sense, transcendentalist art does not have to be *made* compelling. The work convinces, if at all, simply because, like any other fact or event in the world, it exists. It is its own authentication, differing in no essential way from other existent things, save perhaps that it has been signed, sold, and exhibited. Traditionalist art compels belief by virtue of its similarity—represented directly or symbolically—to objects, events, and experiences previously known in the "real" world. Its authenticity, tested and vouched for by our extra-aesthetic experience, is derived and contingent.

Because it constructs its own realities—whether using existing materials (including other art works), stimulating the "real" world, or employing free invention—formalist art must convince primarily in terms of what takes place within the work of art itself.[78] It is not, as with traditionalist art, primarily accuracy of representation, plausibility of plot, power of psychological insight, depth of feeling, or righteousness of moral doctrine that persuades and convinces. Rather, it is elegance of design and ingenuity of process, precision of rhetoric and adroitness of language, refinement of conceit and nuance of probability, or some combination of these, that enforces belief in and validates formalist art.[79] This is not to assert that content is necessarily irrelevant or unimportant, but that the *what* and the *why* of content are seen as inseparable from the *how* of structure and process—from the craft by which content is communicated.

The connection between formalism and craft is both a logical and a necessary one. Since it has been implicit or, often, explicit in much of the preceding discussion, as well as in the statements of artists and critics, one final affirmation of the relationship may serve as a summary. According to Logan Pearsall Smith,

> One of the great defects of our critical vocabulary is the lack of a neutral, non-derogatory name for these great artificers, these artists who derive their inspiration more from the formal than the emotional aspects of their art, and who are more interested in the masterly control of their materials, than in the expression of their own feelings, or the prophetic aspects of their calling.[80]

To show, as I have done in chapter 8 and in this chapter, that formalism with its attendant attitudes is becoming the prevalent, but not

---

[78] Examples of uncompromising statements of this viewpoint are those of Milton Babbitt, "A musical system can provide only the possibility of musical coherence in its own terms" ("Twelve-Tone Rhythmic Structure . . . ," p. 79); and M. Barthes: "On retrouve ici, transposée à l'échelle d'un science du discours, la tâche de la linguistique récente, qui est de décrire la *grammaticalité* des phrases, non leur signification. De la même façon, on s'efforcera de décrire l'acceptabilité des oeuvres, non leur sens" (quoted in "Crisis in Criticism," p. 546).

[79] One striking instance of the coupling of formalist values with a belittling of subject matter is that of Oriental calligraphy. And it may be that one of the shortcomings of much abstract expressionist painting is not that it lacks subject matter, but that in emphasizing the element of personal feeling it tends to neglect the values of skill and virtuosity which are needed in this sort of art in order to compel conviction.

[80] Quoted in Blackmur, *Form and Value in Modern Poetry,* p. 195 n.

the *only*, ideology of contemporary culture or, correlatively, to point to a decline in the significance attributed to subject matter and fidelity of representation is, therefore, to assert the growing importance of skill and elegance as criteria of aesthetic value.[81] In addition to the direct evidence cited, there is a considerable amount of indirect evidence of the growth and prevalence of formalist attitudes, not only in the arts but in culture generally.

It is, as we have seen, the view of many contemporary artists and critics that making a work of art is a species of problem-solving or a kind of experiment. Not only is the notion of art as objective discovery (indicating, as it does, a concern with structure and process rather than subject matter or expression) further evidence of the presence of a tendency toward formalism, but it again emphasizes (at least implicitly) the importance of skill and elegance as criteria of value. For, to the committed problem-solver or the dedicated experimentalist, value does not depend solely or even primarily upon the importance of the problem, where "importance" is defined in terms of social or other goals. It depends rather upon the structure of the solution itself, though the problem-solver must always remember that his solutions should be consonant with and relevant to the wider field or tradition of which they are invariably a part.

This attitude prevails in varying degrees in most disciplines—the sciences, social sciences, and philosophy, as well as the arts. Indeed, it would appear that one of the differences between pure science and technology (see above, p. 217) lies in the fact that for the scientist the value of a piece of research is, to an important degree, a function of the complexity and difficulty of the problem in relation to the ingenuity of experimental design and the elegance of inferential reasoning which yield a viable result. The technologist, on the other hand, caring not a whit for parsimony and polish, values a research project almost entirely in terms of its social or other utility.[82] Similarly, as philosophy becomes

---

[81] This assumes, of course, that communication is a relevant aspect of aesthetic experience, which it is *not* in the art of "pure" transcendentalism.

[82] For these reasons, Rosenberg is, I think, mistaken when he likens a painter's idea of "No more black; or, No straight lines" (see above) to a plumber's way of preventing a toilet tank from sweating. For the painter's "solution"—the consequences he draws from his idea—is judged, if at all, in terms of elegance and skill, while the plumber's solution is essentially evaluated in terms of practical result. And this is, as it were, confirmed by the fact that we attribute craftsmanship to the plumber, not because of his results, but, after we have verified these, in terms of his ingenuity.

concerned with the structure of theories (form) and the design of arguments (process)—with what might be termed the artifice(s) of knowledge—rather than with the true content of reality, elegance and precision, nuance and ingenuity become increasingly important measures of quality. And, as the study of the past gradually reduces the number and importance of facts (content) still to be discovered, historians, too, will probably place increasing emphasis upon methodological refinement and narrative skill.

The reference to history calls attention to an evidence of the prevalence of formalism which has already been discussed, namely, the tendency of a considerable number of contemporary writers to "use" past works, styles, and traditions in the construction of new works. For, as noted earlier, it is the formalists who can employ the past most freely and most fully. And in so doing, their chief interest is not in content, expression, or symbolism, but in manipulating materials, forms, and processes with ingenuity and discrimination.

The discovery of and interest in "Camp" art is yet another indication of the cresting wave of formalism [83] and of its connection with the values of skill and refinement. Two quotations from Susan Sontag's famous essay, "Notes on 'Camp,' " will suffice to show that Camp art is formalism in, so to speak, its "mannerist" phase:

> Camp is the consistently aesthetic experience of the world. It incarnates a victory of "style" over "content," "aesthetics" over "morality," of irony over tragedy. . . .
> Style is everything. Genet's ideas, for instance, are very Camp. Genet's statement that "the only criterion of an act is its elegance" is virtually interchangeable as a statement with Wilde's "in matters of great importance, the vital element is not sincerity, but style." But what counts finally, is the style in which ideas are held.[84]

Another interesting sign of the general acceptance of formalist beliefs and attitudes may be seen in recent judicial decisions on censorship. For in allowing the publication of dialogue and description which would previously have been judged obscene or pornographic, the courts have by implication asserted that means and materials—skill of construction, precision of language, and the like—rather than subjects represented, constitute the essential criteria of value. Content is considered less important than form and process. And, recalling the last quotation, one is tempted to suggest that "the courts are Camp." For, to paraphrase

---

[83] Let us not forget that the crest may at times become a trough.

[84] *Against Interpretation,* pp. 287, 288.

Miss Sontag, they have legalized "the victory of 'style' over 'content,' 'aesthetics' over 'morality' "—though not as yet the victory of irony over tragedy.

The reasons for the prevalence of formalism are many and varied. A number of these have already been discussed. But several important ones—important because they touch upon fundamental aspects of contemporary art and aesthetics—remain to be considered. Before turning to these, it must be stressed once again that, though formalism will tend to function as the ideological-aesthetic "center of gravity" in the stasis predicted for the future, other philosophies, paradigms, and kinds of art will be neither discarded nor subverted. Indeed, one reason for the dominance of formalism lies precisely in its ability to tolerate and comprehend a multiplicity of disparate, competing viewpoints and practices many of which are themselves antithetical to formalism.

The future, like the present, will hold an array of coexisting views of reality, ethical positions, styles of art, and so forth. The differences separating these positions—for instance, between Pop art and abstract expressionism, traditionalism and transcendentalism, neurophysiology and social psychology—will be profound and, at times, irreconcilable. They will stem not from inaccuracy of observation, incompleteness of knowledge, or doubtful lines of reasoning, but from their use of different sorts of reference and, consequently, different premises, data, and methods. These disparities may well be reflections of real and inescapable hierarchic discontinuities. And though it may become possible to describe more precisely how hierarchic discontinuities are articulated—how different levels are related to one another—it will probably not be possible to devise an all-inclusive model or paradigm for a single field, let alone for quite different ones.

For most men, then, one of the central problems of our time—perhaps *the* central problem—is, and will continue to be, that of learning how to live in a relativistic and pluralistic world, a world without scientific, metaphysical, or aesthetic absolutes. In such a world the attraction of formalism is obvious. For, as an objective, neutral method, it can—without respect to the ultimate validity of premises and data, hypotheses and procedures—describe and analyze the structure of systems and constructs and the plausibility of arguments and techniques, whether scientific, philosophical, or aesthetic. And it can evaluate these, not in terms of absolute, final truth values, but in terms of consistency, precision, and ingenuity.

In short, formalism seeks to satisfy the human need for pattern and simplicity not by attempting to discover that unitary truth which from the seventeenth to the twentieth century has been sought in vain, but by developing a method and outlook which is able to embrace the diversity of truths presented by pluralism. For the parsimony of paradigms sought in the past, formalism substitutes a parsimony of method and standard.

Or, to look at the connection between pluralism and formalism from a more specifically aesthetic point of view, a refined appreciation of content requires an intimate awareness of nuances of cultural meaning. Such an awareness, which is acquired only as the result of prolonged and intense experience, is not inter-stylistic—let alone cross-cultural. Consequently, the greater the number of styles of art an individual cultivates, the greater the tendency to direct appreciative attention to formal values rather than to content. For instance, most Western devotees of Hindu music lack the depth of cultural experience needed to appreciate the subtle connotative-referential meanings communicated by Indian *ragas*. What they respond to and enjoy are the intricate play of melodic-rhythmic process and the skill of the improvised structural relationship. That this is the case, is indicated by comparisons made between such improvisations and jazz—for here referential content is clearly not the common denominator.[85] The pluralistic aficionado who appreciates a wide variety of kinds of art—for instance, primitive sculpture, the metaphysical poets, and Japanese court music—must of necessity neglect the cultural content of art, directing his attention to "significant form." Thus in the arts, too, pluralism fosters formalism.

A second, and related, reason why formalism is likely to be the ideological center of gravity in the coming years is that it provides a middle ground between the goalless world of extreme transcendentalism, which is psychologically untenable and intolerable for most men, and the severely shaken world of traditionalism, which has been left without either divinely or naturally authenticated goals.

The world of extreme transcendentalism is, as we have seen, one without causation or purpose, structure or time. It is a world without implication, a world in which prediction, goals, and control are either impossible or irrelevant. Though logically consistent, it is not a world in which man can for long endure. This is so because man is, perhaps above all else, a *predicting* animal.

Belief in the existence of causation and purpose, in the possibility of prediction, and in the efficacy of choice have their origin in the biopsychological nature of man. In less complex animals a relatively large proportion of behavior is genetically determined. The animal comes into

---

[85] This point was called to my attention by my student Steven Crockett.

existence with built-in reaction patterns or with marked tendencies to respond in specific ways to its environment. Man, on the other hand, is born with a much smaller proportion of pre-established behavior patterns. Though our reflexes are taken care of by relatively fixed neural nets, for the most part man must *learn* how to respond to the world.[86] Because his behavior patterns are not genetically specified, man must choose among alternative courses of action, if he is to survive at all. To choose intelligently and successfully man must envisage and predict. He must, that is, make inferences about what will probably follow from a particular set of decisions.

In order to make inferences man must conceptualize, categorize, and symbolize his experience of the world. He must pattern the world. The attempt to give up concepts and patterns, except as a momentary exercise in mysticism, is both futile and misguided. For to abandon one set of categories is invariably to imply some other set. And once an object, attribute, or process has been recognized as separable from all the other things in the universe, it must be conceptualized and categorized in some fashion. Indeed, the act of "separating" is identical with the act of conceptualizing. Thus it is folly to speak of experiencing the world naïvely, without preconceptions. Even unique particulars are experienced categorically. Our perception and awareness of the unique particularity of a specific sunset is not separable from our conceptualization of the event *as being a sunset*.

Predictions, inferences, and categorizations presuppose the existence of a law-like, causal universe. Once this is supposed, the "existence" of time, purpose, and self follow. And though they are frequently based upon inadequate information, mistaken classification, or inept inferences, predictions—particularly relatively short-range ones—are generally quite successful. Indeed, were this not the case, man would have long since gone the way of the dinosaurs, or would have radically revised his behavior.

Though the world pictured by transcendentalism may not be psychologically viable, from a cultural-historical point of view it is neither captious nor fatuous. For this viewpoint is one way of dealing with what for many men is probably the most disturbing and revolutionary aspect of modern culture, namely, that the rising tide of empirical science has, on the one hand, faced man with the proposition that death is oblitera-

---

[86] In this connection, see, for instance, A. L. Kroeber, *An Anthropologist Looks at History*, pp. 200–201; John Pfeiffer, *The Human Brain*, p. 37; Colin Cherry, *On Human Communication*, p. 269, and Clifford Geertz, "The Impact of the Concept of Culture on the Concept of Man," p. 108 and *passim*.

tion and, on the other hand, left him without a unitary world view—whether a divine plan or a natural order—in terms of which the possibility of non-being could be comprehended.

Recent developments in science, particularly in biology, have made it increasingly difficult for thoughtful, educated men and women to believe in the existence of a mind or soul differentiable from the physiological processes of the body.[87] If mind and body are one,[88] then immortality which not only constituted a meaningful life goal, but tempered and mitigated the prospect of death, is no longer credible—save perhaps for those few who are able to believe in the literal resurrection of the body. Death, as literal and total obliteration, is today a stark and pressing fact of human existence.

The confutation of the mind-body dichotomy, together with the general acceptance of the outlook and conclusions of science, has effectively destroyed belief both in the existence of a divine order and in the absolute human and ethical goals which that order affirmed. Little is left but what Susan Sontag has aptly dubbed "religious fellow-travelling"—a vestigial, routine piety.[89] If faith in the existence of a divine order has faded, so has confidence in the possibility of developing a single, comprehensive picture of reality upon which a verified and permanent "natural" metaphysics might be based.

The lack of a fixed and authoritative order, validating human activities and goals, has faced contemporary man with what is perhaps the ultimate question: in the light of the finality of death and considering the inscrutability of the universe—the capriciousness of events, the possibility of injustice and unmerited misfortune—what is the meaning, the purpose, of human existence? This question has received a multitude of diverse answers.

At one extreme are the transcendentalists. Whether viewed from a

---

[87] It is obviously impossible to cite even a small part of the evidence for this statement. But the point is so important that some should be presented: Kroeber tells us that "it seems exceedingly "doubtful that the majority of humanists still believe in spirit or spirituality, except as a metaphor" (*An Anthropologist Looks at History*, p. 128); and Herbert Kohl writes that for the existentialists "Death has made the possibility of nonbeing, Nothingness, a reality" (*The Age of Complexity*, p. 133).

[88] It must be emphasized that to contend that there is no separable entity, "mind," to be found in the world is not to assert that mental activity is identical with neurophysiological process. The relationship of the hierarchic level of mind—of thinking—to lower levels of chemical and biological activity is still very problematic.

[89] See her essay, "Piety without Content," in *Against Interpretation*, pp. 249–55.

hierarchic level of cosmic scope in which a mystic unity is sensed or revealed, or from the lowest level on which only unique particulars are granted reality, existence is seen as One. Distinctions between life and death, man and nature, mind and matter, means and ends, are all considered to be arbitrary and artificial orderings imposed by man upon a fundamentally unarticulated universe. Consequently goals and meanings are impossible and irrelevant, and the search for a specifically human significance is misguided. For those who genuinely espouse this view—and, for reasons presented above, I suspect that they are very few—the question of the meaning of human existence does not have to be answered, because it was never real or pertinent to begin with.

At the opposite extreme is the traditionalist. Because he believes that distinctions such as those just mentioned have a categorical reality, the traditionalist is vitally concerned with meanings and goals, content and expression. Hence the question of the significance of human existence is particularly poignant and pressing for him. (Indeed, for the existentialists it is THE question.) And it should be observed that even when he declares—in defiance or in despair—that existence is meaningless or absurd, the traditionalist is still in basic disagreement with the transcendentalist. For implicit in his declaration is the belief that existence *should* be meaningful.

But few traditionalists have given way to total despair—to nihilism. Most have sought and found some sort of meaning and purpose in existence. Often these have been found to lie in the discovery and perfection of the self—a state of secular grace in which the human will or spirit is specified, shaped, and refined by the choices and commitments made by the individual.[90] Such purification and self-realization through what we undergo—what we suffer—is not a new goal. Rather, as Susan Sontag points out, it is a secular "translation" of an established doctrine, an instance of "the latest and most powerful legacy of the Christian tradition of introspection, opened up by Paul and Augustine, which equates the discovery of the self with the discovery of the suffering self. For the modern consciousness, the artist (replacing the saint) is the exemplary sufferer." [91]

In a universe in which the meaning and purpose of human existence are culturally validated and defined, to accept suffering and to risk destruction are acts of courage and nobility. And because it can be

---

[90] Obviously this was essentially my own point of view when I wrote chapter 2. And perhaps it was the only one possible for a non-believing traditionalist.

[91] *Against Interpretation*, p. 42.

construed within a larger, yet understandable, order, even failure may be significant and admirable. But to court anguish and invite annihilation in the absence of faith in an orderly universe guaranteeing human values—where pain and disappointment, misfortune and death, cannot be comprehended as part of some larger plan—is either a posture of rash romanticism or, in the extreme case, an act of superhuman heroism.[92] "If one can attain a break-through—a bravely irrational one unmediated by universals—he can reach the glories of transcendence; if he fails, he must live in the comtemplation of nothingness." [93] But even were such a Kierkegaardian "leap of faith" successful, it would constitute a flight from the hierarchic level of the human condition—from meanings and purposes, action and passions, community and communication—to that of a solipsistic mysticism in which, for reasons presented above, few men can for long endure.

Both traditionalism and transcendentalism will continue to attract adherents and to have staunch defenders. And within both, a number of specific philosophies and viewpoints—each selecting different data, emphasizing different relationships, and conceiving of reality somewhat differently—will coexist. But none will for long be the predominant position in the fluctuating, yet static, pluralism of the future. This is so, not only for reasons already discussed, but because neither traditionalism nor transcendentalism is, so to speak, ideologically consonant with the contemporary cultural situation.

Though traditionalism and transcendentalism will allow of a number of variant positions, both are fundamentally monistic and absolutist: transcendentalism insisting upon direct, intuitive experience, unme-

---

[92] It is not alone, I suspect, because man is no longer considered to be the center of the universe, "the paragon of animals," that contemporary artists have for the most part forsaken the vision of sublime and cosmic monumentality which has been so important in Western art since its beginning. Partly it is because few artists really believe in the existence of a cohesive, fundamental order within which the diversity and scope, the hazard and mystery, of the universe can be understood.

To tremble on the brink of chaos, sensing the brute grandeur and uncertainty of creation through the shocking conjunction of incomparables, may be a magnificent and exhilarating experience as long as beneath the arbitrary event and behind the inescapable oblivion some sort of reason and order are thought to exist. But to attempt to communicate a vision of monumentality in the absence of such beliefs is almost invariably to produce vacuous bombast rather than grandeur, and self-indulgent sentimentality rather than emotion.

The "aesthetics" of monumentality was discussed at the end of chapter 2; the relationship of monumentality to functionalism and hierarchic structure in music is touched upon at the end of chapter 12.

[93] Murray Krieger, "Tragedy and the Tragic Vision," p. 17.

diated by concepts and categories, as the only true and valid knowledge of reality, and traditionalism positing the existence of an all-embracing, eternal truth—a single, ultimate reality—as the source for the meaning and purpose of human life.

Formalism, on the other hand, is relativistic and pluralistic. Because it admits the provisional validity of alternative constructs and because, as we have seen, it shares important beliefs and attitudes with both traditionalism and transcendentalism, formalism is congruent with the current cultural condition and, for this reason, its influence will be both deep and broad in the years ahead.

And this, I suggest, will be true not only in philosophy, science, and the arts, but in our attitudes toward the activity of living itself. For if we consider death to be final, long-range goals uncertain or ephemeral, and the validity of beliefs and paradigms not absolute but provisional, then we will tend to see the meaning and value of human existence as "contextual" and formal. Emphasis will be less upon *what* happens or is accomplished in a life (upon content and goals) and more upon *how* life is lived—upon the coherence and elegance of its design and structure.[94] In this coming-together of means and ends in a formally constructed artifice, I am reminded not only of the lines from "Sailing to Byzantium," quoted at the beginning of this chapter, but of those which close Yeats's poem "Among School Children":

> O chestnut tree, great rooted blossomer,
> Are you the leaf, the blossom or the bole?
> O body swayed to music, O brightening glance,
> How can we know the dancer from the dance?

---

[94] This tendency may well be encouraged by other circumstances. It has frequently been suggested in recent years that the rapid development of automation will create a vast increase in leisure time and that, as a result, the concept of "work" will have to be redefined in less puritanical terms. If this is correct, the traditional view of work as a goal-oriented *chore* (notice the connection of suffering to value) may well give way to a view in which "work"—whether gainful or not, such as amateur chamber music, Sunday painting, or fishing—is valued *as an activity*. And once again, as emphasis moves from content and goals toward form and process, a dualism—this time, the work-play dichotomy—tends to disappear.

PART III

---

*Formalism in Music:
Queries and
Reservations*

INTRODUCTION

Evidence presented in the preceding chapters indicates that the arts have entered a period in which a multiplicity of styles and techniques, attitudes and ideologies, will coexist for a considerable period of time. Because it can comprehend and tolerate the diversity of multiplicity, formalism will tend to be the dominant ideology not only in the arts but in culture generally. By emphasizing that works of art are artificial constructs whose validity is internal or contextual and that creating a work of art is an act of objective, impersonal discovery, formalism has strongly encouraged experimentalism in the arts.[1]

Particularly in music, the conscious search for new materials, techniques, and principles of organization has led to a significant reduction in the levels of both cultural and compositional redundancy. Or, looked at from the opposite viewpoint: experimentalism has produced a marked increase in the perceptual complexity (information) which listeners are required to comprehend. It is therefore of some importance to consider the arguments for and the consequences of experimentalism in music, especially because both the temptations and the dangers of complexity are greater in music than in the other arts.

Experimentation in literature is limited by the fact that language is a conventional, learned sign system. With the possible exception of Joyce's *Finnegan's Wake*, writers have not attempted to create new

---

[1] See pp. 182–84, above; and Susan Sontag, *Against Interpretation*, p. 100.

vocabularies, grammars, and syntaxes. Certainly, they have not done so on a large scale or in a systematic way. Complexity, too, tends to be limited, both because a sign system which must be shared by a whole culture tends to be conservative and because languages are themselves inherently redundant.[2]

The visual arts, on the other hand, employ "natural," iconic signs, though these are often highly conventionalized. That is, the properties of a painting or a sculpture—its lines and color, volumes and textures—are the same as those seen in the extra-aesthetic world. Consequently, visual signs do not have to be learned in the same way that verbal ones do. Because comprehension and appreciation do not depend upon learning a particular vocabulary, grammar, and syntax, radical experimentation is possible, and has been common, in the plastic arts. Moreover, since they are not syntactic and time-directed, the integrative power of memory, relating later to earlier events, is considerably less important in the appreciation of the plastic arts than in the understanding of music and literature. As a result, complexity does not generally constitute a problem for the art audience. Rather, the problem in the visual arts has been that of extending categorical sensibility. And it is perhaps partly for this reason that, once novelty was accepted as a facet of contemporaneity, modern art was able to attract a large and devoted following, while avant-garde music and literature were not.

Musical sign systems fall somewhere between the conventional ones of language and the iconic ones of the plastic arts. The materials and syntax of music are partly "natural" in the sense that they derive from the operation of *Gestalt*-like modes of pattern perception; partly they are conventional and associatively learned, as are the progressions of tonal harmony—though even these may have their roots in innate perceptual tendencies.[3] Because music is not exclusively a learned sign system, a considerable amount of experimental innovation is evidently possible.

Experimentation has been encouraged not only by the ideological attitudes discussed earlier but by the fact that music has, since its beginnings, been associated through practice, tradition, and theory with various sorts of formal systematization. A syntactic, abstract time-art which is vitally dependent upon aural memory, however, can reduce

---

[2] Because of difference among the arts, mentioned earlier as well as here, Susan Sontag is, I think, mistaken when she suggests that the novel can or should be experimental in the sense that art and music have been so. See *Against Interpretation,* pp. 100–101.

[3] See below, pp. 288–89.

Introduction

cultural and compositional redundancy too far. It can, that is, exceed the perceptual-cognitive capacities of the human mind.

Because the final section of this book will be concerned, directly or indirectly, with the perceptual-cognitive problems posed by highly complex music, it is important to emphasize that the amount of information which can be comprehended by the human mind depends upon both native ability and experience. Therefore, the limits of complexity cannot be fixed with precision but will vary considerably from one listener to another. No doubt some listeners are able to remember and comprehend a remarkable amount of musical information. But it does not follow from this that anything is possible—that there are no limits whatever.

Experimentation in music has produced a host of new methods, techniques, and constructive principles, and it has extended existing ones in various ways. In fact, as we shall see, each new composition tends to employ a unique set of syntactic premises.[4] Because there is no single, or even pre-eminent, experimental music, but rather a plethora of different methods and kinds of music, I have chosen to direct my remarks primarily to the theory and practice of what is called "total serialism." I have done so, not because total serialism is more important or more prevalent than other kinds of experimental music—indeed, it is perhaps already passé—but because its theory and practice have been carefully formulated and explicitly employed. Though the theory and practice of total serialism will be my point of departure as well as the

---

[4] It is important to notice that there is no necessary correlation between compositional method and aesthetic viewpoint. Many composers, beginning with Schönberg and Berg, have employed the twelve-tone method for traditional, expressive ends. Some serialists—for instance, Webern and more recently Babbitt—have tended strongly toward formalism, while others—for example, Pousseur and Berio—have inclined toward transcendentalism. Similarly, there have been tonally oriented formalists, such as Stravinsky, as well as traditionalists. It is difficult, however, to imagine the possibility of a tonal transcendentalist. And though a thoroughgoing use of aleatoric method is probably suited only to the goals of transcendentalism, the randomization of *parts* of a work—perhaps using improvisation—may be useful in articulating structure even in a traditionalist composition.

Just as a composer may change methods from one work to another without changing aesthetic viewpoint (for instance, Stravinsky's recent works are serial, though he remains a formalist), so a composer may, as Krenek has done, change his aesthetic position without changing his basic method. Nor is there any necessary correspondence between aesthetic viewpoint and style. Ralph Shapey's music is clearly traditionalist—passionately expressive and intensely goal-oriented. But his style is radically different from that of more conventional traditionalists such as Copland and Hindemith.

main focus of attention, however, many of the aesthetic, theoretical, and empirical questions posed and explored are, I believe, pertinent and relevant to highly complex music which is not organized along serial lines.

Since it may appear to some readers that what follows constitutes a condemnation of experimental music, whether serial or not, let me state unequivocally that this is not the case. Because the issues and problems upon which attention must be focused are so basic—transcending the parochialism of the present—a dispassionate analysis of the difficulties involved in the perception and comprehension of this music seeks to enhance our understanding of the nature of musical structures and musical experience regardless of style or method.

More than ever before, it is, I think, pointless and misleading to base critical judgments upon stylistic biases. Though it is about as audacious as being "Pro God and Country" (mother-love is taboo), it is important, particularly in an age of stylistic pluralism, to stress that the only music one should be "for" is *good* music—whatever its style or method. And there have been some first-rate serial and experimental compositions.

The time for partisan polemic has long since passed. It is foolish to assume categorical positions, invoke a priori arguments, and make absolute judgments, whether about the propriety of writing tonal music in the mid-twentieth century, about the legitimacy of the method and practice of serialism, or about the validity of the aesthetic goals of transcendental particularism. All these ways of making music are with us and, as I have suggested, will probably continue to be with us for many years.

What is needed is not contention but sympathetic, yet critical, understanding. In what follows, I shall try to be as detached and objective as possible—soberly examining theoretical assumptions and the consequences said to follow from them, pointing to difficulties which seem to be involved in the perception and understanding of highly complex music, raising questions about possible formal and structural results of total serialization, and, in summary, striving to identify and formulate the fundamental problems posed by recent music theory and practice.

DEFINITIONS AND BACKGROUND

Total serialism may be generally defined as "the extension of the serial concept over all aspects (or parameters) of the musical process.

Introduction

. . . everything from pitch succession to density to dynamics to time values is regulated by serial statements derived from one single archetype (usually the order of magnitude shown in the intervals of the basic tone-row) so that literally everything is intricately and inextricably related to everything else." [5]

Although a rigid ordering of the parameters of sound may be prescribed within any one composition, however, the manner in which the several serial orderings of time, timbre, dynamics, and so forth is derived from the tone row and how these orderings are related to one another will vary from work to work—even within the oeuvre of one composer. For instance, Boulez, Babbitt, and Krenek all derive their durational series [6] from their tone rows, but they do so in very different ways and with very different compositional results.[7] What Ernst Krenek has referred to as the "primary and indispensable motivation of serialism—so to speak, its ethics—the idea that all phenomena of the work ought to be traceable to one unique perceivable source" [8] does not oblige composers to follow the same procedures any more than it requires that they select the same tone rows.

Serial composers, as well as their hostile critics, have tended to emphasize the number, rigidity, and importance of the operational rules of this method. This is because, in the absence of common, traditional practice, compositional constraints become tremendously important. The parallel with Thomas S. Kuhn's description of the development of scientific theories is very striking.

> Normal science can proceed without rules only so long as the relevant scientific community accepts without question the particular problem-solutions already achieved. *Rules should therefore become important and the characteristic unconcern about them should vanish whenever paradigms or models are felt to be insecure.* That is, moreover, exactly what does occur. The preparadigm period, in particular, is regularly marked by frequent and deep debates over legitimate methods, problems, and standards of solution, though these serve rather to define schools than to produce agreement.[9]

---

[5] Ernst Krenek, "Tradition in Perspective," p. 35.

[6] A durational series is a set of twelve different time lengths whose ordering gives rise to all the temporal events in a composition.

[7] See György Ligeti, "Pierre Boulez"; Ernst Krenek, "Extents and Limits of Serial Techniques"; and Milton Babbitt, "Twelve-Tone Rhythmic Structure and the Electronic Medium."

[8] "Serialism," p. 67.

[9] *The Structure of Scientific Revolutions,* pp. 47–48. Italics mine.

But the fact is that the compositional constraints imposed by the rules of serialism are much *less* comprehensive than those imposed by the traditional constraints involved in the composition of tonal music.

The serial composer has enormous freedom. He selects this twelve-tone series rather than some other, decides which set-form (out of the forty-eight available) to use at any particular time, establishes his own procedures for combining different set-forms, and makes his own rules for verticalizing the row. The rules, as stated by George Perle, are minimal:

1. The set comprises all twelve notes of the semitonal scale, arranged in a specific linear order.
2. No note appears more than once within the set.
3. The set is statable in any of its linear aspects: prime, inversion, retrograde, and retrograde-inversion.
4. The set, in each of its four transformations (i.e., linear aspects), is statable upon any degree of the semitonal scale.[10]

And although the compositional constraints are somewhat more severe when the serialization of other parameters is added to that of pitch, the composer's prerogative to select materials, rules of derivation, methods for ordering and relating parameters to one another, as well as his freedom to make compositional choices within this self-established set of rules allows for very diverse kinds of music, not only between the music of different composers, but even within the music of one composer.

Indeed, the precompositional systems and the compositional practices of serialism are so various that the only way to describe the method and the music in greater detail than we have done would be to examine the rules employed and procedures followed in specific pieces. Such an examination is beyond the scope and purpose of this volume.

The difficulty is that, while the rules of serialism—whether partial or total—tend to preclude certain kinds of musical organization, they do not establish a particular set of implicative and formalized relationships; that is, they do not specify a syntax and grammar of their own. Consequently, the rules and compositional procedures of serialism do not define a style or style system; [11] what they have in common is rather their opposition to the traditional style system of tonal music.

This should not surprise us. For a piece of music is specified not by an exhaustive set of rules which can be preformulated, but by a tradi-

---

[10] *Serial Composition and Atonality*, p. 3.
[11] See Milton Babbitt, quoted on p. 279, below.

tional practice which cannot be fully explicated in rules. "Rules of art can be useful," writes Michael Polanyi, "but they do not determine the practice of an art; they are maxims, which can serve as a guide to an art only if they can be integrated into the practical knowledge of the art. They cannot replace this knowledge." [12] What is needed if serialism is to become a viable and intelligible musical style is not more rules but a common practice—a musical paradigm.

Although the rules of serialism do not, and are not intended to, establish a musical syntax, twelve-tone pieces often sound alike—and so do totally serialized pieces. They do so partly because the composers' common musical experiences tend to produce a shared taste for particular sounds. In other cases such similarities are, as we shall see, due to explicitly stated aesthetic beliefs and attitudes, held in common by groups of composers. To some extent serial music—particularly the compositions of the Viennese twelve-tone composers—constitutes a kind of stylistic family because of the origins of the twelve-tone method.

The musical practice of the nineteenth century was characterized by a markedly increased use of the ambiguous chords, the less probable harmonic progressions, and the more unusual melodic and rhythmic inflections possible within the style of tonal music. The distinction between the exceptional and the normal became more and more blurred; and, as a result, there was a concomitant loosening of the syntactical bonds through which tones and harmonies had been related to one another. The connections between harmonies were uncertain even on the lowest—the chord-to-chord—level. On higher levels, long-range harmonic relationships and implications became so tenuous that they hardly functioned at all. At best, the felt probabilities of the style system had become obscure; at worst, they were approaching a uniformity which provided few guides for either composition or listening. Schönberg's conscious abandonment of tonality (in his non-serial atonal works) merely recognized the situation for what it was and carried the dissolution a bit further.

Atonality, however, created two serious problems for the composer. The first was that, by removing the last vestige of traditional melodic, harmonic, and formal constraints, it presented the composer with a theoretically unlimited number of compositional choices. Nothing was impossible. All the composer had to guide him were his own taste and as much of tradition as he cared to bring into play. Faced with the

---

[12] *Personal Knowledge,* p. 50.

awesome task of perhaps having to choose every single pitch from scratch, the composer had to invent constraints if he was to compose at all.

The particular constraints that Schönberg developed were designed to solve the second problem facing the composer of atonal music: how was he to avoid implying functional relationships appropriate to the syntax of traditional tonality but irrelevant and misleading in a non-tonal idiom? Schönberg himself stated the matter thus: "Even a slight reminiscence of the former tonal harmony would be disturbing, because it would create false expectations of consequences and continuations."[13] From this reasonable premise almost all the basic rules of twelve-tone composition follow. For instance, the stipulation that the row should contain all twelve tones of the chromatic scale, the rule of non-repetition within the row, and the precept about the avoidance of octaves are all essentially designed to assure as far as possible that no tone is so emphasized that it might be understood as a tonic, related in some functional and traditional way to other tones.[14]

Although the rules and constraints of the twelve-tone method may help to keep the composer from inadvertently writing passages that sound tonal, they do not preclude the possibility of functionalism. There are several reasons for this. First, the freedom allowed the composer in selecting or constructing the twelve-tone row enables him to introduce elements similar to those of tonal music into the series if he so desires; and the latitude permitted in the verticalization of the series makes it

---

[13] *Style and Idea*, p. 108.

[14] Because the first of these rules—the requirement that all twelve tones be used—has not always been followed, it might be worth pointing out why the rule is reasonable, particularly since it is a consequence of a fundamental psychological principle.

Recent literature in perception indicates that visual or auditory stimuli tend to be organized into patterns; and, when the stimuli follow one another in time, the patterns that emerge will be interpreted as functional—that is, earlier events will be understood as implying later ones—particularly if the relationships between the stimuli involve some sort of differentiation. On the other hand, a series of uniform intervals, such as the equal-tempered half-tone scale or the whole-tone scale which contain no intervallic differentiation, is usually perceived as non-functional—at least when taken merely as a collection of available pitches. Thus, Schönberg was correct to insist upon the use of the full semitonal scale in the construction of tone rows. For to omit one or more tones from the chromatic series necessarily destroys uniformity or, conversely, creates differentiation and hence tends to produce some sort of tonal functionalism. It is perhaps for this reason that, as Curt Sachs writes, "there has always been an inhibition against equality [of interval]" (*The Wellsprings of Music*, p. 153).

possible for the composer to emphasize traditional tonal patterns. Both these points are clearly illustrated in Alban Berg's *Lyric Suite:* the main row, divided into two distinguishable tonal areas, gives rise to various kinds of tonal configurations—triadic melodic lines, chords built on thirds, and so forth; and, in the last movement (mm. 26–27), the opening measures of *Tristan* are quoted within the "framework" of the tone row.

Second, functional implication is by no means a product only of the relationships between immediately adjacent pitches and harmonies. Higher-level connections between non-adjacent tones tend to produce high-level melodic lines which may be perceived as functional. And such high-level hierarchic relationships can, of course, be emphasized by register, dynamics, timbre, and formal ordering (e.g., motivic repetition). Most important of all, they can be emphasized, indeed created, by metric placement and rhythmic organization. Although particular musical styles exhibit characteristic metric-rhythmic norms, these tend to be so diverse that they have not given rise to traditionally established sets of syntactical functions to the extent that pitch relationships have. And perhaps it was partly for this reason that Schönberg did not find it necessary to serialize this parameter. Nevertheless, particularly when coupled with motivic repetition, rhythmic organization can create a very strong sense of implicative, goal-directed motion. And such motion tends to make pitch relationships *seem* functional.

Indeed, the unique and unforgettable flavor of, say, Schönberg's music is to a considerable extent a product of the way in which goal-directed motives, structural lines, and rhythmic patterns are combined with serial procedures which preclude the possibility of traditional harmonic goals. The music seems almost hysterically emotional because its intensely directive motion can find no points of real repose. It is driven frantically toward the unattainable.

It would, of course, be a mistake to believe that Schönberg's music has this character because of the rules of serialism. For it had very much the same character—for instance, in *Pierrot Lunaire*—before serial procedures were invented. In short, as we have already noted, the rules of serialism do not define syntax or determine style. Webern's music, though based upon the same serial procedures, is syntactically and stylistically quite different from Schönberg's. For by avoiding high-level, registral melodic motion as well as directively organized rhythmic patterns and sequentially structured motivic relationships, Webern weakens the listener's sense of goal-directed motion. It is because of this tendency toward non-functionalism on all levels and for all parameters that the composers of the avant-garde feel that "modern" music begins, not with Schönberg, who represents the end of romanticism, but with Webern.[15]

---

[15] Webern did *not*, as is sometimes implied, serialize parameters of sound other than pitch. See, in this connection, Herbert Eimert, "The Composer's Freedom of Choice," who writes that "it would be a mistake to think that Anton Webern was already aiming at such 'ordering in time'" (p. 3). For a similar view see Peter Westergaard, "Webern and 'Total Organization,'" p. 107.

CHAPTER

IO

The Arguments for Experimental Music

Although the validity of the reasons given by composers and theorists for a particular set of compositional procedures must not be confused with the merit of the actual music—for good musical choices can be made for bad theoretical reasons—a review of the arguments and the evidence presented in its favor by the advocates of totally ordered music will serve to raise fundamental theoretical issues and to call attention to significant practical problems relating to the perception and cognition of highly complex music whether serial or not. The arguments may be grouped into four general categories: (1) the argument from the nature of the acoustical materials of music; (2) the argument from the isomorphism of pitch and time; (3) the argument by analogy to physical or mathematical models; and (4) the argument from historical necessity.

ARGUMENTS FROM THE NATURE OF THE ACOUSTICAL MATERIALS OF MUSIC

According to Herbert Eimert, the music of Webern and of the total serialists who followed him "is based upon the fundamental unity of all acoustical material—on the recognition that everything is identical." [1]

---

[1] "The Composer's Freedom of Choice," p. 3.

Several important consequences are evidently drawn from this imprecise, but seemingly plausible, statement. The line of reasoning apparently runs something like this: All the parameters of sound—pitch, duration, timbre, loudness, and so on—have as their single, unitary source a periodic wave form. This being so, it follows, so the argument goes, that: (1) All the parameters of sound can be reduced to the acoustic properties of sound waves; or, in Stockhausen's words, "all differences of acoustic perception can be traced to differences in the temporal structure of sound waves." [2] (2) Because the acoustic source is unitary in the sense that frequency, timbre, duration, and intensity are all manifestations of a single basic temporal process (a sound wave), the parameters of sound must necessarily be equivalents of one another. [3] (3) If this is correct, then all the parameters ought to be equally important in the composition of music. Thus Dieter Schnebel writes that "the aim is to annul the principle of dominance. No longer are the elements . . . to be subordinated to one dominant element; they are to co-exist as individualities." [4] And, finally, (4) it follows from this that all the parameters should be treated equally—that is, all should be serialized within some encompassing plan.

The whole argument is both logically confused and empirically unsound. In the first place, it is an inexcusable error to equate acoustical phenomena with qualitative experiences. The former are abstract scientific concepts, the latter are psychological perceptions. One measures frequency, but one perceives pitch. Stockhausen's phrase "acoustic perception" is a self-contradictory absurdity.

Nor is there any simple one-to-one relationship between an acoustical event and its concomitant perceptual experience. Pitch, for instance, is a complex function of both frequency and intensity. One can keep frequency constant and, by changing intensity, alter pitch. [5] Similarly, loudness and volume, which probably combine to form what we designate as the dynamic level (though this is obviously also a function of context), are complex tonal attributes which cannot be equated in any simple way with any single physical characteristic of sound. [6] And so it is also with the other qualitative attributes of sound.

---

[2] Karlheinz Stockhausen, "The Concept of Unity in Electronic Music," p. 40.

[3] Or, viewed somewhat differently, since "all acoustic events . . . are time processes [it is] possible to dissolve the traditional dimensions of music . . . to form the superior category 'articulation of time'" (Heinz-Klaus Metzger, "Intermezzo I," p. 72).

[4] "Karlheinz Stockhausen," p. 133.

[5] See S. S. Stevens and H. Davis, *Hearing*, pp. 70–73.

[6] *Ibid.*, chaps. 4 and 5.

Arguments for Experimental Music

These remarks do not rule out the possibility of relating psychological phenomena to acoustical events. The difficulty is that our knowledge of the neurophysiology of auditory perception and cognitive processes is at present so rudimentary that this ignorance, taken together with the complexity of the stimulus itself, makes the possibility of discovering precise and verifiable connections seem very remote indeed. But even if one could in principle reduce perceptual experience to elementary acoustical events, it does not necessarily follow that any benefit would be gained thereby. For, as Ernest Nagel points out, "the possibility should not be ignored that little if any new knowledge or increased power for significant research may actually be gained from reducing one science to another at certain periods of their development, however great may be the potential advantages of such reduction at some later time." [7] Nor does it follow that perceptual experience would therefore be monolithic. To argue that the differences among pitch, duration, dynamics, timbre, and so on are unreal or unimportant because they can all be traced or reduced to frequency and amplitude is as preposterous as to assert that the differences between rocks, trees, and men are illusory and trivial because they can be reduced to protons and electrons.

If the spurious argument for the unity and equivalence of the parameters of sound is discarded, the notion that all the parameters are equally important does not necessarily follow. And, in fact, ordinary experience shows that it is mistaken. Pitch and time are primary, pattern-forming parameters; dynamics, timbre, and mode of playing (attack, touch, etc.) are dependent variables relative to each other as well as to pitch and duration. After experimenting with the serialization of secondary qualities, Boulez has concluded that "in regard to compositional dialectic, pitch and duration hold priority whereas dynamics and timbre belong to categories of a secondary character." [8] The distinction is important not only theoretically but practically—and for the performer as well as the composer.[9]

To put the matter briefly, pitch-time articulations generate relatively stable relationships that usually remain recognizably the same even when the secondary parameters are considerably changed. But timbre, dynamics, and touch do not form recognizable patterns; and one finds it difficult to imagine such a "pattern" enduring if the primary parameters

[7] *The Structure of Science*, p. 362.

[8] Quoted by Karl Kohn in "Current Chronicle—Los Angeles," p. 368. Also see Pierre Boulez, "'At the ends of fruitful land . . . ,'" pp. 26–27; and H. H. Stuckenschmidt, "Contemporary Techniques in Music," p. 11.

[9] See György Ligeti, "Pierre Boulez," pp. 40 and 42; and Leonard Stein, "The Performer's Point of View," pp. 65–66.

were even modestly varied. These perceptual facts are clearly reflected in our notation, which provides for much more precise definition of the primary qualities, and in ordinary as well as technical language, both of which contain a host of terms for pitch-time patterns, but very few for dynamics, timbre, touch, and so on.

It could be argued that the tendency to group pitch and time, rather than dynamics, timbre, and touch, into patterned relationships is a culturally conditioned kind of behavior and that it therefore might be possible to learn to perceive the secondary parameters as stable organized relationships. Perhaps. But cross-cultural evidence seems to indicate that this is not so. For pitch-time relationships are also the primary categories of organization in the theory, notation, and musical terminology of most non-Western cultures. Even nuances of ornamentation which might at first seem to involve patternings of timbre and intensity are, as a rule, really facets of melodic organization. It thus appears that there is, at the very least, a marked psychological (and perhaps neurological) predisposition for pitch and time to become the primary perceptual parameters.

Two significant points emerge from this discussion. (1) Whatever its compositional merits may be, total serialism cannot, on the basis of the argument examined here, be regarded as a necessary consequence of the nature of either the acoustics of sound or the psychology of perception. (2) Since the secondary parameters are not essentially pattern-forming, total serialism, as a method for organizing musical processes and structures, need not be really "total." That is, it may involve only the serialization of pitch and time. Hence I shall, hereafter, use the term "total serialism" to mean music in which these two parameters are serialized—whether the secondary parameters are so or not.

THE ARGUMENT FROM THE ISOMORPHISM OF PITCH AND TIME

The fact that it is not a necessary consequence of the acoustics of sound does not, of course, imply that total serialism—the serialization of pitch and duration—is arbitrary or unreasonable. Indeed, from a historical point of view the tendency toward more stringent constraints is quite understandable.

Because they were supplemented by limitations derived from the melodic, formal, and rhythmic tradition of late Romantic music, the rules of twelve-tone composition provided adequate compositional constraints for Schönberg and Berg. Evidently these constraints were less adequate for Webern because he tended to reinforce them with the use of strict contrapuntal devices. In the next generation many composers of serial music rejected not only the ethos of late Romantic music but the tradition of Western tonal music as a whole. These composers found that the rules of the twelve-tone method were too liberal. New constraints had to be invented if music was to be composed at all. And what could be more natural than to use the constraints already in existence and extend their scope to include duration? Moreover, by subjecting the other parameters of sound to limitations similar to, or derived from, those used in the serialization of pitch, the composer-theorist could satisfy the deeply felt human need for systematic economy and elegance.

The fact that a course of action can be explained in terms of its history does not prevent the action itself from being arbitrary. The behavior of a psychotic may be explicable in terms of his genetic inheritance and his environment; yet his actions may be judged arbitrary.

The decision to apply serial procedures to parameters other than pitch and to derive such serializations from the twelve-tone row was, and still is, an arbitrary one. The same end—the invention of new constraints—could have been achieved in different ways. Thus, while Schönberg's use of twelve pitches derives both from the *de facto* existence of the equal-tempered chromatic scale and from a desire to avoid suggesting traditional tonal implications, the use of twelve durations or twelve time points finds no sanction within common practice, or in the acoustic properties or psychological characteristics of temporal events. There is no finite number of durations or "time points," let alone merely twelve. "The assumption of 'twelve' time points," writes Milton Babbitt, "is an arbitrary derivative of the pitch system. Obviously, the time-point system is applicable to any number of set elements." [10]

Professor Babbitt seems a bit uneasy not only about the arbitrariness of the number twelve, but about the whole notion of serializing duration. And he is at considerable pains to point out "the immanently temporal nature of the twelve-tone pitch class system." [11] But he does not attempt to prove that the serialization of time or his own time-point system necessarily follow from the twelve-tone system. Rather, he seeks to show that it is not unreasonable to construct a system of durational values that is an exact analogue of, and isomorphic with, the twelve-tone pitch class system.

---

[10] "Twelve-Tone Rhythmic Structure . . . ," p. 72.
[11] *Ibid.*, p. 52.

What is arbitrary is not necessarily unreasonable; and there is no reason why one system should not be so constructed that it is isomorphic with another. The difficulty is that it is not the compositional realizations of the systems which are isomorphic and analogical, but the systems themselves. They have the same logical properties and involve analogous sets of operations and manipulations.

It cannot be assumed, merely because analogical operations can be used to derive and order both time and pitch, that the resulting patterns will be perceptually plausible.[12] Nor does it follow that procedures yielding perceptually viable results when applied to one parameter of sound will necessarily do so when applied to some other parameter. If pitch and time are not in some sense perceptually and experientially analogical, then subjecting them to isomorphic premusical manipulation is not merely arbitrary but presents the listener with really different perceptual problems.

Professor Babbitt himself suggests that there are perceptual problems involved in the analogical serialization of time: "At the outset, I do not wish to attempt to avoid the manifest differences between the elements of the pitch system and those of the time-point system, that is, perceptual—not formal—differences. A pitch representative of a pitch-class system is identifiable in isolation; a time-point representative cannot conceivably be, by its purely dispositional character." [13] In other words, time events are purely relational, while pitches and pitch events are phenomenal as well as relational.[14] The perceptual and cognitive consequences of this difference are momentous.

The phenomenal character of pitch perception is indicated by the fact that it is frequently related either directly or by analogy to visual or spatial perception. And there is considerable evidence to show that this is more than a plausible metaphor. In the first place, ordinary language constantly uses spatial terms to characterize the pitch parameter—for

---

[12] Colin Cherry's observation is pertinent, "Logicians work with language, frequently with freely invented or set-up systems of signs and rules (*pure* systems); and a competent logician does not confuse logic with life" (*On Human Communication*, p. 221).

[13] "Twelve-Tone Rhythmic Structure . . . ," p. 63.

[14] This is similar to a distinction made by Asch and Ebenholtz between phenomena of order and products of association. The latter are reversible, while the former are not. And "there is reason to hold that temporal organization is not an associative phenomenon." That is, temporal order is not reversible. See Solomon E. Asch and Sheldon M. Ebenholtz, "The Principle of Associative Symmetry," p. 156.

example, high-low, large-small, bright-dark, round-pointed, far-near, and so on. There is a sizable amount of experimental evidence which indicates that these are more than mere conventions of speech.[15] Second, the fact that cultures all over the world tend to characterize pitches in spatial terms—or in predominantly visual and hence, by implication, spatial terms—supports the view that this way of perceiving pitch is at least partly innate.[16] Third, the phenomenon of "color-hearing"—whether innate or learned—invariably connects such subjective visual "sensation" with pitch or tonal perception, rather than with the relational facts of rhythmic experience.[17]

Corroboration also seems to be provided by recent work in the physiology of hearing. Like visual stimuli, particular pitches (auditory stimuli) are literally mapped—have particular places—on the cerebral cortex, and different pitches evidently stimulate different parts of the basilar membrane of the inner ear as well.[18] And it does not seem unreasonable to suppose that some of the spatial qualities attributed to pitch are correlates of such neurophysiological localization.

If pitch perception is indeed akin to spatial perception, physiologically as well as psychologically, then, where durational asymmetry is not a distracting factor, inversion, retrograde, or both should be practicable. For visual experience is similarly reversible—we can understand the visual-spatial relationships of a painting even if a slide of it is projected backwards or upside down. And it is significant that when Krenek argues for invertibility and reversibility in contemporary music, he argues by analogy to abstract painting.[19]

But time is not reversible. It moves in one direction only. And if retrograde rhythms are to give rise to perceptually significant patterns, they must be composed of equal (♩♩♩♩) or symmetrically constructed

---

[15] See Stevens and Davis, *Hearing*, chap. 5; and James L. Mursell, *The Psychology of Music*, pp. 62–64 and 80.

[16] See Curt Sachs, *The Rise of Music in the Ancient World* . . . , pp. 69–70.

[17] See Mursell, *The Psychology of Music*, p. 23–25.

[18] See Stevens and Davis, *Hearing*, pp. 97–98; M. H. Goldenstein, S. Kiang, and R. H. Brown, "Responses of the Auditory Cortex to Repetitive Stimuli," p. 356; and Fritz Winckel, "The Psycho-Acoustical Analysis of Structure . . . ," pp. 205–6. Still more recent evidence has appeared indicating that there is a neurological connection between the auditory and visual systems. See J. M. Harrison and R. Irving, "Visual and Nonvisual Auditory Systems in Mammals."

[19] "Serialism," p. 67. From Krenek's point of view time *can* be reversed, for he is interested in creating a timeless, transcendental music in which implication and temporal order are undesirable.

(♩♪♩♪.) temporal values—as was indeed the case with most retrogrades in traditional tonal music.[20] Note, however, that in such symmetrical temporal orderings there is no difference between the retrograde and
the model. A symmetrical durational retrograde cannot be identified *as
such* in the absence of a pitch retrograde. Indeed, symmetrical temporal
orderings are employed precisely because they allow pitch retrogrades
to be understood as reversed patterns.[21]

Because pitches are perceived as phenomenal, existent events, pitch
patterns are better able to maintain their relational identity in the face
of variation than time patterns are. It is possibly for this reason that we
have names for pitches and pitch relationships (intervals, chords, etc.)
and are able to perceive the inversion or retrograde of a pitch series as
being related to its model. But time events are not phenomenal. Consequently, a change in relationship is perceived not as a variation, but as a
totally different event. To reverse the order of an asymmetric time event,
such as ♩♩ ♪ , is to alter its basic structure—its perceptual-cognitive
identity.

One final, if perhaps minor, point with regard to retrograde rhythms:
at least in live performance, rhythms are played and heard as relational
patterns or groupings rather than as precisely measured durations; and
performers make slight but significant adjustments in duration, beat-
placement, and intensity in order to articulate such patterns.[22] When a
time series is reversed, new groupings will arise and different interpretive displacements will take place.

The argument from isomorphism is at least open to serious question. If
pitch and time are not analogical or even perceptually comparable as we
experience them, why should it be perceptually useful to subject them to
isomorphic operations? One suspects that the "reasonableness" is largely
premusical and systematic. But the appeal to systematization is arbitrary
and unconvincing because, despite protestation to the contrary, the postulates of the system are not empirically (aurally) verified. "All that remains of a theory after *complete* generalization," writes J. H. Woodger,

> is its *logical form,* and it is this logical form which determines the
> relation of premise to consequence in a scientific theory, not the par-

---

[20] See, for instance, J. S. Bach, *The Musical Offering,* "Canones diversi, No. 1";
and Joseph Haydn, Piano Sonata in E-flat, Op. 13, No. 6, "Minuetto al Rovescio."

[21] Perhaps it is because Webern, too, wants the listener to perceive pitch retrogrades, etc., that he so often employs symmetrical temporal relationships. See, for
instance, his Symphony, Op. 21.

[22] See G. W. Cooper and L. B. Meyer, *The Rhythmic Structure of Music,* pp.
11, 15.

ticular subject-matter constants which may be substituted for its variables. On the other hand, *it is our knowledge of the subject matter which guides us in determining the logical form of the theory*, because we choose our undefined signs, and frame our definitions, with a view to the precise denotation of the things about which we wish to speak, *and we choose our postulates in such a way that their consequences will agree with our observations regarding the subject matter.*[23]

To extend the scope of serialism, for the sake either of systemic consistency or operational convenience, does disservice to art and violence to reason. "Clearly, the whole pattern of the perceived world is extended both in space and in time," writes W. Grey Walter, "but there is reason to believe that the methods of perception are different for the two classes. . . . The obvious radical difference between space-patterns and time-patterns is that the latter are projected upon a uni-directional parameter; time, for us, has an arrow that points to the grave." [24]

ARGUMENTS BY ANALOGY TO PHYSICAL OR MATHEMATICAL MODELS

The theory of music has always sought support and warrant from other disciplines—notably, mathematics and physics. Music theorists have assumed that musical structures and processes are similar to those of some model discipline—favored because of the elegance of its theory, the cultural acceptability of its doctrine, its genuine relevance for music, or some combination of these.[25] Today's theorists are no exception. Indeed, the crisis in style has produced an almost frantic search for plausible models for music and music theory.

There is, of course, nothing inherently wrong with borrowing suggestive concepts and formulations from other disciplines, particularly since such models have generally been used to rationalize already existing musical practice. Such "borrowing," however, may lead to unfortunate consequences when the model, taken to be the "main event," begins to influence and mold the actual practice of music.

The fallacies involved in the attempt to rationalize the procedures of

---

[23] *The Technique of Theory Construction*, p. 65. Italics in last two passages are mine.

[24] "Activity Patterns in the Human Brain," p. 181; also see Norbert Wiener, quoted on p. 165, above.

[25] At times the situation has been reversed; that is, music has been a model for other disciplines.

total serialism by an appeal to the unity of the acoustic materials of music have already been considered; and the dubious logic of subjecting pitch and time to a single set of quasi-mathematical operations has been discussed. Now I want to deal, first, with the use of terms and concepts drawn from contemporary physics—usually quantum theory—which imply that there are real relationships between this science and music; and, second, with the use of statistical concepts, more particularly the mathematical theory of information, to explain and justify the procedures of experimental music.

The writing of the composer-theorists of the avant-garde—particularly the European branch—is replete with terms like space-time, field relations, phase, quanta, statistics, and Heisenberg's uncertainty principle which are appropriated from contemporary physical theory and mathematics. Here are two brief samples:

> Here the passage of time can be determined only statistically—time as the effect of juxtaposed quanta. . . . Thus the vital thing is that real time is produced by the shooting together of the effect of quanta, their density, their direction and the speed that becomes evident in them. . . . But in addition one will apply the theory of relativity.[26]

> Such field-sizes are now the "elements" and compositions thus include the *statistical character of mass-structure among the elements*. A "pointillistic" time-structure can now be presented, vice-versa, as a special case of mass-structure—the case when field-size equals zero, and each time-process is fixed in the time-continuum by a *point* instead of by a *field*.[27]

The meaninglessness of such vacuous fustian has been discussed by John Backus [28] and the fallacy of inappropriate quantification has been pointed out by Mel Powell.[29] The number of technical or theoretical terms and concepts borrowed from quantum mechanics, relativity theory, and acoustics—but left undefined in the writings of the European serialists—is so vast that it would be futile to try to discuss them all. Rather, I should like to consider more fundamental difficulties, both theoretical and substantive, with the use of physics and mathematics as models for music theory.

---

[26] Dieter Schnebel, "Karlheinz Stockhausen," pp. 125, 134. It should be noted that such "composer-theorists" need not have actually read (let alone understood) the writings of Einstein, Heisenberg, *et al.* They may merely have acquired what one of my students aptly labeled "cultural scuttlebutt."

[27] Karlheinz Stockhausen, "How Time Passes," pp. 32–33.

[28] *"Die Reihe:* A Scientific Evaluation."

[29] "A Note on Rigor."

Arguments for Experimental Music

Theory reduction.—Any valid attempt to reduce the theory of music to, or make it congruent with, the theory of some other discipline—whether physics, information theory, set theory, or neurophysiology—depends upon an explicit and precise formulation of the theoretical and experimental framework of both the science which is to serve as a model (physics, etc.) and music as an art. Such rigorous conditions can hardly be said to obtain with respect to the pseudo-reductions currently prevalent in writings about music. Discussing the possibility of reducing biology to physics and chemistry, Nagel comments that mechanistic explanations in biology "will remain impossible until the descriptive and theoretical terms of biology can be shown to satisfy the first condition for the reduction of that science to physics and chemistry—that is, until the composition of every part or process of living things, and the distribution and arrangement of their parts at any time, can be exhaustively specified in physiochemical terms." [30] How much more impossible must it then be, given our current ignorance of musical processes, to reduce the aesthetics and psychology of music to acoustical, physical, or even to biological terms! The speculations of these theorists are at best vaguely metaphorical, not scientific. [31]

Analogy to physical theory.—The theories of statistical mechanics, from which some contemporary music theorists borrow their vocabulary and in terms of which they have sought to "explain" their music, were designed to deal with the realm of miscroscopic particles in which individual behavior is unpredictable. But this indeterminate world of subatomic phenomena is only *part* of the physical universe and of the universe of physics. The macroscopic world—the world of molecules and planets, of paramecia and people—is highly predictable. "It needs no poetical imagination," writes Erwin Schrödinger, "but only clear and sober scientific reflection to recognize that we are [in biology] obviously faced with events whose regular and lawful unfolding is guided by a 'mechanism' entirely different from the 'probability mechanism' of physics." [32] To fabricate a theory and a practice for an art addressed to macroscopically organized human beings—whose receptors and neurophysiological organization are designed to deal with a macro-

---

[30] *The Structure of Science,* p. 434. And even where reduction is possible there will probably be a "remainder" where one system is more complex than the other.

[31] These remarks do not assert that the data and experimental results of other disciplines may not, if scrupulously employed, be relevant to and valid in the formulation of music theory and aesthetics.

[32] *What Is Life?* . . . , p. 77. Later in the book Schrödinger observes that "quantum indeterminacy plays no biologically relevant role" (p. 85) in the space-time events of a living being.

scopic world—by suggesting analogies to and using terms derived from a theory which was invented to account for the behavior of a subatomic part of the physical universe seems, to say the least, implausible.

The attempt to rationalize the use of chance—whether produced by total serialization or by aleatoric compositional procedures—is mistaken, not only because the universe of macrostates is not random, but because even the assertion that microstates are in principle indeterminate is inaccurate. Since this point is a highly technical one, on which a musician can scarcely be counted an authority, let me again quote Professor Nagel:

> There is . . . no warrant for the conclusion that because quantum theory does not predict the detailed individual behaviors of electrons and other subatomic elements, the behavior of such elements is "inherently indeterminate" and the manifestation of "absolute chance." It is of course true that quantum mechanics in its current formulation does not describe such detailed behavior of individual electrons or predict their individual trajectories. However, if the fundamental assumptions of quantum theory have only a statistical content, as indeed they do have on the standard interpretation given to them, it is neither surprising nor paradoxical that all conclusions derivable from those assumptions exclusively should likewise have only a statistical import.[33]

And even more to the point, Nagel concludes his discussion of indeterminacy with these words:

> The statistical content of quantum mechanics does not annul the deterministic and nonstatistical structure of other physical laws. It also follows that conclusions concerning human freedom and moral responsibility, when based on the alleged "acausal" and "indeterministic" behavior of sub-atomic processes, are built on sand. Neither the analysis of physical theory, nor the study of the subject matter of physics, yields the conclusion that "There is no strict causal behavior anywhere."[34]

The speciousness of the "scientism" current, particularly among European music theorists, is clearly exemplified by the way in which they mix terms and concepts borrowed from quantum mechanics (e.g., indeterminacy and quanta) with those appropriated from relativity theory (e.g., space-time and field forces). These theories, though related, are

---

[33] *The Structure of Science*, p. 309. Also see Norwood R. Hanson, *Patterns of Discovery*, pp. 141, 150. Hanson points out that "indeterminacy" is a necessary consequence of the conceptual framework used in quantum theory.

[34] *The Structure of Science*, p. 316.

conceptually and methodologically distinct; and their assumptions and outlooks are quite different. Yet the alchemists of the avant-garde have, to stir a metaphor, concocted their musico-theoretical witches brew by blandly and indiscriminately mixing terms borrowed from both physical theories.

I should like to close this brief discussion with what appear to be two amusing paradoxes arising out of the somewhat free use of terms and concepts derived from physical theory. The first is that what is predictable in total serialism is the pitch (read: "position") and the duration (read: "velocity") of a tone (read: "particle"), that is, microscopic behavior; but *not* their combination into "harmonies," motives, and so on, that is, their macroscopic behavior. But physical science, which these theorists pretend to use as a model, posits precisely the reverse relationship: macroscopic events are predictable; microscopic ones are not.

The second paradox is this. Probably the single most important new theoretical concept promulgated by avant-garde theory is that which asserts that time is reversible and that the order of events makes no difference. In modern science, however, one of the most fundamental laws—the law of entropy—stipulates, "But for a few exceptions, which really are exceptions, all events in nature are irreversible." [35] And, to compound the paradox, it should be noted that the physical theory in which events *could* conceivably be reversible is the "old-fashioned" world of Newtonian mechanics [36]—a world in which one could not tell from a motion picture whether the planets were moving backward or forward in their orbits. Yet this world is in theory the most predictable ever devised!

The assumption of hierarchic uniformity.—The failure to distinguish between the organization and behavior of microscopic events and those of macroscopic events calls attention to a fundamental characteristic of complex musical structures. And, because they have not, as a rule, taken sufficient account of this characteristic, both serial theory and the theory of tonal music have tended to fall into the error which I earlier called the "assumption of hierarchic uniformity." [37]

---

[35] Schrödinger, *What Is Life?* . . . , p. 248.

[36] Norbert Wiener writes that "even in a Newtonian system, in which time is perfectly reversible, questions of probability and prediction lead to answers asymmetrical as between past and future, because the questions to which they are answers are asymmetrical" (*Cybernetics*, p. 43).

[37] See pp. 96–97. The characteristics of hierarchic structures are discussed in more detail in chapter 12.

Complex musical works, like complex physical or biological structures, tend to be hierarchic. Low-level events, made up of one or two "entities" (pitches), combine to form larger structural units; these in turn unite in various ways and produce still more extensive and complex organizations; and so on, until the highest level, that of the whole entity or the complete musical work, is reached.

It is, as we have seen a serious mistake to assume that the principles or "laws" governing the organization of one hierarchic level are necessarily the same as those of some other level. As a rule, the forces creating structure and organization do not remain the same—are not uniform—from one level to another. "The fallacy of reductionism," writes one biologist, "lies in assuming a one-one relation between different levels of organization." [38] Similarly, in the physical world, as Norwood R. Hanson points out, "There is no logical staircase running from the physics of 10^{-28} cm. to the physics of 10^{28} light-years. There is at least one sharp break; that is why one can make intelligible assertions about the exact co-ordinates and momentum of Mars, but not about the elementary particles of which Mars is constituted." [39] Similarly in the theory and analysis of music it is doubtful that the several different hierarchic levels are governed by the same syntactical and grammatical principles of organization.

This point is important in relation to the theory of serial music because the concept of "acoustic unity" discussed earlier is implicitly based upon the assumption that the shaping forces of music remain the same from level to level—that there is hierarchic continuity. To argue that "all differences in acoustic perception can be traced to differences in the temporal structure of sound waves" (see p. 246, above) is wrong not only for the reasons already mentioned, but because the statement assumes that the same set of organizing forces is operative on all levels.

The world—including the world of music—is not, however, in this sense homogeneous; and it is not so precisely because hierarchic differentiation and articulation are non-uniform. Just as the forces governing the ways in which chemicals unite to form molecules are different from the forces involved in the organization of molecules into cells, so the ways in which tones combine to form motives are different from the ways in which motives are organized to create larger, more complex musical events.

The theory and analysis of tonal music have also tended to assume,

---

[38] Jerry Hirsch, "Behavior Genetics and Individuality Understood," p. 1438.
[39] *Patterns of Discovery*, p. 157.

usually tacitly, the existence of some sort of hierarchic uniformity. As a rule, books on harmony or harmonic analysis do not consider the ways in which harmonic syntax changes from one hierarchic level to another; for instance, that chords built, say, on the mediant very rarely occur on the lowest—chord-to-chord—level, but that mediant harmony is quite probable on higher structural levels. Perhaps because they are not even aware of the possibility that different hierarchic levels may exhibit really different sorts of harmonic syntax, theoreticians often "explain" these matters by suggesting that chords built upon the mediant are really substitutes for the dominant—though it seems difficult, at least for me, to hear the second theme of, say, Beethoven's *Waldstein Sonata* as dominant in function. Likewise, I feel that those who use the analytical techniques developed by Schenker have not always been sufficiently aware of the differences between those musical forces which dominate the organization of the foreground and those which are critical in determining the structure of higher levels—the middle ground and the background. And lest I seem to be saying, "Do as I say, not as I do," I should add that these criticisms also apply to my own work— particularly to parts of the book on rhythm.[40]

The world is understandable, not because it is uniform and homogeneous, but because its rich variety can be organized into complex but functionally related structures. To my mind, these matters are of highest importance because, if we are to build a sensitive and precise theory of music and musical communication, we must discover how the resources and materials of music function differently on different hierarchic levels and thus shape musical processes and articulate musical structures.

Statistical analysis of music and information theory.—The fact that hierarchic structures are not uniformly continuous is an important one to keep in mind when considering the theories of those who suggest that music is a statistical phenomenon and who, consequently, employ statistical methods for its analysis and, at times, its composition as well. While it is undoubtedly true that *some* aspects of music are statistical, it does not follow that all levels of a musical hierarchy are so. This observation is particularly relevant to those avant-garde composers who would contend that because, in some undefined sense, the level of microscopic frequency fluctuation is "statistical" all hierarchic levels must be so as well. Once again the metaphorical parallels suggested with physical theory do not support such a position. As usual Professor Nagel is clear and unequivocal; he observes that quantum mechanics

---

[40] Cooper and Meyer, *The Rhythmic Structure of Music, passim.*

is then a statistical theory with respect to microstates, and microstates succeed each other only with statistical regularity. But it by no means follows that the succession of *macrostates* will also exhibit only a statistical regularity; on the contrary, the macrostates of the system may be related to each other in accordance with a strictly universal, nonstatistical law. It is therefore a *non sequitur* to conclude that, because quantum mechanics is the foundation for all other parts of physics but is a statistical theory, all physical laws deducible from quantum mechanics must also be statistical.[41]

Similarly in music, it does not follow from what seems to be the statistical character of first- and second-order harmonic relationships that all parameters are statistical or that all hierarchic levels are so. The laws of mental behavior, formulated by *Gestalt* psychology, are important shaping forces in composition—and they are not basically statistical. We are not, as a purely statistical account of music might imply, Pavlovian products of conditioned reflexes. As Austin Riesen has observed, it is generally agreed that "even in very simple organisms conditioned and unconditioned responses are not identical," and therefore that "unless innate releasive mechanisms and innate action patterns are carefully worked out for a given organism, any effort to understand its developing repertoire of learned behavior will remain quite superficial."[42]

Two other serious, though not insurmountable, problems confront those who would use statistical data and techniques for the analysis of music. The first concerns the size of the sample; the second concerns what shall be counted, for statistical purposes, as an instance of a particular event *or* as an event worth counting.

Because musical styles change slowly and continuously, the limits of a statistical sample must be carefully controlled if the frequency of a particular musical event is to be related to or be a reflection of our subjective feelings about its probability. For instance, a statistical account of the harmonic style of the later music of Richard Wagner which confined itself to counting the frequency with which Wagner resolves dominant-seventh chords to tonic chords would not accurately represent the experienced listener's feeling that this progression was highly probable and other resolutions of the dominant-seventh were "irregular." An adequate sample in this case would have to include the music of at least the preceding seventy-five years. The problem is a touchy one: because styles change gradually, there are, as a rule, no clear "breaks" indicat-

---

[41] *The Structure of Science*, p. 315. Also see Hanson, *Patterns of Discovery*, pp. 153–55.

[42] "Varying Behavioral Manifestations of Animals," p. 344.

ing what the limits of a sample should be. On the other hand, it will not do to use all the music of western Europe as a sample. For it is clear that we "abstract" sub-sets from such a total sample when we listen to the music of a particular style period. But the limits proper to such a sub-set sample are by no means clear.

The second problem is even more interesting and perplexing than the first. What shall be counted, for statistical purposes, as an instance of a particular event? For example, does it make any sense to count all the A's (440 cps) lasting a quarter-note in Mozart's music? Clearly not. For the syntactical significance of a tone depends upon its context in a particular work and even in the part of the work. An "A" can be a tonic, a dominant, a leading tone, an enharmonic tone, and so on. And the same observation will be true for harmonies, first-order transitions, and even higher-level musical events.

The case seems to be this: Our knowledge of syntax and grammar is antecedent to, and determines, the kinds of units we choose to count for our statistical samples—not the other way around. We could probably never discover the syntax of a style if we had to do it purely statistically. In short, statistics can be meaningful only if we understand syntax; but they can never lead to the discovery of syntax. Statistics is a method of analyzing data and its intelligent use presupposes the existence of an understanding—tacit or explicit—of the way in which a musical style works.

This does not, however, mean that our understanding of music is not "probabilistic," only that "in the study of human communication both statistical and inductive probabilities are relevant—but they should be carefully distinguished." [43] Based upon innate patterns of action and perception, upon a complex array of cultural beliefs and attitudes, and upon learned experience, which depends partly upon frequency, listeners (including composers and performers) form complex systems of subjective probability feelings about musical events. Such internalized, subjective probability systems are the "beliefs" about which Charles Peirce writes. They are, so to speak, habits which, according to Colin Cherry,

> may be regarded as forming your prior set of hypotheses, weighted hypotheses, as though you had in your brain a physiological representation of a *likelihood function* in a space of very large dimensionality—a message space of syntactical and semantical aspects of messages such as had been built up from the evidence of the preceding

---

[43] Colin Cherry, *On Human Communication*, p. 233; also see John Cohen, "Subjective Probability."

conversation, and dependent upon your whole past experience. . . . Your "beliefs" here include not only beliefs about syntactics and semantic attributes of the conversation [read: "piece of music"], and about the whole environment, but, in particular *beliefs about your friend's beliefs* [read: "composer's style"].[44]

One of the conclusions to be drawn from these observations is that, while the concepts and methods of the mathematical theory of information are suggestive and illuminating, their usefulness in the analysis of the grammar and syntax of music is limited by the purely statistical character of the theory. Noam Chomsky's discussion of the application of information theory to language seems also to apply to music.

> Despite the undeniable interest and importance of semantic and sta-
> tistical studies of language, they appear to have no direct relevance
> to the problem of determining or characterizing the set of grammati-
> cal utterances. I think that we are forced to conclude that grammar
> is autonomous and independent of meaning, and that probabilistic
> models give no particular insight into some of the basic problems of
> syntactic structure.[45]

These remarks should not be taken to assert that statistical studies of style and the concepts of information theory are useless or irrelevant as tools for the study of music. Quite the contrary. "Given the grammar of a language," writes Chomsky, "one can study the use of the language statistically in various ways; and the development of probabilistic models for the use of language (as distinct from the syntactic structure of language) can be quite rewarding." [46] But music cannot be reduced in any simple and direct way to statistical variation, as some composers and theorists have implied. Nor can the statistical and mathematical aspects of information theory be applied to music directly and without qualification.[47] On the other hand, it seems to me possible that, given a knowledge of the syntactical functioning of a primarily syntactical art such as music, many of the concepts of information theory can, if "translated" into non-statistical terms—into terms of subjective or in-ductive probability—be relevant and illuminating.[48]

---

[44] *On Human Communication*, p. 247–48.

[45] *Syntactic Structures*, p. 17.

[46] *Ibid.*, p. 17 n.

[47] See Joel E. Cohen, "Information Theory and Music."

[48] The preceding discussion of the relevance of statistics and statistical models has assumed that music is a syntactic mode of ordering experience—a mode of communication. It is possible, however, to write music that is exclusively statistical. Such music would be one facet of the music of transcendental particularism.

Arguments for Experimental Music

The partisans of serialism, whether twelve-tone or total, have from time to time sought, by explaining and describing its historical development, to justify its methods and defend its aesthetic validity. Their appeal to history has generally involved several separate but interrelated steps.

The first step attempts to show that the underlying concepts, methods, and ideals of serialism were prefigured or implicit in earlier music. For instance, writing of Bach's *Art of Fugue*, Anton Webern finds:

> All these fugues are created from one single theme, which is constantly transformed. . . . What does this all mean? An effort towards an all-embracing unity. . . . So we see that this—our—kind of thought has been the ideal for composers of all periods. . . . To develop everything from a single principle idea! [49]

Not only does the past prefigure the present, but the historical process is evolutionary, leading the past to the present in some "logical" fashion. The serial method of Schönberg, writes Adorno, "is today as historically necessary as ever." [50] Here, as stated by Ernst Krenek, is how many serial composers see the development of the twelve-tone method:

> Atonality, then, appears as a state of the musical language that must be accepted as the result of evolution so long as the existence of a permanent motivating force behind the chain of historical events is acknowledged—a force which because of its one-way directedness is identified with progress.
>
> Seen in this light, the introduction of the twelve-tone technique does not indicate a break of traditional continuity either. For as the transition from the area of highly weakened tonal delineation into the uncharted realm of atonality is motivated by the urge of moving onward in the direction of relentless progress, so is the establishment of secure lines of communication, of sign posts and milestones in the new province, necessitated by the same energy that propels history on its forward course. [51]

And total serialism, too, is merely a consequence "drawn from Schoenberg's basic idea of organizing the twelve semitones." [52]

---

[49] "Towards a New Music," p. 30.
[50] Quoted by Metzger, "Intermezzo I," p. 67.
[51] "Tradition in Perspective," p. 32.
[52] Stuckenschmidt, "Contemporary Techniques in Music," p. 12.

The present, then, is not merely an effect or product of historical processes—a view that would be unobjectionable, if perhaps truistic, but it is said to be a *necessary* consequence of the processes. The coupling of such discredited nineteenth-century notions of "historical necessity" with metaphors imported from twentieth-century quantum mechanics would be merely ludicrous were it not for the insidious final steps in the argument.

Here either of two somewhat different lines of reasoning can apparently be used to reach the same conclusion. In both, the lines of reasoning must be conjectural—for they are too obviously questionable to have have been explicitly stated. The first argument moves from the assumption that total serialism is *a* necessary consequence of a historical process to the insolent assumption that it is the *one and only* valid consequence of the process. Such an assumption must underlie Milton Babbitt's assertion—made, I am sure, in a moment of mental aberration—that if new music (by which he must, in the context of the article, mean new serial and experimental music, not the music of, say, Barber or Thomson or Kirchner) is not supported by universities and enlightened devotees, "music will cease to evolve, and, in that very important sense, will cease to live." [53]

Even were it granted that serialism and experimentation were "necessary" consequences of the development of nineteenth-century music—a plausible contention if one does not scrutinize the meaning of "necessary" with too much care—it by no means follows that they are the *only* possible or "valid" consequences. The implications of the past are many and diverse, and, consequently, the possible futures are plural. Nor has it been demonstrated that music must "evolve" (whatever that means) in order to "live" (whatever that means).[54] The musical traditions of India and Japan were relatively stable for centuries. Does this mean that the music was dead? Or, if Western music has, as I am suggesting, reached a point of fluctuating stasis, will it then be dead? But then, it is not entirely clear how long stasis must continue before a certificate of death is issued from Princeton or Darmstadt.

The second and often correlative line of "reasoning" is immoral as well as misguided. It apparently depends upon the assumption, implied in Krenek's statement (quoted above), that whatever happens as a

---

[53] "Who Cares If You Listen?" p. 127. As an alternative and as a verifiable definition, one might contend that music ceases "to live" when no one wants to listen to it.

[54] See chaps. 6 and 7.

necessary consequence of historical forces is therefore valid and valuable: "a force which because of its one-way directedness is identified with progress." And since serialism—whether partial or total—is, so the tacit argument goes, a necessary consequence of the historical process, it must be good. But since the whole dialectic ultimately rests on the belief that whatever happens is necessary, one could, using this line of reasoning, contend that since Hitler's tyranny was a "necessary" consequence of nineteenth- and twentieth-century political and economic history, the Treaty of Versailles, and so on, it was valid and valuable.

History may be able to help us to understand the development of total serialism, but it cannot justify or validate it, either as a method of composition or as a musical style. Only the interest, significance, and persuasive power of the music itself can do these things.

CHAPTER

II

The Perception and Cognition of Complex Music

The preceding chapter attempted to show that the arguments advanced to explain and justify the application of serial methods to all parameters of sound are arbitrary or naïve, illogical or illegitimate, and, hence, unconvincing or absurd. The merit of a composition is tested, however, not by the theoretical constructs upon which it is based or is supposed to be based, but by the only real, "empirical" verification available: the ability of experienced, sensitive listeners to understand and respond intelligently to the implicative sound relationships being presented.[1] Let us therefore turn to a consideration of the organization of total serial music itself and of the possible problems involved in perceiving, understanding, and responding to it.[2]

In considering the methods and practices of total serialism, I do not plan to present an exhaustive study or a detailed argument. For the

---

[1] See Milton Babbitt, "Twelve-Tone Rhythmic Structure . . . ," pp. 50–51. Babbitt emphasizes the *perceptual* aspects of "empirical verification," while I would place more emphasis upon the *cognitive* aspects.

[2] It should be emphasized again that I am not concerned in what follows with the uses which transcendentalists may have made of total serialism (or of other experimental methods), but only with those composers for whom the sound patterns presented in a composition constitute a form of communication between a composer (often through a performer) and listeners.

procedures currently employed by different composers are so various and the resulting compositions are so different in style that any general or comprehensive judgment would be impossible, even if it were desirable. What I hope to do is to point out what appear to me to be genuine problems and important questions relating to the perception and cognition of this music.

Understanding, Perception, and Learning

UNDERSTANDING WHAT?

At the outset an important distinction—though one often glossed over—must be made. I refer to the difference between understanding the musical structure and process presented to the listener's mind, on the one hand, and understanding, or discovering, the repertory of tonal materials and the rules for their manipulation upon which the composition was based. They are not *necessarily*, or even usually, the same. Just as one can speak or listen to a familiar language without knowing anything about its structural linguistic principles—without being able, for instance, to identify parts of speech, types of sentences, prosodic devices, and so on—so one can (and most educated listeners do) understand a series of musical events without knowing the syntactical or other rules that guided the composer's choices. "The user of signs," writes Colin Cherry, "does not need to know the rules; we can read, speak, or write effectively, and we can laugh at jokes with little or no knowledge of rules." [3] Indeed, were this not so, our understanding of language or music or jokes would be severely limited; for in none of these cases do we really have accurate and systematic—let alone exhaustive—knowledge of the rules upon which communication is based. "A great deal is necessarily omitted when a language is described as a finite set of signs and rules." [4]

The rules of music—whether tonal or serial—are, so to speak, a set of instructions which define operations to be performed on selected materials. They are not to be confused with the perceptual patterns and relationships—a piece of music—which are a particular, unique realization of the rules. A computer can, for instance, be programmed to

---

[3] *On Human Communication*, p. 221.
[4] *Ibid.*

compose music, write verse, or play chess. But such a program, or set of instructions, is not the same thing as the music or verse produced or the chess game actually played—any more than the genetic code (set of instructions) in a fertilized human ovum is to be identified or confused with the living child that it generates.

Similarly, an account of the repertory of materials (pitches, durations, etc.) used in a piece of music and their manipulation cannot serve as an analysis of the work of art itself. To "explain" a piece of serial music by discovering its row structure and detailing its permutations and combinations in the work is almost as pointless as trying to explain a joke by discussing theories of humor. As George Perle has observed, "A mere description of the set and the transpositions and transformations to which it is subjected cannot be advanced as an 'explanation' of the work itself but only of the substructure, the system of tone relations upon which the work is based." [5] One does not understand a piece of serial music by "discovering" the tone rows or rhythmic rows, watching for inversions, retrogrades, and the like any more than one listens to the *Eroica* by "conceptualizing" the E-flat major scale and the rules of harmony and counterpoint. Thus, the typical "analysis" of serial music in terms of rows and their manipulation is almost always, aesthetically speaking, irrelevant.[6]

It may seem that I have been too absolute about this matter. It is clear that at times one does perceive the row and is aware of its transformations. In many of the works of Schönberg, Berg, and Webern, for instance, the tone row is used thematically or motivically and we are perceptually aware not only of the row but of its inversions and its retrogrades. But in such cases our perception is of a pattern or set of relationships which happens *also* to be the row. Understanding is not dependent upon the fact that we are hearing the row. At other times the row is not perceptually apparent. It is a source for the entities in the pattern, but is not itself used as a pattern. And even where a tone row is stated as a series, its audibility as a pattern will depend upon the emphasis it receives "from other musical components: rhythm, dynamics, register, phrasing, timbre, etc." [7] And these remarks are relevant to

---

[5] *Serial Composition and Atonality*, p. 61.

[6] See, for example, György Ligeti's analysis of Boulez's *Structures Ia* in "Pierre Boulez"; Henry Weinberg's analysis in "Donald Martino: Trio (1959)"; and, despite his own cautions, many of Perle's analyses in *Serial Composition and Atonality*.

[7] Milton Babbitt, "Twelve-Tone Invariants as Compositional Determinants," p. 254.

durational rows as well as pitch rows.[8] That is, a series of durations or a time-point set is not necessarily a rhythm (pattern) any more than the pitch set is necessarily a motive (pattern).

Whether the listener *should* be aware—though not necessarily conscious—of the row structure has been much debated in the literature. Roberto Gerhard, for instance, denies the relevance of perceiving the serial thread in audition. For him serialism is not an aspect of aesthetic significance but a facet of the composer's technique.[9] David Lewin, on the other hand, believes that segments of a tone row will eventually reveal the nature of the row aurally: ". . . every nesting which involves a given row yields a certain amount of structural information about that row. . . . Even in cases where we do not have sufficient harmonic information to 'define' a row, I feel it is legitimate to conceive of several harmonic ideas as being collectively highly definitive or not very definitive in serial terms." [10] It is not entirely clear, however, what Lewin takes the aesthetic significance of such "discoveries" of the row structure to be. For, insofar as a particular handling of the set structure presents the listener with regularities which are perceptible, what is added to his *musical* understanding, as distinguished from his technical and theoretical knowledge, by referring these regularities back to a tone row? Even if, as Donald Martino contends, the use of the row can create "normative, thus predictable, as well as non-normative, thus dramatic procedures," [11] these would seem to be aurally understandable without the listener's being aware of, or consciously considering, the existence of the source sets. Of course, this does not deny the theoretical and, from the composer's point of view, practical interest in understanding the relationships between the characteristics of a row and the kinds of manipulation appropriate to it on the one hand, and the realization of these in the particular experiential musical structure, on the other. At this point in the history of this "style," however, it seems doubtful whether the "valid" connection which George Perle feels "one ought to be able to establish . . . between the 'serial thread' and the musical correspondences and structures . . . *as they are made to sound*" [12] can be organized into a general structural theory; rather, the connection must be analyzed for each case separately.

---

[8] "The compositional time-point set need not . . . appear as the explicit, foreground rhythm" (Babbitt, "Twelve-Tone Rhythmic Structure . . . ," p. 75).

[9] "Apropos Mr. Stadlen."

[10] "A Theory of Segmental Association . . . ," pp. 112–13.

[11] "The Source Set and Its Aggregate Formations," p. 226.

[12] "Theory and Practice in Twelve-Tone Music," p. 59.

PERCEPTION AND COGNITION

I do not wish to imply by these remarks that knowledge and experience are irrelevant to understanding. Quite the opposite is the case. For instance, knowledge about—as well as the more important knowledge acquired through experience in listening to—fugal processes influences our perception of a particular fugue by directing attention to the contrapuntal interplay of subject and counter-subject, the articulation of the parts into fugal statements and episodes, and so on. Similarly, our acquaintance with the procedures of serialism necessarily influences our perception of the music of, for example, Webern or Babbitt or Boulez, by making us aware of the likelihood of and therefore ready to perceive canonic relationships, motivic inversions, retrogrades, and the like. But to be experientially relevant and influential, knowledge must be, not of the rules per se, but of their manifestation as perceivable processes and relationships.

This calls attention to the important interaction between perception and cognition. The composer-theorists of total serialism evidence considerable concern about the perceptual problems involved in listening to this music: Stockhausen refers to psycho-acoustics; Boulez assigns timbre and dynamics to a secondary role evidently on the basis of "perception"; and, if I read him correctly, Milton Babbitt warns of the danger of employing overly subtle rhythms merely because the electronic medium makes them possible:

> In constructing a musical system for an electronically produced work, whether this system be exemplified in but a single work or a body of works, there is a particular temptation to proceed in this "nontraditional" fashion, since one can presume as the values associated with notationally separable components (the range of discrete values that each component of the musical event may assume) those which are obtainable as the result of the medium's providing measurable and regulable values of frequency, intensity, duration, and spectrum to a a degree of differentiation far exceeding the, at least, present discriminative capacity of the auditory apparatus under the most generous temporal conditions, and further providing those values at time points whose precise specifications similarly can produce measurably different quantities which surpass the discriminative and memorative abilities of the most appropriately qualified observers.[13]

---

[13] "Twelve-Tone Rhythmic Structure . . . ," p. 50.

Perception and Cognition of Complex Music

But perceptual capacities, though dependent on physiological and neural capabilities, are not "given" or genetically imprinted in the nervous system. Perception in any meaningful sense is not the naïve act of an empty, primitive neural receptor; it is an act of learned discrimination. The world is not presented to us as a set of intelligible relationships and processes. We have to learn to see even such primitive shapes as circles, triangles, and the like.[14] Thus while it is commendable for composers to be concerned with the limitations of the senses, it is well to remember that music is directed, not *to* the senses, but *through* the senses and *to the mind*. And it might be well if more serious attention were paid to the capacity, behavior, and abilities of the human mind.

Perception of pitch is limited at both ends of the spectrum. Frequencies above 20,000 cycles per second, essentially inaudible, are not used, even in electronic music. Frequencies below 15 cps are experienced as discrete pulses. As frequency rises above this point, the pulses become "fused" into a single persisting tone—i.e., they are experienced as *pitch*. The experience of sound waves *as pitch* depends in the lower frequency levels upon stimulation of up to 50 per cent of the area of the basilar membrane, an organ apparently incapable, at levels below 15–20 cps, of the mode of response required to produce the pitch experience. Also, the response of the ear to the total auditory range is not uniform: *place* of neural excitation is most crucial for pitch perception of frequencies above 5,000 cps. Below this rate, *frequency* of neural excitation is the primary determinant up to around 400 cps, where *place* joins as a co-determinant. Thus the pitch response can be divided into three overlapping areas of 15–400, 400–5,000, and 5,000–20,000 cps.[15]

This description calls attention to several important considerations:

1. Despite pretension to scientific rigor, the continuum of "time" events, upon which Stockhausen bases his theory of the unity of acoustical materials and which he uses to rationalize the serialization of duration, is a speculative fancy rather than empirical, verified fact. His statement that "between ca. 1/30 and 1/16 sec. our perception of duration gradually changes into perception of rhythm and meter"[16] is mistaken on two counts: (*a*) One cannot assume that the hierarchy of frequency perception is uniform. It is not so. Our perception of frequency in the form of discretely experienced pulses changes, both

---

[14] See Colin Cherry, *On Human Communication*, p. 261; and Donald O. Hebb, *The Organization of Behavior*, chap. 2.

[15] I am most grateful to Professor William Thomson of Indiana University for pointing out mistakes in my first account and for suggesting changes.

[16] "The Concept of Unity in Electronic Music," p. 43.

physiologically and psychologically, at about 20 cycles per second to a perception of pitch. (*b*) Acoustical events, pulses, are confused with psychological events, rhythm and meter. Pulses are not meters; and meters are not rhythms.[17]

2. The maximum frequency which limits the perception of separable pulses is, not surprisingly, of the same order of magnitude as that which limits neural activity generally. *"The maximum speed of making conscious decisions or independent perceptions is one per transit or 1/T. This is the flicker frequency, the bass threshold, the word-scanning frequency in an easy book; of the order of 20 per second . . . and evidently a general fundamental constant for human beings."* [18] And this frequency probably also sets an upper limit on the speed at which pitches can succeed one another. For, as Platt observes, *"the maximum muscle response frequency matches the maximum perception frequency, or 1/T.* Otherwise either some perceptions or decisions would be wasted or some movements would be unguided. This is the phonetic frequency, the letter-frequency of a fast typist, and the tremor frequency, when the muscle moves as fast as its chemistry and inertia will permit."* [19]

This "fundamental constant" evidently limits the speed of both perception and performance and, as one approaches the maximum speed, affects the accuracy of both.[20] It is perhaps because the demand for extreme speed led to a considerable number of performance errors that a number of contemporary composers turned to the electronic medium. It is worth noting, however, that, to paraphrase Platt,[21] the rate of pitch succession is probably set by the listener rather than by the composer or the performer. For the composer or the performer, because of his foreknowledge of the music, knows what to expect; he can be set and ready to execute and perceive each successive event. The listener, on the other hand, must take time to relate pitches and durations to one another—even when the style is quite familiar.

The less well-known a style or a particular work is, the more slowly must the discrete events follow one another if communication is to be accurate. The cognitive perception of an unfamiliar work requires a

[17] See G. W. Cooper and L. B. Meyer, *The Rhythmic Structure of Music,* chap. 1. The confusion between rhythm and other aspects of the temporal dimension of music is common in the literature about music generally.
[18] John R. Platt, "Amplification Aspects of Biological Response . . . ," p. 188. Also see Fritz Winckel, "The Psycho-Acoustical Analysis of Music . . . ," p. 230.
[19] "Amplification Aspects of Biological Response . . . ," p. 189.
[20] See H. Quastler, "Studies of Human Channel Capacity," p. 361.
[21] "Amplification Aspects of Biological Response . . . ," p. 189.

greater number of neural-mental decisions—in which relationships are patterned and their implications comprehended—than does a familiar work or a work in a familiar style. "Until it is resolved, an equivocal decision uses up [neural] network time that could be used for other decisions, and perhaps distorts what other decisions are made." [22] The speed and accuracy of communication thus depend in a fundamental way upon stylistic learning. And it is to problems of learning that we now turn.

PERCEPTION AND LEARNING

If perception depends thus critically upon learning, it might be well before discussing the problems involved in the perception (and hence the learning) of serial music, to consider how we learn to perceive the structure of the world in general and music in particular.

We can learn to perceive and understand the world only because the events of the world are themselves constant and orderly enough to allow us to group and classify them. Were the phenomenal world in constant flux—or if it consisted of a host of independent variables—not only would it be impossible to "decode" the world (to discover the regularities), but probably we could not even guess that there *were* any regularities there to be discovered.

The particular groupings, classifications, and relationships which we derive from such natural regularities are so to speak only potentially present in the world. The way in which we organize and perceive the world is partly a function of the mind's natural modes of pattern perception—the laws of mental behavior. For instance, though the senses receive a series of highly variable stimuli impressions, what the mind comprehends is a series of more or less stable, invariant relationships. We see a circle tilted so that the retinal image is that of an elipse, but we understand it as a circle. Things tend to be perceived as being as constant and regular as possible. Our knowledge of these invariants is at least partly (perhaps largely) learned. Where we do not know, or cannot orient ourselves to, a pattern type, we are like congenitally blind men who have just gained their sight—the world is a welter of confused and disorganized sensations.

We perceive, understand, and respond to the world, including music, in terms of the patterns and models, concepts and classifications, which have been established in our traditions—linguistic, philosophical, musi-

---

[22] *Ibid.*, p. 192. Also see above, chap. 1, n. 12.

cal, and so on. And there are probably events or patterns in the world that we cannot perceive, or comprehend, because they fall outside of our models of, our preconceptions about, the way the world is. Once one has experienced and learned how to deal with the world at all, perception is not passive and indifferent; it is an active and a biased force that structures the universe in accordance with natural and learned modes of organization.

These remarks apply with special force in the perception and cognition of human communication. For communication depends, even more than does our understanding of the natural world, upon our having learned a traditionally established system of sign relationships. Communication depends, that is, upon our having learned a musical style (a system of subjective probabilities) as a set of strongly ingrained habits and dispositions of perception, expectation, cognition, and so forth.

Problems Involved in Learning Serial Music

The habits and dispositions which facilitate perception and make communication possible are acquired not with one, two, or perhaps even a hundred encounters with a particular style or style-class, but become part of our very being through countless experiences that begin in infancy. This fact points to two serious, though not insurmountable, difficulties in the ability of even willing listeners to learn to understand highly complex experimental music.

CHILDHOOD LEARNING

Because our most firmly rooted habits of thought and discrimination are learned in infancy and early childhood, the musical style system we first experience is the one that tends to dominate our perception and cognition of music throughout our lives. And the style thus embedded in the minds of listeners in our culture is not that of serialism but that of tonal music—our musical "vernacular." [23] There have in the past, of course, been differences between the style of "art" music—the music of the high culture—and that of vernacular music, which is generally

_____

[23] See Curt Sachs, *The Wellsprings of Music,* pp. 78–79: "The ages of the machine, of electricity, and of the atom may have remodeled our thought and our vision, but have not touched the ears of our majorities."

learned in early childhood by performance as well as listening. But both kinds of music have heretofore belonged to the same general style-class. They have, that is, generally employed a similar vocabulary of tones, set of melodic archetypes, and a closely related musical syntax. This situation has, as far as I can discover, also prevailed in non-Western cultures. But serial music does *not* belong to the same style system as the music which audiences even today learn to perform and comprehend in early childhood, when enduring and powerful patterns of behavior and response are most readily established. For this reason, until total serial music becomes part of early musical experience, it will probably continue to present serious problems for most listeners.

It is important to remember that early learning is critical, not merely because it is *first*, but because in childhood the connections and pathways of the nervous system are still largely unspecified. John Pfeiffer writes:

> At birth the entire brain of an average male infant weighs eleven to twelve ounces, about the same as an adult chimpanzee. By the age of two it weighs more than two pounds, and the cortex begins a new period of rapid development. Between two and six the cortex completes the major part of its growth, a fact that jibes nicely with theories concerning the importance of early-childhood experiences.[24]

Of course the brain continues, as we shall observe later, to develop new patterns throughout life, and it develops physically even into middle age. But once established these first patterned pathways become tremendously powerful. Like a deeply channeled river bed, they function as the conduits through which sensory input, motor behavior, and cognitive patterns tend "naturally" to flow. The formation later in life of new channels and pathways deep and clear enough to insure new modes of perception and cognition is not an impossible task, but certainly it is a formidable one.

In this connection, it should be noted that early learning is not merely mental. Our ability to learn to perceive visual and auditory patterns is not solely a function of what the senses feed into our nervous system but depends in important ways upon the presence of concurrent motor behavior which is, so to speak, fed back into and thereafter guides the discoveries of the senses. "The maintenance and development of sensorily guided behavior," say Held and Freedman, "depend in part upon bodily movement in the normal environment. Ordered information entailed in the motor-sensory feedback loop is responsible for the stable

---

[24] *The Human Brain*, pp. 42–43.

functioning of the plastic systems of coordination. It is found, from the results of experiments on vision and hearing, that the introduction of disorder into the motor-sensory loop changes the state of these systems and makes performance imprecise." [25] Thus early experience both in listening and in performance (using the motor system of the body, or the vocal chords, or both) seems to be important if audiences are to learn to understand total serialism.[26]

Insofar as serial music is perceptually highly complex and irregular, it is difficult for children, and perhaps even adults, to bring relevant sensory-motor behavior into play. On the other hand, since it is also clear that the human mind is capable of astonishing feats of learning, the point at which complexity and irregularity inhibit or thwart learning must be left open.

One final point needs to be made here. It is sometimes suggested that serial music cannot become a "successful" style because we cannot ignore our early learning of tonal music. This argument does not seem convincing to me. The human mind is capable of maintaining many different and even contradictory behavior systems simultaneously and of bringing these into play at appropriate times. One part of the brain can, so to speak, shut out of perceptual-behavior what other parts have learned. So that once a listener has learned to perceive totally serialized works in a particular style, he can bring proper habits, dispositions, and so forth into play.

LEARNING, PERCEPTION, AND REDUNDANCY

But even if total serial music were regularly presented to the very young, major learning difficulties would still be encountered. And these difficulties also confront even the most favorably disposed adult listener today. Because learning and perception are mutually dependent, each reinforcing and supplementing the other, new learning is contingent upon the possibility of discovering—of perceiving—some sort of manifest order and regularity in experience. For this reason, we begin to perceive something new by attending to simple relationships, stable schemata, and predictable, regular processes which are patently and manifestly organized. The order thus learned (through our *total* sen-

---

[25] Richard Held and Sanford J. Freedman, "Plasticity in Human Sensorimotor Control," p. 461. Also see Richard Held, "Plasticity in Sensory-Motor Systems."

[26] The absence of such motor experience might become a critical problem were electronic music to become the exclusive medium of musical "performance."

sory-motor behavior) is fed back into the perceptual-cognitive network, where it subsequently facilitates more subtle, complex perceptions. Learning also makes possible more rapid and accurate responses to the original orderings because the perceived regularities become "coded" as schemata—that is, archetypal patterns. The perception-learning-*re*perception cycle continues until it is possible for the human mind to comprehend very complex relationships and processes.

I shall call the totality of patterned structure and orderly process available to the mind of an ideally experienced listener *perceptual redundancy.*[27] As our description of learning makes clear, not all listeners—or perhaps even a large proportion of them—realize or experience all of the redundancy potentially present in a musical work. And it appears that, as the listener's experience with a style or a particular work increases, the amount of order perceived will increase and will tend to approach the maximum possible. The ability of listeners to realize the perceptual redundancy in a composition depends upon:

1. The psychology of human mental processes. Those musical events, whatever their particular stylistic-syntactic premises, which are so structured that they conform to the *Gestalt* laws of pattern perception (the principles of good continuation, closure, return, and the like)—laws which are themselves perhaps reflections of the neurophysiological organization of the central nervous system (CNS)—will be more redundant than events which are incongruous with the natural modes of cognitive ordering.[28]

2. The degree to which a listener has learned the syntactic-formal premises of a style. Redundancy will be high where there is a marked correspondence between the objective relationships presented by a composition and the listener's learned habits of discrimination, derived from his experience with stylistically established modes of progression and organization—modes which are themselves probably partly specified and defined by the psychology of human mental processes mentioned above. Moreover, patterns which in general adhere to the syntactic processes and formal procedures that are normative in a style are more redundant than those which are deviant and less probable.

It is important to realize that redundancy is never total. Disorder, ambiguity, and the less probable are always part both of a style and of a

---

[27] "Perceptual," because I wish to distinguish this concept from the purely statistical redundancy of information theory.

[28] The term "redundancy" as used here is in no way perjorative. Were an event or object without redundancy (in this sense), we could not understand it at all. Indeed, we might not discover that there was anything there to be understood.

particular work in that style. Were a composition totally redundant, the result would be complete predictability and, consequently, total tedium—at least from a syntactical point of view. The relative disorder or randomness that necessarily complements redundancy may be called *perceptual information.*

Redundancy facilitates learning not only because order is easier to remember and comprehend than disorder, but because order and regularity make prediction possible. And the mental satisfaction of being able to predict reinforces learning. That is, the arrival of a predictable, regular event rewards the listener, giving him a sense of control and psychic security, and thereby encourages and reinforces his learning, not only of the particular sequence of events, but of the total repertory of events of which the particular event is a part. Manifest irregularity or randomness, on the other hand, precludes predictability; and, by weakening the listener's sense of control, discourages learning.[29] It is probable that new music angers listeners not because their aesthetic sensibilities are offended but because their psychic security—their sense of control—is seriously threatened.

Redundancy is also important because it tends to make communication self-correcting. In aural experience memory is crucial. Even where style is familiar, a sequence of events, musical or linguistic, must have enough internal redundancy to combat "errors" arising from inattention, performance mistakes, acoustical noise (see chap. 1), and the like. For instance, in tonal music or in language, if we miss part of the message, we can, as a rule, reconstruct the missing parts and are therefore still able to comprehend the relationships and progressions between earlier and later events in the entire message. But total serial music, for instance, presents the listener with so little potential redundancy that if anything at all is missed, he is in trouble.

From this point of view, experimental music is often a set of relationships to be studied, not music to be heard. It is not, like language, a means of communication but, like mathematics, an object of investigation. As W. Wesley Peterson has observed, "When we turn from language to information expressed numerically, we find that there is usually too little natural redundancy to be useful for error detection and correction."[30] Of course, mathematical messages can be checked for

---

[29] See Michael I. Posner, "Components of Skilled Performance," p. 1714: "Practice is effective, however, only when the signals in the reaction-time task are regular, so that the subject can learn to anticipate them."

[30] "Error Correcting Codes," p. 98.

errors—and so can total serial music. But they can scarcely be checked, and corrected, *aurally*.

Thus it is not merely because the style is unfamiliar and the notes difficult to play that experimental music must be carefully rehearsed and expertly performed; it is also because compositional redundancy is often so low that almost all the information in the music must be perceived and used if the composition is to be understood. The listener cannot correct mistakes in performance or fill in parts masked by poor performance. A bad performance of Bach or Hindemith may be dull or distorted, yet still understandable; but a sloppy performance of Webern or Boulez will probably be incomprehensible.

THE PROBLEM OF STYLISTIC PLURALITY

There is, of course, no philosophical or psychological reason why new styles should not be developed or invented. Indeed, the history of Western music is the history of changes in musical style. Because such changes have, until now, generally been gradual and evolutionary, however, only a small part of the listener's habits of perception have had to be modified to adjust to them. Moreover, the changes that took place were, as a rule, common to all the works of a particular period. Hence, though style changes have always tended to present problems for the listener, they have in the past generally been absorbed without too much difficulty into his repertory of learned modes of perception, discrimination, understanding, and response.

Listeners have difficulty learning to perceive and understand both serialism and total serialism not only because it is truly revolutionary—in the sense that, for the first time in the history of music, the relationships between pitches are intentionally non-functional (see below)—but also because serial music does not constitute a single style or style system. Though the methods of serialism provide certain limiting conditions for composition, each piece of serial music essentially established its own set of grammatical-syntactical rules and operations. And this may even be the case for different works by the same composer. Thus Milton Babbitt remarks that "the twelve-tone system (and this is one of its virtues) does not imply a specific style or idiom. Indeed, there are already a multitude of styles within the system, and whereas change of idiom in the tonal system has been a gradual and linear process, in twelve-tone music there is no homogeneous core of style to serve as a point of origin." [31]

---

[31] In his review of Boulez's "Le Système dodécaphonique," p. 266.

It is partly because each serial piece is in a different style that listeners find this music so hard to perceive, learn, and understand. Professor Babbitt again states the case clearly and concisely:

> Musical compositions of the kind under discussion possess a high degree of contextuality and autonomy. That is, the structural characteristics of a given work are less representative of a general class of characteristics than they are unique to the individual work itself. Particularly, principles of relatedness . . . are more likely to evolve in the course of the work than to be derived from generalized assumptions. Here again greater and new demands are made upon the perceptual and conceptual abilities of the listener.[32]

But an absolute and arbitrary (in the sense of non-dependence on any established tradition) contextualism precludes not only the possibility of communication but also the possibility of any but fortuitous perception and cognition. For, as Gilbert King points out, "every system of communication presupposes . . . that the sender and the receiver have agreed upon a certain set of possible messages." [33] Our ability to perceive relationships depends in part upon what our past experience has told us constitutes a relationship. In other words, meanings and relationships are functions not merely of what *exists* in the external world but of the habits, dispositions, and traditions which competent observers or listeners bring into play when they perceive and organize the world. "The syntactical constraints of a language," writes Colin Cherry, "ensure that, *to some extent,* we know already what will be said, or written, in a given situation or at a certain point in a speech or text." [34] Indeed, were any event or relationship really unique it would probably escape our attention—we could neither understand nor perceive it.

That a position of such extreme contextualism seems to be based upon an implicit, but illicit, use of non-musical models is indicated by Professor Babbitt's analogy between the listener's understanding of serial music and the student's understanding of mathematics, logic, and science. "Advanced music," he tells us, "to the extent that it reflects the knowledge and originality of the informed composer, scarcely can be expected to appear more intelligible than these arts and sciences [mathematics, philosophy, and physics] to the person whose musical education usually has been less extensive than his background in other

---

[32] "Who Cares If You Listen?" p. 39.

[33] "What Is Information?" p. 90.

[34] *On Human Communication,* p. 115.

fields." [35] Aside from the insidious suggestion that understanding music is a matter of discovering the rules which guided its composition, the analogy is mistaken and misleading, for the following reasons:

1. In mathematics, a formally complete and explicit set of propositions is presented in a persistent medium (words and symbols on paper), while music presents a series of transient events (pitches and durations) which are derived from, but do not constitute a statement of, an unsystematized, formally incomplete set of rules or procedural guides. To show the disparity between the demands on memory of mathematics, which is visual, and of music, which is aural, one need merely ask: Could one learn Euclidian geometry or symbolic logic aurally?

2. Music differs from natural science in that the objects or events studied by the scientist are not *created* by him. This is, I think, a point of some importance. The scientific community can, as Kuhn points out, isolate itself "from the demands of the laity and of everyday life"; [36] and no doubt the ability of science to "progress" is in part a product of the agreement which such isolation makes possible. But the composer cannot, as Babbitt suggests that he perhaps should, withdraw from the world of public concerts and consensus "to one of private performance and electronic media, with its very real possibility of complete elimination of the public and social aspects of musical composition." [37] For while the scientist discovers or chooses a particular paradigm within

---

[35] "Who Cares If You Listen?" p. 40. I do not question the composer's right to employ special private compositional constraints or the legitimacy of constructing orders that are inaudible, or audible only to the initiate. As Leo Treitler points out, ". . . music has always been, in some measure, a mode of discourse among specialists. . . . If this seems to be more the case today, when composers discuss one another's music without having heard it, the change is only one of degree" ("Musical Syntax in the Middle Ages . . . ," p. 76). In some contemporary music, however, "the change in degree" has become a difference in kind.

Certainly musicians have always had "trade secrets"—even jazz has had its *musica reservata*, as Frank Tirro has shown ("The Silent Theme Tradition in Jazz"). But heretofore the unheard order—the private constraint, the inaudible relationship—was embodied in an audible structure and process which could be understood and enjoyed by the uninitiate. Knowledge that a motet was isorhythmic, a mass was a parody of a chanson, or that a theme was being played backward was not a prerequisite for comprehension and appreciation. Indeed, the composer's ingenuity and skill were challenged not by the secret art or unheard patterning per se—it is not difficult to devise ciphers—but in creating an audibly significant composition in which the hidden "meanings" were embedded.

[36] *The Structure of Scientific Revolutions*, p. 163.

[37] "Who Cares If You Listen?" p. 126.

which to work, he does not create the objective world which the paradigm was designed to illuminate. And it is the existence of such an objective world which makes it possible for the scientist to test and validate his theories. The composer of experimental music, however, often creates *both* the paradigm and the sound relationships which the paradigm makes possible. The composer's "reality" must, as Babbitt points out elsewhere,[38] be the *aural* perceptual-cognitive capabilities of sensitive knowledgeable listeners. And though the number of such listeners may vary considerably, there must be enough of them to assure that the coterie is not solipsistic—that admiration is not for the abstract system or theory and its manipulation rather than for the particular work of art as a unique source of insight and illumination.

3. In the present context, however, the crucial point is that neither mathematics nor science is in fact a unique system, contextually isolated. Each depends for its existence upon a culturally shared repertory of stable symbols and operations. And, in addition, physics is possible only because of the assumption—apparently a tenable one—that the laws of nature are constant and enduring.[39] Understanding the world—whether of physics, mathematics, or music—depends both upon a relatively stable universe and upon a relatively constant universe of discourse. And in music that universe of discourse is what we call style. A valid contextualism does not seek to supplant musical style; rather, it presupposes its existence.

The existence of a shared and relatively stable musical style constitutes a kind of *cultural* redundancy. When such redundancy is low (as in the case of recent serial music, where each new work involves a somewhat different syntax), *compositional* redundancy must be proportionately higher if the organization is to be perceived and learning is to take place. Looked at in another way, the less familiar we are with the grammar and syntax of a style, with the ways in which musical events are related to and imply one another, the slower must be the rate at which the events are presented if they are to be intelligible. Thus, for instance, we ask speakers of an unfamiliar language to talk slowly. (The reason for this seems to be that the perception and cognition of a relatively unfamiliar series of events requires the listener to make more

---

[38] "Twelve-Tone Rhythmic Structure . . . ," pp. 50–51.

[39] When a law of nature is said to change, this is only a way of speaking. It is always assumed that nature's "behavior" remains constant and that what changes is our ability to formulate the patterns of that behavior accurately.

decisions, which habits cannot take care of, than perception of a series generated by a familiar grammar and syntax.) [40] Because a novel grammar and syntax necessarily involves a low level of cultural redundancy, works in a new style must show a high level of compositional redundancy if they are to be intelligible—and if subsequent learning is to take place. Even the learning of our native language depends at first upon the repetition of easy words, simple syntactical constructions, and so on.

That these observations are relevant to the learning of musical styles is shown by the course of development followed by particular styles in the history of music. New styles tend, as we have seen,[41] to begin with relatively high levels of compositional redundancy and move toward lower levels as the style becomes familiar and audiences learn, or internalize, its grammar and syntax. If the history of style is viewed in this fashion, total serialism and experimental music, which generally have very low rates of compositional redundancy, should perhaps be thought of as representing the final stage of the style that began around 1750, rather than as a new style. Such a view would, however, be misleading, though not completely so. Other evidence (see pp. 312–16) indicates that serialism is in the early stages of its development; and whatever debts serialism may owe to the past, it is in many respects revolutionary. The picture is confused because serialism has yet to establish a viable, common stylistic practice. It is in what Kuhn calls the "pre-paradigm" period. Once again the similarity to scientific change is clear: "The proliferation of competing articulations, the willingness to try anything, the expression of explicit discontent, the recourse to philosophy and to debate over fundamentals, all these are symptoms of a transition from normal to extraordinary research." [42]

PERCEPTUAL REDUNDANCY AND TOTAL SERIALISM

The compositional redundancy of most total serial music is so low that even were composers to agree upon a common set of rules and procedures—a stable stylistic process—these works would still present tremendous perceptual problems. Indeed, as George Rochberg has pointed out, it is a striking paradox that, though theoretically and

---

[40] See above, pp. 272–73; and Colin Cherry, *On Human Communication*, pp. 280–81; D. E. Broadbent, *Perception and Communication*, p. 78, and "Information Processing in the Nervous System."

[41] Pp. 114–22, above.

[42] *The Structure of Scientific Revolutions*, p. 90.

operationally this is music of total order, perceptually and experientially it sounds like music of total chance.[43] From a methodological point of view, Ernst Krenek explains the paradox in this way: "Whatever happens at any given point is a product of the preconceived serial organization, but by the same token it is a chance occurrence because it is as such not anticipated by the mind that invented the mechanism and set it in motion."[44] In general, it seems clear that the more totally ordered and predetermined music is, the less perceptually patterned and organized it seems to be. Redundancy is systematic and precompositional rather than compositional and perceptual.

Let us see why this is so.

Compositional redundancy.—We have already emphasized that the parameters of sound are not perceptually equivalent. Hence operations which produce perceptual redundancy in one parameter will not necessarily produce equivalent redundancy in another parameter. This is particularly true of the most important pattern-forming parameters: pitch and duration. The serialization of pitch may produce perceptual redundancy. Because, as noted earlier, pitch is phenomenal, it is possible, given a relatively stable time pattern, to perceive the transposition, inversion, or retrograde of a pitch series as being similar to an original series—as being more or less redundant. While pitch patterns are able to maintain their identity when subjected to such variation, durational patterns are not. Save for special instances, durational relationships are asymmetrical with respect to time. We do not perceive the retrograde of a temporal pattern as being a varied repetition. Hence serial operations which produce redundancy in the realm of pitch produce disorder—or rather a new, different order—in the realm of time.

While the serialization of other parameters of sound—dynamics, timbre, touch, and so on—involves a theoretical ordering, the ordering again does not become perceptual. This is so, in the first place, because, as observed earlier, they are not really pattern-forming attributes of sound. A series of timbres does not easily become an independent order and, consequently, whatever patterning it might create will tend to be obscured or nullified by concomitant variations in the time or pitch series. Moreover, because those parameters are neither physically nor psychologically independent of one another or of pitch and time, they cannot be varied independently. A change in duration or pitch necessar-

---

[43] "Indeterminacy in the New Music," pp. 11–12.
[44] "Extents and Limits of Serial Techniques," p. 228.

ily creates a change in loudness or timbre. Even where pitch, register, and duration are kept constant, other parameters (e.g., loudness and timbre) will appear altered, if what precedes and follows them has been varied. Here total order is not merely difficult to perceive—the very notion is a premusical fantasy.

But the really important reason why systemic or precompositional redundancy fails to become perceptual is that when the serial orderings of time and pitch combine to form a total, simultaneous sound pattern, they co-vary in such a way that there is a strong tendency for potentially perceptual redundancy in one parameter (usually pitch) to be masked and subverted by concurrent changes in the other parameter (time). The problem must be discussed in general terms. For since different precompositional rules and procedures give rise to different types of co-variation among the parameters, each serial work would have to be discussed separately.

Two basic types of combinational relationships among the parameters of sound are possible. In the first, the parameters of sound are treated as dependent analogues or variables of one another (as in the music of Stockhausen or in Babbitt's time-point series) so that particular pitches or pitch relationships are always accompanied by correlative durations or durational relationships, intensities, and so forth. In the second, the parameters of sound vary simultaneously but independently of one another—as, for instance in Boulez's *Structures Ia*. That is, the pitch series and time series, whether originally related or independently invented, are treated either as entirely independent of each other or are related as rows rather than as separate pitches and durations. While much depends upon the particular time and pitch series used and upon the ways in which they are combined, the probabilities are such that the parameters will not vary in a co-ordinate, congruent, or regular fashion. And, as a result, perceptual redundancy is minimized.

The fact is that what we perceive and respond to is not the order or regularity of individual parameters, but the pattern—or lack of pattern—which their combination creates. To put it simply, a perceptual pattern is more than, and different from, the sum of the parameters that create it. And though each serialization of a particular parameter *may* be precompositionally redundant, the unique combinations of such parameters does not necessarily—or even ordinarily—produce regularity and order.

It should also be noted that pitch redundancy can be self-masking. That is, because it is possible to verticalize the row—presenting it in part, or even as a whole, simultaneously—the perceived relationships among its pitches can be so variable that the same series may produce quite different perceptual orders. In such a case pitch redundancy will not give rise to motivic (pattern) redundancy.

The perceptual problems involved in the simultaneous variation of several sound parameters is one which the composer of experimental music must consider carefully. In most music that we know—whether Western or Oriental, cultured or primitive—one or at the most two parameters are changed at one time. For instance, if rhythm is varied, pitch relationships usually remain relatively constant. And, in general, it is probably fair to say that the greater the changes in one of the parameters of sound, the smaller must be the changes in other parameters if the redundancy-variation relationship is to be perceived.

Related to these considerations is the problem of the perception of very subtle shades of difference among simultaneously sounding parameters. The situation seems to be that where a large amount of information is communicated by the subtle variation of one or two parameters of music, the other variables must be more constant and less complex, if the small perceptual differences are to be perceived. Thus in an essentially melodic style, like that of India, much of the musical information and meaning is contained in the host of very slight pitch changes, the nuances of ornamentation, and small rhythmic modifications of the melodic voice. Consequently, the variability and information of the other aspects of sound—harmony, dynamics, counterpoint, and so on—tend to be minimized. Conversely, where contrapuntal or harmonic organization is complex and rich in variability, as in the music of Bach or Wagner, melodic and particularly rhythmic materials will tend to be relatively constant and without very subtle nuance.[45]

Where different kinds of information are combined in a single work—as in vocal music, the dance, and opera—the amount of purely musical information included will in general depend upon the amount and importance of the information to be communicated in other ways. For instance, where the text or its general import is known beforehand or its precise meaning is considered relatively unimportant, the amount of musical information will, as a rule, be quite high—for example, an opera ensemble. Where, on the other hand, the text is to be the center of attention and information, as in television commercials, folk music, Gilbert and Sullivan patter songs, or recitatives, the information com-

---

[45] In this connection, see Broadbent, "Information Processing in the Nervous System," p. 458.

municated by the music will tend to be small.[46] And though it seems that the greatest conflicts develop between modes of perception which use the same sense—hearing a text versus hearing music—even different modes of perception tend to obscure one another. Witness the fact that we are barely conscious of the musical background of an exciting movie.

These matters are of some importance in the perception of total serial music because its procedures usually produce very subtle gradations and differences—particularly in the realm of rhythm. But in experimental music such increases in subtlety are not as a rule complemented, or compensated for, by a lowering of the complexity and variability of the other parameters of sound. As a result potentially perceptible redundancy is often masked by competition among subtly varied parameters.

Schemata and perception.—The problem of the perception of simultaneous variables is particularly acute in experimental music because this music provides the listener with no archetypal, traditional schemata as aids to memory and guides to listening. We perceive, comprehend, and remember our experiences—musical or other—in terms of more or less learned schematic types.[47] Particular experiences and objects are comprehended and remembered as deriving from, and deviating from, schemata which serve as methods for "encoding" and remembering large amounts of information easily and efficiently. Without such schemata, memory and perception would be forever bogged down in an incomprehensible welter of isolated particulars. Antecedent-consequent relationships, gap-filling melodic patterns, cadential chord progressions, anapestic rhythmic groups, imitative counterpoint, formal plans, and the like are examples of such schematic archetypes in tonal music. Because they enable us to comprehend complex patterns as a whole, such forms of cultural and compositional redundancy allow us to direct our attention to those parameters of sound which are less stable and regular. The more patent and better known a particular schema is, the more the other parameters of sound can be varied without obscuring the

---

[46] On the interference of one kind of information with the perception of another, see T. Shipley, "Auditory Flutter-Driving of Visual Flicker"; D. E. Broadbent, "Attention and the Perception of Speech"; Paul Spong, M. Haider, and D. B. Lindsley, "Selective Attentiveness and Cortical Evoked Responses . . ."; and Michael I. Posner, "Components of Skilled Performance," who writes that "As the difficulty of a task increases, it demands more of man's limited attention, and the space capacity available for dealing with other signals is reduced" (p. 1714).

[47] See E. H. Gombrich, *Art and Illusion*, pp. 87–90. The presence of schemata or archetypal patterns also enhances the speed of perception and of response, since these are related to the familiarity and expectedness of the sequence of stimuli. See Cherry, *On Human Communication*, pp. 280–81.

totality of pattern relationships. The almost complete absence of such archetypal patterns in much experimental music increases immeasurably the tasks of perception, comprehension, and memory.

"Natural" redundancy.—The listener's ability to perceive and comprehend patterns and relationships is not merely a function of the organizations invented by the composer and the frequency with which these are stated. Because of the nature of the human mind and structure of the human body, some tone combinations and sequences are more easily perceived and learned than others. And because totally ordered music, whether of necessity or by design, tends to exclude these combinations and sequences, its patterns are more difficult to grasp and comprehend than might otherwise be the case. To put the matter somewhat differently, there *are* "natural" modes of perceptual ordering, and where the musical organization allows these to function—is congruent with them—perception is easier and learning is reinforced. Where such natural redundancies are excluded from a musical style, the simplicity of "composed" relationships—frequency of pattern repetition and so on—and the degree of "cultural" redundancy must be increased if the music is to be intelligible.

In raising the "nature versus nurture" question, I realize that I am treading on troubled ground. But it seems to me that the record needs to be set straight.

For two thousand years music theorists searched for a "natural" explanation of musical pitch systems and syntax. Their point of departure was, as a rule, some sort of acoustical data—the lengths of vibrating strings, the overtone series, or some other natural property of sound. Using such data, an attempt was made to show that this or that system was natural—and hence, by extension, necessary or valid. Toward the beginning of the twentieth century this search for a natural justification for music was abandoned. The development of new tonal systems in the West, the study of the history of Western music, and research in comparative musicology made it clear that musical styles are not natural forms of communication, but are learned and conventional.

The fact that something is conventional and learned, however, does not mean that it is arbitrary, any more than showing that it is "natural" is to assert that it is necessary. The central nervous system, acting in conjunction with motor behavior, is not neutral with respect to incoming stimuli and their organization into perceptual patterns. It is a decision network which selects and orders stimuli in terms of its own capacities and structural organization. The situation can be put concisely by saying that the redundancy which we are able to discover in the world is partly a function of the organization—the redundancy—built into the nervous system.

Considerable evidence, both experimental and cultural, indicates that the central nervous system, acting in conjunction with motor systems, predisposes us to perceive certain pitch relationships, temporal proportions, and melodic structures as well shaped and stable. For instance, the octave, fifth, and fourth are basic, normative intervals in the music of almost all cultures.[48] And it does not seem far fetched to say that each of these is quite literally redundant—in the sense that the partials of one tone duplicate the fundamental of the other. Similarly, it appears that relatively simple durational proportions—1:1, 1:2, 1:3, or 2:3—are more easily perceived as stable, memorable patterns [49] than more complex ratios. These observations do not, I hasten to emphasize, assert that such intervals or durational proportions are in any way a necessary condition for the existence of a musical style or syntax. But it seems hard to doubt that when they do act as norms of musical syntax, they function, like other forms of redundancy, to facilitate perception and learning. And their absence increases the amount of information which the nervous system must process.

Both of these examples are instances of the more general laws of pattern-perception, discovered by the *Gestalt* psychologists, which tell us that regular, symmetrical, simple shapes will be more readily perceived, appear more stable, and be better remembered than those which are not. Thus, for instance, conjunct pitch sequences (the law of proximity), continuing timbres (the law of similarity), cyclic formal structures (the law of return)—all help to facilitate perception, learning, and understanding. Though these normative modes of perceptual patterning need not necessarily be present in a particular kind of music, they must be taken into account even when—or perhaps particularly when—they are excluded from the syntactical norms of a style. For where they are not present (as they are not in most advanced music), providing a basis for structural reinforcement, then the rate of other aspects of redundancy—for instance, cultural redundancy—must be substantially increased.

It is important to realize that in our century a new kind of redundancy has become available: that made possible by the development of

---

[48] In this connection, see Sachs, *The Wellsprings of Music*, pp. 56, 148, 177.

[49] This is probably partly a result of our bilateral motor symmetry, the on-off character of nerve responses, the systolic action of the heart, and so forth. See *ibid.*, pp. 111–12.

phonograph and tape recordings. By playing a recording over and over again listeners can undoubtedly "learn" the materials and relationships presented in a particular work. Thus the existence of technological redundancy compensates, so to speak, for the decrease in compositional and cultural redundancy in much contemporary music. Of course, there are still problems. The first is that of arousing audience interest in such seemingly forbidding music in the first place. Will listeners buy recordings of such works and, through repeated hearings, learn their materials? (One can, of course, join Babbitt and argue that it makes no difference whether people listen, that a very few sophisticated peers who can truly understand the skill of the composer are more important than a mass of "appreciators.") The second problem is related to the first. One of the difficulties with the use of repeated hearings in learning new works is that what is learned in one work of advanced serial or experimental music does not as a rule carry over—is not applicable to—the perception and understanding of other works, even those employing the same precompositional rules. One can only hope that the rewards arising from admiration of the composer's skill in one instance will be sufficient to encourage listeners to learn other works.

The channel capacity of the listener.—As the preceding discussion indicates, it is not the level of any particular facet of perceptual redundancy that makes it very difficult for even the most favorably disposed listener to learn to perceive and understand highly complex music. Rather the absence of a stable stylistic syntax, archetypal schema, audible compositional order, and patent "natural" patterning results in a level of redundancy so low that communication is virtually precluded. The theorists of total serialism are not unaware of the new demands being made upon the listener. "The increase in *efficiency*," writes Milton Babbitt, "necessarily reduces the 'redundancy' of the language, and as a result the intelligible communication of the work demands increased accuracy from the transmitter (the performer) and activity from the receiver (the listener). . . . [This reduction in redundancy] makes ever heavier demands upon the training of the listener's perceptual capacities." [50]

The semantic snare in this statement is, of course, the word "efficiency." Efficiency for what? For whom? Would it increase efficiency to send two or three programs over a radio or television channel simultaneously? Obviously not; for they would mask one another. Does the English language lack efficiency because it is about 50

---

[50] "Who Cares If You Listen?" p. 39. Italics mine.

per cent redundant? Not at all; English is an efficient means of communication precisely because it is redundant enough to combat noise and thereby assure relatively accurate and error-free transmission. Unless the noise component in communication—particularly what I have called "cultural noise" [51]—is reduced, lowering the level of perceptual redundancy will produce inaccuracy and confusion, not efficiency. Even if, as Babbitt suggests,[52] a coterie of aficionados devoted their full perceptual capacities to this music, it is doubtful that they would ultimately succeed in really learning to *understand* it aurally. (It is important to note that neither memorization nor performance necessarily entail understanding. Just as it is possible to learn to read, to memorize, and to recite [perform] a series of meaningless syllables or a text in a language one does not know, so it is possible to read, memorize, and perform music that one does not really understand.)

The real difficulty, though, is that not merely the listener's perceptual capacities are involved, but his cognitive capacities as well—his ability to comprehend what he perceives. And when all aspects of redundancy are very low, the effect is not merely additive. To understand what happens, let us look at the communication process from the standpoint of information rather than that of redundancy.

The absence of redundancy means the presence of information. Because its level of redundancy is extremely low, total serial music presents the listener with so much novel, densely packed material that even those parts of the musical message which might have been intelligible are often masked and confused by the welter of incoming information. The listener's channel capacity—his perceptual, cognitive neural network—is so overloaded that it is unable to process the musical message. The situation is succinctly described by Warren Weaver:

> A general theory [of communication] . . . will surely have to take into account not only the capacity of the channel but also (even the words are right!) the capacity of the audience. If you overcrowd the capacity of the audience, it is probably true, by direct analogy, that you do not fill the audience up and then waste only the remainder by spilling. More likely, and again by direct analogy, you force a general error and confusion.[53]

It is, moreover, not merely a matter of the amount of information, but the *rate* of information. Experiments suggest that "there is a limit to the

---

[51] See chap. 1.

[52] "Who Cares If You Listen?" p. 126.

[53] "The Mathematics of Information," pp. 108–9. Also see Fritz Winckel, "The Psycho-Acoustical Analysis of Music . . . ," p. 238.

amount of information which a listener can absorb in a certain amount of time; that is, he has a limited capacity." [54] It is probably at least partly because of the overloading of the audience's channel capacity that total serial music and totally random music sound so much alike. And it is also partly because of this that such music is difficult to learn to understand.

Style changes have, of course, almost always presented problems for listeners. For until habits, dispositions, and expectancy sets appropriate to such changes have become learned, the listener's channel capacity will probably *appear* to be overloaded. Once cultural redundancy has risen to appropriate levels, however, the listener will be able to comprehend and respond to the sequence of musical events intelligently and sensitively. And it might, for these reasons, be urged that the level of redundancy in total serial music is not really as low as the preceding analysis has suggested—that even if the likelihood of learning the norms of such music is much more remote than the learning of past changes has been, it may nevertheless be possible. Perhaps. But indirect evidence from those who should know most about this music—the composers and theorists of total serialism—indicates that the lack of perceptual redundancy has probably not been exaggerated.

Almost all analyses of total serialism that I have encountered are made in terms of the permutations and combinations to which the serialized parameters of sound are subjected. Why should this be so? The answer lies at least in part in its lack of compositional redundancy. For, as Herbert Simon has pointed out, "If a complex structure is completely unredundant—if no aspect of its structure can be inferred from any other—then it is its own simplest description. We can exhibit it but we cannot describe it by a simpler structure." [55]

To put the matter briefly, insofar as total serialism lacks compositional (as distinguished from systematic or precompositional) redundancy, it cannot be analyzed, nor can it be described either in terms of simpler structures or in terms of common processes. All one can do—and it is significant that this is what *has* been done—is to *exhibit* its systemic, precompositional materials. [56] The situation is concisely, if

---

[54] Broadbent, *Perception and Communication*, p. 17. Also see James G. Miller, "Information Input Overload . . ."; and Michael I. Posner, "Components of Skilled Performance."

[55] "The Architecture of Complexity," p. 478.

[56] See Edward T. Cone, "Analysis Today," pp. 174–76. For confirmation of this statement one need only scan the "analyses" printed in *Die Reihe, Perspectives of New Music*, and the *Journal of Music Theory*.

somewhat vitriolically, summed up by T. W. Adorno: "One can not reproach the critic with not understanding these recent products of rampant rationalism, since according to their own programme, they are not to be understood *but only to be demonstrated*. Ask what is the function of some phenomenon within a work's total content and meaning, and the answer is a further exposition of the system." [57]

---

[57] Quoted by Heinz-Klaus Metzger, "Intermezzo I . . . ," p. 79. Italics mine.

CHAPTER
I 2

Functionalism and Structure

In any discussion of serialism (whether total or partial) and of experimental music in general, the question, raised by Adorno, of the existence and relevance of functional relationships in music is perhaps *the* central and critical one. For the composer's attitude toward functionalism is inextricably linked both to his compositional procedures and to his basic aesthetic position—his conception of the role of music in human experience. Indeed from the point of view of musical theory and compositional practice, it is a fundamental difference on this issue that divides the traditionalists and formalists, on the one hand, from the transcendentalists, on the other.

The traditionalists and the formalists, for whom musical communication arises out of the implications which tones, motives, phrases, and even sections have for one another, still seem to admit the possibility and propriety of functional relationships of some sort, though their views on this subject are not entirely clear. Thus Donald Martino, while showing that tonal music and twelve-tone music "belong to different classes of musical systems," asserts that "important objectives—the creation of normative, thus predictable, as well as non-normative, thus dramatic, procedures which help to determine as many pitch aspects of the total composition as the composer deems consistent with his compositional intentions—may be realized in each case by exploiting those properties which are peculiar to the system." [1] What is set forth here is a goal-oriented, teleological view of communication. And I shall try to show that such a view necessarily entails the possibility of some sort of functionalism.

The transcendental particularists, on the other hand, espousing a fundamentally different aesthetic in which implication, goal-directed musical process, and a teleological view of communication play no part, can and do deny both the propriety and the relevance of any sort of functional relationships altogether. The position is clearly stated by Herbert Eimert:

> It would never have occurred to a musician of the 19th century to define a note by its pitch, duration, and intensity. At that time a note was understood through its relationship to other notes and through its relationships to tensions within the structure of a chord. The 19th century did not ask *"what was"* a note, but only *"how did it function?"* [2]

More precisely and accurately, the nineteenth century (as well as the preceding centuries going back to Greek times) defined tones in terms of their functions as the language of theory clearly shows: "What a note was" *was* "how it functioned."

The matter of definition is significant because it indicates how intimately the question of functionalism is linked to our conception of the nature of musical communication. Insofar as one wishes to *understand* an event or an object, particularly one involving human purposes or needs, one defines it operationally or functionally. One asks what it *does*, what function it performs. In very simple-minded terms, a finger is to move, a piano is to play, and a piece of music is to enjoy through understanding. Even our explanations of the physical world are in terms of functional processes. The properties of crystals are discussed and analyzed in terms of the reasons why their constituent atoms and molecules combine in particular ways: how chemical bonds function in relation to one another.

If, of course, one's activity is restricted to simply sensing the world as a physical stimulus, then what something *is* can be specified in a detailed description—and perhaps only as a detailed description. In

---

[1] "The Source Set and Its Aggregate Formations," p. 226.
[2] "What Is Electronic Music?" pp. 7–8.

such a case redundancy is unnecessary and irrelevant.[3] The value of the redundancy in the world is that it enables us to describe it simply [4] and through such description to understand its process. Hence those who contend that music is non-functional are completely consistent in creating a non-redundant music and in equating its analysis with a detailed description of its pitches and so forth. And the concept of perception must be radically different from that described in the previous chapter. For in a functional system perception involves ordering and selection, while in the non-functional aesthetic espoused by transcendental particularism perception (*sensing* is a more accurate term) is passive and non-selective.

Those who contend that understanding music is something more than the passive sensing of a sequence of sounds must, then, adopt some sort of functional position not only compositionally, but analytically. And here it should be noted that analysis is in a sense a one-way operation. That is, it must proceed from a guess, however vague, about how the whole piece of music functions to hypotheses about the operations of its parts. From a logical point of view the analysis of music is like that of mechanical or biological systems. Just as "Physical and chemical knowledge can form part of biology only in its bearing *on previously established biological shapes and functions*," [5] so knowledge of acoustics, psychology, combinatorial procedures, and the like can become relevant for musical analysis only in terms of their bearing on musical shapes and functions. As Michael Polanyi has said, "We must start from some anterior knowledge of the system's total performance and take the system apart with a view to discovering how each part functions in conjunction with the other parts." [6]

THE REQUIREMENTS OF FUNCTIONALISM

Broadly speaking, functionalism in music may be defined as the implications which one musical event—be it a tone, a motive, a phrase, or a section—has for some other musical event either on its own hierarchic level or some other. Since one musical event implies, or is a sign of, some other musical event only for an observer or listener, the

---

[3] But not impossible. A "system" can be highly redundant, but non-functional, e.g., a collection of buttons, sandstone, a coral reef, or a series of exactly repeated notes or motives.

[4] See Herbert A. Simon, "The Architecture of Complexity," p. 479.

[5] Michael Polanyi, *Personal Knowledge*, p. 342.

[6] *Ibid.*, p. 357.

perception of functional relationships is the result of inferences made by the listener about the possible implications of a musical event. The proclivity of listeners to make such inferences—to interpret a musical event functionally—depends on their experience with the musical style out of which the event arises, the formal or syntactical characteristics of the event itself, and the nature of human mental processes. Since we have already dealt with the first two of these in some detail (chap. 2), let us turn our attention to the third.

Man is, as noted earlier, a predicting animal.[7] Because a relatively small amount of his behavior is genetically specified, man must choose among alternative courses of action. And he can choose intelligently only if he can predict what the probable outcome of a chosen course of action will be. Because it is vital to our very survival, we tend whenever possible to interpret events predictively—in terms of antecedent and consequent, cause and effect, means and ends.

A temporal sequence of events is particularly susceptible to such interpretation. Though we tend, if possible, to interpret temporally ordered events in this way, our ability to do so depends not only upon our natural proclivity to predict but also upon the characteristics of the series itself. In general, the more similar in kind and proximate in space and time two different events are, and the more often they are experienced in a particular order, the more likely the first is to be interpreted as implying, as being the sign of, the second. The more likely, that is, are they to be understood as being functionally related. Several significant points follow from this.

1. The less proximate in time and pitch, the less similar in timbre and dynamics and the less often they are placed in a particular relationship with one another, the smaller will be the likelihood that a series of notes will be interpreted functionally. From this it appears that those who espouse a non-functional view of music, are entirely correct in emphasizing pitch and time disjunctions and the absence of compositional and cultural redundancy in their music. Henri Pousseur states the position uncompromisingly: ". . . is it not precisely this criterion of organic quality that is called in question? Must we not therefore carry further our research, with an eye to this fragmentation, discontinuity, asymmetry and even more integral eccentricity?"[8]

2. On the other hand, total redundancy—the exact repetition of an event—will also weaken the sense of functionalism. The events to be

---

[7] See above, pp. 227–28.

[8] "Outline of a Method," p. 80.

related must be different in some respect. The relationship between a note or motive and its exact repetition is not usually interpreted functionally on the hierarchic level of the repetition. An event does not, as a rule, imply itself.

Actually, of course, two temporally ordered events can never really be the same, since they differ in that one is first and the other second. The psychological situation is complex. Much depends upon our opinion whether the repeated note or pattern is a "figure" or is part of the "ground." When a repeated note or pattern is understood as part of a ground—as is, for instance, an ostinato figure—we tend to take its repetition for granted and not to interpret the series of notes or figures as being functionally related to one another. When the pattern and its repetition are understood to be *the* figure, however, then a functional interpretation is attempted. What generally happens is that the first musical event is not understood to imply its repetition but rather both the event *and* its repetition combine to form a compound event which implies some different, new event. And the functional relationship thus established exists on a higher hierarchic level than that of the repeated event itself.

This is a point of some moment because it shows that functionalism need *not* be hierarchically continuous. For instance, on the lowest hierarchic level, the pitch-time events comprising an ostinato figure will be functionally related to one another, but the repetitions of the figure itself on the second hierarchic level will not be so related. On a higher level, however, the repetitions of the ostinato figure may be interpreted as being functionally related to the following texture.[9]

3. It is clear from this and from our earlier discussion of perception and cognition that perceptual redundancy, which is a necessary and, given man's predictive needs, perhaps also sufficient condition for inferences of a functional sort, is by no means entirely dependent upon traditionally established norms and regularities.[10] If musical events are patterned at all, the laws of proximity, good continuation, closure, return, and the like will operate, making it possible and likely that relationships will be understood as functional even in the absence of a set of traditionally established syntactical norms. This is because the human mind searching for control, through prediction, will discover

---

[9] It should be remembered that we understand music both in *pro*spect and *ret*rospect. Consequently, a functional relationship may become apparent only when the implications of the antecedent event are realized.

[10] But when these are not present, it is important, as we have seen, that the level of other kinds of redundancy be higher if communication is to take place.

implicative relationships wherever and whenever a modicum of redundancy exists.

4. It should be emphasized that functional differentiation of some sort is a *sine qua non* of every kind of morphological structure whether natural or artificial. An atom is a structure by virtue of the functional relationships understood to exist between its positively charged nucleus and its negatively charged outer rings; the organization of the simplest living organism is dependent upon functional differentiation among its interacting parts; and so it is with even the most rudimentary forms of human communication, whether linguistic or musical. Furthermore, as we shall see, the more complex a structure is, the greater the number of functionally differentiated hierarchies required for its articulation. Only if the desire for structure and communication is given up altogether, as the most extreme transcendental particularists are apparently willing to do, can one imagine a functionally undifferentiated music.

FUNCTIONALISM AND THE FORMALIST-TRADITIONALIST POSITION

Because he considers tonal implications, morphological structure, and intelligible communication to be aesthetically irrelevant and indeed undesirable, the nature of functional relationships in contemporary music—whether totally ordered or totally random—is no problem for the composer-theorist of transcendental particularism.[11] He simply does his best to avoid any pitch-time sequences which might be interpreted functionally. For the formalist or the traditionalist serial composer, however, the existence, status, and nature of functional relationships is apparently a problem. I say "apparently," because the problems— whether compositional or theoretical—are at bottom, I think, quixotic rather than real. They arise from a misguided historicism coupled with mistaken theoretical-aesthetic conceptions.

As we have seen, Schönberg's method of composing with twelve tones was, at least from an aesthetic point of view, invented in order to avoid suggesting melodic-harmonic relationships derived from the major-minor tonal system which had been the basis of musical syntax since the Renaissance. From this traditional point of view, serial music is un-

---

[11] At least it is no problem from a theoretical point of view, but from a practical point of view it is. For if I am correct in contending that it is of the very essence of human behavior to predict, then it will be no easy matter to invent a series of sounds, no matter how disjunct and disjointed, which cannot be made to serve as the basis for some sort of functionally interpreted inferences.

doubtedly nonfunctional. But without denying the importance of this fact, one may question the logic of the conclusions, both stated and implied, which have evidently been derived from it.

Let us begin with a statement by Ian Hamilton: "As we no longer consider tonality to be the overriding power, it is no longer logical to employ these forms, sonata, rondo, and fugue, which rely for their true meaning on it. As we no longer, therefore, have these forms it is equally invalid to think in terms of the symmetries which they condition." [12] Implicit in this quotation are a host of interrelated assumptions that will not bear serious scrutiny.

The difficulty is that it is not at all clear what the terms "logical" or "invalid" really mean. Why is it "no longer logical" to employ the dramatic forms—sonata, rondo, and others—in music? What evidence is there that these forms depend in some *necessary* way upon the existence of tonality? The evidence is quite to the contrary. Schönberg, Berg, and even Webern employed these forms successfully in the absence of traditional tonality. To be sure, they did not use the forms in exactly the same way as did, say, Beethoven. But then Beethoven's fugues are very different from Bach's, and Brahms's sonata forms are very different from Mozart's. In what sense and on what grounds are these theorists prepared to say that Schönberg's music is "illogical" or "invalid"?

The view that there is some sort of contradiction "between the forms dictated by tonality" [13] and those which are appropriate to serial music apparently rests upon the unstated assumption that the negation of the functionalism of traditional tonality entails the impossibility of all forms of functionalism. As we have seen, this is simply not so. Even if George Rochberg's interesting suggestion that "equal tempered chromaticism, organized hexachordally, incorporates in an organic way fundamental tonal functions having to do with the connection between intervals while discarding the exhausted machinery of historical tonality" [14] should prove to be mistaken, traditional tonality is not—and never has been—the only means of defining functional musical processes and organizing formal structures. The definition of process and the organization of structure depend in the last analysis upon the much more basic cognitive fact that the patterned parameters of sound, by articulating a complex set of stability-instability relationships on different hierarchic

---

[12] "Serialism," pp. 51–52.

[13] Pierre Boulez, "Schönberg Is Dead," p. 20.

[14] "The Harmonic Tendency of the Hexachord," p. 223.

levels, are understood as functional and implicative. No composer has ever relied—at least in a work of any size and complexity—upon tonality alone to create implication and specify structure. Rhythmic patterns, melodic motives, formal repetition, contrasts of texture, differences in the palpability of shape, as well as other compositional resources implicit in the laws of human perceptual-cognitive behavior have always supported, complemented, and at times even contradicted the implications and goal-directed tendencies created by traditional tonality. That these forces can be effective in the absence of historical tonality is shown—no, proved!—by the compositions of the classical twelve-tone composers, Schönberg, Berg, and Webern.[15]

Regardless of the system out of which a series of musical events arises, the human mind will, if possible, discover order in the series and will tend to interpret such order in functional terms. But to conclude from this that there are no significant differences, both in practice and theory, between serial music and traditional tonal music would be a serious mistake. Because it is in many respects new in both practice and theory, serial music poses new compositional problems and demands new theoretical formulations. To cite but a few obvious examples: In the absence of traditionally established tonal functions, dissonance—and, consequently, consonance as well—conceived of as the tendency of one vertical configuration to move toward, resolve to, or imply another, is no longer meaningful. Furthermore, formal structures, such as the archetypal antecedent-consequent phrase, which depended upon traditionally established tonal functions for their articulation are no longer possible, though other means of achieving similar aims may be. On the positive side, variation of foreground patterns through inversion, retrograde, and retrograde-inversion can play a far more important role in serial music than in tonal music precisely because such relationships are not obscured by the uni-directionality of traditional tonal functions.

The compositional differences between serial music and tonal music are undoubtedly important. But they should not be made to seem greater

---

[15] As well as many others: Blackwood, Carter, Sessions, Wolpe, to name four composers who write non-tonal, yet functional, music. The claim by some of the theorists of total serialism that Webern's music represents a fundamental break with the past is not supported by a study of his works. Peter Westergaard has pointed out that, in Webern's music, dynamics, rhythm, and timbre "are still playing their traditional role of differentiation. They interact with one another and with pitch to clarify pitch relationships, sorting out for the ear those pitch relationships which are to shape the movement" ("Webern and 'Total Organization'. . . ," p. 109).

than they really are. And this is what usually occurs when, as Milton Babbitt does, one contrasts the formal structure of the precompositional systems with one another instead of comparing the perceptual-cognitive logic of the resultant musical structures. For instance, having pointed to "the profound differences between the twelve-tone *system* and musical *systems* in which the 'historical forerunners' of the twelve-tone operations appear," [16] Babbitt emphasizes that serial music is a *permutational* system, while tonal music is a *combinational* one. The differences between them are described as follows:

> Given a collection of available elements, the choice of a sub-collection of these as a referential norm provides a norm that is distinguishable by content alone; such a system, and the traditional tonal system is such, is therefore combinational. But if the referential norm is the totality of elements, there is but one such norm in terms of content, and deviations from this norm cannot exist within the system. [17]

This, I take it, means that, if from the chromatic scale (the "collection of available elements") you choose the notes which make up, say, the C major scale, you have provided a set of relationships ("norm") which can be distinguished by its particular tones from some other scale. But if the chromatic scale taken as a whole (the "totality of elements"), constitutes your norm, there can be no deviations, since there is only one chromatic scale. "But," writes Babbitt, "if an ordering is imposed upon this totality, and taken as a norm, this norm is so distinguished, in the case of twelve pitch class elements, from the 12!—1 other possible orderings, that is, other possible permutations." [18] In other words, if a particular ordering of the chromatic scale (a twelve-tone row) is taken as a norm, it is different from all the other possible orderings of the chromatic scale. But this means that once a particular set has been chosen, the twelve-tone system is also combinational, a fact which Babbitt makes clear when, at the end of the article, he writes that he has "led the discussion more in the direction of those aspects which suggest the 'macrocosmically' combinational features of this basically permutational system." [19] Conversely, in the traditional tonal system, once a scale has been chosen, the melodic-harmonic manipulation of the scale is permutational. In short, these and many of the other differences

---

[16] "Twelve-Tone Invariants . . . ," p. 246. Italics mine.
[17] *Ibid.*, pp. 247–48.
[18] *Ibid.*, p. 248.
[19] *Ibid.*, p. 258.

which Babbitt calls our attention to are theoretical and systematic, not compositional.

Babbitt's confusion is evident when he notes that the subject he has discussed—the possible manipulations and combinations to which twelve-tone rows may be subjected—is important "analytically in the 'rational reconstruction' of compositions, and compositionally in comprehending and mastering the materials of the system." [20] As noted earlier, to analyze the row structure on the lowest architectonic level —and Babbitt's analyses do not go beyond this—is like trying to understand the behavior of a living organism by "analyzing," really describing, the ways in which hydrogen, oxygen, and all the other elements are distributed and combined in its physical structure. Compositionally what are comprehended and mastered are *not* the materials of the systems, but the constraints within which compositional choices are made. The system is, moreover, patently incomplete. That is, it provides no rules for determining the succession of rows or row forms, for choosing pitch register, for verticalizing the series, for deciding durational relationships, and so on. [21]

The contention that there is something improper about using serial methods to write in traditional forms seems, in some cases at least, to rest upon a veiled, but questionable, historicism. The argument might run as follows: since sonata form, fugue, rondo, and the like arose within the style system of tonal music, they are out of place, or perhaps even impossible, in the absence of tonality. But this line of reasoning is mistaken both theoretically and philosophically. Theoretically, the "dramatic" procedures of tonal music, though undoubtedly fostered by the system of tonality, are, as we have seen, not dependent upon tonality. Philosophically, there is no evidence that in human activities a change in materials and their microscopic organization necessitates a change in macroscopic form, though the former may make the latter possible. Bottles were once made of clay, later of glass, and today often of plastic—but the macroscopic form has remained quite constant. The patterns and relationships which human beings create, though possibly modified by changes in material, are what they are, have a particular form, not because of their materials per se, but because of human physical and spiritual needs. Thus Boulez's criticism of Schönberg rests on questionable grounds: "Schönberg uses the tone-row simply as a

---

[20] *Ibid.*
[21] Also see above, Introduction to Part III.

lowest common denominator to ensure the semantic unity of each work; but the elements of the language thus obtained are organized according to an already existing rhetoric, and so there is no intrinsic unity." [22] But the "rhetoric" one chooses depends only partly upon one's language; it depends mostly upon what one wants to say. One can exclaim, "Nonsense!" in many different languages.

FUNCTIONALISM, HIERARCHIES, AND COMPLEXITY

The possibility of functional differentiation in the absence of traditional tonality is of tremendous importance. For without such differentiation musical events could not give rise to formally articulated hierarchic structures. And were such structures impossible, the level of musical complexity, the scope of human understanding, or both would be severely limited.

Functionalism and hierarchic structure are, in a sense, but two ways of looking at a single processive organization. For the presumption of functionalism arises only where the elements of a structure or the events of a process exhibit some sort of relatively stable implicative relationships to one another. And such implicative relationships are, at the same time, the basis for hierarchic organization. Specifically, just as a collection of identical, independent cells, which are, by definition, functionally *un*related, can never generate higher-level organic structures; just as a conglomeration of independent and functionally identical individuals do not produce organized social behavior; and just as a sequence of words consisting only of nouns can never combine to form a sentence—so a concatenation of unrelated, isolated pitch-time events can never create a hierarchically ordered musical structure.

The connection between functionalism and hierarchic organization seems to be something like this: In order for a hierarchic structure or process to arise, it must be developed out of "potential," intermediate, and relatively stable forms. These intermediate forms can arise only because functional, dependency relationships make closure (or partial closure) possible. If no implicative or "tendency" relationships existed between an atomic nucleus and its outer rings, between a subject and a predicate, or between the notes of a motive, closure and stability would be impossible. But because the structures or events which organize lower

---

[22] "Schönberg Is Dead," p. 21.

architectonic levels are only partially complete and stable, other complementary structures are implied. That is, still higher levels will arise.[23]

Hierarchic structure enables the composer to invent and the listener to comprehend complex, inter-reactive musical organizations. If musical stimuli (pitches, durations, timbres) did not produce brief, but partially complete events (motives, themes, etc.), and if these did not, in turn, combine with one another to form more extended, higher-order patterns (phrases, sections, etc.), all relationships would necessarily be transient and purely local. Thus Seymour Shifrin wonders whether serial procedure "gives rise to more than motivic connections between transpositions. . . . The danger . . . is in the suggestion of an all-inclusiveness that is achieved too much at the price of distinctions and where the symmetrical niceties tend to be local, static, and simply motivic." [24] In such music, significance would be restricted to the immediate connections between discrete sounds and the meaning of the whole would tend to be additive. Or looked at in a somewhat different way, Herbert Simon writes:

> If there are important systems in the world that are complex without being hierarchic, they may to a considerable extent escape our observation and understanding. Analysis of their behavior would involve such detailed knowledge and calculation of the interactions of their elementary parts that it would be beyond our capacities of memory or computation.[25]

Until recently—that is, until the advent of totally ordered or totally random composition—all music, from the most primitive to the most complex, was hierarchically structured to some extent. Indeed, most of the terms ordinarily used in the analysis of music—motive, antecedent phrase, first-theme group, bridge passage, subject, episode, exposition, and so on—point either explicitly or implicitly to the functions of different parts and levels of the musical hierarchy. And analytic methods such as those developed by Schenker, Lorenz, and Kurth, as well as more traditional ones, all essentially aim at exhibiting the hierarchic-functional structure of musical events.

---

[23] See Herbert A. Simon, "The Architecture of Complexity," pp. 470–71; C. H. Waddington, "The Character of Biological Form," pp. 40–45; and Lancelot Law Whyte, *Accent on Form*, chap. 6.

[24] "A Note from the Underground," p. 152. As we have seen, this *need* not be the case, though it is undoubtedly a "danger" of uncritical serialism.

[25] "The Architecture of Complexity," p. 477.

While emphasizing the importance of hierarchic structure, the systematic formulations and practical procedures of analytic theory have tended to neglect and underestimate the significance of differences among hierarchic levels within particular works. That is, theorists have, as noted earlier (pp. 258–59), often assumed that the principles of hierarchic organization remain constant from level to level. But though the fundamental laws of pattern organization may perhaps remain constant—be truly "general"—the particular parameters of sound used to articulate process and structure will vary in kind as well as in emphasis from one level to another. For example, durational relationships are more important in shaping low-level events such as motives and phrases, while tonal relationships and texture are particularly effective in shaping higher-level processes.

Moreover, the ways in which a particular parameter is used may vary from one level to another. Orchestration is often used to articulate rhythmic groups on low levels, but it also acts to delineate large-scale formal relationships. And it should also be recalled that the probability relationships exhibited by a particular parameter may be different for different hierarchic levels. For instance, it is more likely that, in the music of the classical period, a low-level event like a phrase will begin with a triad than that the melodic connection between phrases will be triadic (though this is not impossible—see Mozart Symphony No. 40, "Minuetto"). For in this style, high-level melodic events generally move either by step (see Beethoven Symphony No. 1, First Movement, allegro theme) or by fourths or fifths (see Mozart Symphony in E-flat, K.543, "Minuetto," mm. 1–8). Or again, with respect to a single parameter, the probabilities of organization may vary for differently functioning parts on the same hierarchic level. Thus the probability of chromatic alteration is greater in a developmental passage than, say, in a thematic one. Again it seems clear that such probabilities will change from style to style. For instance, the chances of a serial piece beginning with a triad are close to zero.

Finally, and perhaps most important of all, it cannot be assumed that the hierarchic articulations created by the several parameters of sound are necessarily always congruent. Harmonic relationships, for instance, may articulate a structural event on one level, while on a higher level melodic events create a different hierarchic span. Indeed, it is partly such interplay among the shaping forces of music which prevents a musical event from being so congruently and definitively structured that the piece stops—has no further implications.

It is also clear that even within a single style, different kinds of musical organization exhibit different sorts of hierarchic structure. Indeed, since at least part of what we mean by "form" is the kind of hierarchic structure a piece has, even works ostensibly in the same "form" will have individual and peculiar hierarchic organizations. Unfortunately there is at present no adequate theory of what might be called "music techtonics." This is an important area for the music theorist. For a carefully worked out and empirically validated theory would make possible a more general and more sensitive understanding of musical structure, musical process, and their interconnection. The situation is evidently strikingly similar to that in biology where, according to Ernst Nagel, "the subject matters of their inquiry have compelled biologists to recognize not just a single type of hierarchical organization in living things, but several types, and that a central problem in the analysis of organic developmental processes is the discovery of the precise interrelations between such hierarchies." [26] A theory of music techtonics could also be of immense value because of the light it would throw upon the nature and the development—the "natural history"—of musical form. The subject of hierarchic structure is of such importance, however, that, even in the absence of an adequate theory, I would like to hazard a few provisional observations.

In order for hierarchic structures to arise, the organizing forces—the functional-syntactical processes which produce closure and stability—must be at least somewhat different for each level of the hierarchy. Without such differentiation, structural relationships would, so to speak, get stuck. That is, lower levels would continue to produce cohesive, relatively stable patterns, but these would not combine with one another to form higher-level shapes. Thus, as we have already observed, pitch-time relationships play a central role in the articulation of low-level patterns (motives or half-phrases). Harmony, dynamics, and timbre as a rule support this articulation. On a somewhat higher level (that of the phrase or period), harmonic progression plays a major role in shaping musical structure. So do pitch-time relationships, but the normative modes of processive structuring are probably somewhat different. As one moves to the level of the succession of periods and sections, instrumental color, dynamics, and perhaps tempo become important shaping forces. Harmonic relationships are still crucial in the articulation of structure. But syntax changes; harmony becomes tonality. That is, the probability system within which implicative relationships arise changes as we move from lower to higher levels. For instance, the probability of

---

[26] *The Structure of Science*, p. 439.

tonic harmony (I) moving to mediant harmony (III) in low-level, chord-to-chord progression is very low; but the probability of a section built on the tonic being followed by a section built on the mediant is fairly high—particularly in the minor mode.

The fact that hierarchies are discontinuous seems to be of major importance for the understanding of the nature of musical structure. For it means that an event which is itself syntactically ordered may, taken as a unit, act as an aspect of formal organization on another hierarchic level. Consider again the example of the ostinato (see p. 298)—that is, a musical figure of, say, six notes which is repeated several times. As a pattern it depends for coherence upon the syntax of the lowest level, upon the functional relationships among the pitches and durations that make up the figure. On the next level—that of the exact repetition of the figure as a whole—no functional organization arises. The relationship between the several statements of the ostinato is purely formal—that of repetition. On the third level, however, the group of, say, five statements of the pattern may be understood to imply—though perhaps mainly in retrospect—the changes in organization and texture which follow the ostinato. As a total group, the ostinato measures are again functional.

The interaction between the formal and the syntactical, processive modes of organization is as a rule both simultaneous—in the sense of being hierarchic—and successive. Usually in a complex musical work the highest level—that which characterizes the form as a whole—is both formal (in that established and relatively stable themes are repeated) and syntactical (in that such stable events are functionally related to less stable parts). But there are musical structures that are almost purely one or the other.

The first two Preludes from Book I of Bach's *Well-Tempered Clavier* are essentially syntactical processes. On the highest level there are no repetitions of closed stable events (motives or themes). Structural coherence is the result of the functional relationships between (*a*) the beginning, which has a relatively closed harmonic shape; (*b*) the middle, in which a less stable, goal-directed, harmonic-melodic process moves to stablized tension on the dominant; and (*c*) the conclusion, which consists of an elaborated cadential formula. The only repetition there is, that of the keyboard figure within the measure, which serves to sustain the harmony, is not syntactically structured. Its constant repetitions preclude process. Consequently it is understood as an active ground rather than as a implicative event. Both Preludes are examples of what might be called "arched" hierarchies. But because they lack the scope and complexity made possible by the mixture of stable, formal events with kinetic, processive ones, neither is *highly* arched.

At the opposite end of the structural spectrum is the theme and variations. The first movement of Mozart's Piano Sonata in A Major, K. 331, may serve as an example. The theme itself, and consequently each variation based upon it, is both syntactically and formally structured. The first part (mm. 1–8) consists of an antecedent-consequent phrase which is harmonically processive but melodically formal. Each of the half-phrases is constructed in such a way that the first two measures are both formal and syntactical, but they are related to the next two measures mainly syntactically. On the highest level, the whole first part functions as a stable, relatively closed shape in relation to what follows. The second part (mm. 9–12) is primarily syntactical in function, creating sufficient tension and variety to call for a return to the consequent half of the first part, but not so much that the form requires further elaboration. The conclusion, which consists of the second half of the first part plus a two-measure affirmation of the cadence, emphasizes closure and makes the shape of the whole theme particularly stable.

Though the theme is thus both hierarchic and mixed, the movement as a whole is purely—or almost purely—formal. The theme and its variations are related to one another not in terms of function but in terms of motivic repetition and structural congruence. The organization is additive, not processive. Observe that because the highest level is not syntactical, the series has no internally structured point of probable termination. That is, the number of variations might be extended indefinitely—their number depending upon the ingenuity of the composer, the patience of the audience, and the taste of the time.

Of course, the series of variations may be ordered in some non-syntactic fashion—for instance, in terms of an alternation of tempi, dynamics, or mode or as a progression in the direction of faster tempi, increased dynamics, and the like. In the first case, the "ordering" will tend to produce a kind of active steady-state. In the second, the generally consistent direction of change may make the form seem goal-directed. But unless there is functional differentiation among the variations, no real process will structure the whole.

A theme and variations is like what Simon has called a "flat" hierarchy. A diamond, for example, "is hierarchic for it is a crystal structure of carbon atoms that can be further decomposed into protons, neutrons, and electrons. However, it is a 'flat' hierarchy, in which the number of first-order subsystems can be indefinitely large. . . . Similarly a linear polymer is simply a chain, which may be very long, of identical sub-parts, the monomers. At the molecular level it is a very flat hierarchy." [27] It is interesting to note that the history of the theme and variations in the eighteenth and nineteenth centuries may, from this point of view, be understood as the search for a way of making a naturally flat hierarchy (as in most variations of the Baroque and early classical periods) into an arched hierarchy with functionally differentiated parts (as in the variations of Beethoven, Schumann, and César Franck).

In the Mozart theme, the formal and syntactical modes of organization are congruent, each supporting the other, even on lower levels, in the articulation of structure. But such congruence does not always occur. Some of the most interesting musical structures are those in which these modes of organization act independently of one another on the same hierarchic level. In order to keep the discussion brief, I shall use an example that I have analyzed elsewhere in more detail.[28]

In the development section of the first movement of Beethoven's String Quartet in B-flat, Op. 130, a marked and regular harmonic process—a motion through the cycle of fifths (D–G–C–c–F)—is begun. When in the course of this progression the tonic, B-flat, is reached, the first theme, somewhat altered, returns. The arrival of the tonic and the restatement of the first theme mark the beginning of the recapitulation. That is, they define an important structural point in the formal organization of the movement. But when this formal articulation takes place, the harmonic process begun in the development section does not stop or change markedly. Instead, the motion through the cycle of fifths continues—as though its momentum were too great to be halted by formal structuring—until the second theme is reached. In short, there is a bifurcation in which, as I would now put it, the syntactical and formal modes act independently of one another for a time, becoming congruent again only when the second theme arrives in the tonic.

Thus the relationship between the modes of musical organization may itself play a significant role in the articulation of structure. That is, non-congruence may create an instability—a tension—which is kinetic and processive on the highest hierarchic level, and the return to

---

[27] "The Architecture of Complexity," p. 469.
[28] *Emotion and Meaning in Music*, pp. 126–27.

congruence of syntax and form creates a kind of structural resolution which, because it re-establishes stability, both permits and emphasizes closure.

From a purely musical point of view, a strophic song such as Schubert's "Tränenregen" (from *Die schöne Müllerin*) is a very flat hierarchy indeed. That is, if one considers only the music of the song, there is no differentiation among the parts. Such a "purist" view, however, misrepresents the structure of the work. The text, which is in no sense an irrelevant, superfluous addition to the music but an integral part of the work, provides clear and significant functional differentiation among the several strophes. Similarly, the unity and structure of large medieval and Renaissance forms is often, and significantly, literary. This is by no means an unimportant consideration. The generally flat hierarchies of such music—and, consequently, the kind of melodic-rhythmic and harmonic relationships appropriate for their articulation—are in part at least a function of the arched hierarchies provided by the text. If this is the case, then it is evidently a mistake to search for arched, over-all hierarchic structures either between or within parts of, say, an Ockeghem Mass, or a Josquin motet. And attempts to apply variants of analytical methods like those of Heinrich Schenker to such music may be quite inappropriate.

(This calls attention to a point of some moment, namely, that concepts and methods designed to analyze and illuminate the process and structure of one sort of music need not be directly relevant or applicable to the analysis of music in some other style or idiom; and, further, that the techniques and procedures appropriate to the analysis of one architectonic level may not be valuable for the analysis of other levels. Useful and suggestive analytic concepts and procedures are generally discovered and developed in connection with particular styles. That this is so is indicated by the fact that the most generally accepted and illuminating modes of analysis—for instance, the concepts of form and harmonic relationship—have been developed in connection with particular stylistic practices. On the other hand, when theorists have posed questions too broadly—asking, for example, "What is melody?"—the answers have generally been vacuous and useless generalities. And the tendency for "analyses" of serial music to consist of accounts of premusical relationships may be partly due to the fact that the absence of any common stylistic practice precludes the development of adequate analytic concepts.)

Rondo and ritornello forms are also, as a rule, rather flat hierarchies. But they differ in important ways from the hierarchic type exemplified by a theme and variations or by a strophic song. In a theme and variations there is generally no alternation of *function* among the parts on the level of the total form. Unity is the result of structural isomorphism, motivic similarity, or both; but the total structure is *additive*. Such additive hierarchic structures may, as we have seen, involve some over-all patterning without creating a higher-level architectonic process. In a rondo or a ritornello movement, on the other hand, the parts, though often on the same hierarchic level, are functionally connected through an alternation of stable parts with less stable ones. Such an alternation creates what might be called *conjunctive* flat hierarchies. It is worth noting that in such conjunctive hierarchies, the presence of functional differentiation may make possible a transformation of the basic form into an arched hierarchy. This is clearest in the rondo, which may be a relatively flat hierarchy or, as it approaches sonata form, a markedly arched one.

Because the imitative relationship between the voices generally precludes simultaneous functional differentiation, canons, too, tend to be flat hierarchies. But they are not additive. Rather, an interlacing of complementary, but similar, strands of music creates what might be called a *braided* or helix-like hierarchy.

THE TECHTONICS OF SERIALISM

Those familiar with contemporary music since Webern will, no doubt, have noticed that additive and braided hierarchies are particularly prevalent in this music—for instance, canons, variations, and additive structures whose parts are often defined by the limits of serial statements. Despite perceptual and relational complexities within the several segments, such constructions are from a formal point of view quite rudimentary. They are, so to speak, like sponges or corals in which the parts are more or less hierarchically organized, but the whole is essentially the same as the sum of the parts. Complexity and interaction tend to be purely local and unity is confined to immediate connections between events.

These observations are corroborated by two striking characteristics of much recent experimental and serial music.

1. As my colleague Grosvenor W. Cooper has pointed out,[29] one of the salient ideals of Western culture and a hallmark of "greatness" in Western art, at least since the Renaissance, has been that of *monumen-*

---

[29] In an unpublished lecture.

tality. To capture and communicate a sense of the scope and magnitude of creation—the variety and multiplicity of things, composers as well as artists and writers have found it appropriate to bring together a wealth of diverse materials, often placing these in sudden and violent juxtaposition. (One need only think of a Bach Passion, a Beethoven symphony, or a play of Shakespeare.) One way of combining and uniting contrasting ideas into a coherent whole, reconciling seemingly incompatible events, is to subsume them under some higher order—to embody them within a hierarchic structure.

When monumentality ceases to be a cultural value,[30] however—when the possibility or necessity of an encompassing order seems remote—then the need for hierarchic structuring becomes less urgent, and functionalism can be more or less abandoned. Indeed, perhaps the test of the rejection of monumentality as an ideal is the degree to which one gives up functionalism. To put the matter the other way around, when functional differentiation and hierarchic structuring are minimized, variety tends to become inconsequential in the literal as well as the figurative sense. Contrasts remain local and transient. The monumental is replaced by the momentary.

2. The tendency to forgo complex, hierarchic organization is also evident in the avoidance of direct and observable pattern repetition, whether strict or varied. Let me explain. While I was working on this part of the book, I happened to go to a concert of traditional tonal music and was struck by the number of phrases and sections based upon either literal or sequential repetition (e.g., A–A′, A–A–B, or A–A′–B). How is it possible to get away with such obvious, even blatant, redundancy? I suspect the most important reason is that because the repetition is embedded in a hierarchic context, it is only partly perceived in terms of the model from which it derives. Mostly it is understood as a part, a building block, in the organization of a more extensive, higher-level structure. Perceptual attention is directed not to the redundancy relationship itself, but toward the implications of the whole event of which the repetition is a part. The redundant event is heard as belonging to a process—as leading toward some more remote goal.

When hierarchic structure is minimized and functionalism abandoned, however, perceptual attention is necessarily directed to the relationship between the model and its repetition. The tedium of redundancy is not mitigated by context. Consequently, there is a strong tendency in non-hierarchic music to mask the precompositional, systemic redun-

---

[30] See pp. 230–31 above, particularly n. 92.

dancy inherent in serial technique—to make the compositional order complexly non-redundant. To put the matter briefly, the non-redundancy in recent experimental music is in an important sense the result of the decay of functional-hierarchic organization.

That recent serial music and particularly totally ordered music is limited to low-level flat hierarchies is not surprising. Such additive structures might be expected for the following reasons.

a) The theory and constraints of serial composition do not deal with the articulation of hierarchic structure. Of course, it might be pointed out that music theory has only recently concerned itself with this aspect of tonal music. The hierarchic organization of tonal music has, however, from the beginning been implicitly acknowledged in the terminology used to describe it. Almost all the technical talk about serialism—discussions of row forms, combinatoriality, segmentation, and the like—has, on the other hand, to do with precompositional permutations of the set.

Moreover, the fact that one finds, in all the rash of theoretical discussion by serial composers, almost no reference to the matter of hierarchic organization is not due to ignorance or naïveté. All these composer-theorists are well aware of the hierarchic structures of tonal music and most are probably familiar with the theories of Heinrich Schenker. Partly, no doubt, this is because they have usually assumed that a denial of traditional tonality necessarily rules out any functional-ism whatsoever. Or, like Milton Babbitt, they have concluded that functionalism is limited to the normative effect of the twelve-tone row. "The functionality of a twelve-tone composition is defined by the specific twelve-tone set. A functional norm is stated, and deviations from this norm appear; but there is no degree of deviation, no hierarchy of deviations such as is present in tonal music, to make possible process and growth—stated in terms of the functional context—through various stages of compositional expansion." [31]

b) As I have tried to show, neither the theory nor the practice of serialism necessarily precludes the possibility of hierarchically organized music. The contention by theorists that this *is* the case, however, has influenced the composer's outlook and inevitably his music. This view, coupled with an aesthetic attitude that tends to find goal-directed processes distasteful, leads the composer to write music in which functionalism and, consequently, hierarchic structure are in practice slighted. In other words, the more complex and multilevel a hierarchic

---

[31] Babbitt, Review of Leibowitz, *Schoenberg et son école*, pp. 58–59.

structure is, the greater must be the functional differentiation among its parts. Complex, arched hierarchies like sonata form, large-scale fugues, and the like must be differentiated on many levels into functionally distinct subgroups. And the more functionally differentiated a piece of music is, the more goal-directed it will appear to be.

d) Finally, if their music represents a radically new stylistic beginning as post-Webern composers claim, then hierarchically simple, additive, or braided structures are to be expected. For the history of musical form, like the history of biological organisms, seems to indicate, as Lancelot Whyte has observed, that "Structure is not a thing that comes into being arbitrarily, it grows from simpler to more complex forms by a series of connected steps." [32] In order for complex, hierarchically arched forms to evolve, low-level, flat hierarchical norms must be established as part of some sort of traditional practice. Thus Schönberg wrote that

> it seemed at first impossible to compose pieces of complicated organization or of great length.
>
> A little later I discovered how to construct larger forms by following a text or a poem. The differences in size and shape of its parts and the change in character and mood were mirrored in the shape and size of the composition, in its dynamics and tempo, figuration and accentuation, instrumentation and orchestration. Thus the parts were differentiated as clearly as they had formerly been by the tonal and structural functions of harmony. [33]

I am aware that these remarks (to the effect that the presence of only low-level hierarchic structures indicates that serialism is still in an early stage of development) contradict the suggestion made earlier that lack of perceptual redundancy shows that post-Webern serialism represents the end of a style. The variance is not, however, empirically absurd. An established set of stylistic premises—traditional tonality—has been rejected by some composers. But the organizational complexity which characterized the later stages of the style has endured. The new methodological paradigm has not yet given rise to multilevel hierarchic structures capable of making the existing complexity coherent and

---

[32] *Accent on Form*, p. 98. The notion that musical forms, like biological forms, "evolve" in an orderly way does not imply a teleological view of history. As Herbert Simon points out, "complex forms can arise from the simple ones by purely random processes. . . . Direction is provided to the scheme by the stability of the complex forms, once these come into existence" ("The Architecture of Complexity," p. 471).

[33] *Style and Idea*, p. 106.

understandable. Indeed, experimental serialism is perhaps still in the process of developing low-level forms, relationships, and processes with the capacity for survival.

If the "Queries and Reservations" presented in Part III have focused attention primarily upon the possible dangers of experimental serialism, it is not because I doubt the validity of serial methods or the value of many of the compositions it has already produced but because I suspect that its natural connection with analytic formalism will make serialism one of the most significant schools of composition in the years ahead. If it is to be so—if it is to coexist alongside the varieties of traditional music (tonal and non-tonal) and the musics of transcendental- ism—experimental serialism must be perceptually and cognitively vi- able, as well as systematically interesting.

Fascinating problems abound. Method and theory may play an im- portant role in their identification, formulation, and solution. But if method and theory are to transcend the private pleasures of ingenuity, the unheard order must be validated in the public arena—in the realm of aural experience. To present the complex simply and the convoluted plainly is to meet the most formidable challenge, to demonstrate the highest skill, to achieve the greatest elegance.

BIBLIOGRAPHY

Ackerman, James S. "A Theory of Style," *Journal of Aesthetics*, 20 (Spring, 1962) : 227–37.

Ames, Van Meter. "The New in the Novel," *Journal of Aesthetics*, 21 (Spring, 1963) : 243–50.

Arp, Hans. "Concrete Art." In *The Modern Tradition*, edited by Richard Ellmann and Charles Feidelson, pp. 49–53. New York: Oxford University Press, 1965.

Asch, Solomon E., and Ebenholtz, Sheldon M. "The Principle of Associative Symmetry," *Proceedings of the American Philosophical Society*, 106 (April, 1962) : 135–63.

Ashton, Doré. "Mark Tobey," *Evergreen Review*, 4 (January–February, 1960) : 29–32.

Attneave, Fred. "Stochastic Composition Processes," *Journal of Aesthetics*, 17 (June, 1959) : 503–10.

Babbitt, Milton. "Review of René Leibowitz, *Schoenberg et son école, Journal of the American Musicological Society*, 3 (Spring, 1950) : 57–60.

———. Review of *Quatrième Cahier: Le Système dodécaphonique, ibid.* (Fall, 1950) : 264–67.

———. "Who Cares If You Listen?" *High Fidelity Magazine*, February, 1958, p. 38+.

———. "Twelve-Tone Invariants as Compositional Determinants," *Musical Quarterly*, 46 (April, 1960) : 246–59.

———. "Twelve-Tone Rhythmic Structure and the Electronic Medium," *Perspectives of New Music*, 1 (Fall, 1962) : 49–79.

Bach, C. P. E. *Essay on the True Art of Playing Keyboard Instruments.* Translated and edited by William Mitchell. New York: W. W. Norton & Co., 1949.

Backus, John. "*Die Reihe*: A Scientific Evaluation," *Perspectives of New Music*, 1 (Fall, 1962) : 160–71.

317

Bagby, Philip. *Culture and History*. Berkeley and Los Angeles: University of California Press, 1963.

Baker, Robert Allen. "A Statistical Analysis of the Harmonic Practice of the 18th and Early 19th Centuries." Ph.D. dissertation, University of Illinois, 1963.

Barron, Frank. "The Psychology of Imagination," *Scientific American*, 199 (September, 1958): 151–66.

Barth, John. *End of the Road*. New York: Avon Books, 1958.

Beardsley, Munro. "On the Creation of Art," *Journal of Aesthetics*, 23 (Spring, 1965): 291–304.

Békésy, Georg von. "The Ear," *Scientific American*, 147 (August, 1957): 66–78.

Bell, Clive. *Art*. London: Chatto & Windus, 1949.

Berenson, Bernard. *Aesthetics and History*. New York: Doubleday Anchor Books, 1954.

Berio, Luciano. "Form." In *The Modern Composer and His World*, edited by John Beckwith and Udo Kasemets, pp. 140–45. Toronto: University of Toronto Press, 1961.

Berlin, Isaiah. "Determinism, Relativism, and Historical Judgments." In *Theories of History*, edited by Patrick Gardiner, pp. 320–29. Glencoe, Ill.: Free Press, 1962.

Berlyne, D. E. "Curiosity and Exploration," *Science*, 153 (July 1, 1966): 25–33.

Blackmur, R. P. *Form and Value in Modern Poetry*. New York: Doubleday Anchor Books, 1957.

Bloch-Michel, Jean. "The Avant-Garde in French Fiction," *Partisan Review*, 25 (Summer, 1958): 467–71.

Boulding, Kenneth. *The Meaning of the 20th Century*. New York: Harper & Row, 1964.

Boulez, Pierre. "Schönberg Is Dead," *The Score*, no. 6 (May, 1952), pp. 18–22.

———. " 'At the ends of fruitful land . . . ,' " *Die Reihe*, vol. 1: *Electronic Music*, pp. 19–29. Bryn Mawr, Pa.: Theodore Presser Co., 1958.

———. "Sonate, que me veux-tu?" *Perspectives of New Music*, 1 (Spring, 1963): 32–44.

Brady, Joseph V. "Ulcers in 'Executive' Monkeys," *Scientific American*, 199 (October, 1958): 95–100.

Brindle, Reginald Smith. "Current Chronicle—Italy," *Musical Quarterly*, 44 (January, 1958): 95–101.

———. "Current Chronicle—Italy," *ibid.*, 47 (April, 1961): 247–55.

Broadbent, D. E. *Perception and Communication*. New York: Pergamon Press, 1958.

———. "Attention and the Perception of Speech," *Scientific American*, 206 (April, 1962): 143–51.

———. "Information Processing in the Nervous System," *Science*, 150 (October 22, 1965): 457–62.

Brown, G. Spencer. "Chance and Control: Some Implications of Randomization." In *Information Theory*, edited by Colin Cherry, pp. 8–17. New York: Academic Press, 1956.

318

Bibliography

Burt, Francis. "An Antithesis," *The Score*, no. 19 (March, 1957), pp. 60–74.

Bury, J. B. *The Idea of Progress*. New York: Macmillan Co., 1932.

Cage, John. *Silence*. Middletown, Conn.: Wesleyan University Press, 1961.

Cahill, James F. "Confucian Elements in the Theory of Painting." In *The Confucian Persuasion*, edited by Arthur F. Wright, pp. 115–40. Stanford, Calif.: Stanford University Press, 1960.

Chaudhury, Pravas Jivan. "The Theory of Rasa," *Journal of Aesthetics*, 11 (December, 1952): 147–50.

———. "Indian Poetics," *ibid.*, 19 (Spring, 1961): 289–94.

Cherry, Colin. *On Human Communication*. New York: Science Editions, 1961.

Chomsky, Noam. *Syntactic Structures*. The Hague: Mouton & Co., 1963.

Clarke, Henry Leland. Review of Benjamin Britten's *War Requiem, Notes*, 22 (Winter, 1965–66): 958.

Cogan, Marc R. "Homo Faber: The Process of Poetry," *Chicago Literary Review*, 3 (April–May, 1966): 2.

Cohen, I. Bernard. "Science and the Nonscientist," *New York Times Book Review*, April 4, 1965, p. 2.

Cohen, Joel E. "Information Theory and Music," *Behavioral Science*, 7 (April, 1962): 137–63.

Cohen, John. "Subjective Probability," *Scientific American*, 197 (November, 1957): 128–38.

Cohen, Morris R. *A Preface to Logic*. New York: Henry Holt & Co., 1944.

———. *Reason and Nature*. Glencoe, Ill.: Free Press, 1964.

Cohen, Sidney. "LSD and the Anguish of Dying," *Harper's Magazine*, 231 (September, 1965): 69–72.

Cone, Edward T. "Analysis Today," *Musical Quarterly*, 46 (April, 1960): 172–88.

Cooke, Deryck. *The Language of Music*. London: Oxford Paperbacks, 1962.

Coons, Edgar, and Kraehenbuehl, David. "Information as a Measure of Structure in Music," *Journal of Music Theory*, 2 (November, 1958): 127–61.

Cooper, Grosvenor W., and Meyer, Leonard B. *The Rhythmic Structure of Music*. Chicago: University of Chicago Press, 1960.

"Crisis in Criticism," *The Times Literary Supplement*, June 23, 1966, pp. 545–46.

"The Cybernated Generation," *Time*, April 2, 1965, pp. 84–91.

Deutsch, Babette. *Poetry in Our Time*. New York: Doubleday Anchor Books, 1963.

Dewey, John. *Art as Experience*. New York: Minton, Balch & Co., 1934.

Dray, William. " 'Explaining What' in History." In *Theories of History*, edited by Patrick Gardiner, pp. 403–8. Glencoe, Ill.: Free Press, 1962.

Eimert, Herbert. "What Is Electronic Music?" *Die Reihe*, vol. 1: *Electronic Music*, pp. 1–10. Bryn Mawr, Pa.: Theodore Presser Co., 1958.

———. "The Composer's Freedom of Choice," *ibid.*, vol. 3: *Musical Craftsmanship*, pp. 1–9. Bryn Mawr, Pa.: Theodore Presser Co., 1959.

Einstein, Alfred. *Essays on Music*. New York: W. W. Norton & Co., 1962.

Eliot, T. S. *Selected Essays*. London: Faber & Faber, 1941.

————. *Notes toward the Definition of Culture.* New York: Harcourt, Brace & Co., 1949.

————. *Selected Prose.* Edited by John Hayward. Harmondsworth: Penguin Books, 1955.

————. "Myth and Literary Classicism." In *The Modern Tradition,* edited by Richard Ellman and Charles Feidelson, pp. 679–81. New York: Oxford University Press, 1965.

Ellman, Richard, and Feidelson, Charles, eds. *The Modern Tradition.* New York: Oxford University Press, 1965.

Etzioni, Amitai. "On the Process of Making Decisions," *Science,* 152 (May 6, 1966): 746–47.

Eyring, Henry. "This Changing World," *AAAS Bulletin,* 10 (September, 1965): 1–4.

Ferguson, Donald N. *Music as Metaphor.* Minneapolis: University of Minnesota Press, 1960.

Fiske, D. W., and Maddi, S. R. *Functions of Varied Experience.* Homewood, Ill.: Dorsey Press, 1961.

Fitts, Paul M. "The Influence of Response Coding on the Performance of Motor Tasks." In *Current Trends in Information Theory,* edited by Brockway McMillan and others, pp. 47–75. Pittsburgh: Pittsburgh University Press, 1953.

Frankel, Charles. "Explanation and Interpretation in History." In *Theories of History,* edited by Patrick Gardiner, pp. 408–27. Glencoe, Ill.: Free Press, 1962.

Freud, Sigmund. *Group Psychology and the Analysis of the Ego.* Translated by James Strachey. New York: Bantam Books, 1960.

Friedländer, Max J. *On Art and Connoisseurship.* Boston: Beacon Press, 1960.

Gardiner, Patrick (ed.). *Theories of History.* Glencoe, Ill.: Free Press, 1962.

Gardner, Martin. "Can Time Go Backward?" *Scientific American,* 216 (January, 1967): 98–108.

Geertz, Clifford. "The Impact of the Concept of Culture on the Concept of Man." In *New Views of the Nature of Man,* edited by John R. Platt, pp. 93–118. Chicago: University of Chicago Press, 1965.

Gellner, Ernest. "Holism versus Individualism in History and Sociology." In *Theories of History,* edited by Patrick Gardiner, pp. 489–503. Glencoe, Ill.: Free Press, 1962.

Genauer, Emily. "Some Forgeries We Have Loved," *Herald Tribune* ("The Lively Arts"), February 19, 1961, p. 19.

Gerhard, Roberto. "Apropos Mr. Stadlen," *The Score,* no. 23 (July, 1958), pp. 50–57.

Getzels, J. W., and Jackson, P. W. "The Highly Intelligent and Highly Creative Adolescent: A Summary of Recent Research Findings." In *The Third Research Conference (1959) on the Identification of Creative Scientific Talent,* edited by Calvin W. Taylor. Salt Lake City: University of Utah Press, 1960.

Gilman, Richard. "Total Revolution in the Novel," *Horizon,* 4 (January, 1962): 96–101.

Bibliography

Glass, Bentley. "The Ethical Basis of Science," *Science*, 150 (December 3, 1965): 1254–61.

Goldenstein, M. H.; Kiang, S.; and Brown, R. H. "Responses of the Auditory Cortex to Repetitive Stimuli," *Journal of the Acoustical Society of America*, 31 (March, 1959): 356–64.

Goldwater, Robert. "Reflections on the Rothke Exhibition," *Arts*, 35 (March, 1961): 42–45.

Gombrich, E. H. *Art and Illusion*. New York: Bollingen Foundation, 1960.

Gradenwitz, Peter. "The Performer's Role in the Newest Music," *The Chesterian*, 34 (Autumn, 1959): 61–64.

Hamilton, Edith. *The Greek Way to Western Civilization*. New York: Mentor Books, 1948.

Hamilton, Ian. "Serialism." In *The Modern Composer and His World*, edited by John Beckwith and Udo Kasemets, pp. 49–56. Toronto: University of Toronto Press, 1961.

Hanslick, Eduard. *The Beautiful in Music*. Translated by Gustav Cohen. London: Novello, Ewer & Co., 1891.

Hanson, Norwood R. *Patterns of Discovery*. London: Cambridge University Press, 1965.

Harris, Richard. "The Forgery of Art," *The New Yorker*, 37 (September 16, 1961): 112–45.

Harrison, J. M., and Irving, R. "Visual and Nonvisual Auditory Systems in Mammals," *Science*, 154 (November, 1966): 738–43.

Hatch, Robert. "Laughter at Your Own Risk," *Horizon*, 3 (September, 1960): 113–16.

Hebb, Donald O. *The Organization of Behavior*. New York: Science Editions, 1961.

Heilbroner, Robert L. *The Future as History*. New York: Grove Press, 1961.

Heisenberg, Werner. *Physics and Philosophy*. New York: Harper Torchbooks, 1962.

———. "Non-Objective Science and Uncertainty." In *The Modern Tradition*, edited by Richard Ellmann and Charles Feidelson, pp. 444–50. New York: Oxford University Press, 1965.

Held, Richard. "Plasticity in Sensory-Motor Systems," *Scientific American*, 213 (November, 1965): 84–94.

Held, Richard, and Freedman, Sanford J. "Plasticity in Human Sensorimotor Control," *Science*, 142 (October 25, 1963): 455–61.

Heron, Woodburn, "The Pathology of Boredom," *Scientific American*, 196 (July, 1959): 52–56.

Hess, Eckhard. "Attitude and Pupil Size," *Scientific American*, 212 (April, 1965): 46–54.

Hildebrand, Joel H. "Order from Chaos," *Science*, 150 (October 22, 1965): 441–50.

Hiller, Lejaren A. "Computer Music," *Scientific American*, 201 (December, 1959): 109–20.

———. "Information Theory and Musical Analysis." Unpublished manuscript, 1961.

Hiller, Lejaren A., and Bean, Calvert. "Information Theory Analyses of Four Sonata Expositions," *Journal of Music Theory*, 10 (Spring, 1966): 96–137.

Hiller, Lejaren A., and Beauchamp, James. "Research in Music with Electronics," *Science*, 150 (October 8, 1965): 161–69.

Hiller, Lejaren A., and Isaacson, Leonard M. *Experimental Music.* New York: McGraw-Hill Book Co., 1959.

Hirsch, Jerry. "Behavior Genetics and Individuality Understood," *Science*, 142 (December 13, 1963): 1436–42.

Hofstadter, Albert. "Validity versus Value: An Essay in Philosophical Aesthetics," *Journal of Philosophy*, 59 (1962): 607–17.

Hoijer, Harry. "The Relation of Language to Culture." In *Anthropology Today*, edited by Sol Tax, pp. 258–77. Chicago: University of Chicago Press, 1962.

Hughes, H. Stuart. *Consciousness and Society.* New York: Vintage Books, 1958.

Huizinga, Johan. "A Definition of the Concept of History." In *Philosophy and History*, edited by Raymond Klibansky and H. J. Paton, pp. 1–10. New York: Harper Torchbooks, 1963.

James, William. *Principles of Psychology.* New York: Dover Publications, 1950.

Kaprow, Allan. "The Legacy of Jackson Pollock," *Art News*, 57 (October, 1958): 24–26.

Keats, John. *Letters.* Edited by Maurice Buxton Forman. New York: Oxford University Press, 1935.

Kenner, Hugh. "Waiting for Godot To Begin," *WFMT Perspective* (Chicago), January, 1962, p. 49.

King, Gilbert. "What Is Information?" In *Automatic Control*, edited by the Editors of *Scientific American*, pp. 83–86. New York: Simon & Schuster, 1955.

Klammer, Armin. "Webern's Piano Variations, Op. 27, 3rd Movement," *Die Reihe*, vol. 2: *Anton Webern*, pp. 81–92. Bryn Mawr, Pa.: Theodore Presser Co., 1959.

Koestler, Arthur. "The Anatomy of Snobbery." In *The Anchor Review*, no. 1, pp. 1–25. New York: Doubleday Anchor Books, 1955.

Koffka, Kurt. *Principles of Gestalt Psychology.* New York: Harcourt, Brace & Co., 1935.

Kohl, Herbert. *The Age of Complexity.* New York: Mentor Books, 1965.

Kohn, Karl. "Current Chronicle—Los Angeles," *Musical Quarterly*, 49 (July, 1963): 360–69.

Kraehenbuehl, David, and Coons, Edgar. "Information as a Measure of the Experience of Music," *Journal of Aesthetics*, 17 (June, 1959): 510–22.

Krenek, Ernst. "Extents and Limits of Serial Techniques," *Musical Quarterly*, 46 (April, 1960): 210–32.

———. "Serialism." In *The Modern Composer and His World*, edited by John Beckwith and Udo Kasemets, pp. 65–71. Toronto: University of Toronto Press, 1961.

———. "Tradition in Perspective," *Perspectives of New Music*, 1 (Fall, 1962): 27–38.

Bibliography

Krieger, Murray. "Tragedy and the Tragic Vision," *Midway* (Chicago), no. 27 (Summer, 1966), pp. 2–25.

Kris, Ernst. *Psychoanalytic Explorations in Art*. New York: International Universities Press, 1952.

Kroeber, A. L. *Anthropology*. New York: Harcourt, Brace & Co., 1948.

————. *An Anthropologist Looks at History*. Berkeley and Los Angeles: University of California Press, 1963.

————. *Style and Civilizations*. Berkeley and Los Angeles: University of California Press, 1963.

Kuhn, Thomas S. *The Structure of Scientific Revolutions*. International Encyclopedia of Unified Science, vol. 2, no. 2. Chicago: University of Chicago Press, 1962.

Lancaster, Clay. "Keys to the Understanding of Indian and Chinese Painting: The 'Six Limbs' of Yasodhara and the 'Six Principles' of Hsieh Ho," *Journal of Aesthetics*, 11 (December, 1952): 95–104.

Langer, Susanne K. *Philosophy in a New Key*. New York: Mentor Books, 1951.

Lewin, David. "A Theory of Segmental Association in Twelve-Tone Music," *Perspectives of New Music*, 1 (Fall, 1962): 89–116.

Ligeti, György. "Pierre Boulez," *Die Reihe*, vol. 4: *Young Composers*, pp. 36–62. Bryn Mawr, Pa.: Theodore Presser Co., 1960.

Lockspeiser, Edward. *Debussy*. London: J. M. Dent & Sons, 1936.

Loehr, Max. "Some Fundamental Issues in the History of Chinese Painting," *Journal of Aesthetics*, 24 (Fall, 1965): 37–43.

Longman, Lester D. "Criteria of Criticism in Contemporary Art," *Journal of Aesthetics*, 18 (March, 1960): 285–93.

Lord, Catherine. "Organic Unity Reconsidered," *Journal of Aesthetics*, 22 (Spring, 1964): 263–68.

Lowell, Robert. *The Old Glory*. New York: Noonday Press, 1966.

Lowinsky, Edward E. "Musical Genius—Evolution and Origins of a Concept," *Musical Quarterly*, 50 (July and October, 1964): 321–40, 476–95.

Luchtung, Wolfgang A. " 'Hiroshima, Mon Amour,' Time, and Proust," *Journal of Aesthetics*, 21 (Spring, 1963): 299–313.

Maison, K. E. *Art Themes and Variations*. New York: Harry N. Abrams, n.d.

Malm, William P. *Japanese Music and Musical Instruments*. Rutland, Vt.: Charles E. Tuttle Co., 1959.

Malraux, André. "The Triumph of Art over History." In *The Modern Tradition*, edited by Richard Ellmann and Charles Feidelson, pp. 541–622. New York: Oxford University Press, 1965.

Mandelbaum, Maurice. "Societal Facts." In *Theories of History*, edited by Patrick Gardiner, pp. 476–88. Glencoe, Ill.: Free Press, 1962.

Manzoni, Giacomo. "Bruno Maderna," *Die Reihe*, vol. 4: *Young Composers*, pp. 114–20. Bryn Mawr, Pa.: Theodore Presser Co., 1960.

Margenau, Henry. "Meaning and Scientific Status of Causality." In *Philosophy of Science*, Readings selected, edited, and introduced by Arthur Danto and Sidney Morgenbesser, pp. 435–49. New York: Meridian Books, 1960.

Martino, Donald. "The Source Set and Its Aggregate Formations," *Journal of Music Theory*, 5 (November, 1961): 224–73.

323

Mathieu, Georges. *From the Abstract to the Possible*. Paris: Editions du Cercle d'Art contemporain, 1960.

McLuhan, Marshall. *The Gutenberg Galaxy*. Toronto: University of Toronto Press, 1964.

McNeill, William H. *The Rise of the West*. Chicago: University of Chicago Press, 1963.

Mead, George Herbert. *Mind, Self, and Society*. Chicago: University of Chicago Press, 1934.

————. "The Test of the Accepted Past," *Midway* (Chicago), no. 22 (Spring, 1965), pp. 70–79.

"Medici Slot Machine," *Time*, July 8, 1966, p. 57.

Melzack, Ronald. "The Perception of Pain," *Scientific American*, 204 (February, 1961): 41–49.

Melzack, Ronald, and Wall, Patrick D. "Pain Mechanisms: A New Theory," *Science*, 150 (November 19, 1965): 971–78.

Merriam, Alan P. *The Anthropology of Music*. Evanston, Ill.: Northwestern University Press, 1964.

Metzger, Heinz-Klaus. "Intermezzo I (Just Who Is Growing Old?)," *Die Reihe*, vol. 4: *Young Composers*, pp. 63–80. Bryn Mawr, Pa.: Theodore Presser Co., 1960.

Meyer, Leonard B. *Emotion and Meaning in Music*. Chicago: University of Chicago Press, 1956.

————. "Universalism and Relativism in the Study of Ethnic Music," *Ethnomusicology*, 4 (May, 1960): 49–54.

Miller, Dorothy C., ed. *Fifteen Americans*. New York: Museum of Modern Art, 1952.

————. *Sixteen Americans*. New York: Museum of Modern Art, 1959.

Miller, James G. "Information Input Overload and Psychopathology," *American Journal of Psychiatry*, 116 (February, 1960): 695–704.

Moles, A. "Informationstheorie der Musik," *Nachrichten technische Fachberichte*, 3 (1956): 47–55.

————. *Théorie de l'information et perception esthétique*. Paris: Flammarion & Cie., 1958.

Morrissette, Bruce. "The New Novel in France," *Chicago Review*, 15 (Winter–Spring, 1962): 1–19.

Muller, Herbert J. "Misuses of the Past," *Horizon*, 1 (March, 1959): 4–13.

Munro, Thomas. "Do the Arts Evolve: Some Recent Conflicting Answers," *Journal of Aesthetics*, 19 (Summer, 1961): 407–17.

————. "What Causes Creative Epochs in the Arts?" *ibid.*, 21 (Fall, 1962): 35–48.

Mursell, James L. *The Psychology of Music*. New York: W. W. Norton & Co., 1937.

Nagel, Ernest. *Principles of the Theory of Probability*. International Encyclopedia of Unified Science, vol. 1, no. 6. Chicago: University of Chicago Press, 1939.

————. *The Structure of Science*. New York: Harcourt, Brace & Co., 1961.

Nagel, Ernest, and Newman, James R. "Gödel's Proof," *Scientific American*, 194 (June, 1956): 71–86.

Bibliography

Oppenheimer, Jane. "Perspectives in Biology," *Natural History*, 74 (February, 1965): 6–8.

Ortega y Gasset, José. "History as a System." In *Philosophy and History*, edited by Raymond Klibansky and H. J. Paton, pp. 283–322. New York: Harper Torchbooks, 1963.

Pascal, Blaise. *Pensées*. Translated by H. F. Stewart. New York: Pantheon Books, 1950.

Perle, George. "Theory and Practice in Twelve-Tone Music: Stadlen Reconsidered," *The Score*, no. 25 (June, 1959), pp. 58–64.

———. "Atonality and the Twelve-Note System in the United States," *ibid.*, no. 27 (July, 1960), pp. 51–66.

———. *Serial Composition and Atonality*. Berkeley and Los Angeles: University of California Press, 1963.

Peterson, W. Wesley. "Error Correcting Codes," *Scientific American*, 206 (February, 1962): 96–108.

Pfeiffer, John. *The Human Brain*. New York: Pyramid Publications, 1962.

Platt, John R. "Amplification Aspects of Biological Response and Mental Activity," *American Scientist*, 44 (April, 1956): 180–97.

———. "The Fifth Need of Man," *Horizon*, 1 (July, 1959): 106–11.

———. "The Step to Man," *Science*, 149 (August 6, 1965): 607–13.

Podhoretz, Norman. "The New Nihilism and the Novel," *Partisan Review*, 25 (Fall, 1958): 576–90.

Poirier, Richard. "Wescac and the Messiah," *Book Week: Chicago Sun-Times*, August 7, 1966, pp. 1, 12.

Polanyi, Michael. *Personal Knowledge*. Chicago: University of Chicago Press, 1958.

Popper, Karl R. *The Poverty of Historicism*. New York: Harper Torchbooks, 1964.

Posner, Michael I. "Components of Skilled Performance," *Science*, 152 (June 24, 1966): 1712–18.

Potter, Van Rensselaer. "Society and Science," *Science*, 146 (November 20, 1964): 1018–22.

Pousseur, Henri. "Outline of a Method," *Die Reihe*, vol. 3: *Musical Craftsmanship*, pp. 44–88. Bryn Mawr, Pa.: Theodore Presser Co., 1959.

Powell, Mel. "A Note on Rigor," *Perspectives of New Music*, 1 (Spring, 1963): 121–24.

Quastler, H. "Studies of Human Channel Capacity." In *Information Theory —Third London Symposium*, edited by E. C. Cherry, pp. 361–71. New York: Academic Press, 1956.

Richards, I. A. *Principles of Literary Criticism*. London: Kegan Paul & Co., 1947.

Richardson, John Adkins. "Dada, Camp, and the Mode Called Pop," *Journal of Aesthetics*, 24 (Summer, 1966): 549–58.

Riesen, Austin. "Varying Behavioral Manifestations of Animals," *Science*, 141 (July 26, 1963): 344–45.

Robbe-Grillet, Alain. "Dehumanizing Nature." In *The Modern Tradition*, edited by Richard Ellmann and Charles Feidelson, pp. 361–78. New York: Oxford University Press, 1965.

Rochberg, George. "The Harmonic Tendency of the Hexachord," *Journal of Music Theory*, 3 (November, 1959): 208–30.

———. "Indeterminacy in the New Music," *The Score*, no. 26 (January, 1960), pp. 9–19.

———. "Duration in Music." In *The Modern Composer and His World*, edited by John Beckwith and Udo Kasemets, pp. 56–64. Toronto: University of Toronto Press, 1961.

Rosenberg, Harold. *The Tradition of the New.* New York: Horizon Press, 1959.

———. "The New as Value," *The New Yorker*, 39 (September 7, 1963): 136–46.

Rosenthal, M. L. *The Modern Poets.* New York: Oxford University Press, 1965.

Russell, Bertrand. "Dialectical Materialism." In *Theories of History*, edited by Patrick Gardiner, pp. 286–95. Glencoe, Ill.: Free Press, 1962.

Sachs, Curt. *The Rise of Music in the Ancient World.* New York: W. W. Norton & Co., 1943.

———. *The Wellsprings of Music.* Edited by J. Kunst. New York: McGraw-Hill Book Co., 1965.

Santi, Piero. "Luciano Berio," *Die Reihe*, vol. 4: *Young Composers*, pp. 98–102. Bryn Mawr, Pa.: Theodore Presser Co., 1960.

Sapir, Edward. "Language," *Encyclopedia of the Social Sciences*, 9: 155–68. New York: Macmillan Co., 1934.

Sargeant, Winthrop. "Twin Bill," *The New Yorker*, 42 (May 28, 1966): 85–88.

Schapiro, Meyer. "Style." In *Anthropology Today*, edited by Sol Tax, pp. 278–303. Chicago: University of Chicago Press, 1962.

Schnebel, Dieter. "Karlheinz Stockhausen," *Die Reihe*, vol. 4: *Young Composers*, pp. 121–35. Bryn Mawr, Pa.: Theodore Presser Co., 1960.

Schönberg, Arnold. *Style and Idea.* New York: Philosophical Library, 1950.

Schonberg, Harold C. "Very Big Man of Avant-Garde," *New York Times*, May 9, 1965, sec. 2, p. 11.

Schroeder, Eric. "The Wild Deer Mathnawi," *Journal of Aesthetics*, 11 (December, 1952): 118–34.

Schrödinger, Erwin. *What Is Life? & Other Scientific Essays.* New York: Doubleday Anchor Books, 1956.

Schuller, Gunther. "American Performance and New Music," *Perspectives of New Music*, 1 (Spring, 1963): 1–8.

Seckler, Dorothy Gees. "The Artist Speaks: Robert Rauchenberg," *Art in America*, 54 (May–June, 1966): 73–84.

Seitz, William C. *The Responsive Eye.* New York: Museum of Modern Art, 1965.

Shafer, Boyd C. "The Study of History in the United States," *AAUP Bulletin*, 50 (September, 1964): 232–40.

Shifrin, Seymour. "A Note from the Underground," *Perspectives of New Music*, 1 (Fall, 1962): 152–53.

Shipley, T. "Auditory Flutter-Driving of Visual Flicker," *Science*, 145 (September 18, 1964): 1328–30.

Bibliography

Simon, Herbert A. "The Architecture of Complexity," *Proceedings of the American Philosophical Society*, 106 (1962): 467–82.

Sontag, Susan. *Against Interpretation*. New York: Noonday Press, 1966.

Spong, Paul; Haider, Manfred; and Lindsley, Donald B. "Selective Attentiveness and Cortical Evoked Responses to Visual and Auditory Stimuli," *Science*, 148 (April 16, 1965): 395–97.

Stebbing, L. Susan. "Some Ambiguities in Discussions concerning Time." In *Philosophy and History*, edited by Raymond Klibansky and H. J. Paton, pp. 107–23. New York: Harper Torchbooks, 1963.

Stein, Leonard. "The Performer's Point of View," *Perspectives of New Music*, 1 (Spring, 1963): 62–71.

Stevens, S. S., and Davis, H. *Hearing*. New York: John Wiley & Sons, 1938.

Stewart, Julian H. "Toward Understanding Cultural Evolution," *Science*, 153 (August 12, 1966): 729.

Stockhausen, Karlheinz. *Klavierstüke XI*. London: Universal Edition, 1957.

———. "How Time Passes," *Die Reihe*, vol. 3: *Musical Craftsmanship*, pp. 10–40. Bryn Mawr, Pa.: Theodore Presser Co., 1959.

———. "The Concept of Unity in Electronic Music," *Perspectives of New Music*, 1 (Fall, 1962): 39–48.

Stone, Kurt. "Ives's Fourth Symphony: A Review," *Musical Quarterly*, 52 (January, 1966): 1–16.

Stravinsky, Igor. *Poetics of Music*. Translated by Arthur Knodel and Ingolf Dahl. Cambridge: Harvard University Press, 1947.

———. *Stravinsky in Conversation with Robert Craft*. Harmondsworth: Pelican Books, 1962.

Stuckenschmidt, H. H. "Contemporary Techniques in Music," *Musical Quarterly*, 49 (January, 1963): 1–16.

Suzuki, D. T. *Zen Buddhism*. Edited by William Barrett. New York: Doubleday Anchor Books, 1956.

Sypher, Wylie. *Loss of the Self in Modern Literature and Art*. New York: Vintage Books, 1964.

Teggart, Frederick J. *Theory and Processes of History*. Berkeley and Los Angeles: University of California Press, 1962.

Thoreau, Henry David. *Walden and Other Writings*. New York: Modern Library, 1937.

Tilden, Freeman. "Not by Truth Alone," *Science*, 148 (June 11, 1965): 1415.

Time, August 12, 1966, p. 50.

Tirro, Frank. "The Silent Theme Tradition in Jazz." Unpublished manuscript, 1966.

Tolstoy, Leo. "Man as the Creature of History." In *The Modern Tradition*, edited by Richard Ellmann and Charles Feidelson, pp. 265–67. New York: Oxford University Press, 1965.

Treitler, Leo. "Musical Syntax in the Middle Ages: Background to an Aesthetic Problem," *Perspectives of New Music*, 4 (Fall–Winter, 1965): 75–85.

Tustin, Arnold. "Feedback." In *Automatic Control*, edited by the Editors of *Scientific American*, pp. 10–23. New York: Simon & Schuster, 1955.

Waddington, C. H. "The Character of Biological Form." In *Aspects of Form*, edited by Lancelot Law Whyte, pp. 43–56. London: Percy Lund Humphries & Co., 1951.

Walsh, W. H. " 'Meaning' in History." In *Theories of History*, edited by Patrick Gardiner, pp. 296–307. Glencoe, Ill.: Free Press, 1962.

Walter, W. Grey. "Activity Patterns in the Human Brain." In *Aspects of Form*, edited by Lancelot Law Whyte, pp. 179–95. London: Percy Lund Humphries & Co., 1951.

Warren, Robert Penn. "Pure and Impure Poetry," *Kenyon Review*, 5 (Spring, 1943): 228–54.

Watts, Alan W. "Beat Zen, Square Zen, and Zen," *Chicago Review*, 12 (Summer, 1958): 3–11.

Weaver, Warren. "Recent Contributions to the Mathematical Theory of Communication," *Etc.: A Review of General Semantics*, 10 (1953): 261–81.

———. "The Mathematics of Information." In *Automatic Control*, edited by the Editors of *Scientific American*, pp. 97–110. New York: Simon & Schuster, 1955.

Webern, Anton. "Towards a New Music," *The Score*, no. 28 (January, 1961), pp. 29–37.

Weinberg, Henry. "Donald Martino: Trio (1959)," *Perspectives of New Music*, 2 (Fall–Winter, 1963): 82–90.

Westergaard, Peter. "Webern and 'Total Organization': An Analysis of the Second Movement of Piano Variations, Op. 27," *Perspectives of New Music*, 1 (Spring, 1963): 107–20.

Wever, Ernest Glen, and Lawrence, Merle. *Physiological Acoustics*. Princeton: Princeton University Press, 1954.

Whitehead, Alfred N. *Modes of Thought*. New York: Macmillan Co., 1938.

Whitrow, G. J. *The Natural Philosophy of Time*. New York: Harper Torchbooks, 1963.

Whorf, Benjamin Lee. *Collected Papers on Metalinguistics*. Washington, D.C.: Government Printing Office, 1952.

Whyte, Lancelot Law. *Accent on Form*. New York: Harper & Brothers, 1954.

Wiener, Norbert. *Cybernetics*. New York: John Wiley & Sons, 1948.

———. *The Human Use of Human Beings*. New York: Doubleday Anchor Books, 1954.

Winckel, Fritz. "The Psycho-Acoustical Analysis of Music as Applied to Electronic Music," *Journal of Music Theory*, 7 (Winter, 1963): 194–246.

Woodger, J. H. *The Technique of Theory Construction*. International Encyclopedia of Unified Science, vol. 2, no. 5. Chicago: University of Chicago Press, 1939.

Youngblood, Joseph E. "Style as Information," *Journal of Music Theory*, 2 (April, 1958): 29–35.

Zimbardo, Philip G., *et al.* "Control of Pain Motivation by Cognitive Dissonance," *Science*, 151 (January 14, 1966): 217–19.

Zola, Emile. "The Novel as Social Science." In *The Modern Tradition*, edited by Richard Ellmann and Charles Feidelson, pp. 270–89. New York: Oxford University Press, 1965.

Index

Ackerman, James S., 95, 99, 104–5, 111, 121–22, 127, 169
Acoustics, music not reducible to, 246–47. *See also* Theory reduction
Adams, Robert M., 96
Adorno, T. W., 263, 293, 294
Aeschylus, 83
Aesthetic emphasis: recent changes in, 210; away from content, 211; on form and materials, 211, 214; kinds of, exhausted, 214; on means as against ends, 210–17; compositional method not correlated with, 237 n. *See also* Arts, The; Formalism; Traditionalism; Transcendentalism
Aesthetic experience: cultural beliefs and, 48, chap. 4 *passim* (*see also* Beliefs, cultural); charisma enhances, 48; and history, 65–66; in primitive culture, no separate category, 54; differentiated in Western culture, 54
Alain-Fournier, Henri, 166
Aleatoric (aleatory). *See* Chance
Analysis: limitations of, 28 n.
Analysis of music: functionalism and, 296; hierarchic structure and, 292–93, 305; redundancy and, 292, 295–96; style and, 311; twelve-tone rows and, 268–69, 292, 303

Analytic formalism. *See* Formalism
Angelico, Fra, 110
Anonymity in the arts, 157. *See also* Impersonality
Anti-teleological art. *See* Radical empiricism; Transcendentalism
Architectonic levels. *See* Hierarchic structure
Arp, Hans, 157, 161
Art: artificiality of, and experimentation, 182–83; not egalitarian, 178–79; history as, 162, 225; philosophy as, 224–25, 232; as problem-solving, 157, 183, 188, 224–25; science as, 162, 216, 232
Art, popular (commercial): emphasis of, on content, 213, 221; role of, in cultural change, 109
Art and nature, relationship between. *See* Formalism; Radical empiricism; Traditionalism; Transcendentalism
Arts, The, differences among: aesthetic emphasis and, 44 n., 214 n.; experimentation and, 235–36; style change and, 81–82, 112–14
Asch, Solomon E., 250 n.
Ashton, Doré, 78
Audience(s): artists' relationship with, 178; fragmentation of, 176–77; for literature, 176; for music, 175–76; for

Index

Change: discovery fosters, 135–36; fluctuation and varied transformation prolong stylistic vitality, 107–8; ideology and, 101, 137–39; variables governing, 101, 119–20, 132; Western view of, modified, 146–48

Change, kinds of: developmental, 99; fluctuating, 101 (*see also* Stasis); mutational, 100, 116 (*see also* Mutational change); trended, 99; varied transformation, 101. *See also* Style change

Channel capacity of listeners (audience), 17, 290–93. *See also* Information

Chaucer, Geoffrey, 177

Chaudhury, Pravas Jivan, 158 n.

Cherry, Colin, 117, 250 n., 261–62, 267, 280

Choice: creation and, 59–60; decision-making time and, 11 n., 272–73; existentialist and radical empiricist attitudes toward, 79; individualization and, 35, 230; prediction and, 79, 227–28, 297–99

Chomsky, Noam, 262

Chopin, Frédéric, 37

Cimabue, Giovanni, 177

Clarke, Henry Leland, 203

Cogan, Marc R., 211

Cognition. *See* Learning; Perception; Redundancy; Understanding

Cohen, I. Bernard, 185

Cohen, Morris R., 6, 111–12

Cohen, Sidney, 168

Communication: accuracy of, and redundancy, 16–17, 278–79; functionalism necessary for, 299; learning and, 274; prediction and, 79–80; value implied in account of, 23. *See also* Hierarchic structure; Information; Learning; Understanding

Complexity: ability of listeners to cope with, 237; in experimental music, 183–84, 235–38, chap. 11 *passim*; value related to, 37. *See also* Experimentation; Information

Compositional constraints: need for, 241–42, 248–49; status of private, 281 n.

Compositional redundancy. *See* Redundancy, compositional

Computer music, electronic music distinguished from, 70

Conceptual categories, psychological

importance of, 28 n., 57 n., 216, 228, 273–74

Cone, Edward T., 52

Construct: art as, 183; history as, 92, 143; knowledge as, 145, 216

Content (in the arts): criticism often overemphasizes, 212–13; central in commercial (popular) art, 213; greatness depends on, 37–38; irrelevant in Pop art, 156 n., 212–13

Contextualism: in the arts, 183; absolute, precludes communication, 280; in music and science, different, 281–82; extreme statements of, 223 n.; valid, presupposes style, 282

Coons, Edgar, 45

Cooper, Grosvenor W., 312

Copland, Aaron, 237 n.

Cornell, Joseph, 202

Courbet, Gustave, 195

Cranach, Lucas the Elder, 194

Creation: belief in, and aesthetic experience, 62; dependent on choice and freedom, 59–60; purposefulness of, 58; risk-taking and, 59–60

Crockett, Steven, 227 n.

Cultural redundancy. *See* Redundancy, cultural

Culture, Western: complexity of, 111, 189, 208–9; continuing diversity of, 184–85. *See also* Beliefs, cultural; Ideology; Pluralism

cummings, e.e., 110

Dante, 201

Darwin, Charles R., 131

David, Jacques Louis, 72, 110, 192, 202 n.

Death: traditionalist (existentialist) and transcendentalist (radical empiricist) attitudes toward, compared, 76, 228–30

Debussy, Claude, 34, 35, 36, 38, 39, 44, 73, 182, 198

de Kooning, Willem, 88, 153

Delacroix, Eugène, 72, 110, 198

Delius, Frederick, 36

Democritus, 67

Derain, André, 198

Designative meaning. *See* Meaning

Determinate meaning. *See* Meaning

Determinism: artists free us from, 59–60; free will and, 97, 111; historical, used to justify serialism, 263–65; style theories and, 104–5; no longer

Index

Index

Information: amount and rate limited by listener, 11n., 272–73, 291–92; channel capacity overloaded by (*see* Channel capacity); combination of different media and, 286–87; and complexity, 36–37, 235; defined, 11; deviation and, 27, 29; tends toward maximum, 117–18; meaning and, chap. 1 *passim*; and meaning differentiated, 21; perceptual, 277–78; probability, uncertainty and, 11, 27, 28–32; psychic economy and evaluation of, 37; schemata aid in processing, 287; style change and, 117, 120–22; an aspect of value, 28, 32, 36; related to need for varied stimulation, 33n. *See also* Information theory; Redundancy; Statistics

Information theory: music and, chaps. 1–3 *passim*; relevance of, to music qualified, 262. *See also* Information; Statistics

Internal-dynamic hypothesis: confirmation of, 118n., 121; and revision of history, 121; not a law, 115, 119; mutational change not explained by, 119–20; qualified, 115–16, 119–22; socio-cultural changes and, 115–16; statistical character of, 120–21; teleology not implied by, 121–22. *See also* Style change

Ionesco, Eugène, 162, 176, 312

Ives, Charles, 200

James, William, 97

Job, 39

Johnson, Lyndon B., 150

Josquin des Prés, 206, 311

Joyce, James, 37, 83, 178, 194, 206–7, 235

Jung, Carl, 166

Kant, Immanuel, 77

Kaprow, Allan, 80

Keats, John, 40–41

Keck, Sheldon, 64n.

Kenner, Hugh, 76n.

King, Gilbert, 280

Kipling, Rudyard, 182

Kirchner, Leon, 264

Klimt, Gustav, 182

Koestler, Arthur, 56

Kohl, Herbert, 160, 229n.

Kohn, Karl, 247n.

Kraehenbuehl, David, 45

Krenek, Ernst, 156–57, 238–39, 251, 263, 264–65, 284

Krieger, Murray, 231

Kroeber, A. L., 105, 115, 229n.

Kuhn, Thomas, 141, 239, 281, 283

Kurth, Ernst, 305

Learning: brain growth and, 275; in childhood, 274–76; motor behavior important in, 275–76; perception and, 270–71; redundancy facilitates, 116–17, 276–79; role of schemata in, 277; stylistic, 7–8, 116–17, 236, 274–77, 283

Lancaster, Clay, 98–99

Langer, Susanne K., 43

Lassus, Roland de, 117

Leibnitz, Gottfried Wilhelm von, 97

Leonardo da Vinci, 202

Lewin, David, 269

Ligeti, György, 156, 211

Lockspeiser, Edward, 73n.

Loehr, Max, 158n.

Lorenz, Alfred O., 305

Louis XIV, 146

Lowinsky, Edward E., 154

Luchtung, Wolfgang A., 168

Machaut, Guillaume de, 118, 177

MacLeish, Archibald, 211

MacLow, Jackson, 72

Magritte, René, 221

Mahler, Gustav, 201

Maison, K. E., 198n.

Malm, William P., 99

Malraux, André, 90, 205

Mandelbaum, Maurice, 143

Manet, Edouard, 202, 206

Mann, Thomas, 166

Margenau, Henry, 77

Marisol (Escobar), 202

Markoff process, 5, 15

Martino, Donald, 269, 294–95

Marvell, Andrew, 201

Marx, Karl, 90, 146, 222

Marxism, 40, 96, 212

Mathieu, Georges, 68, 72, 80, 83–84

Matisse, Henri, 198

McLuhan, Marshall, 150, 208

McNeill, William H., 99, 135, 136, 138, 179

Mead, George H., 6, 35, 144

Meaning: defined, 6, 11; designative, 6–7, 10n. (*see also* Signification, modes of, referential); determinate,

Index

Offenbach, Jacques, 204
O'Neill, Eugene, 206
Oppenheimer, Jane, 141
Originality: distinguished from bizarre, 61; novelty confused with, 218; attitude toward repetition related to, 61; risk-taking and, 59–60; highly valued in Western culture, 61. See also Creation; Novelty; Personal expression
Ortega y Gasset, José, 129
Ossario, Alfonso, 81

Parameters of sound: not equivalent psychologically, 247–48; hierarchic level modifies use of, 306; pitch and time primary, 247–48; secondary, not pattern-forming, 247–48, 284–85; serialization of (see Serialism; Total serialism); subtle variation among, hard to perceive, 286–87. See also Pitch; Time
Paraphrase: defined, 195; in literature, 197–98; in music, 195–96; in plastic arts, 198–99. See also Past art
Paraphrase distinguished from: adaptation, 198; copying, 199; transcription and arrangement, 196
Pascal, Blaise, 38
Past, the: arguments against use of, examined, 186–87; attitude toward, changed, 150–51; changed by use in present, 47, 65, 91–92, 192, 210; distinguished from present, 90–91, 92; ideological accessibility of, 151–53, 187–91; implications of, plural, 59, 89–90 n., 264; knowledge increases relevance of, 149–50, 192–93; new media increase relevance of, 150; relation of present to, not nostalgic, 192–93; presence of, 185–208; present becomes one with, 192; present problems make relevant, 193, 194; psychological accessibility of, 191–93; realization of implications characterizes, 90–91, 192. See also History; Past art; Present
Past art, uses of, 193–208; borrowing, 199–201 (see also Borrowing); eclecticism in, 199, 203–4, 215, 217; by formalists, 191, 207, 225; new implications permit, 65, 192; intra-artistic, 194–95; not literal, 194; modeling, 205–6 (see also Modeling); paraphrase, 195–99 (see also Para-

phrase); pluralism intensified by, 185–86; simulation, 202–5 (see also Simulation); skill and elegance in, 225. See also History; Past
Pavlov, Ivan P., 260
Peirce, Charles, 261
Perception: acoustics not identical with, 246; cognition distinguished from, 270–71; hierarchically discontinuous, 271–72; learning influences, 270–71; motor behavior and, 275–76; of pitch and time, 250–52 (see also Pitch; Time); physiological limitations of, 271–73; of secondary sound parameters (see Parameters of sound); speed and accuracy of, 272–73. See also Central nervous system; Information; Mental behavior
Perceptual information. See Information
Perceptual redundancy. See Redundancy, perceptual
Performance: accuracy of, and redundancy, 279; changes in, explained, 50–51; expectation and, 48; information and, 48; secondary sound parameters and, 247; speed and accuracy of, limited, 272–73
Pergolesi, Giovanni Battista, 195, 196 n.
Perle, George, 240, 268, 269
Personal expression: and cultural expression, 188; cumulative change fostered by, 154–55; decline of, as an ideal, 155, 183, 188 (see also Impersonality); eclecticism precluded by, 174, 191; use of past precluded by, 189, 191; important in traditionalism, 61, 174, 187–88
Perugino, 194
Peterson, W. Wesley, 278
Pfeiffer, John, 275
Phidias, 83
Picasso, Pablo, 37, 59, 67, 72, 83, 102, 174, 194, 195, 198, 205, 207
Pitch: distinguished from frequency, 246, 272; a pattern-forming parameter, 247–48; perception of, 271–72; phenomenal character of, 250–52; retrogrades and inversion of, perceptible, 252, 284; serialization of, 242, 249, 250, 284–86 (see also Serialism; Twelve-tone row); time not isomorphic with, 252 (see also Time)
Plato, 25, 40, 67
Platt, John R., 137, 272–73

337

Index